RESEARCH METHODS FOR BUSINESS

A Skill-Building Approach

Fourth Edition

Uma Sekaran
Southern Illinois University at Carbondale

John Wiley & Sons, Inc.

http://www.wiley.com/college

ACQUISITIONS EDITOR	Jeff Marshall
MARKETING MANAGER	Ilse Wolfe
SENIOR PRODUCTION EDITOR	Patricia McFadden
SENIOR DESIGNER	Harry Nolan
PRODUCTION MANAGEMENT SERVICES	Hermitage Publishing Services
COVER IMAGE	José Ortega/Stock Illustration Source

This book was set in 10/12 Garamond by Hermitage Publishing Services and printed and bound by Malloy Lithographing, Inc. The cover was printed by Von Hoffmann Press, Inc.

This book is printed on acid-free paper. ∞

ISBN 0-471-20366-1
ISBN 0-471-38448-8 (WIE)

Printed in the United States of America

10 9 8 7 6 5 4 3 2 1

To Sudha Pennathur
&
Edward Messerly

With Love

ABOUT THE AUTHOR

Uma Sekaran is Professor Emerita of Management, Southern Illinois University at Carbondale (SIUC), Illinois. Sekaran obtained her MBA degree from the University of Connecticut at Storrs, and Ph.D. from UCLA. She was the Chair of the Department of Management and also the Director of University Women's Professional Advancement at SIUC when she retired from the University and moved to California to be closer to her family.

Dr. Sekaran has authored or co-authored 8 books, 12 book chapters, and more than 55 refereed journal articles in the management area, and has presented more than 70 papers at national, international, and regional management conferences. Professor Sekaran has won recognition for significant research contributions to cross-cultural research from U.S. and international professional organizations. She is the recipient of Meritorious Research Awards both from the Academy of Management and SIUC. She has also been conferred the Best Teacher Award by the University.

Dr. Sekaran continues to teach courses from time to time. During the summer of 2000 she taught a specially designed course titled "Management in the New Millennium" at the Memorial University of Newfoundland in Canada, which highlighted the need for change in management styles in the face of technological advancements. She also continues to engage in research.

PREFACE

Revising *Research Methods for Business* for this fourth edition has been an enjoyable experience. As in previous editions, the simple and informal style of presenting information has been maintained and the focus on practical skill building preserved. The book provides several examples to illustrate the concepts and points presented. Users will also note throughout the book the variety of examples in the different areas of business—production, operations management, business policy and strategy, organizational behavior, human resources management, information systems, marketing, accounting, and finance—cited to illustrate that research finds application in all areas of business. It is hoped that students will find research to be interesting, nonintimidating, and of practical use.

In addition to the inclusion of more miniexercises at the end of chapters from cases adapted from business journals, the chapter on *technology* has been substantially revised to keep in line with the changing trends. The application of software for collecting data, analyzing them, and presenting the results is also discussed in the relevant chapters. The final chapter on *managerial decision making and research* elucidates the research cycle as encompassing the full gamut from qualitative data analysis to quantitative hypothesis testing empirical studies. An additional case is presented to emphasize the need for research by exemplifying a company's failure due to lack of investigation.

Data analysis is illustrated through the current SPSS Version 11.0 in the data analysis chapter and the student version thereof is available with this edition of the book for the interested student.

Most chapters in the book include *managerial implications* of the contents discussed, emphasizing the need for managers to understand research. The *ethical considerations* involved in conducting research are also clearly brought out. The dynamics of *cross-cultural research* in terms of instrument development, surveys, and sampling are discussed, which in the context of today's global economy will be useful to students. The final chapter of the book discusses two case studies, one set in a cross-cultural context further highlighting the need to be culture-sensitive, and the other illustrating how, for lack of research intervention, an organization can be obliterated.

The Refresher Module on Statistical Terms and Tests at the end of the book should help instructors to assign the material to students when they are ready to do so. It is presented in a simple way without discussing derivation of formulas, so that the student has enough knowledge to conduct research applying appropriate statistical tests.

Many have helped in the development of this edition. The valued comments of Usha Sekar, President and CEO of CRIA Technologies, Inc., on the draft version of the chapter on technology have been duly taken into account. Lakshmi

V. Thiyagarajan of Oblix Inc., and Pirasenna V. Thiyagarajan, Sun Microsystems, Inc., supplied information on the security aspects of technology and ERP. Professor Arun Pennathur helped in identifying the software available for questionnaire design, data collection, and data analyses. The help of all these individuals is very much appreciated. My sincere thanks also go to Tom Moellering of SPSS, Inc., who responded promptly to my request for the latest 11.0 version of SPSS software programs for data analysis.

My thanks are due to several other individuals as well. Professor Elizabeth Barclay of Oakland University, Rochester, Michigan, reviewed the third edition and suggested some changes for the revision. Professor Metin Cakici of Isik University, Istanbul, pointed out some inaccuracies in the formulas in the chapter on sampling in the third edition. Thanks to him, these have now been rectified.

Mr. Narayanan Pennathur patiently read the draft versions of the chapters and significantly improved the language and style of writing. Mr. A.R.C. Sekaran helped in getting the manuscript ready for publication. My appreciation to both these individuals. My heartfelt thanks to Sudha Pennathur, President of the House of Pennathur, for an update on the case study in the last chapter and for providing another case for the book. Her help is deeply appreciated.

I expect that students and instructors alike will enjoy this edition. Students should become effective managers, helped by the requisite knowledge and skills acquired by the study of this book. The *Instructor's Manual* that accompanies this text will be a good additional teaching aid for teachers. I hope both the instructors and the students will find this book useful.

Any comments or suggestions may be e-mailed to Chins@Juno.com or mailed to me at the following address: 4571 Latimer Ave, San Jose, California 95130. For additional information check web site http://www.wiley.com/college/sekaran. Good luck!

Uma Sekaran

CONTENTS

**CHAPTER 4
THE RESEARCH PROCESS:
STEPS 1 TO 3: THE BROAD
PROBLEM AREA, PRELIMINARY
DATA GATHERING, PROBLEM
DEFINITION /54**

**CHAPTER 5
THE RESEARCH PROCESS:
STEPS 4 AND 5: THEORETICAL
FRAMEWORK HYPOTHESIS
DEVELOPMENT /85**

CHAPTER 11
SAMPLING /263

CHAPTER 14
MANAGERIAL DECISION MAKING
AND RESEARCH /371

MODULE
A REFRESHER ON SOME
STATISTICAL TERMS AND TESTS
/391

INTRODUCTION TO RESEARCH

TOPICS DISCUSSED

DEFINITION OF RESEARCH

APPLIED AND BASIC RESEARCH

WHY MANAGERS SHOULD KNOW ABOUT RESEARCH

MANAGERS AND THE CONSULTANT–RESEARCHER

- The Manager–Researcher Relationship
- Internal versus External Researchers and Consultants

KNOWLEDGE ABOUT RESEARCH AND MANAGERIAL EFFECTIVENESS

ETHICS AND BUSINESS RESEARCH

CHAPTER OBJECTIVES

After completing Chapter 1 you should be able to:

1. Describe what research is and how it is defined.
2. Distinguish between applied and basic research, giving examples, and discussing why they would fall into one or the other of the two categories.
3. Explain why managers should know about research.
4. Discuss what managers should and should not do in order to interact most effectively with researchers.
5. Identify and fully discuss specific situations in which a manager would be better off using an internal research team, and when an external research team would be more advisable, giving reasons for the decisions.
6. Discuss what research means to you and describe how you, as manager, might apply the knowledge gained about research.
7. Be aware of the role of ethics in business research.

On August 27, 2001, Chunk Orlando, CEO of a 14-year-old automobile company, was mentally assessing and pondering over the state of affairs in his organization. Of late, things had not been going well, and matters seemed to be getting out of hand. The market value of the shares of the company was down 72%, dropping from $60 per share to $16.75. Performance and productivity levels were on the decline and the quarterly loss of $206 million on sales of about 8 billion did not portend a bright future for the company. The advertising agency did not seem to be doing a good job either. To top it all, there was a lawsuit filed for discrimination against female employees in the company. Chuck felt he had to take a very active role in the running of the organization and make a 180 degree change from his hitherto hands-off policy.

Instead of ruminating on the past, Chuck wanted to focus on the present and plan for the future. Apart from the obvious changes like increasing the productivity of workers and getting a more effective advertising agency, Chuck felt that he needed to take stock of "intangible" assets such as patents, customer lists, brand value, intellectual knowledge of designers, and the like. These evaluations would give investors a sense of the value of the assets and whether resources were being effectively utilized. "Unless the accounting process takes stock of these, capital cannot be allocated in a sensible way, analysts will not be able to evaluate the company, and investors will not understand the worth of the company," he said to himself.

There were several great ideas that came to Chuck's mind, such as assessing whether the current models of the vehicles manufactured appealed sufficiently to the trendy tastes of the increasing number of affluent buyers in the 25 to 40 age group. However, Chuck was baffled as to how to go about these enormous tasks. Several questions came to his mind and he posed the following important issues to himself: "How does one increase efficiency and productivity?" "How does one account for intangible assets?" "Does anyone know at all?" and "How does one go about assessing advertising needs and effectiveness?"

A major concern was to decide whether or not he should slash the advertising budget since the anticipated revenues were not forthcoming during this downturn. He remembered having read somewhere that those who did not burnish their brands through increased advertisement budgets might find themselves worth a lot less when the tough times end. IBM, for instance, was stated to have lost only 1% of brand value last year, compared to bigger declines at other hi-tech companies because IBM had increased its advertising budget. "But from where would the advertising funds come?" he wondered. Such thoughts very much taxed his mind.

"Certainly," he said to himself, "the company's problems are a function of industry trends, the economy, idle capacity, and the like. But there is much scope for improvement on various fronts, such as increasing gas mileage, which would find great favor with the government and customers, better designing and engineering, improved marketing, designing for the trendy mod group, as well as catering to clients in the lower economic strata, in addition to increasing the productivity of workers."

Then there were the ethical issues that disturbed Chuck. At the personal level, he wondered if he should give himself a raise in salary and other perks when

(handwritten margin notes at top:) ① why do research?? ② where can good research be applied?

(handwritten margin note left:) Q's

the rest of the company employees had a freeze on their salaries. Did he deserve the compensation he would get when the company was on a downward spiral, at least for now? He also toyed with the idea that a token cut in his salary would serve as a morale booster to company employees.

He wanted answers to several of these issues, but did not know who would help him to find them. He knew that research in these areas would help, but did not know where to seek the necessary guidance. Also, how would he verbalize his various concerns and handle the researchers? He had broad visions for the future of his company, but was at a loss to know how to execute these plans. "Just because one is able to design a rail system and make trains, it does not necessarily follow that one can make them run too," he thought to himself.

It is not infrequently that chief executives and managers at various levels in an organization find themselves facing such dilemmas. This book helps to find solutions to the problems that managers, and those responsible for the execution of projects, often face.

As a manager, you will have to make several decisions each day at work. What would help you to make the right decisions? Will it be your experience on the job, your sixth sense or hunch, or will you just hope for good luck? For sure, all of these will play a part *after* you have thoroughly investigated or researched the problem situation and generated some alternative solutions to choose from. Whether or not managers realize it, they are constantly engaged in research as they try to find solutions to the day-to-day problems, big and small, that confront them at work. Some of the issues are solved with relative ease, as when a machine on the shop floor stops working, and the foreman, with his past experience, hastens to do the necessary repair and gets it to run smoothly again. A few problems may present moderate difficulty, requiring some time and effort for the manager to investigate into and find a solution, as for example, when many employees absent themselves from work frequently. Yet other problems could be quite complex and the manager might proceed to seek the help of an "expert researcher" to study the issue and offer solutions, as in the case of a company consistently incurring losses to the perplexity and dismay of everyone.

(handwritten margin notes left:) life family job school homeowner medical $ $ $ raising kids

WHAT IS RESEARCH?

(handwritten margin notes left:) Better your chances of finding an optimal solution to your problem

Just close your eyes for a minute and utter the word *research* to yourself. What kinds of images does this word conjure up for you? Do you visualize a lab with scientists at work with Bunsen burners and test tubes, or an Einstein-like character writing dissertations on some complex subject, or someone collecting data to study the impact of a newly introduced day-care system on the morale of employees? Most certainly, all these images do represent different aspects of research. Research, a somewhat intimidating term for some, is simply the process of finding solutions to a problem after a thorough study and analysis of the situational factors. Managers in organizations constantly engage themselves in studying and analyzing issues and hence are involved in some form of research activity as they make decisions at the workplace. As is well known, sometimes managers make good decisions and the problem gets solved, sometimes they make poor decisions and the problem persists, and on occasions they make such colossal blunders that the organization gets stuck in the mire. The difference between making good decisions and committing blunders lies in how managers go about the decision-making process. In other words, good decision making fetches a "yes" answer to the following questions: Do managers identify where exactly the problem lies, do they correctly recognize the relevant factors in the situation needing investigation, do they know what types of information are to be gathered and how, do they know how to make use of the information so collected and draw appropriate conclusions to make the right decisions, and finally, do they know how to implement the results of this process to solve the problem? This is the essence of research and to be a successful manager it is important for you to know how to go about making the right decisions by being knowledgeable about the various steps involved in finding solutions to problematic issues. This is what this book is all about.

The Excitement of Research and Why Managers Should Know about Research

Modern technology has made research an exciting and a relatively smooth process. Today a personal computer with a modem or any means to an Internet connection places one within easy reach of knowledge of what is happening in the global markets and how the world economy is impacting on business. Chapter 3 gives a broad idea of how technology has facilitated the research process and decision making, and the later chapters describe the use of technology in information gathering, data collection, data analysis, and data presentation. By grasping the fundamentals of the research process and keeping abreast of modern technology, such as computers with enormous capability to store and retrieve information, you as a manager can face the competitive global market with its multitude of complex and confusing factors with greater confidence.

Knowledge of research not only helps one to look at the available information in sophisticated and creative ways in the fast-paced global environment that businesses face, but this knowledge also helps in other ways. For example, you can interact more effectively with research consultants who work for you, you can discriminate between good and bad studies published in professional journals, and if so desired, you yourself can undertake research to solve problems. Moreover, knowledge in the business area is exploding and there is an overwhelming maze of information available through the Internet, which has to be sifted through to determine its reliability. Identifying the critical issues, gathering relevant information, analyzing the data in ways that would help decision making, and implementing the right course of action, are all facilitated by understanding business research. After all, decision making is merely a process of choosing from among alternative solutions to resolve a problem and research helps to generate viable alternatives for effective decision making.

BUSINESS RESEARCH

Business research can be described as a systematic and organized effort to investigate a specific problem encountered in the work setting, that needs a solution. It comprises a series of steps designed and executed, with the goal of finding answers to the issues that are of concern to the manager in the work environment. This means that the first step in research is to know where the problem areas exist in the organization, and to identify as clearly and specifically as possible the problems that need to be studied and resolved. Once the problem that needs attention is clearly defined, then steps can be taken to gather information, analyze the data, and determine the factors that are associated with the problem and solve it by taking the necessary corrective measures.

This entire process by which we attempt to solve problems is called research. Thus, research involves a series of well-thought-out and carefully executed activities that will enable the manager to know how organizational problems can be solved, or at least considerably minimized. Research thus encompasses the processes of inquiry, investigation, examination, and experimentation. These processes have to be carried out systematically, diligently, critically, objectively, and logically. The expected end results would be the discovery that will help the manager to deal with the problem situation.

The difference between the manager who uses common sense alone to analyze and make a decision in a given situation, and the investigator who uses a scientific method, is that the latter does a systematic inquiry into the matter and proceeds to describe, explain, or predict phenomena based on data carefully collected for the purpose.

Definition of Research

We can now define business research as an *organized, systematic, data-based, critical, objective, scientific inquiry or investigation into a specific problem*, undertaken with the purpose of finding answers or solutions to it. In essence, research provides the needed information that guides managers to make *informed* decisions to successfully deal with problems. The information provided could be the result of a careful analysis of data gathered firsthand or of data that are already available (in the company, industry, archives, etc.). Data can be quantitative (as generally gathered through structured questions) or qualitative (as generated from the broad answers to specific questions in interviews, or from responses to open-ended questions in a questionnaire, or through observation, or from already available information gathered from various sources).

Research and the Manager

A common experience of all organizations is that the managers thereof encounter problems big and small on a daily basis, which they have to solve by making the right decisions. In business, research is usually primarily conducted to resolve problematic issues in, or interrelated among, the areas of accounting, finance, management, and marketing. In **Accounting,** budget control systems, practices, and procedures are frequently examined. Inventory costing methods, accelerated depreciation, time-series behavior of quarterly earnings, transfer pricing, cash recovery rates, and taxation methods are some of the other areas that are researched. In **Finance,** the operations of financial institutions, optimum financial ratios, mergers and acquisitions, leveraged buyouts, intercorporate financing, yields on mortgages, the behavior of the stock exchange, and the like, become the focus of investigation. **Management** research could encompass the study of employee attitudes and behaviors, human resources management, the impact of changing demographics on management practices, production operations management, strategy formulation, information systems, and the like. **Marketing** research could address issues pertaining to product image, advertising, sales promotion, distribution, packaging, pricing, after-sales service, consumer preferences, new product development, and other marketing aspects.

Exhibit 1 gives an idea of some commonly researched topical areas in business.

Exhibit 1: Some Commonly Researched Areas in Business

1. Employee behaviors such as performance, absenteeism, and turnover.
2. Employee attitudes such as job satisfaction, loyalty, and organizational commitment.
3. Supervisory performance, managerial leadership style, and performance appraisal systems.
4. Employee selection, recruitment, training, and retention.
5. Validation of performance appraisal systems.
6. Human resource management choices and organizational strategy.
7. Evaluation of assessment centers.
8. The dynamics of rating and rating errors in the judgment of human performance.
9. Strategy formulation and implementation.
10. Just-in-time systems, continuous-improvement strategies, and production efficiencies.
11. Updating policies and procedures in keeping with latest government regulations and organizational changes.
12. Organizational outcomes such as increased sales, market share, profits, growth, and effectiveness.
13. Brand loyalty, product life cycle, and product innovation.
14. Consumer complaints.
15. Impression management, logos, and image building.
16. Product positioning, product modification, and new product development.
17. Cost of capital, valuation of firms, dividend policies, and investment decisions.

18. Risk assessment, exchange rate fluctuations, and foreign investment.
19. Tax implications of reorganization of firms or acquisition of companies.
20. Collection of accounts receivable.
21. Development of effective cost accounting procedures.
22. Qualified pension plans and cafeteria type of benefits for employees.
23. Deferred compensation plans.
24. Installation of effective management information systems.
25. Advanced manufacturing technologies and information systems.
26. Design of career paths for spouses in dual-career families.
27. Creative management of a diverse workforce.
28. Cultural differences and the dynamics of managing a multinational firm.
29. Alternative work patterns: job sharing, flexitime, flexiplace, and part-time work.
30. Downsizing.
31. Participative management and performance effectiveness.
32. Differences in leadership positions, salaries, and leadership styles.
33. Instrument development for assessing "true" gender differences.
34. Installation, adaptation, and updating of computer networks and software suitable for creating effective information systems for organizations.
35. Installation of an effective Data Warehouse and Data Mining system for the organization.
36. Keeping ahead of the competition in the new millennium.

Not only are the issues within any subarea related to many factors within that particular system, but they must also be investigated in the context of the external environment facing the business. For example, economic, political, demographic, technological, competitive, and other relevant global factors could impinge on some of the dynamics related to the firm. These have to be scrutinized as well to assess their impact, if any, on the problem researched.

TYPES OF BUSINESS RESEARCH: APPLIED AND BASIC

Research can be undertaken for two different purposes. One is to solve a current problem faced by the manager in the work setting, demanding a timely solution. For example, a particular product may not be selling well and the manager might want to find the reasons for this in order to take corrective action. Such research is called ***applied research.*** The other is to generate a body of knowledge by trying to comprehend how certain problems that occur in organizations can be solved. This is called ***basic research.*** It is quite possible that some organizations may later on apply the knowledge gained by the findings of such basic research to solve their own problems. For instance, a university professor may be interested in investigating the factors that contribute to absenteeism as a matter of mere academic interest. After gathering information on this topic from several institutions and analyzing the data, the professor may identify factors such as inflexible work hours, inadequate training of employees, and low morale as primarily influencing absenteeism. Later on, a manager who encounters absenteeism of employees in his organization may use this information to determine if these factors are relevant to that particular work setting.

Thus, research done with the intention of applying the results of the findings to solve specific problems currently being experienced in the organization is called **applied research.** Research done chiefly to enhance the understanding of certain problems that commonly occur in organizational settings, and seek methods of solving them, is called **basic** or **fundamental research.** It is also known as **pure research.** The findings of such research contribute to the building of knowledge in the various functional areas of business. Such knowledge generated is usually later applied in organizational settings for problem solving.

Applied Research

Consider the following two situations cited in *Business Week.*

1. Oxford Health Plans Inc. saw trouble brewing. It was a company in distress experiencing computer problems. Turnover among Oxford's programmers was unusually high and processing of claims became a big nightmare. Clients started canceling their policies, claims for bypass surgery and such were way up, and premiums paid out relative to clients' medical expenses, on a percentage basis, was close to 85%.

2. Xerox is insular and isn't ready for the increasingly competitive, high-tech world. Xerox still relies on old-fashioned and slow-selling analog copiers for more than half its revenue and despite its double-digit growth in digital products and services, its sales rose just 4%.

It is obvious that Oxford has a multitude of problems and an outside consultant–researcher would perhaps be able to design a scientific study that would look into them. Presumably, this would be a lengthy investigation that could result in several different recommended solutions. The company manager could then consider them, make the right decision, and thereby solve Oxford's problems.

In the second situation, Xerox also needs to look into the efficacy of the analog technology used in copiers and examine what should be done to increase efficiency and promote its sales. The two preceding examples illustrate the need for applied research, whereby existing problems can be solved through investigation and good managerial decision making.

Basic or Fundamental Research

Right from her days as a clerical employee in a bank, Sandra had observed that her colleagues, though extremely knowledgeable about the nuances and intricacies of banking, were exerting very little effort to improve the efficiency and effectiveness of the bank in the area of customer relations and service. They took on the minimum amount of work load, availed of long tea and lunch breaks, and seemed not motivated in their dealings with the customers or the management. That they were highly knowledgeable about banking policies and practices was clearly evident from their mutual discussions about these as they processed applications from customers. Sandra herself was very hardworking and enjoyed her work with the customers. She always used to think what a huge waste it was for talented employees to goof off rather than contribute to the GNP. When she left the bank and did her dissertation for her Ph.D., her topic of investigation was Job Involvement, or the ego investment of people in their jobs. The conclusion of her investigation was that the single most important contributory factor to job involvement is the fit or match between the nature of the job and the personality predispositions of the people engaged in performing it. For example, challenging jobs allowed employees with high capabilities to get job-involved, and people-oriented employees got job-involved with service activities. Sandra then understood why the highly intelligent bank employees could not get job-involved or find job satisfaction in the routine jobs that rarely called for the use of their abilities.

Subsquently, when Sandra joined the Internal Research Team of a Fortune 500 Company, she applied this knowledge to solve problems of motivation, job satisfaction, job involvement, and the like, in the organization.

The above is an instance of basic research, where knowledge was generated to understand a phenomenon of interest to the researcher. Most research and development departments in various industries, as well as many professors in colleges and universities, do basic or fundamental research, so that more knowledge is generated in particular areas of interest to industries, organizations, and researchers. Though the objective of engaging in basic research is primarily to equip oneself with additional knowledge of certain phenomena and problems that occur in several organizations and industries with a view to finding solutions, the knowledge generated from such research is often applied later for solving organizational problems.

As stated, the primary purpose of conducting basic research is to generate more knowledge and understanding of the phenomena of interest and to build theories based on the research results. Such theories subsequently form the foundation of further studies of many aspects of the phenomena. This process of building on existing knowledge is the genesis for theory building, particularly in the management area.

Several examples of basic research can be provided. For instance, research into the causes and consequences of global warming will offer many solutions to minimize the phenomenon, and lead to further research concerning if and how global warming can be averted. Although research on global warming might primarily be for the purpose of understanding the nuances of the phenomenon, the findings will ultimately be applied and useful to, among others, the agricultural and building industries.

Many large companies also engage in basic research. For instance, General Electric Company generates knowledge concerning the different applications of electrical energy, their motto being "We bring good things to life." Computer companies in the Silicon Valley are constantly engaged in generating the know-how to increase the usefulness of microcomputers in industry, which benefits managers and technicians in all organizations. This, ultimately, results in increased sales of computers for them.

University professors engage in basic research in an effort to understand and generate more knowledge about various aspects of businesses, such as how to improve the effectiveness of information systems, integrate technology into the overall strategic objectives of an organization, assess the impact of logos, increase the productivity of employees in service industries, monitor sexual harassment incidents at the workplace, increase the effectiveness of small businesses, evaluate alternative inventory valuation methods, change the institutional structure of the financial and capital markets, and the like. These findings later become useful for application in business situations.

As illustrated, the main distinction between applied and basic business research is that the former is specifically aimed at solving a currently experienced problem, whereas the latter has the broader objective of generating knowledge and understanding of phenomena and problems that occur in various organizational settings. Despite this distinction, both types of research follow the same steps of systematic inquiry to arrive at solutions to problems. As current or prospective practicing managers in organizations, you would be directly or indirectly engaged in applied research. You would also be keeping abreast of new basic knowledge generated by being in regular touch with the published research in the business journals related to your sphere of work, some of which could very well be relevant and applicable to your own business organization.

In sum, both applied and basic business research are scientific in nature, the main difference being that the former is undertaken specifically to solve a current business problem whereas the latter is primarily resorted to because of the importance of the subject to the researcher. A deeper understanding of the phenomenon would be useful for its own sake as well as for application later, as needed. Both basic and applied research have to be carried out in a scientific manner (discussed in the next chapter) so that the findings or results generated by them can be relied upon to effectively solve the problem investigated. It is, however, possible that some applied research could have a shorter time frame than some basic research.

MANAGERS AND RESEARCH

Managers with knowledge of research have an advantage over those without. Though you yourself may not be doing any major research as a manager, you will have to understand, predict, and control events that are dysfunctional to the organization. For example, a new product developed may not be "taking off," or a financial investment may not be "paying off" as anticipated. Such disturbing phenomena have to be *understood* and explained. Unless this is done, it will not be possible to *predict* the future of that product or the prospects of that investment, and how future catastrophic outcomes can be *controlled*. A grasp of research methods will enable managers to understand, predict, and control their environment.

A thought that may cross your mind is that, because you will probably be bringing in researchers to solve problems instead of doing the research yourself, there is no need to bother to study about research. The reasons become clear when one considers the consequences of failure to do so. With the ever-increasing complexity of modern organizations, and the uncertainty of the environment they face, the management of organizational systems has become one of constant trouble shooting in the workplace. It would help if managers could sense, spot, and deal with problems *before* they get out of hand. Knowledge of research and problem-solving processes helps managers to identify problem situations before they get out of control. Although minor problems can be fixed by the manager, major problems would warrant the hiring of outside researchers or consultants. The manager who is knowledgeable about research can interact effectively with them. Knowledge about research processes, design, and interpretation of data also helps managers to become discriminating recipients of the research findings presented, and to determine whether or not the recommended solutions are appropriate for implementation.

Another reason why professional managers today need to know about research methods is that they will become more discriminating while sifting through the information disseminated in business journals. Some journal articles are more scientific and objective than others. Even among the scientific articles, some are more appropriate for application or adaptation to particular organizations and situations than others. This is a function of the sampling design, the types of organizations studied, and other factors reported in the journal articles. Unless the manager is able to grasp fully what the published empirical research really conveys, she or he is likely to err in incorporating some of the suggestions such publications offer. By the same token, managers can handle with success their own problems at considerable cost savings by studying the results of "good" (discussed in the next chapter) published research that has addressed similar issues.

There are several other reasons why professional managers should be knowledgeable about research and research methods in business. First, such knowledge sharpens the sensitivity of managers to the myriad variables operating in a situation and reminds then frequently of the multicausality and multifinality of phenomena, thus avoiding inappropriate, simplistic notions of one variable "causing" another. Second, when managers understand the research reports about their organizations handed to them by professionals, they will be equipped to take intelligent, educated, calculated risks with known probabilities attached to the success or failure of their decisions. Research then becomes a useful deci-sion-making tool rather than a mass of incomprehensible statistical information. Third, because managers become knowledgeable about scientific investigations, vested interests inside or outside the organization will not prevail. For instance, an internal research group within the organization will not be able to distort information or manipulate the findings to their advantage if managers are aware of the biases that could creep into research and know how data are analyzed and interpreted. As an example, an internal research team might state that a particu-lar unit to which it is partial (for whatever reason) has shown increased profits and hence should be allocated more resources to buy sophisticated equipment to further enhance its effectiveness. However, the increased profit could have been a one-time windfall phenomenon due to external environmental factors such as market conditions, bearing no relation whatever to the unit's operating efficiency. Thus, awareness of the different ways in which data could be cam-ouflaged will help the manager to make the right decision. Fourth, knowledge about research helps the manager to relate to and share pertinent information with the researcher or consultant hired for problem solving.

In sum, being knowledgeable about research and research methods helps pro-fessional managers to:

1. Identify and effectively solve minor problems in the work setting.
2. Know how to discriminate good from bad research.
3. Appreciate and be constantly aware of the multiple influences and multiple effects of factors impinging on a situation.
4. Take calculated risks in decision making, knowing full well the probabilities associated with the different possible outcomes.
5. Prevent possible vested interests from exercising their influence in a situation.
6. Relate to hired researchers and consultants more effectively.
7. Combine experience with scientific knowledge while making decisions.

THE MANAGER AND THE CONSULTANT–RESEARCHER

As a manager, you will often need to engage a consultant to study some of the more complex, time-consuming problems that you might encounter, as in the case of Oxford Health Plan discussed earlier. It is thus important to be knowledgeable about how to locate and select a researcher, how to effectively interact with the consultant (the terms researcher and consultant are used interchangeably), what the manager–researcher relationship should be, and the advantages and disadvantages of internal versus external consultants. It has to be emphasized that the genuine motive of the manager in hiring con-sultants should be for problem solving and not for promoting self-interests or advancing one's pet projects and ideas.

How to Locate and Select a Researcher

Many organizational consulting firms are listed in telephone directories and can be used for consulting on various types of projects. If a broad indication about what areas or issues need to be researched is stated, the consulting firm will provide lists of individuals that have expertise in those particular areas. The credentials of these individuals are also usually presented by the consulting firm or can be requested. Other organizations that have used their services can also be contacted to ascertain the merits and effectiveness of the individuals and the reputation of the firm.

Many colleges of business also have professors who do organizational consulting work. Some of them have vast experience working with several types of organizations. These individuals can also be contacted and their services utilized, if they have the time and would agree to do the study. In all cases, however, it is advisable to check their credentials and the institutions they hail from before hiring them.

The Manager–Researcher Relationship

During their careers, it often becomes necessary for managers to deal with consultants. Many academicians also have their students do research projects for the class and several organizations allow access to them, asking only that a copy of the research project be made available to them. Some professors interested in publishing the results of basic research also approach organizations and are afforded the facilities to conduct research. If the research has been done scientifically, then the results of the study would be beneficial to the manager, who would have obtained useful information without paying for it. By being able to point out the relevant variables integral to what is of concern to the researchers doing basic research, and by helping them with useful insights, the manager stands to benefit a great deal. When the manager is knowledgeable about research, then the interactions between the manager and the researcher become more meaningful, purposeful, and beneficial both to the organization and the researcher alike.

Quite frequently, organizations also hire outside research agencies to identify and solve problems for them. In such a case, the manager must not only interact effectively with the research team, but must also explicitly delineate the roles for the researchers and the management. The manager has to inform the researchers what types of information could be provided to them, and more important, which of their records would *not* be made available to them. Such records might include the personnel files of the employees, or the ones with certain trade secrets. Making these facts explicit at the very beginning can save a lot of frustration for both parties. Managers who are very knowledgeable about research can more easily foresee what information the researchers might require, and if certain documents containing such information cannot be made available, they can inform the research team about this at the outset. It is vexing for researchers to discover at a late stage that the company will not let them have certain information. If they know the constraints right from the beginning, the researchers might be able to identify alternate ways of tackling the problems and to design the research in such a way as to provide the needed answers.

Values

Beyond specifying the roles and constraints, the manager should also make sure that there is a congruence in the value systems of management and the consultants. For example, the research team might very strongly believe and recommend that reduction of the workforce and streamlining would be the ideal way to significantly cut down operating costs. Management's consistent philosophy, however, might be *not* to fire employees who are experienced, loyal, and senior. Thus, there might be a clash of ideologies between management and the research team. Research knowledge will help managers to identify and explicitly state, even at the outset, the values that the organization holds dear, so that there are no surprises down the road. Clarification of the issue offers the research team the opportunity to either accept the assignment, and find alternative ways of dealing with the problem, or regret its inability to undertake the project. In either case, both the organization and the research team would be better off having discussed their value orientations, thus avoiding potential frustration on both sides.

Exchange of information in a straightforward and forthright manner also helps to increase the rapport and trust levels between the two parties, which in turn motivates the two sides to interact effectively. Under this setup, researchers feel free to approach the management to seek assistance in making the research more purposeful. For instance, the research team is likely to request that management inform the employees of the ensuing research and its broad purpose to allay any fears they might entertain.

To summarize, the manager should make sure while hiring researchers or consultants that:

1. The roles and expectations of both parties are made explicit.
2. Relevant philosophies and value systems of the organization are clearly stated, and constraints, if any, communicated.
3. A good rapport is established with the researchers, and between the researchers and the employees in the organization, enabling the full cooperation of the latter.

INTERNAL VERSUS EXTERNAL CONSULTANTS/RESEARCHERS

Internal Consultants/Researchers

Some organizations have their own consulting or research department, which might be called the Management Services Department, the Organization and Methods Department, R & D (research and development department), or by some other name. This department serves as the internal consultant to subunits of the organization that face certain problems and seek help. Such a unit within the organization, if it exists, would be useful in several ways, and enlisting its help might be advantageous under some circumstances, but not in others. The manager often has to decide whether to use internal or external researchers. To reach a decision, the manager should be aware of the strengths and weaknesses of both, and weigh the advantages and disadvantages of using either, based on the needs of the situation. Some of the advantages and disadvantages of both the internal and external teams are now discussed.

Advantages of Internal Consultants/Researchers

There are at least four advantages in engaging an internal team to do the research project:

1. The internal team would stand a better chance of being readily accepted by the employees in the subunit of the organization where research needs to be done.
2. The team would require much less time to understand the structure, the philosophy and climate, and the functioning and work systems of the organization.
3. They would be available for implementing their recommendations after the research findings are accepted. This is very important because any "bugs" in the implementation of the recommendations could be removed with their help. They would also be available for evaluating the effectiveness of the changes, and considering further changes if and when necessary.
4. The internal team might cost considerably less than an external team for the department enlisting help in problem solving, because they will need less time to understand the system due to their continuous involvement with various units of the organization. For problems that are of low complexity, the internal team would be ideal.

Disadvantages of Internal Consultants/Researchers

There are also certain disadvantages to engaging internal research teams for purposes of problem solving. The four most critical ones are:

1. In view of their long tenure as internal consultants, the internal team may quite possibly fall into a stereotyped way of looking at the organization and its problems. This would inhibit any fresh ideas and perspectives that might be needed to correct the problem. This would definitely be a handicap for situations in which weighty issues and complex problems are to be investigated.
2. There is scope for certain powerful coalitions in the organization to influence the internal team to conceal, distort, or misrepresent certain facts. In other words, certain vested interests could dominate, especially in securing a sizable portion of the available scant resources.
3. There is also a possibility that even the most highly qualified internal research teams are not perceived as "experts" by the staff and management, and hence their recommendations do not get the consideration and attention they deserve.
4. Certain organizational biases of the internal research team might in some instances make the findings less objective and consequently less scientific.

External Consultants/Researchers

The disadvantages of the internal research teams turn out to be the advantages of the external teams, and the former's advantages work out to be the disadvantages of the latter. However, the specific advantages and disadvantages of the external teams may be highlighted.

Advantages of External Consultants

The advantages of the external team are:

1. The external team can draw on a wealth of experience from having worked with different types of organizations that have had the same or similar types of problems. This wide range of experience would enable them to think both divergently and convergently rather than hurry to an instant solution on the basis of the apparent facts in the situation. They would be able to ponder over several alternative ways of looking at the problem because of their extensive problem-solving experiences in various other organizational setups. Having viewed the situation from several possible angles and perspectives (divergently), they could critically assess each of these, discard the less viable options and alternatives, and focus on specific feasible solutions (think convergently).

2. The external teams, especially those from established research and consulting firms, might have more knowledge of current sophisticated problem-solving models through their periodic training programs, which the teams within the organization may not have access to. Because knowledge obsolescence is a real threat in the consulting area, external research institutions ensure that their members are current on the latest innovations through periodic organized training programs. The extent to which internal team members are kept abreast of the latest problem-solving techniques may vary considerably from one organization to another.

Disadvantages of External Consultants

The major disavantages in hiring an external research team are as follows:

1. The cost of hiring an external research team is usually high and is the main deterrent, unless the problems are very critical.

2. In addition to the considerable time the external team takes to understand the organization to be researched, they seldom get a warm welcome, nor are readily accepted by employees. Departments and individuals likely to be affected by the research study may perceive the study team as a threat and resist them. Therefore, soliciting employees' help and enlisting their cooperation in the study is a little more difficult and time-consuming for the external researchers than for the internal teams.

3. The external team also charges additional fees for their assistance in the implementation and evaluation phases.

Keeping in mind these advantages and disadvantages of the internal and external research teams, the manager who desires research services has to weigh the pros and cons of engaging either before making a decision. If the problem is a complex one, or if there are likely to be vested interests, or if the very existence of the organization is at stake because of one or more serious problems, it would be advisable to engage external researchers despite the increased costs involved. However, if the problems that arise are fairly simple, if time is of the essence in solving moderately complex problems, or if there is a systemwide need to establish procedures and policies of a fairly routine nature, the internal team would probably be the better option.

Knowledge of research methods and appreciation of the comparative advantages and disadvantages of the external and internal teams help managers to make decisions on how to approach problems and determine whether internal or external researchers will be the appropriate choice to investigate and solve the problem.

KNOWLEDGE ABOUT RESEARCH AND MANAGERIAL EFFECTIVENESS

As mentioned, managers are responsible for the final outcome by making the right decisions at work. This is greatly facilitated by research knowledge. Knowledge of research heightens the sensitivity of managers to the innumerable internal and external factors of a varied nature operating in their work and organizational environment. It also helps to facilitate effective interactions with consultants and comprehension of the nuances of the research process.

Sophisticated technology such as simulation and model building is now available and may lend itself to profitable application in certain business areas. The recommendations of the external consultant who is proficient in this technology and urges its application in a particular situation may make no sense to, and might create some misgivings, in the manager not acquainted with research. Even a superficial knowledge of these techniques helps the manager to deal with the researcher in a mature and confident manner, so that dealing with "experts" does not result in discomfort. As the manager, *you* will be the one to make the final decision on the implementation of the recommendations made by the research team. Remaining objective, focusing on problem solutions, fully understanding the recommendations made, and why and how they are arrived at, make for good managerial decision making. Although company traditions are to be respected, there may be occasions where today's rapidly changing turbulent environment would demand the substitution or re-adaptation of some of these traditions, based on research findings. Thus, knowledge of research greatly enhances the decision-making skills of the manager.

ETHICS AND BUSINESS RESEARCH

Ethics in business research refers to a code of conduct or expected societal norm of behavior while conducting research. Ethical conduct applies to the organization and the members that sponsor the research, the researchers who undertake the research, and the respondents who provide them with the necessary data. The observance of *ethics* begins with the person instituting the research, who should do so in good faith, pay attention to what the results indicate, and surrendering the ego, pursue organizational rather than self-interests. Ethical conduct should also be reflected in the behavior of the researchers who conduct the investigation, the participants who provide the data, the analysts who provide the results, and the entire research team that presents the interpretation of the results and suggests alternative solutions.

Thus, ethical behavior pervades each step of the research process—data collection, data analysis, reporting, and dissemination of information on the Internet, if such an activity is undertaken. How the subjects are treated and how confidential information is safeguarded are all guided by business ethics. We will highlight these as they relate to different aspects of research in the relevant chapters of this book.

There are business journals such as the *Journal of Business Ethics* and the *Business Ethics Quarterly* that are mainly devoted to the issue of ethics in business. The American Psychological Association has established certain guidelines for conducting research, to ensure that organizational research is conducted in an ethical manner and the interests of all concerned are safeguarded. As stated, we will discuss the role of ethics in the chapters that follow, insofar as it is relevant to the various steps in the research process.

SUMMARY

We opened this chapter with a series of problems facing the CEO of an automobile company, all of which could have been resolved through research. In this chapter we examined what research is, the two types of research (applied and basic), some commonly researched topical areas in business, why managers should know about research for good decision making, effective relationship between the manager and the consultant–researcher, and the advantages and disadvantages of external and internal consultants. We also saw how managerial effectiveness is enhanced by knowledge of research and highlighted some of the areas where ethical issues deserve attention in the conduct of business research. In the next chapter we will examine what "scientific" investigation is.

DISCUSSION QUESTIONS AND POINTS TO PONDER

1. Why should a manager know about research when the job entails *managing* people, products, events, environments, and the like?
2. For what specific purposes is basic research important?
3. When is applied research, as distinct from basic research, useful?
4. Why is it important to be adept in handling the manager–researcher relationship?
5. Explain, giving reasons, which is more important, applied or basic research.

6. Give two specific instances where an external research team would be useful and two other scenarios when an internal research team will be deployed, with adequate explanations as to why each scenario is justified for an external or internal team.

7. Describe a situation where research will help you as a manager to make a good decision.

8. Given the situations below, (a) discuss with reasons whether they fall into the category of applied or basic research, and (b) for Scenario 1, explain with reasons, who will conduct the research.

Scenario 1

To Acquire or Not to Acquire: That is the Question

Companies are very interested in acquiring other firms even when the latter operate in totally unrelated realms of business. For example, Gencore Industries manufacturing asphalt plants for road construction acquired Ingersoll-Rand in 1996, and later acquired yet another company engaged in the business of food processing. Such acquisitions are claimed to "work miracles." However, given the volatility of the stock market and the slowing down of business, many companies are not sure whether such acquisitions involve too much risk. At the same time, they also wonder if they are missing out on a great business opportunity if they fail to take such risk. Some research is needed here!

Scenario 2

Reasons for Absenteeism

A university professor wanted to analyze in depth the reasons for absenteeism of employees in organizations. Fortunately, a company within 20 miles of the campus employed her as a consultant to study that very issue.

Scenario 3

Effects of Nasal Spray on Flu

A research scientist surveys 1,000 employees in different organizational settings to study the efficacy of several types of nasal sprays in controlling the flu virus. He subsequently publishes his findings in a highly respected medical journal.

SCIENTIFIC INVESTIGATION

TOPICS DISCUSSED

THE HALLMARKS OF SCIENCE
- Purposiveness
- Rigor
- Testability
- Replicability
- Precision and Confidence
- Objectivity
- Generalizability
- Parsimony

LIMITATIONS TO SCIENTIFIC RESEARCH IN MANAGEMENT

THE BUILDING BLOCKS OF SCIENCE AND THE HYPOTHETICO-DEDUCTIVE
  METHOD OF RESEARCH

THE SEVEN STEPS OF THE HYPOTHETICO-DEDUCTIVE METHOD
- Observation
- Preliminary Information Gathering
- Theory Formulation
- Hypothesizing
- Further Scientific Data Collection
- Data Analysis
- Deduction

OTHER TYPES OF RESEARCH
- Case Studies
- Action Research

CHAPTER OBJECTIVES

After completing Chapter 2 you should be able to:

1. Explain what is meant by scientific investigation, giving examples of both
   scientific and nonscientific investigations.

2. Explain the eight hallmarks of science.

3. Briefly explain why research in the organizational behavior and management areas cannot be completely scientific.

4. Describe the building blocks of science.

5. Discuss the seven steps of the hypothetico-deductive method, using an example of your own.

6. Appreciate the advantages of knowledge about scientific investigation.

Managers frequently face issues that call for critical decision making. Recall the various issues that confronted Chuck Orlando in Chapter 1. Managerial decisions based on the results of scientific research tend to be effective. In Chapter 1, we defined research as an organized, systematic, data-based, critical, objective, scientific inquiry into a specific problem that needs a solution. Decisions based on the results of a well-done scientific study tend to yield the desired results. It is necessary to understand what the term *scientific* means. Scientific research focuses on solving problems and pursues a step-by-step logical, organized, and rigorous method to identify the problems, gather data, analyze them, and draw valid conclusions therefrom. Thus, scientific research is not based on hunches, experience, and intuition (though these may play a part in final decision making), but is purposive and rigorous. Because of the rigorous way in which it is done, scientific research enables all those who are interested in researching and knowing about the same or similar issues to come up with comparable findings when the data are analyzed. Scientific research also helps researchers to state their findings with accuracy and confidence. This helps various other organizations to apply those solutions when they encounter similar problems. Furthermore, scientific investigation tends to be more objective than subjective, and helps managers to highlight the most critical factors at the workplace that need specific attention so as to avoid, minimize, or solve problems. Scientific investigation and managerial decision making are integral aspects of effective problem solving.

The term *scientific research* applies to both basic and applied research. Applied research may or may not be generalizable to other organizations, depending on the extent to which differences exist in such factors as size, nature of work, characteristics of the employees, and structure of the organization. Nevertheless, applied research also has to be an organized and systematic process where problems are carefully identified, data scientifically gathered and analyzed, and conclusions drawn in an objective manner for effective problem solving.

Do organizations always follow the rigorous step-by-step process? No. Sometimes the problem may be so simple that it does not call for elaborate research, and past experiences might offer the necessary solution. At other times, exigencies of time (where quick decisions are called for), unwillingness to expend the resources needed for doing good research, lack of knowledge, and other factors might prompt businesses to try to solve problems based on hunches. However, the probability of making wrong decisions in such cases is high. Even such business "gurus" as Lee Iacocca confess to making big mistakes due to errors of judgment. *Business Week, Fortune,* and the *Wall Street Journal,* among other business periodicals and newspapers, feature articles from time to time about organizations that face difficulties because of wrong decisions made on the basis of hunches and/or insufficient information. Many implemented plans fail because not enough research has preceded their formulation.

THE HALLMARKS OF SCIENTIFIC RESEARCH

The hallmarks or main distinguishing characteristics of scientific research may be listed as follows:

1. Purposiveness
2. Rigor
3. Testability
4. Replicability
5. Precision and Confidence
6. Objectivity
7. Generalizability
8. Parsimony

Each of these characteristics can be explained in the context of a concrete example. Let us consider the case of a manager who is interested in investigating how employees' commitment to the organization can be increased. We shall examine how the eight hallmarks of science apply to this investigation so that it may be considered "scientific."

Purposiveness

not all "research" is well defined... "fact finding mission"

The manager has started the research with a definite aim or purpose. The focus is on increasing the commitment of employees to the organization, as this will be beneficial in many ways. An increase in employee commitment will translate into less turnover, less absenteeism, and probably increased performance levels, all of which would definitely benefit the organization. The research thus has a purposive focus.

Rigor

A good theoretical base and a sound methodological design would add rigor to a purposive study. Rigor connotes carefulness, scrupulousness, and the degree

theoretical Framework

 # matters how many employees

of exactitude in research investigations. In the case of our example, let us say the manager of an organization asks 10 to 12 of its employees to indicate what would increase their level of commitment to it. If, solely on the basis of their responses, the manager reaches several conclusions on how employee commitment can be increased, the whole approach to the investigation would be unscientific. It would lack rigor for the following reasons: (1) the conclusions would be incorrectly drawn because they are based on the responses of just a few employees whose opinions may not be representative of those of the entire workforce, (2) the manner of framing and addressing the questions could have introduced bias or incorrectness in the responses, and (3) there might be many other important influences on organizational commitment that this small sample of respondents did not or could not verbalize during the interviews, and the researcher would have failed to include them. Therefore, conclusions drawn from an investigation that lacks a good theoretical foundation, as evidenced by reason (3), and methodological sophistication, as evident from (1) and (2) above, would be unscientific. Rigorous research involves a good theoretical base and a carefully thought-out methodology. These factors enable the researcher to collect the right kind of information from an appropriate sample with the minimum degree of bias, and facilitate suitable analysis of the data gathered. The following chapters of this book address these theoretical and methodological issues. Rigor in research design also makes possible the achievement of the other six hallmarks of science that we shall now discuss.

Testability

If, after talking to a random selection of employees of the organization and study of the previous research done in the area of organizational commitment, the manager or researcher develops certain hypotheses on how employee commitment can be enhanced, then these can be tested by applying certain statistical tests to the data collected for the purpose. For instance, the researcher might hypothesize that those employees who perceive greater opportunities for participation in decision making would have a higher level of commitment. This is a hypothesis that can be tested when the data are collected. A correlation analysis would indicate whether the hypothesis is substantiated or not. The use of several other tests, such as the chi-square test and the *t*-test, is discussed in the Module titled Refresher on Statistical Terms and Tests at the end of this book, and in Chapter 12.

Scientific research thus lends itself to testing logically developed hypotheses to see whether or not the data support the educated conjectures or hypotheses that are developed after a careful study of the problem situation. Testability thus becomes another hallmark of scientific research.

Replicability

Let us suppose that the manager/researcher, based on the results of the study, concludes that participation in decision making is one of the most important factors that influences the commitment of employees to the organization. We will place more faith and credence in these findings and conclusion if similar findings emerge on the basis of data collected by other organizations employing the same methods. To put it differently, the results of the tests of hypotheses should be supported again and yet again when the same type of research is repeated in other similar circumstances. To the extent that this does happen (i.e., the results are *replicated* or repeated), we will gain confidence in the scientific nature of our research. In other words, our hypotheses would not have been supported merely by chance, but are reflective of the true state of affairs in the population. Replicability is thus another hallmark of scientific research.

Precision and Confidence

In management research, we seldom have the luxury of being able to draw "definitive" conclusions on the basis of the results of data analysis. This is because we are unable to study the universe of items, events, or population we are interested in, and have to base our findings on a sample that we draw from the universe. In all probability, the sample in question may not reflect the exact characteristics of the phenomenon we try to study (these difficulties are discussed in greater detail in a later chapter). Measurement errors and other problems are also bound to introduce an element of bias or error in our findings. However, we would like to design the research in a manner that ensures that our findings are as close to reality (i.e., the true state of affairs in the universe) as possible, so that we can place reliance or confidence in the results.

Precision refers to the closeness of the findings to "reality" based on a sample. In other words, precision reflects the degree of accuracy or exactitude of the results on the basis of the sample, to what really exists in the universe. For example, if I estimated the number of production days lost during the year due to absenteeism at between 30 and 40, as against the actual of 35, the precision of my estimation compares more favorably than if I had indicated that the loss of production days was somewhere between 20 and 50. You may recall the term *confidence interval* in statistics, which is what is referred to here as precision.

Confidence refers to the probability that our estimations are correct. That is, it is not merely enough to be precise, but it is also important that we can confidently claim that 95% of the time our results would be true and there is only a 5% chance of our being wrong. This is also known as confidence level.

The narrower the limits within which we can estimate the range of our predictions (i.e., the more precise our findings) and the greater the confidence we have in our research results, the more useful and scientific the findings become. In social science research, a 95% confidence level—which implies that there is only a 5% probability that the findings may *not* be correct—is accepted as conventional, and is usually referred to as a significance level of .05 ($p = .05$). Thus, precision and confidence are important aspects of research, which are attained through appropriate scientific sampling design. The greater the precision and confidence we aim at in our research, the more scientific is the investigation and the more useful are the results. Both precision and confidence are discussed in detail in Chapter 11 on Sampling.

Objectivity

[handwritten margin notes: "Why would someone pay is that their is "no such thing"]

[handwritten margin notes: me" one of Research's greatest shortcomings"]

*[handwritten margin notes: * difficult in a complex system - even choosen's what to study is subjective - what articles to read, who to hire...]*

The conclusions drawn through the interpretation of the results of data analysis should be objective; that is, they should be based on the facts of the findings derived from actual data, and not on our own subjective or emotional values. For instance, if we had a hypothesis that stated that greater participation in decision making will increase organizational commitment, and this was not supported by the results, it makes no sense if the researcher continues to argue that increased opportunities for employee participation would still help! Such an argument would be based, not on the factual, data-based research findings, but on the subjective opinion of the researcher. If this was the researcher's conviction all along, then there was no need to do the research in the first place!

Much damage can be sustained by organizations that implement non-data-based or misleading conclusions drawn from research. For example, if the hypothesis relating to organizational commitment in our previous example was not supported, considerable time and effort would be wasted in finding ways to create opportunities for employee participation in decision making. We would only find later that employees still keep quitting, remain absent, and do not develop any sense of commitment to the organization. Likewise, if research shows that increased pay is not going to increase the job satisfaction of employees, then implementing a revised increased pay system will only drag down the company financially without attaining the desired objective. Such a futile exercise, then, is based on nonscientific interpretation and implementation of the research results. *[handwritten: But, doesn't always give best results in the long run]*

The more objective the interpretation of the data, the more scientific the research investigation becomes. Though managers or researchers might start with some initial subjective values and beliefs, their interpretation of the data should be stripped of personal values and bias. If managers attempt to do their own research, they should be particularly sensitive to this aspect. Objectivity is thus another hallmark of scientific investigation. *[handwritten: not completely possible - a second opinion can help]*

Generalizability

[handwritten: This is part of the reason publishing is so important]

Generalizability refers to the scope of applicability of the research findings in one organizational setting to other settings. Obviously, the wider the range of applicability of the solutions generated by research, the more useful the research is to the users. For instance, if a researcher's findings that participation in decision making enhances organizational commitment are found to be true in a variety of manufacturing, industrial, and service organizations, and not merely in the particular organization studied by the researcher, then the generalizability of the findings to other organizational settings is enhanced. The more generalizable the research, the greater its usefulness and value. However, not many research findings can be generalized to all other settings, situations, or organizations.

For wider generalizability, the research sampling design has to be logically developed and a number of other details in the data-collection methods need to be meticulously followed. However, a more elaborate sampling design, which would doubtless increase the generalizability of the results, would also increase the costs of research. Most applied research is generally confined to research within the particular organization where the problem arises, and the results, at best, are generalizable only to other identical situations and settings. Though such limited applicability does not necessarily decrease its scientific value (subject to proper research), its generalizability is restricted.

Parsimony

[handwritten marginalia: Sometimes forgotten. Especially w/ the increase in technology ↳ *daughters IM.ing each other,* ↳ *calling from store* ↳ *mapquesting ansloo of just getting diredn* ↳ *collecting too many variables & running useless stats]*

Simplicity in explaining the phenomena or problems that occur, and in generating solutions for the problems, is always preferred to complex research frameworks that consider an unmanageable number of factors. For instance, if two or three specific variables in the work situation are identified, which when changed would raise the organizational commitment of the employees by 45%, that would be more useful and valuable to the manager than if it were recommended that he should change 10 different variables to increase organizational commitment by 48%. Such an unmanageable number of variables might well be totally beyond the manager's control to change. Therefore, the achievement of a meaningful and parsimonious, rather than an elaborate and cumbersome, model for problem solution becomes a critical issue in research.

Economy in research models is achieved when we can build into our research framework a lesser number of variables that would explain the variance far more efficiently than a complex set of variables that would only marginally add to the variance explained. Parsimony can be introduced with a good understanding of the problem and the important factors that influence it. Such a good conceptual theoretical model can be realized through unstructured and structured interviews with the concerned people, and a thorough literature review of the previous research work in the particular problem area.

In sum, scientific research encompasses the eight criteria just discussed. These are discussed in more detail later in this book. At this point, a question that might be asked is why a scientific approach is necessary for investigations when systematic research by simply collecting and analyzing data would produce results that can be applied to solve the problem. The reason for following a scientific method is that the results will be less prone to errors and more confidence can be placed in the findings because of the greater rigor in application of the design details. This also increases the replicability and generalizability of the findings.

SOME OBSTACLES TO CONDUCTING SCIENTIFIC RESEARCH IN THE MANAGEMENT AREA

In the management and behavioral areas, it is not always possible to conduct investigations that are 100% scientific, in the sense that, unlike in the physical sciences, the results obtained will not be exact and error-free. This is primarily because of difficulties likely to be encountered in the measurement and collection of data in the subjective areas of feelings, emotions, attitudes, and perceptions.

These problems occur whenever we attempt to quantify human behavior. Difficulties might also be encountered in obtaining a representative sample, restricting the generalizability of the findings. Thus, it is not always possible to meet all the hallmarks of science in full. Comparability, consistency, and wide generalizability are often difficult to obtain in research. Still, to the extent that the research is designed to ensure purposiveness, rigor, and the maximum possible testability, replicability, generalizability, objectivity, parsimony, and precision and confidence, we would have endeavored to engage in scientific investigation. Several other possible limitations in research studies are discussed in subsequent chapters.

THE BUILDING BLOCKS OF SCIENCE IN RESEARCH

One of the primary methods of scientific investigation is the hypothetico-deductive method. The deductive and inductive processes in research are described below.

Deduction and Induction

Answers to issues can be found either by the process of deduction or the process of induction, or by a combination of the two. *Deduction* is the process by which we arrive at a reasoned conclusion by logical generalization of a known fact. For example, we know that all high performers are highly proficient in their jobs. If John is a high performer, we then conclude that he is highly proficient in his job. *Induction,* on the other hand, is a process where we observe certain phenomena and on this basis arrive at conclusions. In other words, in induction we logically establish a general proposition based on observed facts. For instance, we see that the production processes are the prime features of factories or manufacturing plants. We therefore conclude that factories exist for production purposes. Both the deductive and the inductive processes are applied in scientific investigations.

Theories based on deduction and induction help us to understand, explain, and/or predict business phenomena. When research is designed to test some specific hypothesized outcomes, as for instance, to see if controlling aversive noise in the environment increases the performance of individuals in solving mental puzzles, the following steps ensue. The investigator begins with the theory that noise adversely affects mental problem solving. The hypothesis is then generated that if the noise is controlled, mental puzzles can be solved more quickly and correctly. Based on this a research project is designed to test the hypothesis. The results of the study help the researcher to deduce or conclude that controlling the aversive noise does indeed help the participants to improve their performance on mental puzzles. This method of starting with a theoretical framework, formulating hypotheses, and logically deducing from the results of the study is known as the hypothetico-deductive method.

The building blocks of scientific inquiry are depicted in Figure 2.1 and include the processes of initially observing phenomena, identifying the problem, constructing a theory as to what might be happening, developing hypotheses,

Figure 2.1
The building blocks of science.

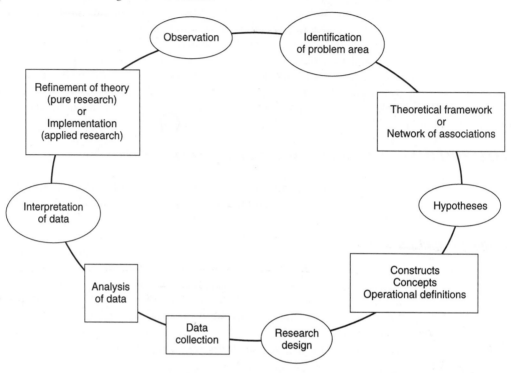

determining aspects of the research design, collecting data, analyzing the data, and interpreting the results.

The significance of these building blocks can be illustrated through an example.

Example 2.1   A sales manager might *observe* that customers are perhaps not as pleased as they used to be. The manager may not be certain that this is really the case but may experience anxiety and some uneasiness that customer satisfaction is on the decline. This process of ***observation*** or sensing of the phenomena around us is what gets most of the research—whether applied or basic—started. The next step for the manager is to determine whether there is a real problem, and if so, how serious it is. This ***problem identification*** calls for some preliminary data gathering. The manager might talk casually to a few customers to find out how they feel about the products and customer service. During the course of these conversations the manager might find that the customers like the products but are upset because many of the items they need are frequently out of stock, and they perceive the salespersons as not being helpful. From discussions with some of the salespersons, the manager might discover that the factory does not supply the goods on time and promises new delivery dates that it fails on occasions to keep. Salespersons might also indicate that they try to please and retain the customers by communicating the delivery dates given to them by the factory.

Integration of the information obtained through the informal and formal interviewing process has helped the manager to determine that a problem does exist. It also helps the manager to formulate a conceptual model or ***theoretical framework*** of all the factors contributing to the problem. In this case, there is a network of connections among the following factors: delays by the factory in delivering goods, the notification of later delivery dates that are not kept, the promises of the salespersons to the customers (in hopes of retaining them) that cannot be fulfilled, all of which contribute to customer dissatisfaction. From the theoretical framework, which is a meaningful integration of all the information gathered, several ***hypotheses*** can be generated and tested to determine if the data support them. Concepts are then ***operationally defined*** so that they can be measured. A ***research design*** is set up to decide on, among other issues, how to ***collect*** further data, ***analyze*** and ***interpret*** them, and finally, to provide an answer to the problem. The process of drawing from logical analysis an inference that purports to be conclusive is called ***deduction.*** Thus, the building blocks of science provide the genesis for the hypothetico-deductive method of scientific research, a discussion of which follows.

THE HYPOTHETICO-DEDUCTIVE METHOD

The Seven-Step Process in the Hypothetico-Deductive Method

The seven steps involved in the hypothetico-deductive method of research stem from the building blocks discussed above, and are listed and discussed below.

1. Observation
2. Preliminary information gathering
3. Theory formulation
4. Hypothesizing
5. Further scientific data collection
6. Data analysis
7. Deduction

Observation

Observation is the first stage, in which one senses that certain changes are occurring, or that some new behaviors, attitudes, and feelings are surfacing in one's environment (i.e., the workplace). When the observed phenomena are seen to have potentially important consequences, one would proceed to the next step.

How does one observe phenomena and changes in the environment? The people-oriented manager is always sensitive to and aware of what is happening in and around the workplace. Changes in attitudes, behaviors, communication patterns and styles, and a score of other verbal and nonverbal cues can be readily picked up by managers who are sensitive to the various nuances. Irrespective of whether we are dealing with finance, accounting, management, marketing, or administrative matters, and regardless of the sophistication of the machines and the Internet, in the ultimate analysis, it is the people who achieve the goals and make things happen. Whether it is the installation of an effective Management Information System, a new manufacturing technology, distribution channel, strategic plan, cost accounting system, investment plan, or training scheme, it is mainly through the efforts of the employees that the goals are attained. The vast majority react and respond positively or negatively to various factors in the work environment, and knowingly or unwittingly transmit cues, which the manager can easily pick up. When there is indeed a problem in the situation, the manager may not understand what exactly is happening, but can definitely sense that things are not what they should be.

Likewise, a drop in sales, frequent production interruptions, incorrect accounting results, low yielding investments, disinterestedness of employees in their work, and the like, could easily attract the attention of the manager, though why they occur may be an enigma.

Preliminary Information Gathering

Preliminary information gathering involves the seeking of information in depth, of what is observed. This could be done by talking informally to several people in the work setting or to clients, or to other relevant sources, thereby gathering information on what is happening and why. Through these unstructured interviews, one gets an idea or a "feel" for what is transpiring in the situation. Once the researcher increases the level of awareness as to what is happening, the person could then focus on the problem and the associated factors through further structured, formal interviews with the relevant groups. Additionally, by doing library research, or obtaining information through other sources, the investigator would identify how such issues have been tackled in other situations. This information would give additional insights of possible factors that could be operating in the particular situation—over and above those that had not surfaced in the previous interviews.

Thus, a mass of information would have been collected through the interviews and library search. The next step is to make sense of the factors that have been identified in the information-gathering stage by piecing them together in some meaningful fashion.

Theory Formulation

Theory formulation, the next step, is an attempt to integrate all the information in a logical manner, so that the factors responsible for the problem can be conceptualized and tested. The theoretical framework formulated is often guided by experience and intuition. In this step the critical variables are examined as to their contribution or influence in explaining why the problem occurs and how it can be solved. The network of associations identified among the variables would then be theoretically woven together with justification as to why they might influence the problem. This process of theory formulation is discussed in greater detail in Chapter 5.

One might wonder at this juncture why a theory has to be formulated each time a problem is investigated, and why one cannot act on the information contained in the previously published research findings, as one surveys the literature. There are a couple of reasons for this. One is that different studies might have identified different variables, some of which may not be relevant to the situation on hand. Also, in the previous studies, some of the hypotheses might have been substantiated and some others not, presenting a perplexing situation. Hence, problem solving in every complex problem situation is facilitated by formulating and testing theories relevant to that particular situation.

Hypothesizing

Hypothesizing is the next logical step after theory formulation. From the theorized network of associations among the variables, certain testable hypotheses or educated conjectures can be generated. For instance, at this point, one might hypothesize that if a sufficient number of items are stocked on shelves, customer dissatisfaction will be considerably reduced. This is a hypothesis that can be tested to determine if the statement would be supported.

Hypothesis testing is called **deductive** research. Sometimes, hypotheses that were not originally formulated do get generated through the process of **induction.** That is, after the data are obtained, some creative insights occur, and based on these, new hypotheses could get generated to be tested later. Generally, in research, hypotheses testing through deductive research and hypotheses generation through induction are both common. The Hawthorne experiments are a good example of this. In the relay assembly line, many experiments were conducted that increased lighting and the like, based on the original hypothesis that these would account for increases in productivity. But later, when these hypotheses were not substantiated, a new hypothesis was generated based on observed data. The mere fact that people were chosen for the study gave them a feeling of importance that increased their productivity whether or not lighting, heating, or other effects were improved, thus the coining of the term the *Hawthorne effect!*

Further Scientific Data Collection

After the development of the hypotheses, data with respect to each variable in the hypotheses need to be obtained. In other words, further scientific data collection is needed to test the hypotheses that are generated in the study. For instance, to test the hypothesis that stocking sufficient items will reduce customer dissatisfaction, one needs to measure the current level of customer satisfaction and collect further data on customer satisfaction levels whenever sufficient number of items are stocked and made readily available to the customers. Data on every variable in the theoretical framework from which hypotheses are generated should also be collected. These data then form the basis for further data analysis.

Data Analysis

In the data analysis step, the data gathered are statistically analyzed to see if the hypotheses that were generated have been supported. For instance, to see if stock levels influence customer satisfaction, one might want to do a correlational analysis and determine the relationship between the two factors. Similarly, other hypotheses could be tested through appropriate statistical analysis. Analyses of both quantitative and qualitative data can be done to determine if certain conjectures are substantiated. Qualitative data refer to information gathered in a narrative form through interviews and observations. For example, to test the theory that budgetary constraints adversely impact on managers' responses to their work, several interviews might be conducted with managers after budget restrictions are imposed. The responses from the managers who verbalize their reactions in different ways might be then organized to see the different categories under which they fall and the extent to which the same kinds of responses are articulated by the managers.

Deduction

Deduction is the process of arriving at conclusions by interpreting the meaning of the results of the data analysis. For instance, if it was found from the data analysis that increasing the stocks was positively correlated to (increased) customer satisfaction (say, .5), then one can deduce that if customer satisfaction is to be increased, the shelves have to be better stocked. Another inference from this data analysis is that stocking of shelves accounts for (or explains) 25% of the variance in customer satisfaction ($.5^2$). Based on these deductions, the researcher would make recommendations on how the "customer dissatisfaction" problem could be solved.

In summary, there are seven steps involved in identifying and resolving a problematic issue. To make sure that the seven steps of the hypothetico-deductive method are properly understood, let us briefly review two examples in an organizational setting and the course of action taken in the seven steps.

Two Examples of the Application of the Hypothetico-Deductive Method in Organizations

Example 2.2   THE CIO DILEMMA

Observation

The Chief Information Officer (CIO) of a firm observes that the newly installed Management Information System (MIS) is not being used by middle managers as much as was originally expected. The managers often approach the CIO or some other "computer expert" for help, or worse still, make decisions without facts. "There is surely a problem here," the CIO exclaims.

Information Gathering through Informal Interviews

Talking to some of the middle-level managers, the CIO finds that many of them have very little idea as to what MIS is all about, what kinds of information it could provide, and how to access it and utilize the information.

Obtaining More Information through Literature Survey

The CIO immediately uses the Internet to explore further information on the lack of use of MIS in organizations. The search indicates that many middle-level managers—especially the old-timers—are not familiar with operating personal computers and experience "computer anxiety." Lack of knowledge about what MIS offers is also found to be another main reason why some managers do not use it.

Formulating a Theory

Based on all this information, the CIO develops a theory incorporating all the relevant factors contributing to the lack of access to the MIS by managers in the organization.

Hypothesizing

From such a theory, the CIO generates various hypotheses for testing, one among them being: Knowledge of the usefulness of MIS would help managers to put it to greater use.

Data Collection

The CIO then develops a short questionnaire on the various factors theorized to influence the use of the MIS by managers, such as the extent of knowledge of what MIS is, what kinds of information MIS provides, how to gain access to the information, and the level of comfort felt by managers in using computers in general, and finally, how often managers have used the MIS in the preceding 3 months.

Data Analysis

The CIO then analyzes the data obtained through the questionnaire to see what factors prevent the managers from using the system.

Deduction

Based on the results, the manager deduces or concludes that managers do not use MIS owing to certain factors. These deductions help the CIO to take necessary action to rectify the situation, which might include, among other things, organizing seminars for training managers on the use of computers, and MIS and its usefulness.

Example 2.3   THE UNINTENDED CONSEQUENCES OF BUDGET CUTS

Observation

The Vice President in charge of Finance senses that the budgetary process is not working as well as it should. Managers seem to be overcautious, pad their budgets excessively, and all in all, seem to be acting defensively. In essence, the VP observes various phenomena and senses a problem.

Information Gathering through Informal Interviews

The VP chats with a few of the managers and their staff. He finds that there is much anxiety among the managers that the budgets for all departments are likely to be slashed. There is also a perception that the new information system that is planned for installation will take away from the managers much of their original power and control. A general notion that the managers who have bigger budgets will be evaluated more favorably also seems to prevail.

Gathering More Information through Literature Survey

Amused by these findings, the VP reads materials on the subject and finds that many factors, including the ones identified through the interviews, are instrumental in thwarting the idea of effective budgeting.

Formulating Theory about What Is Happening

Piecing together the information obtained from the interviews and the literature, the VP develops a theory of possible factors that may be influencing ineffective budgeting practices. That is, a theoretical framework of the factors that could account for padding of budgets is developed.

Hypothesizing

From the theory, the VP conjectures the relationships among the factors, and one of the hypotheses is that fear of budget cuts influences excessive padding of the budget.

Data Collection

In this phase, the VP collects data from the other managers anonymously through a questionnaire, on various factors such as the extent of anxiety regarding perceived budget cuts, concern regarding the installation of the proposed information systems, and the like.

Data Analysis

The VP then has the data analyzed to see if there are indeed significant correlations between each of the different factors and slack in the budget (i.e., the hypotheses are tested).

Deduction

If significant correlations are in fact found, the VP would deduce (or conclude) that misperceptions about budget cuts and the proposed information system did indeed have an influence on the managers padding their budgets. To solve the problem, the VP may then clarify the real situation to the managers, allay their fears, and educate them on how they would all benefit by proposing realistic budgets.

Review of the Hypothetico-Deductive Method

In summary, the hypothetico-deductive method involves the seven steps of observation, preliminary data gathering, theory formulation, hypothesizing, scientific data collection, data analysis, and deduction. Later chapters in this book will discuss how hypothetico-deductive research might be conducted scientifically in organizations.

OTHER TYPES OF RESEARCH

Case studies and action research are sometimes used to study certain types of issues. These will be briefly discussed now.

Case Studies

Case studies involve in-depth, contextual analyses of similar situations in other organizations, where the nature and definition of the problem happen to be the same as experienced in the current situation. As in the hypothetico-deductive studies, hypotheses can be developed in case studies as well. However, if a particular hypothesis has *not* been substantiated in even a single other case study, no support can be established for the alternate hypothesis developed.

Case study, as a problem-solving technique, is not often undertaken in organizations because such studies dealing with problems similar to the one experienced by a particular organization of a particular size and in a particular type of setting are difficult to come by. Moreover, authentic case studies are difficult to find because many companies prefer to guard them as proprietary data. However, by carefully scrutinizing documented case studies, the manager is in a position to obtain several clues as to what factors might be operating in the current situation and how the problem might be solved. Picking the right cases for study, and understanding and correctly translating the dynamics to one's own situation, are critical for successful problem solving. It should be noted that case studies usually provide qualitative rather than quantitative data for analysis and interpretation. However, the application of case study analysis to certain organizational issues is relatively easy. For example, a study of what contributes to the successful installation of a good MIS system in organizations similar to the one that is planning to install it, and the practical application of that knowledge would be very functional.

Action Research

Action research is sometimes undertaken by consultants who want to initiate change processes in organizations. In other words, action research methodology is most appropriate while effecting planned changes. Here, the researcher begins with a problem that is already identified, and gathers relevant data to provide a tentative problem solution. This solution is then implemented, with the knowledge that there may be unintended consequences following such implementation. The effects are then evaluated, defined, and diagnosed, and the research continues on an ongoing basis until the problem is fully resolved.

Thus, action research is a constantly evolving project with interplay among problem, solution, effects or consequences, and new solution. A sensible and realistic problem definition and creative ways of collecting data are critical to action research. An example of a situation where action research will be useful is given below.

Example 2.4   The vice president of CDS Co. wants to introduce a new system of bookkeeping that is likely to meet with some resistance from the Accounting Department. Based on the past experience in the organization, the VP would like to seek a solution to the problem of employee resistance.

There are several other methods of obtaining data for research purposes, such as through focus groups, panels, observational studies, projective techniques, and interactive media, as we shall see in Chapter 10.

SUMMARY

In this chapter we obtained a general understanding of what constitutes scientific research and examined the hallmarks of scientific investigations. We also discussed, with examples, the steps involved in the hypothetico-deductive method of studying a problem in order to solve it. When managers realize the value of scientific investigation, they are able to understand and readily accept the need for "good" research. This offers the opportunity to effectively solve complex problems encountered at the workplace. The manager also realizes that although organizational research cannot offer 100% accuracy in results, choices and trade-offs among the various criteria of scientific investigation can be made to obtain valid results for good decision making.

In this chapter, we also briefly touched on case studies and action research. Several methods of collecting data and analyzing them for these types of research are discussed at length in Chapter 10.

Because modern technology has befriended the research process in a big way, in the next chapter we will broadly discuss some of the ways in which technology, and in particular the Internet, facilitates exploration of the exciting, wide global world of research.

DISCUSSION QUESTIONS AND POINTS TO PONDER

1. Describe the hallmarks of scientific research.

2. What are the steps in hypothetico-deductive research? Explain them, using an example not in the book.

3. One hears the word *research* being mentioned by several groups such as research organizations, college and university professors, doctoral students, graduate assistants working for faculty, graduate and undergraduate students doing their term papers, research departments in industries, newspaper reporters, journalists, lawyers, doctors, and many other professionals and nonprofessionals. In the light of what you have learned in this chapter, which among the aforementioned groups of people do you think may be doing "scientific" investigations in the areas of basic or applied research? Why?

4. Explain the processes of deduction and induction, giving an example of each.

 5. If research in the management area cannot be 100% scientific, why bother to do it at all? Comment on this statement.

6. Critique the following research done in a service industry as to the extent to which it meets the hallmarks of scientific investigation discussed in this chapter.

The Friendly Telephone Company

Customer complaints were mounting, and letters of complaint detailing the problems they experienced with the residential telephones lines were constantly pouring in at the Friendly Telephone Company. The company wanted to pinpoint the specific problems and take corrective action.

Researchers were called in, and they spoke to a number of customers, noting the nature of the specific problems they faced. Because the problem had to be attended to very quickly, they developed a theoretical base, collected relevant detailed information from a sample of 100 customers, and analyzed the data. The results promise to be fairly accurate with at least an 85% chance of success in problem solving. The researchers will make recommendations to the company based on the results of data analysis.

---

 7. Strictly speaking, would case studies be considered as scientific research? Why or why not?

8. What is action research? Describe a specific situation where action research will be warranted.

9. Comment on the following situation.

The Dilemmas of Dorothy Dunning

Dorothy Dunning, Chief Production Manager, was on top of the world just 2 years ago. In her nontraditional job, she was cited to be the real backbone of the company, and her performance was in no small measure responsible for the mergers the institution was contemplating with other well-known global corporations.

Of late though, the products of the company had to be recalled several times owing to safety concerns. Quality glitches and production delays also plagued the company.

To project a good image to consumers, Dunning developed a very reassuring web site and made sweeping changes in the manufacturing processes to enhance the quality of the product, minimize defects, and enhance the efficiency of the workers.

A year after all these changes, the company continues to recall defective products!

TECHNOLOGY AND BUSINESS RESEARCH

TOPICS DISCUSSED

INFORMATION NEEDS OF BUSINESS

COMMONLY USED TECHNOLOGIES IN BUSINESS RESEARCH

- The Internet
- Electronic Mail
- The Intranet
- Browsers
- Web Sites

SOME SOFTWARE USED IN BUSINESS RESEARCH

- Groupware
- Neural Networks
- CAM/CAD
- Enterprise Resource Planning
- Data Analytic Software Programs

EMERGING TECHNOLOGY APPLICATIONS

- Handheld Devices
- Interactive Voice, CD-ROM
- Digital Boards
- Group Videoconferencing
- Virtual Reality
- Linkage of PCs to Electronic Devices

INFORMATION SYSTEMS AND MANAGERIAL DECISION MAKING

- Data Warehousing, Data Mining, and Operations Research

INTERNATIONAL DIMENSIONS OF CYBERSPACE

DATA STORAGE AND SURVEILLANCE

- Storage of Databases
- Data Security

MANAGERIAL ADVANTAGE OF TECHNOLOGICAL ADVANCEMENTS

ETHICS IN HANDLING INFORMATION TECHNOLOGY

CHAPTER OBJECTIVES

After completing Chapter 3 you should be able to:

1. Explain the advantages of technology for business communication.
2. Be conversant with some of the uses of PC software.
3. Have an idea of what Information Systems can do for business.
4. Know about Internet, Intranet, browsers, and web sites.
5. Understand the usefulness and hazards of e-mail in business communication.
6. Have some knowledge of data warehousing and data mining.
7. Recognize the potential misuse of technology and know how to guard against it.

The centrality of technology in all aspects of business cannot be overstated. Technology, as used in this chapter, refers to all hardware, software, and other communication aids that achieve the desired business results. For instance, if we have to send out a professional business letter, word processing software would be the technology employed for the purpose; if we want to advertise our products, web technology would be an effective means; and if we need to find published material on any topic of interest, recourse to the Internet would ferret out the desired data.

Comparison of the following headline items in 1998 and 2001 mirrors the advances in technology and pinpoints the repercussions in their wake.

Headlines published in 1998

An electronics firm will save big money by replacing six people with one and lose all this paperwork (referring to a mound of papers depicted on the side) using Enterprise Resource Planning software.

Fortune, February 2, 1998, p. 149

Business Secrets of the Billion-Dollar Website—Yes, the Web is already big in business. This website may be the future of retailing.

Fortune, February 2, 1998, p. 142

The arrival of e-business is rewriting the very fundamentals of business: redefining relationships with customers and suppliers, creating new business models, even redrawing the boundaries between industries.

Business Week, March 23, 1998, p. 80

Headlines published in 2001

Terror attacks help boost technologies that help save vital information.

Time, October 2001, p. Y11

The ease with which information can be shared globally, for all its good, also works to the advantage of terrorists, says Howard Perlmutter, professor emeritus of social architecture at the Wharton School of the University of Pennsylvania.

Information Week, September 17, 2001

Russian programmer accused of breaking copyright law tells his side of the story.

San Francisco Chronicle, August 31, 2001, B1

In the present global business environment, research needs to take advantage of the current and emerging technologies to find solutions to problems. We will now offer a *broad overview* of various technologies that facilitate managers in decision making, particularly as they relate to business research. We will particularly highlight those that enhance the effectiveness of organizations insofar as they help research in the preliminary information-gathering phase, and subsequently in obtaining and analyzing data from several sources for enabling business decisions. We will also briefly discuss information technology that helps managers to find ready access to stored data for managerial decision making. The ensuing chapters in this book will provide more specific details of the use of particular software for literature search, data collection, data analysis, and business presentations, as are relevant.

INFORMATION NEEDS OF BUSINESS

To run a business, useful, timely, accurate, reliable, and valid data are needed. When *data* in their raw form are evaluated, analyzed, and synthesized, useful *information* becomes available to managers that helps them make good business decisions. For example, figures of gross sales, profits, and the like, are data of a descriptive nature, which are doubtless informative to the manager (e.g., the amount of dollars received from the sale of the product, and how much profit the company has made). They do not, however, give any indication as to the measures the company could take to promote its growth further. Informed decisions (for instance, sales strategies the company should adopt) would be a function of the analysis of these data and synthesizing them, in conjunction with other relevant information pertaining to different territories, regional sales statistics, competitors' sales and strategies, and the like.

Information gathering, communicating, and decision making go hand in hand. The information age has allowed managers to collect even voluminous data in a short time frame and make sound decisions based on their analyses and interpretation. Apart from the obvious examples of companies whose very survival hinges on research—biotechnology and chemical firms, to cite a few—almost every organization has to engage in research at some level or the other to stay competitive. Companies gather data on a continuing basis, both from within and outside the organization, whether or not they term such activities *research*. For example, firms do engage in the first step of the research process when they gather data from the external environment to assess market trends, competitive practices, and new products. It is also research when they review the effectiveness of internal policies and procedures, or assess their own product performance. Other internal areas of information gathering that a typical business resorts to relate to accounting, administration, budget, finance, sales, marketing, human resources accounting, employee surveys, and the like. Internal and external sources of information often overlap, as when external research on customer preferences, financial markets, and economic indicators determines internal decisions regarding product lines, marketing strategies, and distribution systems.

The methods used to gather, analyze, and synthesize information from the external and internal environments are becoming more and more sophisticated owing to the immense scope of technology, which makes possible timely and efficient research vital to the survival of companies. We will now broadly examine a few of these.

COMMONLY USED TECHNOLOGIES IN BUSINESS RESEARCH

Digital technology has come in handy for research, especially in collecting, storing, and analyzing information. These include all electronic interactive media such as CD-ROM, the DVD, the browser, the Internet and the Intranet, and search engines. Computerized databases on compact disks are available, especially for research in the finance area.

The Internet

The **Internet,** which is a vast global network of computers connecting people and information, has opened up tremendous possibilities for advancing research and expanding the realm of business opportunities throughout the world. . Because the Internet connects us worldwide, any needed research data can be collected from any country through the Internet. For example, customer preferences for packaging a product can be determined and pricing strategies developed for each country, if so desired.

If we want industry information or published materials on any topic of interest, the Internet comes in handy. We can easily download secondary data and print them, for leisurely examination. We can also conduct computer-interactive surveys very efficiently with large global audiences, where the computer will sequence and personalize the questions as we would desire (skip questions and ask appropriate follow-up information). This will require that the respondent at the other end has access to a computer and is willing to respond. The representativeness of the sample will also be compromised, as we shall see in Chapter 11. Companies like SurveyOnLine offer specialized services to conduct Internet surveys for firms that need information of a confidential nature, as for example, the effectiveness of supervisors. Computer-assisted telephone interviews can also be conducted to gather data, as we will see in a later chapter.

The marketing, finance, accounting, sales, and other departments of a company can and do use the Internet frequently for their research. In the business environment, desktop computers can be connected to the local area network (LAN), which in turn, could be hooked to the Internet by a high-speed line. This would help several individual employees to gain simultaneous access to central information. The LAN enables employees with computers in close proximity to share information resources and files, and helps schedule, monitor, and process data from remote locations.

Business research can proceed using the Internet and search engines, even where sources of information on a particular topic are not readily known. Search engines are software programs designed to help the search on the World Wide Web. By keying in the important (key) words that describe the topic in some fashion, the user can address the search engine to suggest the best possible "links" (sites with the requested information) and access them directly to review the needed data. Altavista and Google are two such search engines put to frequent use.

Electronic Mail

The Internet also permits the exchange of **electronic mail** (e-mail), which has increasingly become the primary mode of business communication both within and outside the company, especially in the wake of the anthrax scare following the post–September 2001 events. Prior to the pervasive reach of the Internet, e-mail was primarily used within large technically sophisticated corporations, in the academic environment, and in certain government defense sectors, but not between corporations or other entities. The easy global access to the Internet has enabled all organizations and many individuals to have access to e-mail. The external world comprises both national and global territories. E-mail is inexpensive, almost instantaneous, and has the added advantage of guaranteed delivery subject only to the correctness of the e-mail address. E-mail is a simple and effective way of requesting and obtaining data on a variety of topics from both within and outside the organization. Short surveys could also be conducted via e-mail. Several "cyber cafes" offer access to the Internet for those who do not own or have ready access to a computer.

It should be noted that due to bioterrorism hazards attendant on postal communication, e-mail could well become a safer alternative. According to the *San Francisco Chronicle* (October 23, 2001, p. B1), the volume of e-mail has risen 25% since September 11, 2001. When very valuable and confidential information such as company contracts is conveyed by e-mail, firms that provide encrypted e-mail, digital signatures, and other security features stand to benefit.

E-mail provider Critical Path will be selling a service called "online registered mail," which would allow sensitive documents to be sent online with an extra layer of security, and let the sender keep track of when the document is received and opened. With the increasing number of products in the market offering Internet security, transactions of business via e-mail is becoming simplified. Some companies like Schwab also resort to ordinary e-mails, alerting customers that their statement is ready on the company's *secure* web site.

Privacy of employees using the Internet is, however, not always assured. Some companies keep tabs on the use of Internet and e-mail facilities for private purposes. Companies like AOL have a declared policy of not reading customers' e-mail, not keeping tabs on web hits, and not seeking data from children without their parents' approval.

The Intranet

The **Intranet** is to the internal system of the organization what the Internet is to its external environment. That is, it links internal data networks of the company, but prevents access to others outside the company. It also facilitates data gathering from within the company; for example, surveys can be easily conducted through the Intranet to assess employee morale or the popularity of benefit packages.

The Intranet can be creatively put to use. Cronin (1998) remarked that Ford's Intranet success is so spectacular that the automaker's in-house web site could save billions of dollars and fulfill a cherished dream of building cars on demand. Cronin went on to explain how the carmaker's product development system documents thousands of steps that go into manufacturing, assembling, and testing vehicles. By opening its Intranet to major suppliers, Ford customized every car and truck while reducing costs at the same time. For instance, suppliers could provide car seats in the sequence of colors needed, so that blue seats are ready just when the blue cars reach the seat installation station. By opening up its Intranet to suppliers and coordinating the delivery and assembly of thousands of components, some auto companies tried to move closer to "manufacturing on demand." Now automakers use private "trading exchanges" like Covisint to work with suppliers.

Browsers

The wide use of the Internet will not have been rendered possible without the enabling features of the browser, which front-ends the web sites and web applications. Browser software (like Microsoft's Explorer and Netscape) allows even the nontechnical user easy access to and navigation through the web. Without the browsers, the Internet would have continued to be relegated to the confines of a limited group of highly technical users. In a sense, browsers ignited the "Internet revolution."

Web Sites

Organizations create *web sites* to promote their image, communicate with customers, build relationships, share information, offer attractive inducements to prospective customers, and ensure that they keep returning. In some cases they even allow online purchases by customers, bypassing the traditional sales channels. The built-in audit capability and push technology (using cookies to track details of web sites visited) also provides feedback on the efficacy of the sites. Consumers spend millions of dollars shopping on the web. Practically every business creates its web site. As noted by Wildstrom (1998), the World Wide Web is a powerful tool for business communications and a great way to pass on information to customers or to co-workers. Software to create web sites readily and with greater ease is now becoming available.

SOME SOFTWARE USED IN BUSINESS RESEARCH

We now list some of the software programs and examine their application in the different areas of business. As you read through these, ponder how researchers might be helped by the different software.

Groupware

Groupware is a software that runs on a network so that teams can work on joint projects, and it allows people from different departments to access data jointly. For example, if the accounting, finance, sales, and production departments have to coordinate their efforts to come up with a viable product within a tight budget, they will be served well by groupware. This software is of immense use for efficient and effective completion of specific team projects.

Neural Networks

Neural Networks are designed to trace patterns in a set of data and generalize therefrom. This software enables sales forecasts, stock market predictions, detection of weather patterns, and the like. The California Scientific Software's *Brainmaker* used for managing investments by recognizing patterns and trends influencing stock prices can be cited as a specific example.

CAM/CAD

Computer-aided manufacturing (CAM) software helps engineers to design the manufacturing components and directs the production of the product. *Computer-aided design (CAD)* software creates and displays complex drawings with precision, enabling experimentation with different designs. CAD/CAM software that integrates the two has been in use for a long time in manufacturing and production units of organizations. Design sophistication and product development are made possible by this program, and this software is extensively used by manufacturing organizations.

Enterprise Resource Planning

Enterprise Resource Planning (ERP) packages from software companies that offer all-in-one integrated business applications have slowly replaced traditional manufacturing, finance, and order entry applications, which are usually "home designed" and do not lend themselves for easy integration. The trend is to integrate various ERP packages using "best-of-breed" criteria for specific applications for specialized solutions and for industry-specific needs. For example, the needs of pharmaceutical companies differ from those of automobile manufacturing companies, and these are duly taken into account.

The world's two largest software companies, IBM and Microsoft, are said to run big parts of their business on ERP software from SAP, a company based in Germany (Garten, 1998). The advantage of ERP packages is their capability to provide comprehensive solutions to all the needs of an organization in its day-to-day work. This is so because they provide complete support for the executive support system and the Management Information System (MIS), and can work with all existing data bases built on different platforms. Software developers use various tools to build and modify data tables and develop custom functionality.

ERP solutions were initially targeted for big companies and organizations that had to reengineer to install ERP in their systems, with only one goal as the objective—to increase the return on investment. With the top organizations almost saturated, ERP software companies are now targeting their products to the bottom of the pyramid, facing the challenge of meeting a diverse set of applications while trying to keep their costs down.

Data Analytic Software Programs

As will be discussed in later chapters, software programs are available to *obtain,* *store,* and *analyze* raw data collected through surveys, using SPSS, SAS, Excel, and the like. Sophisticated business presentations of the results obtained from data analysis are also possible through computer graphics and interactive CDs, as described later.

Gathering data is facilitated through **audit capabilities** in software that track and provide information on the extent of usage of any function or feature. As we saw, it is now feasible to analyze online purchase requisitions for office supplies to determine frequency, volume, and type of purchases. A company can track the number of times its web site has been visited and the duration of such visits, so as to evaluate its appeal and improvise it, as needed. With a little more programming effort and the cooperation of the visitors to the site, more information on user profile can be easily obtained to assess buying preferences and market demographics—information useful for developing marketing strategies.

Multimedia computers combine text with sound, video animation, and graphics—all vital in business communication and presentations. Connectivity, which enables even incompatible software and hardware to share information and resources through the use of a communication network, will enable us to access information even more easily in the future.

Designing questionnaires, collecting data, data analysis, and web and e-mail surveys are facilitated by several software programs, including SumQuest or SQ Survey Software, Professional Quest, and Perseus.

EMERGING APPLICATIONS IN TECHNOLOGY

Handheld Devices

The new wave of computer technology represented by small, cost-effective, handheld devices like the Palm, assisted by a new class of software, eases data gathering and immediate analyses, and has initiated a process change in field work. Critical data can be gathered at any time and from any location, and analyzed. The wireless device increases efficiency and enables the field work force to spend more time on field operations.

Personal computers that are fast, accurate, reliable, and economical, and facilitate compact storage by reducing paperwork to the minimum, are slowly yielding to handheld computer technology like the Palm Top, which provides a lot of computing power for daily use by executives on the move. Microsoft's Pocket PC 2002, for instance, has in addition to core applications of Word and Excel, Internet Explorer and Outlook-like-e-mail, with security enhancements. Pocket PCs can also check corporate databases. However, for extensive web applications, the handhelds are not as yet the most useful tool due to size and limitations of speed.

Interactive Voice Technology, CD-ROM, and Relational Databases

These are some of the technological advances that have helped businesses to conduct research and increase their operational efficiency. Relational databases refer to those that can be linked in any desired manner.

Digital Whiteboards

Digital whiteboards allow contents on a board displaying intricate diagrams and voluminous notes to be copied on to the PC notepad and transmitted electronically to others, as needed. For example, brainstorming sessions while problem solving can be easily communicated to others in any part of the world by this method. Now it is even possible to digitally store these contents permanently, using a digital whiteboard. When used in conjunction with an electronic projection system (EPS), the board serves as an electronic flipchart and flips back and forth between "pages" to edit in real time. This is very useful during videoconferencing presentations.

Group Videoconferencing

Group videoconferencing reproduces the face-to-face meeting effect by using large TV monitors or multimedia projectors. Videoconferencing systems have the advantage of integrating with other vital business technologies like spreadsheets and presentation software. Thus, much data (including numerical figures) can be exchanged during videoconferencing as organizations try to engage in consultative decision making and further research and analysis. Videoconferencing has become even more attractive in the postterrorist business environment on considerations of cost and safety.

Virtual Reality

Virtual reality creates 3-D environments in which to create a product in a computer and show it to prospective interested groups with details regarding price, materials, and other relevant information. Greeting messages with virtual flowers can compete with Hallmark cards in a big way in the future.

Linkage of PCs to Electronic Devices

One of the latest efforts being made by Microsoft and Sony is to link PCs and consumer electronic devices. For instance, a company can plug a camcorder to a PC or to a TV set top box for sending video mail over the Internet (Clark & Bank, 1998). Business transactions, communication, and research through this mode will be accelerated multifold when the device is perfected.

Thus far we have discussed the usefulness of software packages, the Internet, and other facilities for collecting data needed for decision making. However, unless the data collected periodically by different departments and from different sources, find a repository in a central system, where the information can be retrieved at any time by any decision maker, organizational effectiveness will be compromised. We will now see how data can be effectively stored for retrieval whenever necessary.

INFORMATION SYSTEMS AND MANAGERIAL DECISION MAKING

As organizations take on expanded functions and grow in size, it is important for them to be equipped with a good information system from which data can be accessed for analysis by executives and managers at different levels. Putting effective information systems in place requires careful architectural planning. Computerized information systems enable the efficient operation of different subsystems in the organization inasmuch as information for any area such as finance, budget, plant maintenance, transportation, distribution, marketing, or human resources, can be readily drawn by any department.

Data Warehousing, Data Mining, and Operations Research

Data warehousing and *data mining* are aspects of information systems. Most companies are now aware of the benefits of creating a *data warehouse* that serves as the central repository of all data collected from disparate sources including those pertaining to the company's finance, manufacturing, sales, and the like. The data warehouse is usually built from data collected through the different departments of the enterprise and can be accessed through various on-line analytical processing (OLAP) tools to support decision making. Data warehousing can be described as the process of extracting, transferring, and integrating data spread across multiple external databases and even operating systems, with a view to facilitate analysis and decision making.

Complementary to the functions of data warehousing, many companies resort to *data mining* as a strategic tool for reaching new levels of business intelligence. Using algorithms to analyze data in a meaningful way, data mining more effectively leverages the data warehouse by identifying hidden relations and patterns in the data stored in it. For instance, data mining makes it possible to trace retail sales patterns by ZIP code and the time of day of the purchases, so that optimal stocking of items becomes possible. Such "mined" data pertaining to the vital areas of the organization can be easily accessed and used for different purposes. For example, staffing for different times of the day can be planned, as can the number of check-out counters that need to be kept open in retail stores, to ensure efficiency as well as effectiveness. We can see that data mining helps to clarify the underlying patterns in different business activities, which in turn facilitates decision making.

Operations research (OR) or *management science* (MS) is another sophisticated tool used to simplify and thus clarify certain types of complex problems that lend themselves to quantification. OR uses higher mathematics and statistics to identify, analyze, and ultimately solve intricate problems of great complexity faced by the manager. It provides an additional tool to the manager by using quantification to supplement personal judgment. Areas of problem solving that easily lend to OR include those relating to inventory, queuing, sequencing, routing, and search and replacement. OR helps to minimize costs and increase efficiency by resorting to *decision trees, linear programming, network analysis,* and *mathematical models.*

Other information systems such as the *Management Information Systems (MIS), Decision Support System, the Executive Information System, and the Expert System* are good decision-making aids, but not necessarily involved with data collection and analyses in the strict sense.

In sum, a good information system collects, mines, and provides a wide range of pertinent information relating to aspects of both the external and internal environments of the organization. By using the wide variety of tools and techniques available for solving problems of differing magnitude, executives, managers, and others entrusted with responsibility for results at various levels of the organization can find solutions to various concerns merely by securing access to these data available in the system and analyzing them.

It should be ensured that the data in the information system are error-free and are frequently updated. After all, decision making can only be as good as the data made available to managers.

INTERNATIONAL DIMENSIONS OF CYBERSPACE

Cyberspace is not free of geographical boundaries or cultural nuances. Foreign governments can use the same firewall and filtering technology that American corporations use to deter computer hackers. Some countries ban access to gambling web sites, and a few others like Singapore and Saudi Arabia censor the web site contents.

A judge in France ruled that Yahoo had violated French law by selling Nazi memorabilia on Internet auctions, and the ruling is contested by Yahoo. As a result of these, unregulated cyberspace is a mythical notion. Local laws do indeed govern what can and cannot appear in cyberspace.

Copyright laws can also be deemed to be broken as in the case of the Russian programmer who was accused of breaking copyright laws in 2001, but pleaded not guilty to charges of violating the U.S. Digital Millennium Copyright Act of 1998. The decision on this case will have an impact on the sale of books and other works in the digital age and the jurisdiction of U.S. law over the Internet.

DATA STORAGE AND SURVEILLANCE

Storage of Databases

The September 11th catastrophe in 2001 has sadly but powerfully dramatized the need for storing company data at more than one site and away from the location of business operations. Fortunately, a devastated financial company that was based at the World Trade Center in New York had a data center in Boston. A member of the storage management company Veritas' "fly-to-site" team drove from New Jersey to Boston, and recovered all the data.

Data is the lifeblood of companies and should be mirrored live in at least two other locations, or at least backed up on tape and stored in other remote locations. There are several firms in the storage industry that offer protection of proprietary data and aid in disaster recovery.

Data Security

Increasingly, organizations and their information systems are faced with security threats that include, among others, computer hacking, Internet fraud, and sabotage, from a wide range of sources. Computer viruses and computer hacking are an incessant threat and everpresent danger.

To protect information from a variety of threats, digital IDs and firewalls are a few of the security measures used to prevent fraud and unauthorized use.

Authentication, authorization, and *encryption* are some basic security methodologies employed to prevent unauthorized people from having access to and interpreting these data. These security measures maintain the integrity of the information by allowing access to only authorized personnel and safeguarding it once it leaves the secure confines of the organization by scrambling the message (encryption).

Though several companies offer security software, as technology advances, so will the ingenuity of the hackers, and vigilance is therefore warranted on a continuing basis.

MANAGERIAL ADVANTAGE OF TECHNOLOGICAL ADVANCEMENTS

Information technology and the development of software to gather, store, and analyze information—the results of which facilitate decision making—are registering advances at an exponential rate. It is important for managers to take full advantage of information technology and keep current on the latest innovations. It should be ensured that persons working with information technology keep abreast of all current advances, and in fact, develop software tailored to the special needs of the system. It cannot be overemphasized that unless information is constantly updated, an organization will not benefit even if it has installed the most sophisticated technology. Hence the information system should be current.

As we have stated, software technology can be put to effective use in the research process for problem identification (as discussed in the next chapter), theory building, collecting data from respondents, analyzing it, and presenting the results—all of which are discussed in the subsequent chapters of this book.

Online terminal-activated systems with massive databases (including text information, graphics, sound, and video) serve businesses more economically and effectively. LAN in the organization, therefore, serves a useful purpose.

Technology is not, however, without its drawbacks. For instance, voice mail and caller IDs can make data collection via telephone difficult, if not impossible, as discussed in Chapter 10. Safety of data access by the appropriate personnel and storage of data at different locations are also important, as we have noted.

ETHICS IN HANDLING INFORMATION TECHNOLOGY

Although technology offers unbounded opportunities for organizations and facilitates decision making at various levels, it also imposes certain obligations on the part of its users. First, it is important that the *privacy* of all individuals is protected, whether they are consumers, suppliers, employees, or others. In other words, businesses have to *balance* their information needs against the individual rights of those they come in contact with, and on whom they store data. Second, companies also need to ensure that *confidential information* relating to individuals is protected and does not find its way to unscrupulous vendors and used for nefarious purposes. Third, care should be taken to ensure that *incorrect information* is not distributed across the many different files of the company. Fourth, those who collect data for the company should be honest, trustworthy, and careful in obtaining and recording the data in a timely fashion. The responsibility of organizations rests in the fact that technology should go hand in hand with the ethical practices followed by their members as they pursue their daily ongoing business activities.

SUMMARY

In this chapter we have examined some aspects of computer technology that facilitate research and decision making by managers in organizations. We have specifically examined some of the current possibilities for research afforded by the use of software—from simple data collection to the development of information systems to facilitate further research and decision making.

We described the role of information technology that readily makes available to managers the data they need and also indicated that functionally rich data marts and data warehouses expand the scope and quality of decision making. We mentioned Management Information System, the Decision Support System, Executive Information System, and Operations Research as facilitators of managerial decision making.

The obligations of the users of technology in organizations were noted. With the development of ever-increasing levels of sophisticated software packages that are easy to understand and use, you as a manager will have in your possession the tools to face the challenges and solve the problems that businesses encounter.

Now that we have had a broad overview of what technology can do to facilitate research, we will examine the steps in doing research in the next chapter.

DISCUSSION QUESTIONS AND POINTS TO PONDER

1. As a manager, what kinds of information do you think you will explore through the Internet for research?

2. How can audit capabilities in software help organizations?

3. How do you think you will apply the concepts of data warehousing and data mining in a company doing retail business?

4. How does technology help in information gathering as well as its dissemination?

5. How can technology be misused? Give some hypothetical instances where this could occur.

6. Specify the types of information that may be stored in a data warehouse in a university, and offer three purposes for which data mining might be used in this context.

7. How would an institution safeguard vital information when it sends important data or discharges payments over the Internet?

8. An article in *Fortune* says: Video conferencing won't take the place of business travel, because it shouldn't. The two have to work together. Can you comment on why this would be so?

hinder

EXERCISES

1. Access the web sites of Intel and Sybase and compare and contrast what you find about these two companies.

2. Send an e-mail to a classmate briefly describing your views on technology.

3. Do a search for references relating to technology and print them.

THE RESEARCH PROCESS

Steps 1 to 3: The Broad Problem Area Preliminary Data Gathering Problem Definition

TOPICS DISCUSSED

APPENDIX:

- Online databases
- Bibliographical Indexes
- Referencing in the APA Format
- Referencing and Quotation in the Literature Review Section

CHAPTER OBJECTIVES

After completing Chapter 4 you should be able to:

1. Identify the steps in the research process.
2. Identify problem areas that are likely to be studied in organizations.
3. Discuss how problem areas can be identified in work settings.
4. State research problems clearly and precisely.
5. Develop relevant and comprehensive bibliographies for any organizational research topic.
6. Write a literature review on any given topic, documenting the references in the prescribed manner.
7. Apply all you have learned to a group project that might be assigned.

Referring back to Chuck Orlando's concerns cited at the beginning of Chapter 1, why was he so confused and bewildered? How could he have had a better handle on how to go about solving the various issues? What were the specific factors he should have investigated?

In this chapter we will examine ways to identify the variables that would operate in any specific situation that might tend to be problematic for the manager. We will also see how a literature survey is done and how problems can be narrowed down and clearly defined.

THE RESEARCH PROCESS FOR APPLIED AND BASIC RESEARCH

In Chapter 2 we discussed and illustrated through Figure 2.1 the foundation or the building blocks of science. Scientific inquiry in the hypothetico-deductive mode can be discussed relating to its two distinct aspects—the **process** of developing the conceptual framework and the hypotheses for testing, and the **design,** which involves the planning of the actual study, dealing with such aspects as the location of the study, the selection of the sample, and collection and analysis of the data. Figure 4.1 captures the research process in the first five boxes. Boxes 6 and 7 embody the design aspects, which will be elaborated later in this book.

Figure 4.1
The research process for basic and applied research.

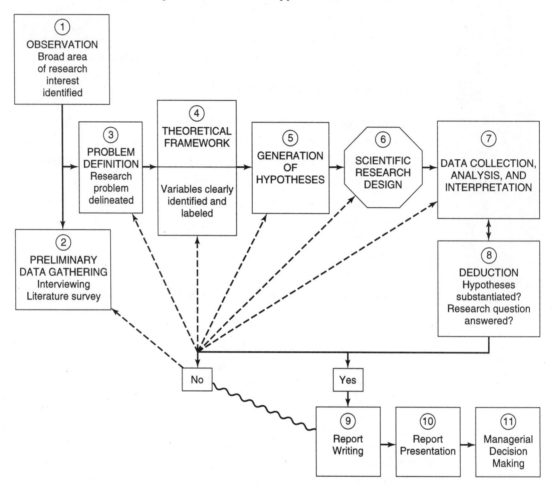

Box 8 denotes the final deduction from the hypotheses testing. When all or most of the hypotheses are substantiated and the research question is fully answered, the researcher writes up the report and makes a presentation, and the manager is able to examine different ways of solving the problem and making a final decision, as represented in boxes 9, 10, and 11. If, however, several of the hypotheses are not substantiated, or are only partially supported, one may go back to examine the reasons for this. Note the broken lines and the arrow headed to several other boxes in Figure 4.1, indicating that the process may have to be restarted at the point where the researcher feels the need for reexamination. But managerial decisions may have to be made on the basis of current findings, either for lack of time or other reasons, in which case the researcher tries to make educated conjectures as to why certain hypotheses were not supported, and then writes the report reflecting these. This is indicated by the curved line in Figure 4.1 leading from the box No to Report Writing.

Despite the fact that the research model is depicted and discussed in this book as if it were a step-by-step *linear* process, one has to bear in mind that it is not actually so in practice. For example, though the literature search and interviews might have been conducted before formulating the theoretical framework, one may have to go back and conduct more interviews and/or seek additional information from the literature for a clearer understanding, so as to refine the theory. The research site, sample, measurement of the variables, and other design issues may also have to be simultaneously considered as one identifies the problem, formulates the theory, and generates the hypotheses.

Each of the components of the research model will be discussed in this book. This particular chapter will discuss steps 1 to 3 of Figure 4.1: (1) the identification of the broad problem area; (2) preliminary information gathering, especially through unstructured and structured interviews and literature survey; and (3) problem definition.

BROAD PROBLEM AREA

Identification of the broad problem area through the process of observing and focusing on the situation was discussed in Chapter 2. Recall that the broad problem area refers to the entire situation where one sees a possible need for research and problem solving. The specific issues that need to be researched within this situation may not be identified at this stage. Such issues might pertain to (1) problems currently existing in an organizational setting that need to be solved, (2) areas that a manager believes need to be improved in the organization, (3) a conceptual or theoretical issue that needs to be tightened up for the basic researcher to understand certain phenomena, and (4) some research questions that a basic researcher wants to answer *empirically*. Examples of each type can be provided taking the issue of sexual harassment, which is a problem that at least some organizations will have to handle at some point in time.

As an example of a problem **currently existing,** a situation might present itself where a manager might receive written complaints from women in some departments that they are not being "treated right" by the bosses. From the generalized nature of these complaints, the manager might become aware that he is facing a gender-related problem situation, but may not be able to pinpoint what exactly it is. That is, the matter calls for further investigation before the exact problem can be identified and attempts are made to resolve it. On the other hand, the following is an example of a situation **requiring improvement.** If the company has already formulated policies on discrimination and sexual harassment, and legitimate complaints of discrimination continue to come in, then it is obvious that the policies are ambiguous and need to be redefined either in how they have been framed, how they are understood, or how they are enforced.

The example of a **conceptual issue that needs to be tightened** would be for the basic researcher to study sexual harassment so as to define that concept in precise terms. Currently, sexual harassment might only be broadly defined as:

Any unwelcome sexual advances, requests for sexual favors, and other verbal and physical conduct of a sexual nature.

However, in practice, certain nonverbal or nonphysical attention, such as ogling, might also be unpalatable to some and could be termed "harassment." Thus, the researcher might want to come up with a precise statement of what sexual harassment is and expand the definition of the term. Here is a clear case for a better understanding and definition of the concept itself. An example of a researcher wanting to find some **answers empirically** might be when the issue of perceived or actual sexual harassment and its impact on the consequences for the individuals (e.g., psychological stress) and organizations (poor performance) is explored by gathering data and testing the relationships. This is a situation where some specific answers are sought to a research question.

Examples of broad problem areas that a manager could observe at the workplace are as follows:

1. Training programs are perhaps not as effective as anticipated.
2. The sales volume of a product is not picking up.
3. Minority group members in organizations are not advancing in their careers.
4. The daily balancing of accounting ledgers is becoming a continuing concern.
5. The newly installed information system is not being used by the managers for whom it was primarily designed.
6. The introduction of flexible work hours has created more problems than it has solved in many companies.
7. The anticipated results of a recent merger have not been forthcoming.
8. Inventory control is not effective.
9. The installation of an MIS keeps getting stalled.
10. The management of a complex, multidepartmental team project is getting out of hand in the R & D department of a firm.

The broad problem area would be narrowed down to specific issues for investigation after some preliminary data are gathered by the researcher. This may be through interviews and literature research.

PRELIMINARY DATA COLLECTION

Nature of Data To Be Gathered

In Chapter 2 we mentioned that unstructured interviews, structured interviews, and library research would help the researcher to define the problem more specifically and evolve a theory, delineating possible variables that might exert an influence on it. The nature of information needed by the researcher for the purpose could be broadly classified under three headings:

1. Background information of the organization—that is, the contextual factors.
2. Managerial philosophy, company policies, and other structural aspects.
3. Perceptions, attitudes, and behavioral responses of organizational members and client systems (as applicable).

Certain types of information such as the background details of the company can be obtained from available published records, the web site of the company, its archives, and other sources. Other types of written information such as company policies, procedures, and rules can be obtained from the organization's records and documents. Data gathered through such existing sources are called *secondary data*. That is, they are data that already exist and do not have to be collected by the researcher. Some secondary sources of data are statistical bulletins, government publications, information published or unpublished and available from either within or outside the organization, data available from previous research, case studies and library records, online data, web sites, and the Internet. In contrast, certain other types of information such as the perceptions and attitudes of employees are best obtained by talking to them; by observing events, people, and objects; or by administering questionnaires to individuals. Such data gathered for research from the actual site of occurrence of events are called *primary data*.

We will now see how the three broad types of information mentioned earlier can be gathered.

Background Information on the Organization

It is important for the researcher or the research team—especially if an outside agency conducts the research—to be well acquainted with the background of the company or organization studied, before even conducting the first interview with their officials. Such background information might include, among other things, the undernoted contextual factors, which may be obtained from various published sources such as trade publications, the *Census of Business and Industry, Directory of Corporations,* several other business guides and services, records available within the organization, and the web.

1. The origin and history of the company—when it came into being, business it is in, rate of growth, ownership and control, and so on.
2. Size in terms of employees, assets, or both.
3. Charter—purpose and ideology.
4. Location—regional, national, or other.
5. Resources—human and others.

6. Interdependent relationships with other institutions and the external environment.

7. Financial position during the previous 5 to 10 years, and relevant financial data.

8.) *law suits* (9) *reputation*

Information gathered on the foregoing aspects will be useful in talking knowledgeably with others in the company during the interview and raising the appropriate issues related to the problem. As an example, the problem of cash flow (which can be gleaned from the balance sheets) may be related to poor quality of raw materials purchased, resulting in a high rate of return of goods sold by the company. This issue can be tactfully investigated during the course of the discussions with the appropriate members in the system if this information is known in advance. Or an industry analysis might reveal that some of the problems encountered are not unique to this company but are faced industrywide, such as competition from foreign producers, consumer resistance to spending money, and the like. In such a case, more questions can be focused toward strategies (such as sales and advertising efforts) developed by the company to promote sales in the face of foreign competition.

Information on Structural Factors and Management Philosophy

Information on company policies, structure, workflow, management philosophy, and the like can be obtained by asking direct questions of the management. When questions are directed at several managers individually, it is quite possible that some of the responses will be conflicting and contradictory. Frequent instances of such contradictions might in themselves indicate problems such as poor communication or misperceptions by members of the organization's philosophy, goals, values, and so forth. These issues can be pursued by the researcher in subsequent interviews to obtain an idea of the extent to which differences in perceptions exist in the organization.

Such information gathering would be particularly useful when newly installed systems, processes, and procedures do not produce the desired results. The failure of many new technologies, well-meant benefit policies, strategic plans, or marketing or production practices is often due to misunderstandings and misperceptions of the cherished goals and motives of top administration rather than any inherent faults in the mechanisms themselves. Once the misperceptions are cleared, the problem might well disappear. Hence, it is useful to gauge the extent to which perceptual and communications problems exist, right at the start.

Questioning about managerial and company philosophy offers an excellent idea of the priorities and values of the company, as for example: (1) whether product quality is really deemed important by the company or if only lip service is being paid to the concept; (2) whether the company has short-term or long-term goals; (3) whether controls are so tight that creativity is stifled, or so loose that nothing gets done, or if they are conductive to good performance; (4) whether the company always wants to play it safe or is prepared to take calculated risks; and (5) whether it is people-oriented or solely profits-oriented.

Quite frequently, aspects of structure also influence the problem and need to be explored. Below are some of the structural factors.

1. Roles and positions in the organization and number of employees at each job level.
2. Extent of specialization.
3. Communication channels.
4. Control systems.
5. Coordination and span of control.
6. Reward systems.
7. Workflow systems and the like.

It is possible that the respondents' perceptions of the structural variables may not match the formal written structural policies and procedures of the organization. Where such is the case, these become relevant leads to follow during further unstructured and structured interviews with various levels of employees in the organization.

Perceptions, Attitudes, and Behavioral Responses

Employees' perceptions of the work and the work environment and their attitudinal and behavioral responses can be tapped by talking to them, observing them, and seeking their responses through questionnaires. A general idea of people's perceptions of their work, the organizational climate, and other aspects of interest to the researcher can be obtained through both unstructured and structured interviews with the respondents. By establishing good rapport with the individuals and following the right questioning techniques—discussed in detail in Chapter 10—the researcher will be able to obtain useful information. An understanding of the attitudinal and behavioral reactions of organizational members is often very helpful in arriving at a precise problem definition.

Attitudinal factors comprise people's beliefs about and reactions to the following:

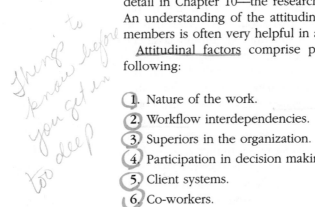

1. Nature of the work.
2. Workflow interdependencies.
3. Superiors in the organization.
4. Participation in decision making.
5. Client systems.
6. Co-workers.
7. Rewards provided by the organization, such as pay raises and fringe benefits.
8. Opportunities for advancement in the organization.
9. Organization's attitudes toward employees' family responsibilities.

10. Company's involvement with community, civic, and other social groups.
11. Company's tolerance of employees' taking time off from the job.

Behavioral factors include actual work habits such as industriousness, extent of absenteeism, performance on the job, and the like.

The respondents could be encouraged at the interviewing stage to talk about their jobs, other work- and non-work-related factors, and their attitudes, values, perceptions, and behaviors, some of which might influence the outcomes at the workplace. Talking to several people at various levels in the organization would give the interviewer a good idea of the dynamics that operate in the system. Detailed discussions on how the unstructured and structured interviews are to be conducted can be found in Chapter 10, where data collection methods are discussed.

At this stage questions might arise as to whether seeking all this information on management philosophy, structure, and perceptions and attitudes is *always* necessary; how the materials will be utilized in the research project; and how much time one should expend in collecting such particulars. The answer to these questions is that there is no substitute for good judgment. Depending on the situation, the type of problem investigated, and the nature of some initial responses received, certain aspects may have to be explored in greater depth than others. For example, if the problem as identified by the manager is related to individuals' attitudes and behaviors, then the value system, the corporate culture, and employee perceptions may have to be delved into more deeply than the structural aspects. On the other hand, if reorganization of the work layout is the subject of the study, then the workflow interdependencies and the coordination aspects will need more attention. The main idea in gathering information on values, structures, and processes (instead of merely dealing with the manifest symptoms), is that these might often reveal the root of the **real problem.** These distinctions are elaborated later in this chapter. For now, as an illustration, many companies are introducing employee stock ownership plans (ESOP). Not all employees are necessarily excited about this. Rather than immediately working toward making the package more attractive through cosmetic changes, talking to individuals might reveal that the employees perceive ESOP merely as a tool to deter takeovers and save taxes, and as providing no true opportunities for employee involvement and participation. The understanding so gained helps the manager to attack the **real issues** (in this case, the concern and fear of the employees), rather than work on the surface **symptoms** (making cosmetic changes in the package to make it more attractive).

As another example, a manager might think that refining the just-in-time (JIT) system will help reduce inventory and production costs, whereas the real problem could be with the type of machinery used in the production process. It is for reasons such as these that conversing with people at different levels helps the researcher to understand what some of their concerns are. Spending 2 or 3 days interviewing individuals at different levels in the system should generally suffice to get a grasp of the establishment and understand the culture of the organization.

Once the interviews are conducted, the next step for the researcher is to tabulate the various types of information that have been gathered during the interviews and determine if there are discernible patterns in the responses. For instance, it might be observed from the qualitative data that some problems are frequently mentioned by employees at several levels in the organization. Certain factors such as insufficient lighting, untrained personnel, or inadequate tools may be brought out forcefully in the interviews by several workers. When the tabulation reveals that such variables have surfaced quite frequently, it gives the researcher some good ideas about how to proceed in the next step of surveying the literature to see how others have perceived such factors in other work settings and defined the problem, before arriving at solutions. Because literature survey is one way of summarizing secondary data and is an important step in the research process for defining the research problem, we will now discuss it in some detail as one of the preliminary data-gathering tools.

It is important to keep in mind that information from secondary data can be extracted from various sources, including books and periodicals, government publications and information sources, the media, census, stock market reports, and mechanized and electronic information of all kinds such as the bar code, scanner data, and the Internet. Secondary data can be culled from the historical records of the organization itself, from information already available on the Intranet, or from external sources such as the ones mentioned above, either through the Internet or otherwise.

LITERATURE SURVEY vs Review of Lit

Literature survey is the documentation of a comprehensive review of the published and unpublished work from secondary sources of data in the areas of specific interest to the researcher. The library is a rich storage base for secondary data, and researchers used to spend several weeks and sometimes months going through books, journals, newspapers, magazines, conference proceedings, doctoral dissertations, master's theses, government publications, and financial, marketing, and other reports, to find information on their research topic. With computerized databases now readily available and accessible, the literature search is much speedier and easier, and can be done without entering the portals of a library building.

should

The researcher could start the literature survey even as the information from the unstructured and structured interviews is being gathered. Reviewing the literature on the topic area at this time helps the researcher to focus further interviews more meaningfully on certain aspects found to be important in the published studies, even if these had not surfaced during the earlier questioning.

Reasons for the Literature Survey

The purpose of the literature review is to ensure that no important variable that has in the past been found repeatedly to have had an impact on the problem is ignored. It is possible that some of the critical variables are never brought out in the interviews, either because the employees cannot articulate them or are unaware of their impact, or because the variables seem so obvious to the interviewees that they are not specifically stated. If there are variables that are not identified during the interviews, but influence the problem critically, then research done without considering them would be an exercise in futility. In such a case, the true reason for the problem would remain unidentified even at the end of the research. To avoid such possibilities the researcher needs to delve into all the important research work relating to the particular problem area.

The following example will help to highlight the importance of the literature survey. In establishing employee selection procedures, a company might be doing the right things such as administering the appropriate tests to assess the applicants' analytical skills, judgment, leadership, motivation, oral and written communication skills, and the like. Yet, it might be consistently losing excellent MBAs hired as managers, within a year, although highly paid. The reasons for the turnover of MBAs may not be identified while conducting interviews with the candidates. However, a review of the literature might indicate that when employees have unmet job expectations (that is, their original expectations of their role and responsibilities do not match actual experiences), they will be inclined to quit the organization. Talking further to the company officials, it might be found that **realistic job previews** are never offered to the candidates at the time of the interview. This might explain why the candidates experience frustration on the job and leave after a while. This important factor significantly influencing the turnover of managerial employees, may not have come to light but for the literature survey. If this variable is not included in the research investigation, the problem may not be solved at all!

Sometimes it might happen that the investigator spends considerable time and effort to "discover" something that has already been thoroughly researched. A literature review would prevent such a waste of resources in reinventing the wheel. However, because every situation is unique, further research has to proceed taking into consideration the relevant variables applicable to it. Finally, a good literature survey could in itself be the basis of qualitative research, as for instance, tracing the origins and progress of technology and predicting where it is headed in the future.

A survey of the literature not only helps the researcher to include all the relevant variables in the research project, but also facilitates the creative integration of the information gathered from the structured and unstructured interviews with what is found in previous studies. In other words, it gives a good basic framework to proceed further with the investigation. A good literature survey thus provides the foundation for developing a comprehensive theoretical framework from which hypotheses can be developed for testing. The development of the theoretical framework and hypotheses is discussed in the next chapter.

A good literature survey thus ensures that:

1. Important variables that are likely to influence the problem situation are not left out of the study.

2. A clearer idea emerges as to what variables would be most important to consider (parsimony), why they would be considered important, and how they should be investigated to solve the problem. Thus, the literature survey helps the development of the theoretical framework and hypotheses for testing.

3. The problem statement can be made with precision and clarity.

4. Testability and replicability of the findings of the current research are enhanced.

5. One does not run the risk of "reinventing the wheel" that is, wasting efforts on trying to rediscover something that is already known.

6. The problem investigated is perceived by the scientific community as relevant and significant.

Conducting the Literature Survey

Based on the specific issues of concern to the manager and the factors identified during the interview process, a literature review needs to be done on these variables. The first step in this process involves identifying the various published and unpublished materials that are available on the topics of interest, and gaining access to these. The second step is gathering the relevant information either by going through the necessary materials in a library or by getting access to online sources. The third step is writing up the literature review. These are now discussed.

Identifying the Relevant Sources

Previously, one had to manually go through several bibliographical indexes that are compiled periodically, listing the journals, books, and other sources in which published work in the area of interest can be found. However, with modern technology, locating sources where the topics of interest have been published has become easy. Almost every library today has computer online systems to locate and print out the published information on various topics.

Global business information, published articles in newspapers and periodicals, and conference proceedings, among other sources, are all now available on databases. Computerized databases include bibliographies, abstracts, and full texts of articles on various business topics. Statistical and financial databases are also easily accessible. Computer hardware and software enable the storage, updating, and display of information on global activities. Economic indicators and other data for various countries can be tracked easily. Statistical abstracts and the like, now available on CD-ROM and on the Internet, bring to the researcher all the information needed for research at the press of the appropriate computer keys.

Basically, three forms of databases come in handy while reviewing the literature, as indicated below.

1. The **bibliographic databases,** which display only the bibliographic citations, that is, the name of the author, the title of the article (or book), source of publication, year, volume, and page numbers. These have the same information as found in the Bibliographic Index books in libraries, which are periodically updated, and include articles published in periodicals, newspapers, books, and so on.

2. The **abstract databases,** which in addition provide an abstract or summary of the articles.

3. The **full-text databases,** which provide the full text of the article.

Databases are also available for obtaining statistics—marketing, financial, and so on—and directories are organized by subject, title, geographic location, trade opportunities, foreign traders, industrial plants, and so on. Some of these online databases are listed in Section I of the Appendix at the end of this chapter.

Online searches provide a number of advantages. Besides saving enormous amounts of time, they are comprehensive in their listing and review of references, and the researcher can focus on materials most central to the research effort. In addition, finding access to them is relatively inexpensive.

Some of the important research databases available online and on the World Wide Web are provided in the Appendix to this chapter. Access to these can be had online or through the Internet. If a source of information is not known, the search strategies on the Internet help to find it. Databases include, among others, listings of journal articles, books in print, census data, dissertation abstracts, conference papers, and newspaper abstracts that are useful for business research. Details of some of these databases can be found in the Appendix to this chapter.

Extracting the Relevant Information

Accessing the online system and getting a printout of all the published works in the area of interest from a bibliographical index (some useful indexes are provided in Section 2 of the Appendix to this chapter) will provide a comprehensive bibliography on the subject, which will form the basis for the next step. Whereas the printout could sometimes include as many as a hundred or more listings, a glance at the titles of the articles or books will indicate which of these may be pertinent and which others are likely to be peripheral to the contemplated study. The abstract of such articles that seem to be relevant can then be obtained through the online system. This will give an idea of the articles that need to be looked into in depth, the full text of which can then be printed out. While reading these articles, detailed information on the problem that was researched, the design details of the study (such as the sample size and data collection methods), and the ultimate findings could be systematically noted in some convenient format. This facilitates the writing up of the literature review with minimum disruption and maximum efficiency. While reading the articles, it is possible that certain other factors are also found to be closely related to the problem at hand. For instance, while reading the articles on the effectiveness of Information Systems, the researcher might find that the size of the company has also been found to be an important factor. The researcher might then want to know more about how the size of organizations is categorized and measured by others and, hence, might want to read materials on organization size. All the articles considered relevant to the current study can be then listed as references, using the appropriate referencing format, which is discussed in Section 3 of the Appendix to this chapter.

Writing Up the Literature Review

The documentation of the relevant studies citing the author and the year of the study is called literature review or literature survey. The literature survey is a

clear and logical presentation of the relevant research work done thus far in the area of investigation. As stated earlier, the purpose of the literature survey is to identify and highlight the important variables, and to document the significant findings from earlier research that will serve as the foundation on which the theoretical framework for the current investigation can be built and the hypotheses developed. Such documentation is important to convince the reader that (1) the researcher is knowledgeable about the problem area and has done the preliminary homework that is necessary to conduct the research, and (2) the theoretical framework will be structured on work already done and will add to the solid foundation of existing knowledge.

A point to note is that the literature survey should bring together all relevant information in a cogent and logical manner instead of presenting all the studies in chronological order with bits and pieces of uncoordinated information. A good literature survey also leads one logically to a good problem statement.

There are several accepted methods of citing references in the literature survey section and using quotations. The *Publication Manual of the American Psychological Association* (2001) offers detailed information regarding citations, quotations, references and so on, and is one of the accepted styles of referencing in the management area. Other formats include *The Chicago Manual of Style* (1993), and Turabian's *Manual for Writers* (1996). As earlier stated, details of the referencing style and quotations based on the APA Manual (2001) are offered in Section 3 of the Appendix at the end of this chapter.

Examples of Two Literature Surveys

Let us take *a portion* of two literature reviews done and examine how the activity has helped to (1) introduce the subject of study, (2) identify the research question, and (3) build on previous research to offer the basis to get to the next steps of theoretical framework and hypotheses development.

Example 4.1   RISK-TAKING BEHAVIORS AND ORGANIZATIONAL OUTCOMES

Managers handle risks and face uncertainties in different ways. Some of these styles are functional and others adversely impact on corporate performance. Living in times of dramatic organizational changes (mergers, for instance), and with the company performance varying vastly in this turbulent environment, it is important to investigate risk-taking behaviors of managers and organizational outcomes.

A vast body of knowledge exists regarding risk-taking behaviors in decision making. Some studies have shown that the context that surrounds the decision maker exerts an influence on the extent of risk the individual is prepared to take (Shapira, 1995; Starbuck & Milken, 2000). Other studies, such as those done by Sankar (1997) and Velcher (1998) indicate that the position of the risk taker, and whether the decision is taken by an individual or is the result of group effort, account significantly for the variance in risk-taking behaviors, and ultimately, to the performance of the organization. Schwartz (2001) has argued that the results of research done using subjects to participate in activities in a lab setting, show different results compared to those found in research done in organizational settings. Additionally, MacCrimmon and Wehrung (1995, 1998, 2001) suggest that the differences in the measurement tools used in research studies account for the differences in the findings of managerial risk attitudes.

You will note that the above example first introduces the subject of risk-taking behaviors and corporate performance, and why it is an important topic to be studied. Through the literature survey, it identifies the problem to be studied as one of investigating the factors that account for risk-taking behaviors. It also indicates the important factors to be considered in the research, which would enable the researcher to formulate a theory, based on which, hypotheses can be formulated and tested.

Example 4.2   ORGANIZATIONAL EFFECTIVENESS

Organization theorists have defined organizational effectiveness (OE) in various ways. OE has been described in terms of objectives (Georgopolous & Tannenbaum, 1957), goals (Etzioni, 1960), efficiency (Katz & Kahn, 1966), resources acquisition (Yuchtman & Seashore, 1967), employee satisfaction (Cummings, 1977), interdependence (Pfeffer, 1977), and organizational vitality (Colt, 1995). As Coulter (2002) remarked, there is little consensus on how to conceptualize, measure, or explain OE. This should, however, not come as a surprise to us since OE models are essentially value-based classification of the construct (the values being those of the researchers) and the potential number of models that can be generated by researchers is virtually limitless. Researchers are now moving away from a single model and are taking contingency approaches to conceptualizing OE (Cameron, 1996; Wernerfelt, 1998; Yetley, 2001). However, they are still limiting themselves to examining the impact of the dominant constituencies served and the organization's life cycle on OE instead of taking a broader, more dynamic approach (Dahl, 2001, p. 25).

From the portion of the above extract, several insights can be gained. The literature review (1) introduces the subject of study (organizational effectiveness), (2) highlights the problem (that we do not have a good conceptual framework for understanding what OE is), and (3) summarizes the work done so far on the topic in a manner that convinces the reader that the researcher has indeed surveyed the work done in the area of OE and wants to contribute to the understanding of the concept, taking off on the earlier contingency approaches in a more creative way. The scholar has carefully paved the way for the next step, which is to develop a more viable and robust model of organizational effectiveness. This model will be logically developed, integrating several streams of research done in other areas (such as cross-cultural management, sociology, etc.), which will be woven further into the literature review. Once the scholar has explicated the framework as to what constitutes OE and what the factors that influence it are, the next step would be to develop testable hypotheses to see if the new model is indeed viable.

The literature survey thus provides the basis or foundation for developing a conceptual framework for looking at the problem in a more useful and/or creative way. This, in turn, helps to develop testable hypotheses that would substantiate or disprove our theory.

Examples of a good literature survey can be found at the beginning of any article in the *Academy of Management Journal* and most other academic or practitioner-oriented journals. Specimens of a literature survey can also be found later in this book.

One important benefit derived from a well-written literature survey section is that the researcher would be able to delineate a logical, well-defined, and sharply focused problem for research investigation. This delineation or definition of the problem, which is the next step in the research process, is now discussed.

PROBLEM DEFINITION

After the interviews and the literature review, the researcher is in a position to narrow down the problem from its original broad base and define the issues of concern more clearly. It is critical that the focus of further research, or in other words, the problem, be unambiguously identified and defined. No amount of good research can find solutions to the situation, if the critical issue or the problem to be studied is not clearly pinpointed.

A problem does not necessarily mean that something is seriously wrong with a current situation that needs to be rectified immediately. A "problem" could simply indicate an interest in an issue where finding the right answers might help to improve an existing situation. Thus, it is fruitful to **define a problem as any situation where a gap exists between the actual and the desired ideal states.** Basic researchers usually define their problems for investigation from this perspective. For instance, we would ideally like to see zero defects, low inventory of unsold goods, high share quotation in the stock market, and so on. These "problems" could then very well become the foci of research. Thus, problem definitions could encompass both existing problems in a current setting, as well as the quest for idealistic states in organizations. Thus, we might find some managers defining their problem as one of severe decline in productivity, or the company fast losing its market share, where the goal is to rectify the situation with a heightened sense of urgency. Other managers might define the "problem" as a situation in which there is considerable interest in attracting highly qualified engineers to the firm, or enhancing the quality of life for their employees.

In either case, one should know what exactly the issue is, for which one seeks answers. It is very important that **symptoms** of problems are not *defined as the real problem*. For instance, a manager might have tried to increase productivity by increasing the piece rate, but with little success. Here the real **problem** may be the low morale and motivation of employees who feel they are not being recognized as valuable contributors to the system and get no "praise" for the good work that they do. The low productivity may merely be a symptom of the deep-rooted morale and motivation problem. Under these conditions, a higher piece rate will not improve productivity! Thus, finding the "right" answers to the "wrong" problem definitions will not help. Hence, it should be recognized that correct problem identification is extremely critical for finding solutions to vexing issues.

Frequently, managers tend to describe the problem in terms of symptoms during the interviews. Rather than accepting it as such, the researcher needs to identify the problem more accurately after talking to the employees and reviewing the literature, as discussed earlier. One way of determining that the problem, rather than the symptom, is being addressed is to ask the question (after gathering sufficient information through interviews and literature search), "Is this factor I have identified an **antecedent,** the real **problem,** or the **consequence?"** These terms can be discussed in the context of the earlier example of low productivity. The real issue or problem here is low morale and motivation. The consequence of the problem is low productivity. Note that the consequence (or effects) of low motivation can also manifest itself in absenteeism, sabotage, or any number of other adverse effects for the firm. The real problem that needs to be addressed in this case, hence, is not productivity, but motivation. The antecedent of the problem (i.e., the contributing factor) in the given situation seems to be nonrecognition of the employees' contributions. Until such time as the employees are recognized for their work, their motivation and morale will not improve, nor will their productivity, as a consequence. Without addressing the central issue, if more money is given, or better equipment installed to increase productivity, the desired results will not ensue because the right problem would not have been addressed.

Problem definition or problem statement, as it is also often referred to, *is a clear, precise, and succinct statement of the question* or *issue that is to be investigated with the goal of finding an answer or solution.* As mentioned earlier, problem definitions could pertain to (1) existing business problems where a manager is looking for a solution, (2) situations that may not pose any current problems but which the manager feels have scope for improvement, (3) areas where some conceptual clarity is needed for better theory building, or (4) situations in which a researcher is trying to answer a research question empirically because of interest in the topic. The first two fall within the realm of applied research, and the latter two under basic research.

Examples of Well-Defined Problems

1. To what extent do the structure of the organization and type of information systems installed account for the variance in the perceived effectiveness of managerial decision making?

2. To what extent has the new advertising campaign been successful in creating the high-quality, customer-centered corporate image that it was intended to produce?

3. How has the new packaging affected the sales of the product?

4. Has the new advertising message resulted in enhanced recall?

5. How do price and quality rate on consumers' evaluation of products?

6. Is the effect of participative budgeting on performance moderated by control systems?

7. Does better automation lead to greater asset investment per dollar of output?

8. Does expansion of international operations result in an enhancement of the firm's image and value?

9. What are the effects of downsizing on the long-range growth patterns of companies?

10. Can cultural differences account for the differences in the nature of hierarchical relationships between superiors and subordinates in Germany, India, Japan, Singapore, and the United States?

11. What are the components of "quality of life"?

12. What are the specific factors to be considered in creating a data warehouse for a manufacturing company?

13. What network system is best suited for Smith Pharmaceuticals?

MANAGERIAL IMPLICATIONS

Managers sometimes look at the symptoms in problematic situations and treat them as if they are the real problems, getting frustrated when their remedies do not work. Understanding the *antecedents–problem–consequences* sequence, and gathering the relevant information to get a real grasp of the problem go a long way in pinpointing it.

Managers' inputs help researchers to define the broad problem area and confirm their own theories about the situational factors impacting on the central problem. Managers who realize that correct problem definition is critical to ultimate problem solution, do not grudge the time spent in working closely with researchers, particularly at this stage. Awareness of information sources and ability to obtain access to the requisite information at will through the Internet are great assets to the manager. Using this facility, the manager can get to know how similar businesses the world over grapple with similar situations and get a better handle on the issues at hand.

ETHICAL ISSUES IN THE PRELIMINARY STAGES OF INVESTIGATION

Once a problem is sensed and an investigation is decided on, it is necessary to inform all employees—particularly those who will be interviewed for preliminary data gathering through structured and unstructured interviews—of the proposed study. Though it is not necessary to acquaint them with the actual reasons for the study (because this might bias responses), letting them know that the research is intended to help them in their work environment will enlist their cooperation. The element of unpleasant surprise will thus be eliminated for the employees. It is also necessary to assure employees that their responses will be kept confidential by the interviewer/s and that individual responses will not be divulged to anyone in the organization. These two steps make the employees comfortable with the research undertaken and ensure their cooperation. Attempts to obtain information through deceptive means should be avoided at all costs as they engender distrust and anxiety within the system. In essence, employers have the right to gather information relating to work, and employees have the right to privacy and confidentiality; but respondent cooperation alone assures good information.

We could draw lessons from the fact that Johns Hopkins University ran into ethical problems for allegedly using human beings for riskly scientific experiments. The Maryland Court of Appeals took issue with the prestigious university for its research in the 1990s when it exposed hundreds of poor and minority infants and toddlers to major health risks without alerting their parents. Some of the children, according to newsprint reports, now suffer learning disabilities and cognitive impairments akin to lead poisoning.

More recently, in June 2001, the same institution practiced deliberate deception on asthma patients to enable doctors to chart the effects of certain medicine. In the process one patient died. In both cases, failure to observe ethical standards brought discredit to this prestigious research organization. The moral of this is quite clear—experiments on human beings may sometimes become worthwhile as a matter of necessity in the larger interests of promoting the health and well being of people, but it is imperative that these should be undertaken only with the full knowledge and unqualified and specific approval of the participating subjects.

SUMMARY

In this chapter, we learned about the first three steps in the research process: identification of the broad problem area to be researched, preliminary data gathering through interviews and literature survey, and problem definition. In particular, we discussed how managers could identify the broad problem area through observation, how preliminary data can be collected through unstructured and structured interviews and literature survey, and how the problem can be honed. We defined the term *problem* as any situation where a gap exists between the actual and desired states. We also touched on the ethical issues confronting researchers.

The Appendix to this chapter offers information on (1) online databases, (2) bibliographical indexes, (3) APA format for references, and (4) notes on referencing previous studies and quoting original sources in the literature review section.

In Chapter 5 we will examine the next two steps in the research process: theoretical framework and hypotheses.

DISCUSSION QUESTIONS AND POINTS TO PONDER

1. How would you describe the research process?
2. Explain the preliminary data collection methods.
3. Why is it important to gather information on the background of the organization?

4. Should a researcher *always* obtain information on the structural aspects and job characteristics from those interviewed? Give reasons for your answer with examples.

5. How would you go about doing a literature survey in the area of business ethics?

6. What is the purpose of a literature survey?

7. Why is appropriate citation important? What are the consequences of not giving credit to the source from which materials are extracted?

8. "The problem definition stage is perhaps more critical in the research process than the problem solution stage." Discuss this statement.

9. Why should one get hung up on problem definition if one already knows the broad problem area to be studied?

10. Offer a clearly focused problem statement in the broad area of corporate culture.

11. After studying and extracting information from all the relevant work done previously, how does the researcher know which particular references, articles, and information should be given prominence in the literature survey?

12. Below is the gist of an article from *Business Week*. After reading it, (a) identify the broad problem area, (b) define the problem, and (c) explain how you would proceed further.

While Chrysler's minivans, pickups, and sport utility vehicles take a big share of the truck market, its cars trail behind those of GM, Ford, Honda, and Toyota. Quality problems include, among other things, water leaks and defective parts.

---

13. Comment on the following research:

From 1932 to 1972, a research study was conducted in Tuskegee, Alabama, to chart the effects of withholding treatment to African American men with syphilis.

14. What is the problem statement in the following situation?

Employee Loyalty

Companies benefit through employee loyalty. Crude downsizing in organizations during the recession crushed the loyalty of millions. The economic benefits of loyalty embrace lower recruitment and training costs, higher productivity of workers, customer satisfaction, and the boost to morale of fresh recruits. In order that these benefits are not lost, some companies while downsizing try various gimmicks. Flex leave, for instance, is one. This helps employees receive 20% of their salary, plus employer provided benefits, while they take a 6 to 12 month sabbatical, with a call option on their services. Others try alternatives like more communication, hand holding, and the like.

---

15. How would you define the problem in the following case?

Accounting Gets Radical

The GAAP (Generally Accepted Accounting Principles) do an unacceptable job of accounting for the principle activities of the information age companies. Today, investors are in the dark because the acounting is irrelevant. The basic purpose of accounting is to provide useful information to help investors make rational invest-ment, credit, and similar decisions, but today's most important assets and activi-ties—intellectual capital and work knowledge—are totally ignored.

Professor Robert A. Howell wants to reform the accounting system with the goal of making clear the measurement of how companies produce cash and create value.

PRACTICE PROJECTS

I. Do the project assigned below, following the step-by-step process delineated therein:

 i. Compile a bibliography on any one of the following topics, or any other topic of interest to you, from a business perspective: (a) day care; (b) product develop-ment; (c) open-market operations; (d) information systems; (e) manufacturing technology; (f) assessment centers; (g) transfer pricing.

 ii. From this bibliography, select 15 references that include books, periodicals, and newspaper items.

 iii. Based on these 15 articles, write a literature review using different forms of cita-tions as described in the Appendix.

 iv. Formulate a problem statement.

II. Visit the following web sites and answer the questions below.

 a. Visit   IBM   http://www.ibm.com   and

   Ford   http://www.ford.com

 What similarities and differences do you notice?

 b. Visit   Intel   http://www.intel.com   Microsoft   http://www.microsoft.com
 and   Apple   http://www.apple.com

 Write a paragraph on each of these companies.

III. Gain access to the online system in your library and (a) generate a list of the refer-ences that relate to the performance of General Motors, and (b) obtain the abstracts of these studies.

IV. Get access to the online system and obtain a list of references that deal with product image.

APPENDIX

Section 1
SOME ONLINE DATABASES USEFUL FOR BUSINESS RESEARCH

ONLINE DATABASES

Databases contain raw data stored on disks or CD-ROM. Computerized databases that can be purchased deal with statistical data, financial data, texts, and the like. Computer network links allow the sharing of these databases, which are updated on a regular basis. Most university libraries have computerized databases pertaining to business information that can be readily accessed.

Online services such as America Online, CompuServe, Prodigy, Delphi, and Microsoft Network provide, among other things, facilities of the electronic mail, discussion forums, real time chat, business and advertising opportunities, stock quotes, online newspapers, and access to several databases. Some of the databases useful for business research are listed below.

1. **ABI/INFORM Global** and **ABI/INFORM** provide the capability to search most major business, management, trade and industry, and scholarly journals from 1971 onward. The information search can be made by keying in the name of the author, periodical title, article title, or company name. Full texts from the journals and business periodicals are also available on CD-ROM and electronic services.

2. **INFOTRAC** has a CD-ROM with expanded academic, business, and investment periodicals index covering over 1,000 periodicals in social sciences and business that are updated monthly.

3. **American Science and Technology Index (ASTI)** is available both online and on CD-ROM, and indexes periodicals and books.

4. **The Business Periodicals Index (BPI)** provides an index of more than 3,000 business and management periodicals, and is available online and on CD-ROM.

5. **Human Resources Abstract** is a quarterly abstracting service that covers human, social, and manpower information.

6. **The Public Affairs Information Service (PAIS)** is available both online and on CD-ROM. This indexing service of books, periodicals, business articles, government documents in business, and so on, is a useful source of reference.

7. **The Wall Street Journal Index** is available in full text by using the Dow Jones News/Retrieval Service. This index covers corporate news as well as general economic and social news. The Dow Jones News/Retrieval Service offers full texts of articles.

OTHER SOURCES OF INFORMATION

Dictionaries and encyclopedias are also accessible in the areas of accounting, business, finance, management, investing, international trade, business and management, marketing and advertising, and production and inventory management.

Information on books in print as well as book reviews are available on CD-ROM. Likewise, census data are also available on CD-ROM.

SOME REFERENCE GUIDES

American Statistical Index is available both online and on CD-ROM as statistical masterfiles.

Prompt-Predicasts provides an overview of markets and technology and offers access to abstracts and some full texts on industries, companies, products, markets, market size, financial trends, and so on.

OTHER DATABASES

The following databases can also be accessed through the Internet:

Business and Industry Database*

Guide to Dissertation Abstracts

Guide to Newspaper Abstracts

Conference Papers

Conference Proceedings

Operations Research/Management Science

Periodicals Abstract

Personnel Management Abstract

Social Science Citation Index

STAT-USA

Conference Board Cumulative Index (covers publications in business, finance, personnel, marketing, and international operations).

Note: A cumulated annotated index to articles on accounting and in business periodicals arranged by subject and by author is also available. The Lexis-Nexis Universe provides specific company and industry information including company reports, stock information, industry trends, and the like.

---

* Includes information on whether the company is private or public, description of business, company organization and management, product lines and brand names, financial information, stock and bond prices and dividends, foreign operations, marketing and advertising, sales, R & D, and articles available on the company in newspapers and periodicals.

ON THE WEB

Some of the many web sites useful for business research that can be accessed through a browser such as the Netscape Navigator or the Internet Explorer are provided below. Please note that each web site can be accessed with the following references, but preceded in each case by http://. For example, the second reference for All Business Network will be:

http://www.webcom.com/~garnet/labor/aa_eeo.html

1. Academy of Management   aom@academy.pace.edu
2. All Business Network   www.webcom.com/~garnet/labor/aa_eeo.html
   This site offers articles, publications, and government resources related to human resources management.
3. ASTD Home Page   www.astd.org
   ASTD (American Society for Training and Development) has information on shifting paradigms from training to performance.
4. AT&T Business Network   www.bnet.att.com
   This site gives access to good business resources and offers the latest business news and information.
5. Bureau of Census   www.census.gov
6. Business Information Resources   www.eotw.com/business_info.html
   Links small business researchers to magazines and journals, government and law, financial services, and other entrepreneurial organizations.
7. Business Management Home Page   www.lia.co.za/users/johannh/index.htm
   This page offers sources dealing with project management, total quality management (TQM), continuous improvement, productivity improvement, and related topics.
8. Business Researcher's Interests   www.brint.com/interest.html
9. Company Annual Reports   www.reportgallery.com/bigaz.htm
10. CNN Financial Network   http://cnnfn.com/index.html
11. Dow Jones Business Directory   www.Businessdirectory.dowjones.com
12. Entrepreneur Forum   http://upside.master.com/forum
13. Entrepreneur's Resources Center   www.herring.com/erc
14. Fidelity Investment   www.fid-inv.com
15. Harvard Business School Publishing   www.hbsp.harvard.edu
16. Human Resources Management on the Internet
    http://members.gnn.com/hrmbasics/hrinet.htm
17. Index of Business Topics www1.usal.com/~ibnet/iccindex.html
    Covers a vast range of subjects for companies engaged in international trade.
18. International Business Directory   www.et.byu.edu/-eliasone/main.html
    This site offered by BYU has valuable sources for international business.

19. I.O.M.A.   www.ioma.com/ioma/direct.html
    This site links to business resources that include financial management, legal resources, small business, human resources, and Internet marketing.
20. MBA Page   www.cob.ohio-state.edu/dept/fin/mba/htm
    Designed by Ohio State University to help MBA students.
21. Multinational Companies   http://web.idirect.com/~tiger/worldbea.htm
22. Operations Management   www.muohio.edu/~bjfinch/ominfo.html
23. Society for Human Resource Management   www.shrm.org
24. STAT-USA   www.stat-usa.gov
25. Systems Dynamics for Business Policy   http://web.mit.edu/15.87/www
26. Wall Street Journal   www.wsj.com
27. Wall Street Research Net   www.wsrn.com

For more information on web sites refer to Leshin (1997).

Section 2
BIBLIOGRAPHICAL INDEXES

The following indexes help in compiling a comprehensive bibliography on business topics.

1. **Bibliographic Index.** A cumulative bibliography of bibliographies—an index that lists, by subject, sources of bibliographies.
2. **Business Books in Print.** This indexes by author, title, and business subjects, the books in print in the areas of finance, business, and economics.
3. **Business Periodicals Index.** This is a cumulative subject index covering 270 business periodicals.
4. **Management Information Guide.** This offers bibliographic references in many business areas.
5. **Human Resource Management Abstracts.** This is an index of articles that deal with the management of people and the subject area of organizational behavior.
6. **Psychological Abstracts.** This summarizes the literature in psychology, covering several hundred journals, reports, monographs, and other scientific documents.
7. **Public Affairs Information Service Bulletin.** This has a selective subject index of books, yearbooks, directories, government documents, pamphlets, and over a thousand periodicals relating to national and international economic and public affairs.
8. **Work Related Abstracts.** This contains abstracts of articles, dissertations, and books relating to labor, personnel, and organizational behavior.

FINANCIAL GUIDES AND SERVICES

1. **Business and Investment Service** analyzes production in basic industries, and presents stock market trends and indexes, as well as earnings and prices of stocks in selected industries.

2. **Dun and Bradstreet Credit Service** collects, analyzes, and distributes credit information on manufacturers, wholesalers, and retailers. Includes information on the enterprise and offers a detailed statement of the methods of operation, financial statement analysis, management progress, and payment record.

3. **Moody's Bond Record** provides information on dividends declared, payment dates, ex-dividend rates, income bond interest payments, payments on bonds and default, stock splits, etc.

4. **Moody's Stock Survey** presents data on stocks, makes recommendations for purchase, sale, or exchange of individual stocks, and discusses industry trends and developments.

5. **Standard and Poor's Corporation Services** offers investment data weekly. They have several publications, one of which is *Standard & Poor's Register of Corporations, Directors, and Executives,* which has three volumes. Volume 1 has an alphabetical listing of over 45,000 U.S. and Canadian companies, Volume 2 furnishes a list of executives and directors with a brief about each, and Volume 3 contains and index of companies by SIC number and by location.

REFERENCE GUIDES IN THE MARKETING AREA

1. **Topicator** is a classified guide to articles in advertising, communications, and marketing periodicals.

2. **Standard Directory of Advertisers** is arranged by industry and gives the names of officers, products, advertising agency, media used, and a "Trade-name List."

NEWSPAPER INDEXES OF CURRENT EVENTS

1. **New York Times Index,** published every 2 weeks, summarizes and classifies news alphabetically by subject, persons, and organizations. It is also accessible online.

2. **Wall Street Journal Index,** published monthly, gives a complete report on current business. Grouped under "Corporate News" and "General News," the subject index of all articles that have appeared in the *Journal* is also given.

Note: Brown and Vasarhelyi (1985) have a database of accounting literature that will be useful to researchers in the accounting area. Ferris (1988) offers topical areas for accounting research as well.

Section 3
APA FORMAT FOR REFERENCING RELEVANT ARTICLES

A distinction has to be made between bibliography and references. A **bibliography** is the listing of the work that is relevant to the main topic of research interest arranged in the alphabetical order of the last names of the authors. A **reference list** is a subset of the bibliography, which includes details of all the citations used in the literature survey and elsewhere in the paper, arranged again, in the alphabetical order of the last names of the authors. These citations have the goals of crediting the author and enabling the reader to find the works cited.

At least three modes of referencing are followed in business research. These are based on the format provided in the *Publication Manual of the American Psychological Association* (APA) (2001), the *Chicago Manual of Style* (1993), and the Turabian style (1996). Each of these manuals specifies, with examples, how books, journals, newspapers, dissertations, and other materials are to be referenced in manuscripts. Since the APA format is followed for referencing by many journals in the management area, we will highlight the distinctions in how books, journals, newspaper articles, dissertations, and so on, are referenced, using this as per the Specimen Referencing format below. We will, in Section 4, discuss how these references will be cited in the literature review section. All the citations mentioned in the research report will find a place in the References section at the end of the report.

SPECIMEN FORMAT FOR CITING DIFFERENT TYPES OF REFERENCES

Specimen Format for Referencing

Book by a single author

Leshin, C. B. (1997). *Management on the World Wide Web*. Englewood Cliffs, NJ: Prentice-Hall.

Book by more than one author

Cornett, M., Wiley, B.J., & Sankar, S. (1998). *The pleasures of nurturing*. London: McMunster Publishing.

More than one book by the same author in the same year

Roy, A. (1998a) *Chaos theory*. New York: McMillian Publishing Enterprises.
Roy, A. (1998b). *Classic chaos*. San Francisco, CA: Jossey Bamar.

Edited Book

Pennathur, A., Leong, F.T., & Schuster, K. (Eds). (1998). *Style and substance of thinking*. New York: Publishers Paradise.

Chapter in an Edited Book

Riley, T., & Brecht, M.L. (1998). The success of the mentoring process. In R. Williams (Ed.) *Mentoring and career success*, pp. 129–150. New York: Wilson Press.

Book Review

Nichols, P. (1998). A new look at Home Services [Review of the book Providing Home Services to the Elderly by Girch, S. *Family Review Bulletin, 45,* 12–13.

Journal Article

Jeanquart, S., & Peluchette, J. (1997). Diversity in the workforce and management models. *Journal of Social Work Studies, 43* (3), 72–85.

Conference Proceedings Publication

Yeshwant, M. (1998). Revised thinking on Indian philosophy and religion. In S.Pennathur (Ed.), *Proceedings of the Ninth International Conference on Religion,* (pp. 100–107). Bihar, India: Bihar University.

Doctoral Dissertation

Kiren, R.S. (1997). *Medical advances and quality of life*. Unpublished doctoral dissertation, Omaha State University.

Paper Presentation at Conference

Bajaj, L.S. (1996, March 13). *Practical tips for efficient work management*. Paper presented at the annual meeting of Enterpreneurs, San Jose, CA.

Unpublished Manuscript

Pringle, P.S. (1991). *Training and development in the '90s*. Unpublished manuscript, Southern Illinois University, Diamondale, IL.

Newspaper Article

The new GM pact. (1998, July 28). *Concord Tribune*, p.1.

REFERENCING NONPRINT MEDIA

Film

Maas, J.B. (Producer), & Gluck, D.H. (Director). (1979). *Deeper into hypnosis* (film). Englewood Cliffs, NJ: Prentice-Hall.

Cassette Recording

Clark, K.B. (Speaker). (1976). *Problems of freedom and behavior modification* (Cassette Recording No. 7612). Washington, DC: American Psychological Association.

Referencing Electronic Sources

Author, I. (1998). Technology and immediacy of information [On-line] Available http://www.bnet.act.com

---

Section 4
REFERENCING AND QUOTATION IN THE LITERATURE REVIEW SECTION

Cite all references in the body of the paper using the author–year method of citation; that is, the surname of the author(s) and the year of publication are given at the appropriate places. Examples of this are as follows:

a. Todd (1998) has shown...

b. In recent studies of dual-career families (Hunt, 1999; Osborn, 1998) it has been...

c. In 1997, Kyle compared dual-career and dual-earner families and found that...

As can be seen from the above, if the name of the author appears as part of the narrative as in the case of (a), the year of publication alone has to be cited in parentheses. Note that in case (b), both the author and the year are cited in parentheses, separated by a comma. If the year and the author are a part of the textual discussion as in (c) above, the use of parenthesis is not warranted.

Note also the following:

1. Within the same paragraph, you need not include the year after the first citation so long as the study cannot be confused with other studies cited in the article. An example of this is:

   Gutek (1985) published her findings in the book titled *Sex and the Work place.* Gutek indicated...

2. When a work is authored by **two** individuals, always cite both names every time the reference occurs in the text.

3. When a work has **more than two** authors but fewer than six authors, cite all authors the first time the reference occurs, and subsequently include only the surname of the first author followed by "et al." as per the example below:

   Sekaran, U., Martin, T., Trafton, and Osborn R. N. (1980) found … (first citation)

   Sekaran et al. (1980) found … (subsequent citations)

4. When a work is authored by **six or more** individuals, cite only the surname of the first author followed by et al. and the year for the first and subsequent citations. Join the names in a multiple-author citation in running text by the word *and*. In parenthetical material, in tables, and in the reference list, join the names by an ampersand (&). Examples are given below.

   a. As Tucker and Snell (1989) pointed out…

   b. As has been pointed out (Tucker & Snell, 1989),…

5. When a work has no author, cite in text the first two or three words of the article title. Use double quotation marks around the title of the article. For example, while referring to the newspaper article cited earlier, the text might read as follows:

   While examining unions ("With GM pact," 1990).

6. When a work's author is designated as "Anonymous," cite in text, the word *Anonymous* followed by a comma and the date: (Anonymous, 1979). In the reference list, an anonymous work is alphabetized by the word *Anonymous*.

7. When the same author has several works published in the same year, cite them in the same order as they occur in the reference list, with the inpress citations coming last. For example:

   Research on the mental health of dual-career family members (Sekaran, 1985a, 1985b, 1985c, 1999, in press) indicates…

8. When more than one author has to be cited in the text, these should be in the alphabetical order of the first author's surname, and the citations should be separated by semicolons as per the illustration below:

   In the job design literature (Aldag & Brief, 1976; Alderfer, 1972; Beatty, 1982; Jeanquart, 1998),…

Personal communication through letters, memos, telephone conversations, and the like, should be cited in the text only and not included in the reference list since these are not retrievable data. In the text, provide the initials as well as the surname of the communicator together with the date, as in the following example:

L. Peters (personal communication, June 15, 1998) feels…

In this section we have seen different modes of citation. We will next see how to include quotations from others in the text.

QUOTATIONS IN TEXT

Quotations should be given exactly as they appear in the source. The original wording, punctuation, spelling, and italics must be preserved even if they are erroneous. The citation of the source of a direct quotation should always include the page number(s) as well as the reference.

Use double quotation marks for quotations in text. Use single quotation marks to identify the material that was enclosed in double quotation marks in the original source. If you want to emphasize certain words in a quotation, underline them and immediately after the underlined words, insert within brackets the words: *italics added*. Use three ellipsis points (...) to indicate that you have omitted material from the original source. See example that follows later.

If the quotation is of more than 40 words, set it in a free-standing style starting on a new line and indenting the left margin a further five spaces. Type the entire quotation double spaced on the new margin, indenting the first line of paragraphs five spaces from the new margin, as shown below.

In trying to differentiate dual-earner and dual-career families, Sekaran (1986) states:

> Various terms are used to refer to dual-earner families: dual-worker families, two-paycheck families, dual-income families, two-job families, and so on. Spouses in dual-earner families may both hold jobs, or one of the partners may hold a job while the other pursues a career...
>
> The distinction between dual-career and dual-earner families also gets blurred when spouses currently holding jobs are preparing themselves both educationally and technically to move up in their organization. (p. 4)

If you intend publishing an article in which you have quoted extensively from a copyrighted work, it is important that you seek written permission from the owner of the copyright. Make sure that you also footnote the permission obtained with respect to the quoted material. Failure to do so may result in unpleasant consequences, including legal action taken through copyright protection laws.

THE RESEARCH PROCESS

Steps 4 and
Theoretical
Hypothesis D

TOPICS DISCUSSED

THE NEED FOR A THEORETICAL FRA
VARIABLES
- Dependent Variable
- Independent Variable
- Moderating Variable
- Intervening Variable

THE THEORETICAL
HYPOTHESIS DEVE
- Definition
- If–Then Statemen
- Directional and N
- Null and Alternate

MANAGERIAL IMPLI

CHAPTER OBJEC

After completing Chap

1. Identify and label
2. Trace and establish
   framework.
3. Develop a set of hy
   alternate.
4. Apply what has been learned to a research project.

etical

nd the

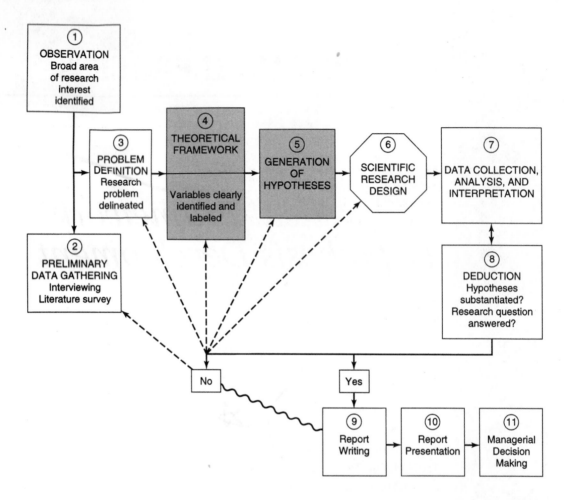

In the previous chapter, the focus was on learning how to narrow down and clearly define the research problem. But mere definition of the problem does not solve it. How, then, does one proceed further? The answer is by going through the entire process as shown in the research process model. The next two steps are designated as steps 4 and 5 indicated by the shaded portions in the figure shown. Step 4 relates to evolving a theoretical framework, and step 5 deals with deriving testable hypotheses. In this chapter we shall discuss both topics in some depth.

You will find as you proceed in this chapter that at various places you are instructed to work out certain exercises. Doing them at that time, before reading further, will help you in becoming adept at formulating theoretical frameworks in a logical manner without getting confused.

THE NEED FOR A THEORETICAL FRAMEWORK

After conducting the interviews, completing a literature survey, and defining the problem, one is ready to develop a theoretical framework. A theoretical frame-

A fend outside definitions

work is a conceptual model of how one theorizes or makes logical sense of the relationships among the several factors that have been identified as important to the problem. This theory flows logically from the documentation of previous research in the problem area. Integrating one's logical beliefs with published research, taking into consideration the boundaries and constraints governing the situation, is pivotal in developing a scientific basis for investigating the research problem. In sum, the theoretical framework discusses the interrelationships among the variables that are deemed to be integral to the dynamics of the situation being investigated. Developing such a conceptual framework helps us to postulate or hypothesize and test certain relationships and thus to improve our understanding of the dynamics of the situation.

From the theoretical framework, then, testable hypotheses can be developed to examine whether the theory formulated is valid or not. The hypothesized relationships can thereafter be tested through appropriate statistical analyses. By being able to test and replicate the findings, we will also have stronger conviction in the rigor of our research. Thus, the entire research rests on the basis of the theoretical framework. Even if testable hypotheses are not necessarily generated (as in some applied research projects), developing a good theoretical framework is central to examining the problem under investigation.

Since the theoretical framework offers the conceptual foundation to proceed with the reasearch, and since a theoretical framework is none other than identifying the network of relationships among the variables considered important to the study of any given problem situation, it is essential to understand what a variable means and what the different types of variables are.

VARIABLES

A variable is anything that can take on differing or varying values. The values can differ at various times for the same object or person, or at the same time for different objects or persons. Examples of variables are production units, absenteeism, and motivation.

Example 5.1   *Production units:* One worker in the manufacturing department may produce one widget per minute, a second might produce two per minute, a third might produce five per minute. It is also possible that the same member could produce one widget the first minute, and five the next minute. In both cases, the number of widgets produced has taken on different values, and is therefore a variable.

Example 5.2   *Absenteeism:* Today three members in the sales department may be absent, tomorrow six members may not show up for work; the day after, there may be no one absent. The value can thus theoretically range from "zero" to "all" being absent, on the absenteeism variable.

Example 5.3   *Motivation:* The levels of motivation of members to learn in the class or in a work team might take on varying values ranging from "very low" to "very high."

An individual's motivation to learn from different classes or in different work teams might also take on differing values. Now, how one *measures* the level of motivation is an entirely different matter. The factor called motivation has to be reduced from its level of abstraction and operationalized in a way that it becomes measurable. We will discuss this in Chapter 8.

Types of Variables

Four main types of variables are discussed in this chapter:

1. The dependent variable (also known as the criterion variable).
2. The independent variable (also known as the predictor variable).
3. The moderating variable.
4. The intervening variable.

Variables can be discrete (e.g., male/female) or continuous (e.g., the age of an individual). Extraneous variables that confound cause-and-effect relationships are discussed in Chapter 7 on Experimental Designs. In this chapter, we will primarily concern ourselves with the four types of variables listed above.

Dependent Variable

The dependent variable is the variable of primary interest to the researcher. The researcher's goal is to understand and describe the dependent variable, or to explain its variability, or predict it. In other words, it is the main variable that lends itself for investigation as a viable factor. Through the analysis of the dependent variable (i.e., finding what variables influence it), it is possible to find answers or solutions to the problem. For this purpose, the researcher will be interested in quantifying and measuring the dependent variable, as well as the other variables that influence this variable.

Example 5.4 A manager is concerned that the sales of a new product introduced after test marketing it do not meet with his expectations. The dependent variable here is sales. Since the sales of the product can vary—can be low, medium, or high—it is a variable; since sales is the main focus of interest to the manager, it is the dependent variable.

Example 5.5 A basic researcher is interested in investigating the debt-to-equity ratio of manufacturing companies in southern California. Here the dependent variable is the ratio of debt to equity.

Example 5.6 A vice president is concerned that the employees are not loyal to the organization, and in fact, seem to switch their loyalty to other institutions. The dependent variable in this case would be *organizational loyalty*.

Here again, there is variance found in the levels of organizational loyalty of employees. The V.P. might want to know what accounts for the variance in the loyalty of organizational members with a view to control it. If he finds that increased pay levels would ensure their loyalty and retention, he can then offer inducement to employees by way of pay raises, which would help control the variability in organizational loyalty and keep them in the organization.

It is possible to have more than one dependent variable in a study. For example, there is always a tussle between quality and volume of output, low-cost production and customer satisfaction, and so on. In such cases, the manager is interested to know the factors that influence all the dependent variables of interest and how some of them might differ in regard to different dependent variables. These investigations may call for multivariate statistical analyses.

Now respond to Exercises 5.1 and 5.2

DV = ORG. PERFORMANCE

Exercise 5.1

An applied researcher wants to increase the performance of organizational members in a particular bank.
What would be the dependent variable in this case?

Exercise 5.2

D.V. = ADVERTISEMENT STRATEGY ?

A marketing manager wonders why the recent advertisement strategy does not work.
What would be the dependent variable here?

Independent Variable

An independent variable is one that influences the dependent variable in either a positive or negative way. That is, when the independent variable is present, the dependent variable is also present, and with each unit of increase in the independent variable, there is an increase or decrease in the dependent variable also. In other words, the variance in the dependent variable is accounted for by the independent variable. To establish causal relationships, the independent variable is manipulated as described in Chapter 7 on Experimental Designs.

Example 5.7   Research studies indicate that successful new product development has an influence on the stock market price of the company. That is, the more successful the new product turns out to be, the higher will be the stock market price of that firm. Therefore, the **success of the new product** is *the independent variable,* and **stock market price** the *dependent variable*. The degree of perceived success of the new product developed will explain the variance in the stock market price of the company. This relationship and the labeling of the variables are diagrammed in Figure 5.1.

Figure 5.1

Diagram of the relationship between the independent variable (new product success:
and the dependent variable (stock market price).

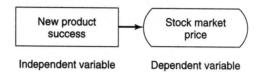

Independent variable   Dependent variable

Example 5.8 Cross-cultural research indicates that managerial values govern the power distance between superiors and subordinates. Here, power distance (i.e., egalitarian interactions between the boss and the employee, versus the high-power
superior in limited interaction with the low-power subordinate) is the subject of
interest and hence the **dependent variable.** Managerial values that explain the
variance in power distance is the **independent variable.** This relationship is
diagrammed in Figure 5.2.

Now do Exercises 5.3 and 5.4

*List the variables in this and the next exercise, individually, and label them
as dependent or independent, explaining why they are so labeled. Diagram
the relationships.*

PRODUCTION = DV
SUPVERVISION = IV
TRAINING = IV

Exercise 5.3

A manager believes that good supervision and training would increase the
production level of the workers.

Exercise 5.4

A consultant is of the opinion that much benefit would accrue by buying
and selling at the appropriate times in a financial environment where the
stocks are volatile.   MKT. TIMING → BENEFIT

Figure 5.2

Diagram of the relationship between the independent variable (managerial values) and
the dependent variable (power distance).

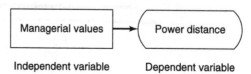

Independent variable   Dependent variable

Figure 5.3A

Diagram of the relationship between the independent variable (availability of reference manuals) and the dependent variable (rejects).

Moderating Variable

The moderating variable is one that has a strong *contingent* effect on the independent variable–dependent variable relationship. That is, the presence of a third variable (the moderating variable) modifies the original relationship between the independent and the dependent variables. This becomes clear through the following examples.

Example 5.9   It has been found that there is a relationship between the availability of Reference Manuals that manufacturing employees have access to, and the product rejects. That is, when workers follow the procedures laid down in the manual, they are able to manufacture products that are flawless. This relationship is diagrammed in Fig. 5.3A.

Although this relationship can be said to hold true generally for all workers, it is nevertheless contingent on the inclination or urge of the employees to look into the Manual every time a new procedure is to be adopted. In other words, only those who have the interest and urge to refer to the manual every time a new process is adopted will produce flawless products. Others who do not will not be benefited and will continue to produce defective products. This influence of the attributes of the worker on the relationship between the independent and the dependent variables can be diagrammed as in Figure 5.3B.

Figure 5.3B

Diagram of the relationship between the independent variable (availability of reference materials) and the dependent variable (rejects) as modulated by the moderating variable (interest and inclination).

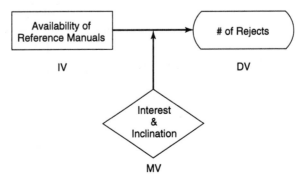

As in the above case, whenever the relationship between the independent variable and the dependent variable becomes contingent or dependent on another variable, we say that the third variable has a moderating effect on the independent variable–dependent variable relationship. The variable that moderates the relationship is known as the moderating variable.

Example 5.10

Let us take another example of a moderating variable. A prevalent theory is that the diversity of the workforce (comprising people of different ethnic origins, races, and nationalities) contributes more to organizational effectiveness because each group brings its own special expertise and skills to the workplace. This synergy can be exploited, however, only if managers know how to harness the special talents of the diverse work group; otherwise they will remain untapped.

In the above scenario, organizational effectiveness is the **dependent variable,** which is positively influenced by workforce diversity—the **independent variable.** However, to harness the potential, managers must know how to encourage and coordinate the talents of the various groups to make things work. If not, the synergy will not be tapped. In other words, the effective utilization of different talents, perspectives, and eclectic problem-solving capabilities for enhanced organizational effectiveness is contingent on the skill of the managers in acting as catalysts. This managerial expertise then becomes the **moderating variable.** These relationships can be depicted as in Figure 5.4.

The Distinction between an Independent Variable and a Moderating Variable

At times, confusion is likely to arise as to when a variable is to be treated as an independent variable and when it would become a moderating variable. For instance, there may be two situations as follows:

Situation 1

A research study indicates that the better the quality of the training programs in an organization and the greater the growth needs of the employees (i.e., where

Figure 5.4
Diagram of the relationship among the three variables: workforce diversity, organizational effectiveness, and managerial expertise.

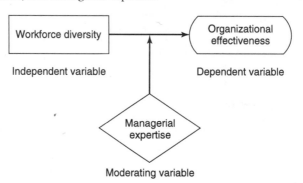

the need to develop and grow on the job is strong), the greater is their willingness to learn new ways of doing things.

Situation 2

Another research study indicates that the willingness of the employees to learn new ways of doing things is *not* influenced by the quality of the training programs offered by the organizations to *all* people without any distinction. Only those with high growth needs seem to have the yearning to learn to do new things through specialized training.

In the above two situations, we have the same three variables. In the first case, the training programs and growth need strength are the independent variables that influence employees' willingness to learn, which is the dependent variable. In the second case, however, the quality of the training program is the independent variable, and while the dependent variable remains the same, growth need strength becomes a moderating variable. In other words, only those with high growth needs show a greater willingness and adaptability to learn to do new things when the quality of the training program is improved. Thus the relationship between the independent and dependent variables has now become contingent on the existence of a moderator.

The above illustration makes it clear that even though the variables used are the same, the decision whether to label them dependent, independent, or moderating depends on how they affect one another. The differences between the effects of the independent and the moderating variables could be visually depicted as in Figure 5.5A and 5.5B (see page 94).

Note the steep incline of the top line and the relative flatness of the bottom line in Figure 5.5B.

Now do Exercises 5.5 and 5.6

Exercise 5.5

List and label the variables in this and the following exercise and explain and diagram the relationships among the variables.

A manager finds that off-the-job classroom training has a great impact on the productivity of the employees in her department. However, she also observes that employees over 60 years of age do not seem to derive much benefit and do not improve with such training.

Exercise 5.6

A visitor to a factory observes that the workers in the packing department have to interact with one another to get their jobs done. The more they interact, the more they seem to tend to stay after hours and go to the local pub together for a drink. However, the women packers, even though they interact with the others as much as the men, do not stay late, nor do they visit the pub after work hours.

Figure 5.5A
Illustration of the influence of independent variables on the dependent variable when no moderating variable operates in the situation.

Training programs
Growth needs

Intervening Variable

An intervening variable is one that surfaces between the time the independent variables start operating to influence the dependent variable and the time their impact is felt on it. There is thus a temporal quality or time dimension to the intervening variable. The intervening variable surfaces as a function of the independent variable(s) operating in any situation, and helps to conceptualize and explain the influence of the independent variable(s) on the dependent variable. The following example illustrates this point.

Figure 5.5B
Illustration of the influence of independent variables on the dependent variable when a moderating variable is operating in the situation.

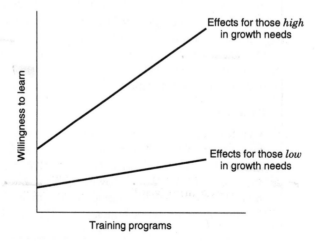

Training programs

Figure 5.6

Diagram of the relationship among the independent, intervening, and dependent variable.

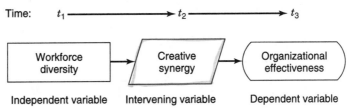

Example 5.11   In Example 5.10 where the **independent variable** workforce diversity influences the **dependent variable** organizational effectiveness, the **intervening variable** that surfaces as a function of the diversity in the workforce is *creative synergy*. This creative synergy results from a multiethnic, multiracial, and multinational (i.e., diverse) workforce interacting and bringing together their multifaceted expertise in problem solving. This helps us to understand how organizational effectiveness can result from having diversity in the workforce. Note that creative synergy, the intervening variable, surfaces at time t_2, as a function of workforce diversity, which was in place at time t_1, to bring about organizational effectiveness in time t_3. The intervening variable of creative synergy helps us to conceptualize and understand how workforce diversity brings about organizational effectiveness. The dynamics of these relationships are illustrated in Figure 5.6.

Example 5.12   It would be interesting to see how the inclusion of the moderating variable *managerial expertise* in the foregoing example would change the model or affect the relationships. The new set of relationships that would emerge in the presence of the **moderator** can be depicted as in Figure 5.7. As can be seen therefrom, managerial expertise moderates the relationship between workforce diversity and creative synergy. In other words, creative synergy will not result from the multifaceted problem-solving skills of the diverse workforce unless the manager is capable of harnessing that synergy by creatively coordinating the different skills. If the manager lacks the expertise to perform this role, then no matter how many different problem-solving skills the diverse workforce might have, synergy will just not surface. Instead of functioning effectively, the organization might just remain static, or even deteriorate.

It is now easy to see what the differences are among an independent variable, intervening variable, and a moderating variable. The **independent variable** helps to *explain* the variance in the dependent variable; the **intervening variable** *surfaces at time t_2* as a function of the independent variable, which also helps us to conceptualize the relationship between the independent and dependent variables; and the **moderating variable** has a *contingent effect* on the relationship between two variables. To put it differently, while the independent variable explains the variance in the dependent variable, the intervening variable does not add to the

Figure 5.7

Diagram of the relationship among the independent, intervening, moderating, and dependent variables.

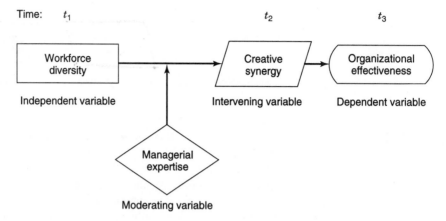

variance already explained by the independent variable, whereas the moderating variable has an interaction effect with the independent variable in explaining the variance. That is, unless the moderating variable is present, the theorized relationship between the other two variables considered will not hold.

Whether a variable is an independent variable, a dependent variable, an intervening variable, or a moderating variable should be determined by a careful reading of the dynamics operating in any given situation. For instance, a variable such as motivation to work could be a dependent variable, an independent variable, an intervening variable, or a moderating variable, depending on the theoretical model that is being advanced.

Now do Exercises 5.7, 5.8, and 5.9

Exercise 5.7

Make up three different situations in which motivation to work would be an independent variable, an intervening variable, and a moderating variable.

Exercise 5.8

List and label the variables in the following situation, explain the relationships among the variables, and diagram these.

Failure to follow accounting principles causes immense confusion, which in turn creates a number of problems for the organization. Those with vast experience in bookkeeping, however, are able to avert the problems by taking timely corrective action.

Exercise 5.9

List and label the variables in the following situation. Explain the relationships among the variables and diagram them. What might be the problem statement or problem definition for the situation?

The manager of Haines Company observes that the morale of employees in her company is low. She thinks that if their working conditions are improved, pay scales raised, and the vacation benefits made attractive, the morale will be boosted. She doubts, however, if an increase of pay scales would raise the morale of all employees. Her conjecture is that those that have supplemental incomes will just not be "turned on" by higher pay, and only those without side incomes will be happy with increased pay with resultant boost of morale.

THEORETICAL FRAMEWORK

Having examined the different kinds of variables that could operate in a situation and how the relationships among these can be established, it is now possible to see how we can develop the conceptual model or the theoretical framework for our research.

The theoretical framework is the foundation on which the entire research project is based. It is a logically developed, described, and elaborated network of associations among the variables deemed relevant to the problem situation and identified through such processes as interviews, observations, and literature survey. Experience and intuition also guide in developing the theoretical framework.

It becomes evident at this stage that to arrive at good solutions to the problem, one should correctly identify the problem first, and then the variables that contribute to it. The importance of conducting purposeful interviews and doing a thorough literature review now becomes clear. After identifying the appropriate variables, the next step is to elaborate the network of associations among the variables, so that relevant hypotheses can be developed and subsequently tested. Based on the results of hypotheses testing (which would indicate whether or not the hypotheses have been supported), the extent to which the problem can be solved would become evident. The theoretical framework is thus an important step in the research process.

The relationship between the literature survey and the theoretical framework is that the former provides a solid foundation for developing the latter. That is, the literature survey identifies the variables that might be important, as determined by previous research findings. This, in addition to other logical connections that can be conceptualized, forms the basis for the theoretical model. The theoretical framework elaborates the relationships among the variables, explains the theory underlying these relations, and describes the nature and direction of the relationships. Just as the literature survey sets the stage for a good theoretical framework, this in turn provides the logical base for developing testable hypotheses.

The Components of the Theoretical Framework

A good theoretical framework identifies and labels the important variables in the situation that are relevant to the problem defined. It logically describes the interconnections among these variables. The relationships among the independent variables, the dependent variable(s), and if applicable, the moderating and intervening variables are elaborated. Should there be any moderating variable(s), it is important to explain how and what specific relationships they would moderate. An explanation of why they operate as moderators should also be offered. If there are any intervening variables, a discussion on how or why they are treated as intervening variables would be necessary. Any interrelationships among the independent variables themselves, or among the dependent variables themselves (in case there are two or more dependent variables), if any, should also be clearly spelled out and adequately explained.

The elaboration of the variables in the theoretical framework thus addresses the issues of why or how we expect certain relationships to exist, and the nature and direction of the relationships among the variables of interest. A schematic diagram of the conceptual model described in the theoretical framework will also help the reader to visualize the theorized relationships.

It may be noted that we have used the terms *theoretical framework* and *model* interchangeably. There are differences of opinion as to what a model actually represents. Some describe models as simulations; others view a model as a representation of relationships between and among concepts. We use the term model here in the latter sense as a conceptual scheme connecting concepts.

In sum, there are five basic features that should be incorporated in any theoretical framework.

1. The variables considered relevant to the study should be clearly identified and labeled in the discussions.
2. The discussions should state how two or more variables are related to one another. This should be done for the important relationships that are theorized to exist among the variables.
3. If the nature and direction of the relationships can be theorized on the basis of the findings of previous research, then there should be an indication in the discussions as to whether the relationships would be positive or negative.
4. There should be a clear explanation of why we would expect these relationships to exist. The arguments could be drawn from the previous research findings.
5. A schematic diagram of the theoretical framework should be given so that the reader can see and easily comprehend the theorized relationships.

Let us illustrate how these five features are incorporated in the following example of Delta Airlines.

Example 5.13   DELTA AIRLINES

With airline deregulation, there were price wars among the various airlines that cut costs in different ways. According to reports, Delta Airlines faced charges of **air-safety violations** when there were several near collisions in midair, and one accident that resulted in 137 deaths in 1987. Four important factors that seem to have influenced these are poor communication among the cockpit crew members themselves, poor coordination between ground staff and cockpit crew, minimal training given to the cockpit crew, and management philosophy that encouraged a decentralized structure. It would be nice to know if these factors did indeed contribute to the safety violations, and if so, to what extent.

Theoretical Framework for Example 5.13

The dependent variable is safety violation, which is the variable of primary interest, in which the variance is attempted to be explained by the four independent variables of (1) communication among crew members, (2) communication between ground control and the cockpit crew, (3) training received by the cockpit crew, and (4) decentralization.

The less the communication among the crew members themselves, the greater is the probability of air-safety violations since very little information is shared among them. For example, whenever safety is threatened, timely communication between the navigator and pilot is most unlikely. Each member will be preoccupied with his or her work and lose sight of the larger picture. When ground crew fail to give the right information at the right time, mishaps are bound to occur with aborted flights and collisions. Coordination between ground and cockpit crew is at the very heart of air safety. Thus, the less the coordination between ground control and cockpit crew, the greater the possibility of air-safety violations taking place. Both of the above factors are exacerbated by the management philosophy of Delta Airlines, which emphasizes decentralization. This philosophy might have worked before the deregulation of the airlines when the number of flights was manageable. But with deregulation and increased flights overall in midair, and with all airlines operating many more flights, centralized coordination and control assume great importance. Thus, the greater the degree of decentralization, the greater is the scope for lower levels of communication both among in-flight staff and between ground staff and cockpit crew, and the greater the scope for air-safety violations. Also, when cockpit crew members are not adequately trained, they may not have the requisite knowledge of safety standards or may suffer from an inability to handle emergency situations and avoid collisions. Thus, poor training also adds to the probability of increased safety violations. These relationships are diagrammed in Figure 5.8.

Note how the five basic features of the theoretical framework have been incorporated in the example.

1. Identification and labeling of the dependent and independent variables have been done in the theoretical framework.

Figure 5.8
Schematic diagram for the theoretical framework in Example 5.13.

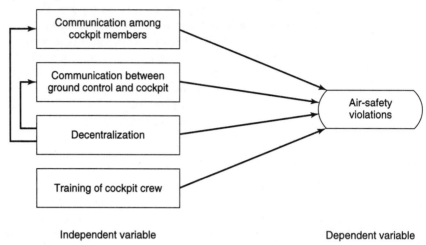

Independent variable   Dependent variable

2. The relationships among the variables were discussed, establishing that the four independent variables are related to the dependent variable, and that the independent variable, decentralization, is related to the other two independent variables, namely, communication among the cockpit members and between ground control and the cockpit crew. The nature and direction of the relationship of each independent variable with the dependent variable and the relationship of decentralization to the two independent variables were clearly stated.

For example, it was indicated that the lower the training level of the cockpit crew, the greater the chances of air-safety violations. Thus, as the training is lowered, the hazard is increased, or conversely, the higher the training, the less likely the air-safety violations, indicating a negative relationship between the two variables. Such a negative relationship exists between each of the independent variables excepting decentralization, and the dependent variable. There is also a negative relationship between decentralization and communication among cockpit members (the more the decentralization, the less the communication) and between decentralization and coordination (the more the decentralization, the less the coordination).

3. Why these relationships can be expected was explained through several logical statements, as for example describing why decentralization, which worked before deregulation, would not now work. More specifically, it was argued that:

a. lower levels of communication among cockpit crew would fail to alert the pilot to the impending hazards;

b. poor coordination between ground control and cockpit crew would be detrimental because such coordination is the very essence of safety;

Figure 5.9
Schematic diagram for the theoretical framework including the intervening variable.

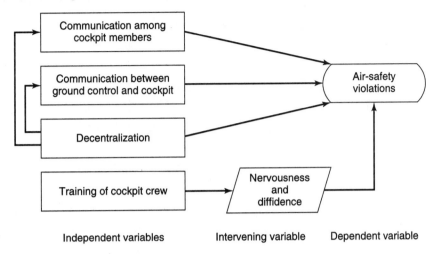

c. encouragement of decentralization would only reinforce poorer communication and coordination efforts;

d. inadequate training of cockpit crew would fail to build survival skills.

4. The relationships among the variables have been schematically diagrammed (see Figure 5.8).

It would now be interesting to see if we can interject an **intervening** variable in the model. For example, we may say that lack of adequate training makes the pilots **nervous and diffident,** and this in turn explains why they are not able to confidently handle situations in midair when many aircraft share the skies. Nervousness and diffidence are a function of lack of training, and help to explain why inadequate training would result in air-safety hazard. This scenario can be depicted as in Figure 5.9.

We may also substantially change the model by using (poor) training as a moderating variable as shown in Figure 5.10. Here, we are theorizing that poor communication, poor coordination, and decentralization are likely to result in air-safety violations only in such cases where the pilot in charge has had inadequate training. In other words, those who have had adequate training in deftly handling hazardous situations through simulated training sessions, and so forth, would not be handicapped by poor communication and coordination, and in cases where the aircraft is operated by well-trained pilots, poor communication and coordination will not result in hazards to safety.

These examples, again illustrate that the same variable could be independent, intervening, or moderating, depending on how we conceptualize our theoretical model.

Figure 5.10

Schematic diagram for the theoretical framework including a moderating variable.

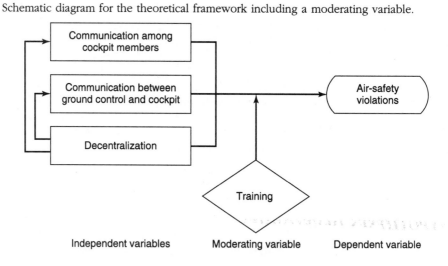

Independent variables   Moderating variable   Dependent variable

---

Now Do Exercises 5.10 and 5.11

Exercise 5.10

Develop a theoretical framework for the following situation after stating what the problem definition of the researcher would be in this case.

A family counselor, engaged in counseling married couples who are both professionals, is caught in a dilemma. He realizes that the focus of the counseling sessions should be on both family satisfaction and job satisfaction; however, he is not sure how they can be integrated in the dual-career family. Husbands, who are the traditional breadwinners, seem to derive more job satisfaction as they get more involved in their jobs and also spend more discretionary time on job-related activities. This, however, does not seem to be true in the case of the wives, who perform the dual role of career person and homemaker. However, both husbands and wives seem to enjoy high levels of family satisfaction when they spend more time together at home and help each other in planning family-oriented activities.

Exercise 5.11

Define the problem and develop the theoretical framework for the following situation.

The probability of cancer victims successfully recovering under treatment was studied by a medical researcher in a hospital. She found three variables to be important for recovery.

(handwritten margin note:) in class for practices? Do ahead of time

- Early and correct diagnosis by the doctor.
- The nurse's careful follow-up of the doctor's instructions.
- Peace and quiet in the vicinity.

In a quiet atmosphere, the patient rested well and recovered sooner. Patients who were admitted in advanced stages of cancer did not respond to treatment even though the doctor's diagnosis was performed immediately on arrival, the nurses did their best, and there was plenty of peace and quiet in the area.

HYPOTHESES DEVELOPMENT

Once we have identified the important variables in a situation and established the relationships among them through logical reasoning in the theoretical framework, we are in a position to test whether the relationships that have been theorized do in fact hold true. By testing these relationships scientifically through appropriate statistical analyses, or through negative case analysis in qualitative research (described later in the chapter) we are able to obtain reliable information on what kinds of relationships exist among the variables operating in the problem situation. The results of these tests offer us some clues as to what could be changed in the situation to solve the problem. Formulating such testable statements is called *hypotheses development.*

Definition of Hypothesis

A hypothesis can be defined as a logically conjectured relationship between two or more variables expressed in the form of a testable statement. Relationships are conjectured on the basis of the network of associations established in the theoretical framework formulated for the research study. By testing the hypotheses and confirming the conjectured relationships, it is expected that solutions can be found to correct the problem encountered.

Example 5.14   Several testable statements or hypotheses can be drawn from the theoretical framework formulated in Example 5.13. One of them could be as follows:

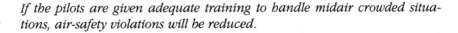

If the pilots are given adequate training to handle midair crowded situations, air-safety violations will be reduced.

The above is a testable statement. By measuring the extent of training given to the various pilots and the number of safety violations committed by them over a period of time, we can statistically examine the relationship between these two variables to see if there is a significant negative correlation between the two. If we do find this to be the case, then the hypotheses is substantiated. That is, giving more training to pilots in handling crowded space in midair will reduce safety violations. If a significant negative correlation is not found, then the hypotheses would not have been substantiated. By convention in the social sciences, to call a relationship "statistically significant," we should be confident that 95 times out of 100 the observed relationship will hold true. There would be only a 5% chance that the relationship would not be detected.

Statement of Hypotheses: Formats

If–Then Statements

As already stated, a hypothesis is a testable statement of the relationship among variables. A hypothesis can also test whether there are differences between two groups (or among several groups) with respect to any variable or variables. To examine whether or not the conjectured relationships or differences exist, these hypotheses can be set either as propositions or in the form of **if–then statements.** The two formats can be seen in the following two examples.

Example 5.15   *Employees who are more healthy will take sick leave less frequently.*

Example 5.16   *If* employees are more healthy, **then** they will take sick leave less frequently.

Directional and Nondirectional Hypotheses

If, in stating the relationship between two variables or comparing two groups, terms such as *positive, negative, more than, less than,* and the like are used, then these hypotheses are **directional** because the direction of the relationship between the variables (positive/negative) is indicated, as in Example 5.17 below, or the nature of the difference between two groups on a variable (more than/less than) is postulated, as in example 5.18.

Example 5.17   *The greater the stress experienced in the job, the lower the job satisfaction of employees.*

Example 5.18   *Women are more motivated than men.*

On the other hand, **nondirectional** hypotheses are those that do postulate a relationship or difference, but offer no indication of the direction of these relationships or differences. In other words, though it may be conjectured that there would be a significant relationship between two variables, we may not be able to say whether the relationship would be positive or negative, as in Example 5.19. Likewise, even if we can conjecture that there will be differences between two groups on a particular variable, we will not be able to say which group will be more and which less on that variable, as in Example 5.20.

Example 5.19   *There is a relationship between age and job satisfaction.*

Example 5.20   *There is a difference between the work ethic values of American and Asian employees.*

Nondirectional hypotheses are formulated either because the relationships or differences have never been previously explored and hence there is no basis for indicating the direction, or because there have been conflicting findings in previous research studies on the variables. In some studies a positive relationship might have been found, while in others a negative relationship might have been traced. Hence, the current researcher might only be able to hypothesize that there would be a significant relationship, but the direction may not be clear. In such cases, the hypotheses could be stated nondirectionally. Note that in Example 5.19 there is no clue as to whether age and job satisfaction are positively or negatively correlated, and in Example 5.20 we do not know whether the work ethic values are stronger in Americans or in Asians. However, in Example 5.20, it would have been possible to state that age and job satisfaction are positively correlated, since previous research has indicated such a relationship. Whenever the direction of the relationship is known, it is better to develop directional hypotheses for reasons that will become clear in our discussions in a later chapter.

Null and Alternate Hypotheses

The null hypothesis is a proposition that states a definitive, exact relationship between two variables. That is, it states that the population correlation between two variables is equal to zero or that the difference in the means of two groups in the population is equal to zero (or some *definite* number). In general, the null statement is expressed as no *(significant)* relationship between two variables or no *(significant)* difference between two groups, as we will see in the various examples in this chapter. The alternate hypothesis, which is the opposite of the null, is a statement expressing a relationship between two variables or indicating differences between groups.

To explain it further, in setting up the null hypothesis, we are stating that there is no difference between what we might find in the population characteristics (i.e., the total group we are interested in knowing something about) and the sample we are studying (i.e., a limited number representative of the total population or group that we have chosen to study). Since we do not know the true state of affairs in the population, all we can do is to draw inferences based on what we find in our sample. What we imply through the null hypothesis is that any differences found between two sample groups or any relationship found between two variables based on our sample is simply due to random sampling fluctuations and not due to any "true" differences between the two population groups (say, men and women), or relationships between two variables (say, sales and profits). The null hypothesis is thus formulated so that it can be tested for possible rejection. If we reject the null hypothesis, then all permissible alternative hypotheses relating to the particular relationship tested could be supported. It is the theory that allows us to have faith in the alternative hypothesis that is generated in the particular research investigation. This is one more reason why the theoretical framework should be grounded on sound, defendable logic to start with. Otherwise, other researchers are likely to refute and postulate other defensible explanations through different alternative hypotheses.

The *null* hypothesis in respect of group differences stated in our Example 5.18 would be:

$$H_0: \mu_M = \mu_W$$

M = man
W = women

or

$$H_0: \mu_M - \mu_W = 0$$

where H_0 represents the null hypothesis, μ_M is the mean motivational level of the men, and μ_W is the mean motivational level of the women.

The *alternate* for the above example would statistically be set as follows:

$$H_A: \mu_M < \mu_W$$

which is the same as

$$H_A: \mu_W > \mu_M$$

where H_A represents the alternate hypothesis and μ_M and μ_W are the mean motivation levels of men and women, respectively. For the **nondirectional** hypothesis of mean group differences in work ethic values in Example 5.20, the null hypothesis would be:

$$H_0: \mu_{AM} = \mu_{AS}$$

or

$$H_0: \mu_{AM} - \mu_{AS} = 0$$

where H_0 represents the null hypothesis, μ_{AM} is the mean work ethic value of Americans and μ_{AS} is the mean work ethic value of Asians.

The alternate hypothesis for the above example would statistically be set as:

$$H_A: \mu_{AM} \neq \mu_{AS}$$

where H_A represents the alternate hypothesis and μ_{AM} and μ_{AS} are the mean work ethic values of Americans and Asians, respectively.

The null hypothesis for the relationship between the two variables in Example 5.17 would be

$$H_0: \text{There is no relationship between stress experienced on the job and the job satisfaction of employees.}$$

This would be statistically expressed by

$$H_0: \rho = 0$$

where ρ represents the correlation between stress and job satisfaction, which in this case is equal to 0 (i.e., no correlation).

The alternate hypotheses for the above null, which has been expressed directionally in Example 5.17, can be statistically expressed as

$$H_A: \rho < 0 \text{ (The correlation is negative.)}$$

For Example 5.19, which has been stated nondirectionally, while the null hypothesis would be statistically expressed as:

$$H_0: \rho = 0$$

The alternate hypothesis would be expressed as:

$$H_A: \rho \neq 0$$

Having thus formulated the null and alternate hypotheses, the appropriate statistical tests (t tests, F tests) can then be applied, which would indicate whether or not support has been found for the alternate—that is, that there is a significant difference between groups or that there is a significant relationship between variables as hypothesized.

The steps to be followed in hypothesis testing are:

1. State the null and the alternate hypotheses.
2. Choose the appropriate statistical test depending on whether the data collected are parametric or nonparametric (discussed in a later chapter).
3. Determine the level of significance desired ($p = .05$, or more, or less).
4. See if the output results from computer analysis indicate that the significance level is met. If, as in the case of Pearson correlation analysis in Excel software, the significance level is not indicated in the printout, look up the critical values that define the regions of acceptance on the appropriate table [(t, F, χ^2)—see tables at the end of the book]. This critical value demarcates the region of rejection from that of acceptance of the null hypothesis.
5. When the resultant value is larger than the critical value, the null hypothesis is rejected, and the alternate accepted. If the calculated value is less than the critical value, the null is accepted and the alternate rejected.

Now do Exercises 5.12, 5.13, and 5.14

Exercise 5.12

For the theoretical framework developed for the Haines Company in Exercise 5.9, develop five different hypotheses.

In-class
Exercises
A work thru

In-class
exercise
work-thru

Exercise 5.13

A production manager is concerned about the low output levels of his employees. The articles that he read on job performance frequently mentioned four variables as important to job performance: skill required for the job, rewards, motivation, and satisfaction. In several of the articles it was also indicated that only if the rewards were valent (attractive) to the recipients did motivation, satisfaction, and job performance increase, not otherwise.

Given the above situation, do the following:

1. *Define the problem.*
2. *Evolve a theoretical framework.*
3. *Develop at least six hypotheses.*

Exercise 5.14

Retention of minority women at the workplace is becoming more and more difficult. Not finding an influential mentor in the system who is willing to help them, lack of an informal network with influential colleagues, lack of role models, and the dearth of high-visibility projects result in dissatisfaction experienced at work and the minority women ultimately decide to leave the organization. Of course, not all minority women quit the system. Only those who have the wherewithal (for example, resources and self-confidence) to start their own business leave the organization.

For the above situation, define the problem, develop a theoretical framework, and formulate six hypotheses.

Before concluding the discussion on hypotheses, it has to be reiterated that hypotheses generation and testing can be done both through deduction and induction. In deduction, the theoretical model is first developed, testable hypotheses are then formulated, data collected, and then the hypotheses are tested. In the inductive process, new hypotheses are formulated based on what is known from the data already collected, which are then tested. Recall from our discussions in Chapter 2, the example of the Hawthorne experiments, where new hypotheses were developed after the data already collected did not substantiate any of the original hypotheses.

In sum, new hypotheses not originally thought of or which have been previously untested might be developed after data are collected. Creative insights might compel researchers to test a new hypothesis from existing data, which, if substantiated, would add new knowledge and help theory building. Through the enlargement of our understanding of the dynamics operating in different situations using the deductive and the inductive processes, we add to the total body of knowledge in the area.

HYPOTHESIS TESTING WITH QUALITATIVE RESEARCH: NEGATIVE CASE ANALYSIS

Hypotheses can also be tested with qualitative data. For example, let us say that a researcher has developed the theoretical framework after extensive interviews, that unethical practices by employees are a function of their inability to discriminate between right and wrong, or due to a dire need for more money, or the organization's indifference to such practices. To test the hypothesis that these three factors are the primary ones that influence unethical practices, the researcher would look for data that would refute the hypothesis. When even a single case does not support the hypothesis, the theory would be revised. Let us say that the researcher finds one case where an individual is deliberately engaged in the unethical practice of accepting kickbacks (despite the fact that he was knowledgeable enough to discriminate right from wrong, was not in need of money, and knew that the organization would not be indifferent to his behavior), simply because he wanted to "get back" at the system, which "would not listen to his advice." This new discovery through disconfirmation of the original hypothesis, known as the negative case method, enables the researcher to revise the theory and the hypothesis until such time as the theory becomes robust.

We have thus far seen how a literature review is done, theoretical frameworks are formulated, and hypotheses developed. Let us now illustrate this logical sequence through a mini example where a researcher wants to examine the organizational factors influencing women's progress to top management positions. The literature survey and the number of variables are deliberately kept small since the purpose is merely to illustrate how a theoretical framework is developed from the literature survey, and how hypotheses are developed based on the theoretical framework.

Example 5.21   EXAMPLE OF LITERATURE REVIEW, THEORETICAL FRAMEWORK, AND HYPOTHESES DEVELOPMENT

Introduction

Despite the dramatic increase in the number of managerial women during the current decade, the number of women in top management positions continues to be very small and static, suggesting a glass ceiling effect that women currently face (Morrison, White, & Vura, 1999; Van Velsor, 2000). Given the projected demographics of the workplace, which forecasts that for every six or seven women entering the workforce in the future, there will be about only three white males joining the labor market, it becomes important to examine the organizational factors that would facilitate the *early* advancement of women to top executive positions. This study is an effort to identify the factors that currently impede women's advancement to the top in organizations.

A Brief Literature Survey

It is often declared that since women have only recently embarked on careers and entered the managerial ranks, it would take more time for them to rise to top executive positions. However, many women in higher middle management positions feel that there are at least two major stumbling blocks to their advancement: gender role stereotypes and inadequate access to critical information (Crosby, 1985; Daniel, 1998; Welch, 2001).

Gender stereotypes, or sex-role stereotypes as they are also known, are societal beliefs that men are better fitted for taking on leadership roles and positions of authority and power, whereas women are more suited for taking on nurturing and helping roles (Eagly, 1989; Kahn & Crosby, 1998; Smith, 1999). These beliefs influence the positions that are assigned to organizational members. Whereas capable men are given line positions and developed to take on higher responsibilities and executive roles in the course of time, capable women are assigned to staff positions and dead-end jobs. With little exposure to management of budgets and opportunities for significant decision making, women are seldom groomed for top-level positions.

Women are also excluded from the "old boys" network because of their gender. Information exchange, development of career strategies, clues regarding access to resources, and such important information vital to upward mobility are thus lost to women *(The Chronicle,* 2000). While many other factors impinge on women's upward mobility, the two variables, sex-role stereotypes and exclusion from critical information, are particularly detrimental to women's advancement to senior level positions.

Theoretical Framework

The dependent variable of advancement of women to top management positions is influenced by the two independent variables—sex-role stereotyping and access to critical information. The two independent variables are also interrelated as explained below.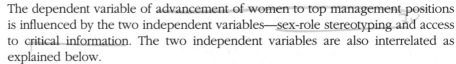

Sex-role stereotypes adversely impact on women's career progress. Since women are perceived as ineffective leaders but good nurturers, they are not assigned line positions in their early career but offered staff responsibilities. It is only in line positions that managers make significant decisions, control budgets, and interact with top-level executives who have an impact on their future careers. These opportunities to learn, grow and develop on the job, and gain visibility in the system help managers to advance to top-level positions. However, since women in staff positions do not gain these experiences or have the visibility to be identified as key people in the organization with the potential to be successful top managers, their advancement to top-level positions is never considered by the system and they are always overlooked. Thus, sex-role stereotypes hinder the progress of women to the top.

Exclusion from the networks where men informally interact with one another (golf course, pubs, and so on) also precludes women from gaining access to crucial information and resources vital for their advancement. For example, many of the significant organizational changes and current events are discussed informally among men outside the work setting. Women are generally unaware of the most recent developments since they are not a part of the informal group that interacts and exchanges information away from the workplace. This definitely is a handicap. For example, knowledge of an impending vacancy for an executive position enables one to strategize to occupy that position. One can become a key contender by procuring critical information relevant to the position, get prepared to present the appropriate credentials to the right people at the right time, and thus pave the way for success. Thus, access to critical information is important for the progress of all, including women. When women do not have the critical information that is shared in informal networks, their chances of advancement to top positions also get severely restricted.

Gender-role stereotypes also hinder access to information. If women are not considered to be decision makers and leaders, but are perceived merely as support personnel, they would not be apprised of critical information essential for organizational advancement, since this would not be seen as relevant for them. When both stereotyping and exclusion from critical information are in operation, there is no way that women can reach the top. These relationships are schematically diagrammed in Figure 5.11.

In sum, both gender-role stereotypes and access to critical information significantly influence women's advancement to top-level positions in organizations and explain the variance in it.

Hypotheses

1. The greater the extent of gender stereotyping in organizations, the fewer will be the number of women at the top.

2. Male managers have more access to critical information than women managers in the same ranks.

Figure 5.11
Schematic diagram of Example 5.21.

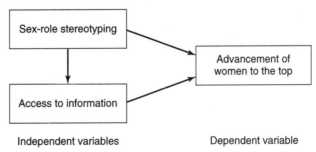

Independent variables   Dependent variable

Sex Roles "stereotypes" = leadership
↳ more wholistic
↳ more people oriented
↳ long-run, fair, just

3. There will be a significant positive correlation between access to information and chances for promotion to top-level positions.

4. The more the sex-role stereotyping, the less the access to critical information for women.

5. Sex-role stereotyping and access to critical information will both significantly explain the variance in promotional opportunities for women to top-level positions.

MANAGERIAL ADVANTAGE

At this juncture, it becomes easy to follow the progression of research from the first stage when managers sense the broad problem area, to preliminary data gathering (including literature survey), to developing the theoretical framework based on the literature review and guided by experience and intuition, to formulating hypotheses for testing.

It is also clear that once the problem is defined, a good grasp of the four different types of variables enlarges the understanding of managers as to how multiple factors impinge on the organizational setting. Knowledge of how and for what purpose the theoretical framework is developed and the hypotheses are generated enables the manager to be an intelligent judge of the research report submitted by the consultant. Likewise, knowledge of what significance means, and why a given hypothesis is either accepted or rejected, helps the manager to persist in or desist from following hunches which, while making good sense, do not work. If such knowledge is absent, many of the findings through research will not make much sense to the manager and decision making will bristle with confusion.

SUMMARY

In this chapter we examined the four types of variables—dependent, independent, moderating, and intervening. We also discussed how the theoretical framework is developed and how testable hypotheses are generated therefrom. We saw examples where the same variable can be a dependent, independent, moderating, or intervening, depending on the situation. We also explained when a null hypothesis would be accepted or rejected, based on whether or not the results of hypothesis testing meet the significance test. Futhermore, we also briefly discussed the test for hypothesis validation in qualitative research. In the next chapter we will examine the basic research design issues.

DISCUSSION QUESTIONS AND POINTS TO PONDER

⭐ Choose Best Examples for in-class discussion

1. "Because literature survey is a time-consuming exercise, a good, in-depth interview should suffice to develop a theoretical framework." Discuss this statement.

2. There is an advantage in stating the hypothesis both in the null and in the alternate; it adds clarity to our thinking of what we are testing. Explain.

3. It is advantageous to develop a directional hypothesis whenever we are sure of the predicted direction. How will you justify this statement?

4. For the following case titled "Sleepless Nights at Holiday Inn" (published in *Business Week* and adapted here):

a. Identify the problem

b. Develop a theoretical framework

c. Develop at least four hypotheses

(handwritten annotations: maintenance; type of building; IV; service level; DV; revenue; enhance Brand awareness; Work thru)

Sleepless Nights At Holiday Inn *(handwritten: owners; self awareness)*

Just a few years ago, Tom Oliver, the Chief Executive of Holiday Hospitality Corp., was struggling to differentiate among the variety of facilities offered to clients under the Holiday flagship—the *Holiday Inn Select* designed for business travelers, the *Holiday Inn Express* used by penny pinchers, and the *Crowne Plaza Hotels,* the luxurious hotels meant for the big spenders. Oliver felt that revenues could be quadrupled if only clients could differentiate among these.

Keen on developing a viable strategy for Holiday Hospitality, which suffered from brand confusion, Tom Oliver conducted a customer survey of those who had used each type of facility, and found the following. The consumers didn't have a clue as to the differences among the three different types. Many complained that the buildings were old and not properly maintained, and the quality ratings of service and other factors were also poor. Furthermore, when word spread that one of the contemplated strategies of Oliver was a name change to differentiate the three facilities, irate franchises balked. Their mixed messages did not help consumers to understand the differences, either.

Oliver thought that he first needed to understand how the different classifications would be important to the several classes of clients, and then he could market the heck out of them and greatly enhance the revenues. Simultaneously, he recognized that unless the franchise owners fully cooperated with him in all his plans, mere face lifting and improvement of customer service would not bring added revenues.

---

5. For the scenario below,

a. What is the problem statement?

b. Develop a theoretical framework.

c. What type of research does the company envisage?

Exxon Mobil (EM) is a well-oiled machine that is pumping profits. How does it do it? By using technology to evaluate potential deposits. It displays a 3-D computer image, IMAX style, on a 32-foot wraparound screen. It then drills underwater. Once oil is found, EM pumps the oil without any significant lapse of time.

Its investment in R & D is over $600 million per year, and it employs 1,500 Ph.Ds. Unlike companies that finance both applied and basic research, EM demands work that produces a measurable impact and competitive advantage. Dissemination of findings among scientists is thus high.

EM is also getting payoffs from older technologies, like increasing the recovery rate from existing deposits. An example is the so-called reservoir analysis that has enabled EM to boost reserves and improve recovery from fields.

The merger of the two companies, Exxon and Mobil was remarkable, given their two divergent philosophies and cultures. Exxon had top efficiency born out of command and control, while Mobil was loose and informal, but the elaborate restructuring worked out well.

The return on capital deployed was 21% in the year 2000, more than double the level of the past 2 years and the best among big oil companies.

6. Develop a theoretical framework for the following case.

Once given, perks are extraordinarily hard to take away without sapping employee morale. The adverse effects of these cuts far outweigh the anticipated savings in dollars. Research has shown that when the reason behind the cuts is explained to employees, morale does not drop.

7. For the following scenario described in *Fortune* dated October 29, 2001, develop a theoretical framework.

Hiring decisions are made without much thought to several aspects pertaining to the candidate. For instance, Schlager, whose resumé did not mention anything at all about attempting to murder his wife and spending 6 years in prison, was hired for a medical director position in one of the largest medical device companies. A simple Googling would have turned up one of the 24 articles in this case, comments *Fortune* magazine. Thirty percent of resumés contain misstatements of facts, according to industry experts. The most common resumé fudge is to expand the dates of employment. When people are fired, it does not feature in the resumé. Discovering crimes committed under an alias and getting information from overseas are practically impossible.

PRACTICE PROJECT

For the topic you chose to work on for the project in the previous chapter, do the following:

1. Go through the computer-generated bibliography again.

2. Define a problem statement that, in your opinion, would be most useful for researchers to investigate.

3. Write up a literature review that would seem to offer the greatest potential for developing a good theoretical framework, using about 20 references.

4. Develop the theoretical framework incorporating its five basic features as discussed in the chapter.

5. Generate a set of testable hypotheses based on the theoretical framework.

THE RESEARCH PROCESS

Step 6: Elements of Research Design

TOPICS DISCUSSED

THE RESEARCH DESIGN

PURPOSE OF THE STUDY: EXPLORATORY, DESCRIPTIVE, HYPOTHESIS
TESTING, CASE STUDY ANALYSIS

TYPE OF INVESTIGATION: CAUSAL VERSUS CORRELATIONAL

EXTENT OF RESEARCHER INTERFERENCE WITH THE STUDY

STUDY SETTING: CONTRIVED VERSUS NONCONTRIVED

UNIT OF ANALYSIS: INDIVIDUALS, DYADS, GROUPS, ORGANIZATIONS,
CULTURES

TIME HORIZON OF STUDY: CROSS-SECTIONAL VERSUS LONGITUDINAL

MANAGERIAL IMPLICATIONS

CHAPTER OBJECTIVES

After completing this chapter you should be able to:

1. Understand the different aspects relevant to designing a research study.
2. Identify the scope of any given study and the end use of the results.
3. Decide for any given situation the type of investigation needed, the study
   setting, the extent of researcher interference, the unit of analysis, and the
   time horizon of the study.
4. Identify which of the two, a causal or a correlational study, would be more
   appropriate in a given situation.

THE RESEARCH DESIGN

Having identified the variables in a problem situation and developed the theoretical framework, the next step is to design the research in a way that the requisite data can be gathered and analyzed to arrive at a solution.

The research design, which involves a series of rational decision-making choices, was originally presented in a simple manner in box 6 of Figure 4.1, and is now represented in the shaded box in Figure 6.1. The various issues involved in the research design and discussed in this chapter are now comprehensively shown in Figure 6.2. As may be seen, issues relating to decisions regarding the purpose for the study (exploratory, descriptive, hypothesis testing), its location (i.e., the study setting), the type it should conform to (type of investigation), the

Figure 6.1
The research process.

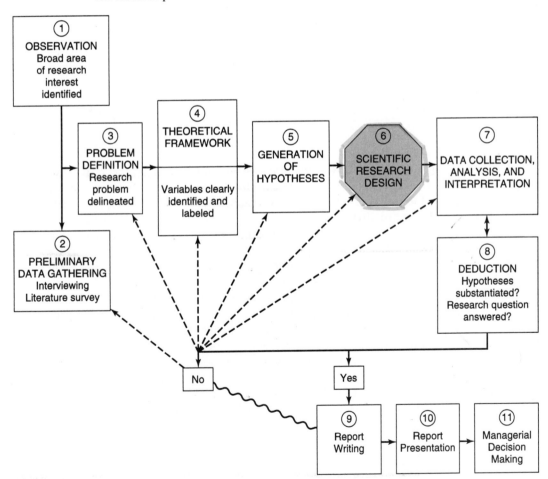

Figure 6.2
The research design.

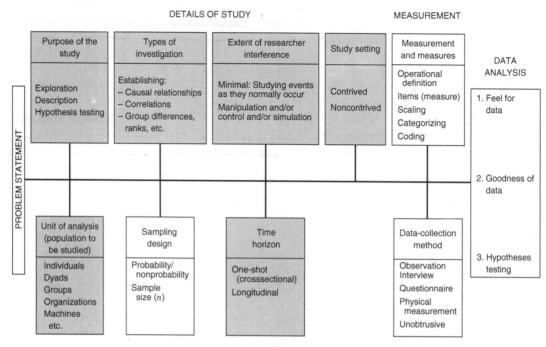

relating to concerned w/or limited by time ⇐

extent to which it is manipulated and controlled by the researcher (extent of researcher interference), its temporal aspects (time horizon), and the level at which the data will be analyzed (unit of analysis), are integral to research design. These are discussed in this chapter. In addition, decisions have to be made as to the type of sample to be used (sampling design), how the data will be collected (data collection methods), how variables will be measured (measurement), and how they will be analyzed to test the hypotheses (data analysis). These are discussed in subsequent chapters.

As shown in Figure 6.2, each component of the research design offers several critical choice points. The extent of scientific rigor in a research study depends on how carefully the manager/researcher chooses the appropriate design alternatives, taking into consideration its specific purpose. For instance, if a critical financial decision to invest millions of dollars in a project is to be based on the results of a research investigation, then careful attention to details is necessary to ensure that the study has precision and has the acceptable level of confidence. This implies, as we will see later in the book, that close attention is paid to sampling, measurement, data collection, and so on. Contrast this to the research goal of generating a profile of managers in an organization to publish a newsletter. This will not call for elaborate research design decisions.

It is important to note that the more sophisticated and rigorous the research design is, the greater the time, costs, and other resources expended on it will be.

It is therefore relevant to ask oneself at every choice point whether the benefits that result from a more sophisticated design to ensure accuracy, confidence, generalizability, and so on, are commensurate with the larger investment of resources.

In this chapter we will examine the six basic aspects of research design. Specifically, we will discuss the purpose of the study, the types of investigation, the extent of researcher interference, the study setting, the unit of analysis, and the time horizon of the study (the shaded parts in Figure 6.2). The other aspects of measurement, data collection methods, sampling design, and data analysis will be elaborated in later chapters.

PURPOSE OF THE STUDY: EXPLORATORY, DESCRIPTIVE, HYPOTHESIS TESTING (ANALYTICAL AND PREDICTIVE), CASE STUDY ANALYSIS

Studies may be either exploratory in nature or descriptive, or may be conducted to test hypotheses. The case study, which is an examination of studies done in other similar organizational situations, is also a method of solving problems, or for understanding phenomena of interest and generating further knowledge in that area. The nature of the study—whether it is exploratory, descriptive, or hypothesis testing—depends on the stage to which knowledge about the research topic has advanced. The design decisions become more rigorous as we proceed from the exploratory stage, where we attempt to explore new areas of organizational research, to the descriptive stage, where we try to describe certain characteristics of the phenomena on which interest centers, to the hypotheses testing stage, where we examine whether or not the conjectured relationships have been substantiated and an answer to the research question has been obtained. We will now look at each of these in some detail.

Exploratory Study

An exploratory study is undertaken when not much is known about the situation at hand, or no information is available on how similar problems or research issues have been solved in the past. In such cases, extensive preliminary work needs to be done to gain familiarity with the phenomena in the situation, and understand what is occurring, before we develop a model and set up a rigorous design for comprehensive investigation.

In essence, exploratory studies are undertaken to better comprehend the nature of the problem since very few studies might have been conducted in that area. Extensive interviews with many people might have to be undertaken to get a handle on the situation and understand the phenomena. More rigorous research could then proceed.

Some qualitative studies (as opposed to quantitative data gathered through questionnaires, etc.) where data are collected through observation or interviews, are exploratory in nature. When the data reveal some pattern regarding the phenomena of interest, theories are developed and hypotheses formulated for subsequent testing. For example, Henry Mintzberg interviewed managers to explore the nature of managerial work. Based on the analysis of his interview data, he formulated theories of managerial roles, the nature and types of managerial activities, and so on. These have been tested in different settings through both interviews and questionnaire surveys.

Exploratory studies are also necessary when some facts are known, but more information is needed for developing a viable theoretical framework. For instance, when we want to get at the important factors that influence the advancement of women in organizations, previous studies might indicate that women are increasingly taking on qualities such as assertiveness, competitiveness, and independence. There is also a perception that a judicious blend of masculine and feminine traits—such as being strong but not tough, kind but not soft—is conducive to women's organizational advancement. These notions apart, there is a need for interviewing women managers who have made it to the top to explore *all* the relevant variables. This will help to build a robust theory.

In sum, exploratory studies are important for obtaining a good grasp of the phenomena of interest and advancing knowledge through subsequent theory building and hypothesis testing.

The following is an example where exploratory research would be necessary.

Example 6.1   The manager of a multinational corporation is curious to know if the work ethic values of employees working in its subsidiary in Pennathur City would be different from those of Americans. There is very little information about Pennathur (except that it is a small city in southern India), and since there is considerable controversy about what work ethic values mean to people in other cultures, the manager's curiosity can be satisfied only by an exploratory study, interviewing the employees in organizations in Pennathur. Religion, political, economic, and social conditions, upbringing, cultural values, and so on play a major role in how people view their work in different parts of the world. Here, since very little is known about work ethic values in India (or even if it is a viable concept for study in that country, as per discussions in a later chapter), an exploratory study will have to be undertaken.

Many topics of interest and concern to management in the management and organizational behavior areas have been studied, and information is available in the library on these subject areas. Although few exploratory studies are currently undertaken in the management area, researchers do explore new grounds from time to time with the changing dynamics that occur at the workplace. Not long ago, for instance, exploratory research on the topics of women in management and dual career families was conducted. Because of subsequent studies, research on these topics has now progressed beyond the exploratory stage to the hypothesis testing stage.

The same is also true of research on quality of life. At one time, exploratory studies were undertaken to understand what the concept *quality of work life* means. After extensive interviews with various groups of people, it was considered to encompass such factors as enriched jobs, healthy work environment, stress-free work relationships, job satisfaction, work role involvement, and other work-related factors. Current thinking is that the concept quality of work life is too narrow and limited to be useful for research and that the concept quality of life is more encompassing since work and nonwork cannot be viewed as two tightly compartmentalized aspects of an individual's life. Current research now takes both the work and nonwork factors (family, community, etc.) into consideration while examining quality of life. This advancement of knowledge would not have been possible without the initial exploratory studies.

Currently, exploratory studies about organizationally relevant differences in race, ethnic, and country origins are being undertaken so that sound theories about managing a diverse work group can be evolved for the future. Such exploratory studies are necessary since we do not now know if there are differences in communication styles, interpretation schemas, superior–subordinate relationship expectations, and the like, among the groups. If conflict and stress in the system are to be reduced and productivity is to be maintained and increased in the years to come, such understanding would be essential. The demographics of the workplace are constantly changing, and learning to value differences and adopting new styles of management are important to organizational success.

Exploratory studies can be done by interviewing individuals and through focus groups. For instance, if a company manufacturing cosmetics wants to obtain a thorough understanding of what it is that arouses emotive appeal for the product and induces people to buy cosmetics, several focus groups can be convened to discuss the related issues. This exploratory study will offer the needed preliminary information for a full-fledged study on the matter, later. With the advancement of technology, the Internet and videoconferencing facilities offer the advantage of contacting focus groups online at minimal cost. An analysis of their views would be very useful for a further in-depth study. Focus groups are discussed further in a later chapter.

It is important to note that doing a study for the first time in a particular organization does not make the research exploratory in nature; only when knowledge is scant and a deeper understanding is sought, does the study become exploratory.

Descriptive Study

A descriptive study is undertaken in order to ascertain and be able to describe the characteristics of the variables of interest in a situation. For instance, a study of a class in terms of the percentage of members who are in their senior and junior years, sex composition, age groupings, number of semesters left until graduation, and number of business courses taken, can be considered as descriptive in nature. Quite frequently, descriptive studies are undertaken in organizations to learn about and describe the characteristics of a group of employees, as for example, the age, educational level, job status, and length of service of Hispanics or Asians, working in the system. Descriptive studies are also undertaken to understand the characteristics of organizations that follow certain common practices. For example, one might want to know and be able to describe the characteristics of the organizations that implement flexible manufacturing systems (FMS) or that have a certain debt-to-equity ratio.

The goal of a descriptive study, hence, is to offer to the researcher a profile or to describe relevant aspects of the phenomena of interest from an individual, organizational, industry-oriented, or other perspective. In many cases, such information may be vital before even considering certain corrective steps, as for example: *Should the organization consider changing its practices?* If a study of the firms in the industry indicates that most of them resort to *just-in-time* systems to cut inventory costs, maybe organization Z should also seriously consider the feasibility of this practice. Or if a descriptive study stresses the need to introduce flexible work hours for parents of children under 3 years of age, this may have to be seriously considered, and a much more focused study initiated to decide on the matter.

A brief description of the study of advances in the textile industry might look something like this:

US Textiles has used high-tech to make huge advances in productivity and innovation. An army of reels surrounds a complex circular knitting machine at Malden Hills, feeding yarn to thousands of needles producing polyester fabric. The 3-dimensional loom has added value utility in the competitive market.

Jacquard looms, which are computer controlled at Burlington, weave miles of intricately patterned materials. Even faster looms use jets of compressed air to move the weft. The industry is being revolutionized with a 3-dimensional loom that weaves the fibers in the shape of the end product, skipping the laborious process of lamination.

Denims, which are difficult to make, are now made by computer controls and electric sensors to a so-called dye range, which ensures a shade perfectly matching customers' samples.

The fastest looms, automated spinning processes, and Sanfmi machines programmed from a desktop computer and capable of producing any type of garment are other innovations in the textile industry.

Such a description of the advances helps textile companies to gauge their progress in keeping up with the technological advances.

Descriptive studies that present data in a meaningful form thus help to (1) understand the characteristics of a group in a given situation, (2) think systematically about aspects in a given situation, (3) offer ideas for further probe and research, and/or (4) help make certain simple decisions (such as how many and what kinds of individuals should be transferred from one department to another).

Below are examples of situations warranting a descriptive study.

Example 6.2   A bank manager wants to have a profile of the individuals who have loan payments outstanding for 6 months and more. It would include details of their average age, earnings, nature of occupation, full-time/part-time employment status, and the like. This might help him to elicit further information or decide right away on the types of individuals who should be made ineligible for loans in the future.

Example 6.3   A CEO may be interested in having a description of organizations in her industry that follow the LIFO system. In this case, the report might include the age of the organizations, their locations, their production levels, assets, sales, inventory levels, suppliers, and profits. Such information might allow comparison later of the performance levels of specific types of companies.

Example 6.4   A marketing manager might want to develop a pricing, sales, distribution, and advertising strategy for her product. With this in mind, she might ask for information regarding the competitors, with respect to the following:

1. The percentage of companies who have prices higher and lower than the industry norm; a profile of the terms of sale; and the percentage where prices are controlled regionally instead of from central headquarters.
2. The percentage of competitors hiring in-house staff to handle sales and those who use independent agents.
3. Percentage of sales groups organized by product line, by accounts, and by region.
4. The types of distribution channels used and the percentage of customers using each.
5. Percentage of competitors spending more dollars on advertising/promotion than the firm and those spending less; a categorization of their target audience, and the types of media most frequently used.
6. Percentage of those using the web ("dot coms") to sell the product.

Descriptive studies thus become essential in many situations. Whereas qualitative data obtained by interviewing individuals may help the understanding of phenomena at the exploratory stages of a study, quantitative data in terms of frequencies, or mean and standard deviations, become necessary for descriptive studies. A report on a descriptive study of the reaction of organizational members to a proposal to introduce an on-site child care facility, for instance, might look somewhat like this:

> *Whereas 30% of the employees were in favor of the idea, at least 40% felt that on-site child care facility was unnecessary. Twenty percent indicated that it would benefit only those with preschool children and hence would be unfair to the others who cannot use the facility. The remaining 10% suggested the introduction of a cafeteria style of benefits, so that employees could opt for what they preferred.*

> *More women than men were favorably inclined toward the proposal (almost 2:1). Parents with two or more preschool children overwhelmingly desired this; employees who did not belong to this category were opposed to the idea.*
>
> *Employees over 50 years of age and those below 25 did not seem to favor this scheme. However, women between 25 and 45 (a total of 45 women) seemed to desire it the most.*
>
> *The mean on the preference scale indicated for the child care facility by all employees is rather low (1.5 on a 5-point scale), but the dispersion is rather high, the standard deviation being 1.98. This indicates that there are some who indicate a strong liking for the proposed project, while some are totally against it.*
>
> *The average preference indicated by women between the ages of 30 and 45 with children is the highest (4.75 on a 5-point scale) with very little disper-sion (the standard deviation for this group of 42 women was .38). This is the group that desires the on-site facility the most.*

Introductory descriptive narratives in some research reports, as you might have noticed, are drawn from government statistical publications such as the Bureau of Labor Statistics, census, and the like, from which data are culled for presenta-tion, as and when appropriate.

Hypotheses Testing

Studies that engage in hypotheses testing usually explain the nature of certain relationships, or establish the differences among groups or the independence of two or more factors in a situation. Examples of such studies are given below. Hypothesis testing is undertaken to explain the variance in the dependent vari-able or to predict organizational outcomes.

Example 6.5   A marketing manager wants to know if the sales of the company will increase if he doubles the advertising dollars. Here, the manager would like to know the nature of the relationship that can be established between advertising and sales by testing the hypothesis: *If advertising is increased, then sales will also go up.*

Example 6.6   Given people's tensions on the subject of purchase of guns in these days of crime in cities big and small, a marketing researcher might be interested in predicting the factors that would significantly account for the variance in people's decision to purchase guns. Here, the researcher would have theorized the factors that would influence people's decision to possess guns (through literature search and interviews) and then test the hypothesis that four specific variables will signifi-cantly account for the variance in people's intention to buy a gun. Here again, the researcher is interested in understanding and accounting for the variance in the dependent variable—gun purchase—through hypothesis testing.

Example 6.7   The testing of a hypothesis such as: *More men than women are whistleblowers,* establishes the difference between two groups—men and women—in regard to their whistle-blowing behavior.

Example 6.8   The independence between two variables that are qualitative in nature can also be established through hypothesis testing. Consider the hypothesis: *Working the night shift (as opposed to the day shift) is related to whether or not one is married.* A chi-square test of independence will easily provide the answer to this question.

As may be seen, in hypotheses testing the researcher goes beyond mere description of the variables in a situation to an understanding of the relationships among factors of interest.

Case Study Analysis

As discussed in Chapter 2, case studies involve in-depth, contextual analyses of matters relating to similar situations in other organizations. We noted earlier that case studies, as a problem-solving technique, are not frequently resorted to in organizations because finding the same type of problem in another comparable setting is difficult due to the reluctance of the companies to reveal their problems. Case studies that are qualitative in nature are, however, useful in applying solutions to current problems based on past problem-solving experiences. They are also useful in understanding certain phenomena, and generating further theories for empirical testing.

Review of the Purpose of the Study

It is not difficult to see that in exploratory studies, the researcher is basically interested in exploring the situational factors so as to get a grip on the characteristics of the phenomena of interest. Also, pilot studies on a small scale, by interviewing individuals or gathering information from a limited number of occurrences, are not uncommon in exploratory research.

Descriptive studies are undertaken when the characteristics or the phenomena to be tapped in a situation are known to exist, and one wants to be able to describe them better by offering a profile of the factors. Hypothesis testing offers an enhanced understanding of the relationship that exists among variables. It could also establish cause-and-effect relationships, as we will see in the next chapter. Hypothesis testing can be done with both qualitative and quantitative data. Case studies are generally qualitative in nature and are sometimes used as a tool in managerial decision making.

Methodological rigor increases as we move progressively from an exploratory study to a hypothesis-testing study, and with this, the costs of research also increase. As we will see in later chapters in this book, increases in sample size, multiple methods of data collection, development of sophisticated measuring instruments, and the like, add to research costs, though they contribute more to testability, accuracy, precision, and generalizability.

TYPE OF INVESTIGATION: CASUAL VERSUS CORRELATIONAL

A manager should determine whether a causal or a correlational study is needed to find an answer to the issue at hand. The former is done when it is necessary to establish a definitive cause-and-effect relationship. However, if all that the manager wants is a mere identification of the important factors "associated with" the problem, then a correlational study is called for. In the former case, the researcher is keen on delineating one or more factors that are undoubtedly *causing* the problem. In other words, the intention of the researcher conducting a causal study is to be able to state that variable X causes variable Y. So, when variable X is removed or altered in some way, problem Y is solved. Quite often, however, it is not just one or more variables that *cause* a problem in organizations. Given the fact that most of the time there are multiple factors that influence one another and the problem in a chainlike fashion, the researcher might be asked to identify the crucial factors *associated* with the problem, rather than establish a cause-and-effect relationship.

or weblike

The study in which the researcher wants to delineate the *cause* of one or more problems is called a **causal study.** When the researcher is interested in delineating the important variables *associated* with the problem, the study is called a **correlational study.** It may be of interest to know that attempts are sometimes made to establish cause-and-effect relationships through certain types of correlational or regression analyses, such as cross-lagged correlations and path analysis (Billings & Wroten, 1978; Namboodiri, Carter, & Blalock, 1975). Whether a study is a causal or a correlational one thus depends on the type of research questions asked and how the problem is defined. The following example will illustrate the difference.

Example 6.9

A *causal* study question:
   Does smoking *cause* cancer?
A *correlational* study question:
   Are smoking and cancer related?
      OR
   Are smoking, drinking, and chewing tobacco *associated* with cancer? If so, which of these contributes most to the variance in the dependent variable?

The answer to the first question will help to establish whether people who do *not* smoke will *not* develop cancer. The answer to the second question will determine if smoking and cancer are correlated. The third situation recognizes that there are perhaps several other factors that influence cancer apart from the three identified, but do these three help to explain a significant amount of the variance in cancer? If they do, then which among the three variables examined is the one that has the greatest association with it, which is the next, and which the third? The answer to the correlational study would help determine the extent of risk of cancer that people expose themselves to by smoking, drinking, and chewing tobacco. The intention here is not to establish a causal connection between one factor and another, but merely to see if a relationship does exist among the variables investigated.

The distinction between causal and correlational studies can be made clear by the following two examples as well.

Example 6.10   Fears of an earthquake predicted recently in the New Madrid fault zone were instrumental (i.e., causal) in an unprecedented number of house owners in the Midwest region taking out an earthquake insurance policy.

[handwritten: ⚹ the difference between causal & correlational is not just the # of variables considered]

Example 6.11.   Increases in interest rates and property taxes, the recession, and the predicted earthquake considerably slowed down the business of real estate agents in the Midwest.

Note that Example 6.10 indicates a causal relationship between the earthquake prediction and earthquake insurance, whereas Example 6.11 indicates that several factors, including the predicted earthquake *influenced* (not caused) the slowdown of real estate agents' business. This is a correlational study, which was not intended to establish a cause-and-effect relationship.

EXTENT OF RESEARCHER INTERFERENCE WITH THE STUDY

[handwritten: Ethical issues w/ causal research #6]

The extent of interference by the researcher with the normal flow of work at the workplace has a direct bearing on whether the study undertaken is causal or correlational. A correlational study is conducted in the natural environment of the organization with minimum interference by the researcher with the normal flow of work. For example, if a researcher wants to study the factors influencing training effectiveness (a correlational study), all that the individual has to do is develop a theoretical framework, collect the relevant data, and analyze them to come up with the findings. Though there is some disruption to the normal flow of work in the system as the researcher interviews employees and administers questionnaires at the workplace, the researcher's interference in the routine functioning of the system is minimal as compared to that caused during causal studies.

In studies conducted to establish cause-and-effect relationships, the researcher tries to *manipulate* certain variables so as to study the effects of such manipulation on the dependent variable of interest. In other words, the researcher deliberately changes certain variables in the setting and interferes with the events as they normally occur in the organization. As an example, a researcher might want to study the influence of lighting on worker performance, and hence manipulates the lighting in the work situation to varying intensities. Here, there is considerable researcher interference with the natural and normal setting. In other cases the researcher might even want to create an altogether new artificial setting where the cause-and-effect relationships can be studied by manipulating certain variables and tightly controlling certain others, as in a laboratory. Thus, there could be varying degrees of interference by the researcher in the manipulation and control of variables in the research study, either in the natural setting or in an artificial lab setting.

Let us give examples of research with varying degrees of interference—minimal, moderate, and excessive.

Example 6.12   **MINIMAL INTERFERENCE**

A hospital administrator wants to examine the relationship between the perceived emotional support in the system and the stresses experienced by the nursing staff. In other words, she wants to do a correlational study.

Here, the administrator/researcher will collect data from the nurses (perhaps through a questionnaire) to indicate how much emotional support they get in the hospital and to what extent they experience stress. (We will learn in a later chapter in this book how to measure these variables.) By correlating the two variables, the answer that is being sought can be found.

In this case, beyond administering a questionnaire to the nurses, the researcher has not interfered with the normal activities in the hospital. In other words, researcher interference has been *minimal.*

Example 6.13   **MODERATE INTERFERENCE**

The same researcher is now no longer content with finding the correlation, but wants to firmly establish a causal connection. That is, the researcher wants to demonstrate that if the nurses had emotional support, this indeed would *cause* them to experience less stress. If this can be established, then the nurses' stress can definitely be reduced by offering them emotional support.

To test the cause-and-effect relationship, the researcher will measure the stress currently experienced by the nurses in three wards in the hospital, and then deliberately manipulate the extent of emotional support given to the three groups of nurses in the three wards for perhaps a week, and measure the amount of stress at the end of that period. For one group, the researcher will ensure that a number of lab technicians and doctors help and comfort the nurses when they face stressful events—for example, when they care for patients suffering excruciating pain and distress in the ward. Under a similar setup, for a second group of nurses in another ward, the researcher might arrange for them only a moderate amount of emotional support and employing only the lab technicians and excluding doctors. The third ward might operate without any emotional support.

If the experimenter's theory is correct, then the reduction in the stress levels before and after the 1-week period should be greatest for the nurses in the first ward, moderate for those in the second ward, and nil for the nurses in the third ward.

Here we find that not only does the researcher collect data from nurses on their experienced stress at two different points in time, but has also "played with" or manipulated the normal course of events by deliberately changing the amount of

moderating & intervening

emotional support received by the nurses in two wards, while leaving things in the third ward unchanged. Here, the researcher has interfered *more than minimally*.

Example 6.14	**EXCESSIVE INTERFERENCE**

The above researcher, after conducting the previous experiments, feels that the results may or may not be valid since other external factors might have influenced the stress levels experienced by the nurses. For example, during that particular experimental week, the nurses in one or more wards may not have experienced high levels of stress because there were no serious illnesses or deaths in the ward. Hence, the emotional support received might not be related to the level of stresses experienced.

The researcher might now want to make sure that such extraneous factors as might affect the cause-and-effect relationship are controlled. So she might take three groups of medical students, put them in different rooms, and confront all of them with the same stressful task. For example, she might ask them to describe in the minutest detail, the surgical procedures in performing surgery on a patient who has not responded to chemotherapy and keep bombarding them with more and more questions even as they respond. Although all are exposed to the same intensive questioning, one group might get help from a doctor who voluntarily offers clarifications and help when students stumble. In the second group, a doctor might be nearby, but might offer clarifications and help only if the group seeks it. In the third group, there is no doctor present and no help is available.

In this case, not only is the support manipulated, but even the setting in which this experiment is conducted is artificial inasmuch as the researcher has taken the subjects away from their normal environment and put them in a totally different setting. Here, the researcher has intervened *maximally* with the normal setting, the participants, and their duties. In the next chapter, we will see why such manipulations are necessary to establish cause-and-effect relationships beyond any doubt.

As seen, the extent of researcher interference would depend on whether the study is correlational or causal and also the importance of establishing causal relationship beyond any doubt whatever.

discuss placebos & why they are important in causal studies

Most organizational problems seldom call for a causal study. In any case, researcher interference through a change in the setting in which the causal study is conducted is rarely done, except in some market research areas.

STUDY SETTING: CONTRIVED AND NONCONTRIVED

As we have just seen, organizational research can be done in the natural environment where work proceeds normally (that is, in noncontrived settings) or in artificial, contrived settings. Correlational studies are invariably conducted in noncontrived settings, whereas most rigorous causal studies are done in contrived lab settings.

discussion ⟹ which are more valuable ???

class debate?

or, just the stat used

Correlational studies done in organizations are called **field studies.** Studies conducted to establish cause-and-effect relationship using the same natural environment in which employees normally function are called **field experiments.** Here, as we have seen earlier, the researcher does interfere with the natural occurrence of events inasmuch as the independent variable is manipulated. For example, a manager wanting to know the effects of pay on performance would raise the salary of employees in one unit, decrease the pay of employees in another unit, and leave the pay of the employees in a third unit untouched. Here there is a tampering with or manipulating of the pay system to establish a cause-and-effect relationship between pay and performance, but the study is still conducted in the natural setting and hence is called a field experiment.

Experiments done to establish cause and effect relationship beyond the possibility of the least doubt require the creation of an artificial, contrived environment in which all the extraneous factors are strictly controlled. Similar subjects are chosen carefully to respond to certain manipulated stimuli. These studies are referred to as **lab experiments.** Let us give another example to understand the differences among a field study (a noncontrived setting with minimal researcher interference), a field experiment (noncontrived setting but with researcher interference to a moderate extent), and a lab experiment (a contrived setting with researcher interference to an excessive degree).

def.

Example 6.15   FIELD STUDY

A bank manager wants to analyze the relationship between interest rates and bank deposit patterns of clients. She tries to correlate the two by looking at deposits into different kinds of accounts (such as savings, certificates of deposit, golden passbooks, and interest-bearing checking accounts) as interest rates changed.

This is a field study where the bank manager has merely taken the balances in various types of accounts and correlated them to the changes in interest rates. Research here is done in a noncontrived setting with no interference with the normal work routine.

Example 6.16   FIELD EXPERIMENT

The bank manager now wants to determine the cause-and-effect relationship between interest rate and the inducements it offers to clients to save and deposit money in the bank. She selects four branches within a 60-mile radius for the experiment. For 1 week only, she advertises the annual rate for new certificates of deposit received during that week in the following manner: the interest rate would be 9% in one branch, 8% in another, and 10% in the third. In the fourth branch, the interest rate remains unchanged at 5%. Within the week, she would be able to determine the effects, if any, of interest rates on deposit mobilization.

The above would be a field experiment since nothing but the interest rate is manipulated, with all activities occurring in the normal and natural work environment. Hopefully, all four branches chosen would be more or less compatible in size, number of depositors, deposit patterns, and the like, so that the interest-savings relationships are not influenced by some third factor. But it is possible that some other factors might affect the findings. For example, one of the areas may have more retirees who may not have additional disposable income that they could deposit, despite the attraction of a good interest rate. The banker may not have been aware of this fact while setting up the experiment.

problem w/ not having randomized groups

Example 6.17

LAB EXPERIMENT

The banker in Example 6.16 may now want to establish the causal connection between interest rates and savings, beyond a doubt. Because of this she wants to create an artificial environment and trace the true cause-and-effect relationship. She recruits 40 students who are all business majors in their final year of study and are more or less of the same age. She splits them into four groups and gives each one of them chips that count for $1,000, which they are told they might utilize to buy their needs or save for the future, or both. She offers them by way of incentive, interest on what they save but manipulates the interest rates by offering a 6% interest rate on savings for group 1, 8% for group 2, 9% for group 3, and keeps the interest at the low rate of 1% for group 4.

Here, the manager has created an artificial laboratory environment and has manipulated the interest rates for savings. She has also chosen subjects with similar backgrounds and exposure to financial matters (business students). If the banker finds that the savings by the four groups increase progressively, keeping in step with the increasing rates of interest, she would be able to establish a cause-and-effect relationship between interest rate and the disposition to save.

In this lab experiment with the contrived setting, the researcher interference has been maximal, inasmuch as the setting is different, the independent variable has been manipulated, and most external nuisance factors such as age and experience have been controlled.

Experimental designs are discussed more fully in the next chapter. However, the above exmaples show us that it is important to decide the various design details before conducting the research study since one decision criterion might have an impact on others. For example, if one wants to conduct an exploratory, descriptive, or a correlational hypothesis-testing study, then the necessity for the researcher to interfere with the normal course of events in the organization will be minimal. However, if causal connections are to be established, experimental designs need to be set up either within the organization where the events normally occur (the field experiment) or in an artificially created laboratory setting (the lab experiment).

In summary, we have thus far made a distinction among (1) *field studies,* where various factors are examined in the natural setting in which daily activities go on as normal with minimal researcher interference, (2) *field experiments,* where cause and effect relationships are studied with some amount of researcher interference, but still in the natural setting where work continues in the normal fashion, and (3) *lab experiments,* where the researcher explores cause-and-effect relationships not only exercising a high degree of control but also in an artificial and deliberately created setting.

In the next chapter, we will see the advantages and disadvantages of using contrived and noncontrived settings for establishing cause-and-effect relationships. Depending on the degree to which establishment of the cause-and-effect relationship *unequivocally* is important to a research project, a contrived or a noncontrived setting would be relevant for causal studies. Thus, the choice of the setting becomes an important issue in research design. As stated earlier, an artificial setting is rarely called for in business research.

UNIT OF ANALYSIS: INDIVIDUALS, DYADS, GROUPS, ORGANIZATIONS, CULTURES

The unit of analysis refers to the level of aggregation of the data collected during the subsequent data analysis stage. If, for instance, the problem statement focuses on how to raise the motivational levels of employees in general, then we are interested in individual employees in the organization and would have to find out what we can do to raise their motivation. Here the unit of analysis is the **individual.** We will be looking at the data gathered from each individual and treating each employee's response as an individual data source. If the researcher is interested in studying two-person interactions, then several two-person groups, also known as **dyads,** will become the unit of analysis. Analysis of husband–wife interactions in families and supervisor–subordinate relationships at the workplace are good examples of dyads as the unit of analysis. However, if the problem statement is related to group effectiveness, then the unit of analysis would be at the group level. In other words, even though we may gather relevant data from all individuals comprising, say, six groups, we would aggregate the individual data into group data so as to see the differences among the six **groups.** If we compare different departments in the organization, then the data analysis will be done at the departmental level—that is, the individuals in the department will be treated as one unit—and comparisons made treating the department as the unit of analysis.

Our research question determines the unit of anlaysis. For example, if we desire to study group decision-making patterns, we would probably be examining such aspects as group size, group structure, cohesiveness, and the like, in trying to explain the variance in group decision making. Here, our main interest is not in studying individual decision making but group decision making, and we will be studying the dynamics that operate in several different groups and the factors that influence group decision making. In such a case, the unit of analysis will be groups.

As our research question addresses issues that move away from the individual to dyads, and to groups, organizations, and even nations, so also does the unit of analysis shift from individuals to dyads, groups, organizations, and nations. The characteristic of these "levels of analysis" is that the lower levels are subsumed within the higher levels. Thus, if we study buying behaviors, we have to collect data from, say, 60 individuals, and analyze the data. If we want to study group dynamics, we may need to study, say, six or more groups, and then analyze the data gathered by examining the patterns in each of the groups. If we want to study cultural differences among nations, we will have to collect data from different countries and study the underlying patterns of culture in each country. Some critical issues in cross-cultural research are discussed in later chapters.

Individuals do not have the same characteristics as groups (e.g., structure, cohesiveness) and groups do not have the same characteristics as individuals (e.g., IQ, stamina). There are variations in the perceptions, attitudes, and behaviors of people in different cultures. Hence, the nature of the information gathered, as well as the level at which data are aggregated for analysis, are integral to decisions made in the choice of the unit of analysis.

It is necessary to decide on the unit of analysis even as we formulate the research question since the data collection methods, sample size, and even the variables included in the framework may sometimes be determined or guided by the level at which data are aggregated for analysis.

Let us examine some research scenarios that would call for different units of analysis.

Example 6.18
INDIVIDUALS AS THE UNIT OF ANALYSIS
The Chief Financial Officer of a manufacturing company wants to know how many of the staff would be interested in attending a 3-day seminar on making appropriate investment decisions. For this purpose, data will have to be collected from each individual staff member and the unit of analysis is the individual.

Example 6.19
DYADS AS THE UNIT OF ANALYSIS
Having read about the benefits of mentoring, a human resources manager wants to first identify the number of employees in three departments of the organization who are in mentoring relationships, and then find out what the jointly perceived benefits (i.e., by both the mentor and the one mentored) of such a relationship are.

Here, once the mentor and the mentored pairs are identified, their joint perceptions can be obtained by treating each pair as one unit. Hence, if the manager wants data from a sample of 10 pairs, he will have to deal with 20 individuals, a pair at a time. The information obtained from each pair will be a data point for subsequent analysis. Thus, the unit of analysis here is the dyad.

Example 6.20
GROUPS AS THE UNIT OF ANALYSIS
A manager wants to see the patterns of usage of the newly installed Information System (IS) by the production, sales, and operations personnel. Here three groups of personnel are involved and information on the number of times the IS is used by each member in each of the three groups as well as other relevant issues will be collected and analyzed. The final results will indicate the mean

usage of the system per day or month for each group. Here the unit of analysis is the group.

Example 6.21

DIVISIONS AS THE UNIT OF ANALYSIS

Proctor and Gamble wants to see which of its various divisions (soap, paper, oil, etc.) have made profits of over 12% during the current year. Here, the profits of each of the divisions will be examined and the information aggregated across the various geographical units of the division. Hence, the unit of analysis will be the division, at which level the data will be aggregated.

Example 6.22

INDUSTRY AS THE UNIT OF ANALYSIS

An employment survey specialist wants to see the proportion of the workforce employed by the health care, utilities, transportation, and manufacturing industries. In this case, the researcher has to aggregate the data relating to each of the subunits comprised in each of the industries and report the proportions of the workforce employed at the industry level. The health care industry, for instance, includes hospitals, nursing homes, mobile units, small and large clinics, and other health care providing facilities. The data from these subunits will have to be aggregated to see how many employees are employed by the health care industry. This will need to be done for each of the other industries.

Example 6.23

COUNTRIES AS THE UNIT OF ANALYSIS

The Chief Financial Officer (CFO) of a multinational corporation wants to know the profits made during the past 5 years by each of the subsidiaries in England, Germany, France, and Spain. It is possible that there are many regional offices of these subsidiaries in each of these countries. The profits of the various regional centers for each country have to be aggregated and the profits for each country for the past 5 years provided to the CFO. In other words, the data will now have to be aggregated at the country level.

As can be easily seen, the data collection and sampling processes become more cumbersome at higher levels of units of analysis (industry, country) than at the lower levels (individuals and dyads).

It is obvious that the unit of analysis has to be clearly identified as dictated by the research question. Sampling plan decisions will also be governed by the unit of analysis. For example, if I compare two cultures, for instance those of India and the United States—where my unit of analysis is the country—my sample size will be only two, despite the fact that I shall have to gather data from several hundred individuals from a variety of organizations in the different regions of each country, incurring huge costs. However, if my unit of analysis is individuals (as when studying the buying patterns of customers in the southern part of the United States), I may perhaps limit the collection of data to a representative sample of a hundred individuals in that region and conduct my study at a low cost!

It is now even easier to see why the unit of analysis should be given serious consideration even as the research question is being formulated and the research design planned.

TIME HORIZON: CROSS-SECTIONAL VERSUS LONGITUDINAL STUDIES

Cross-Sectional Studies

This is what you will do for your D.P.

A study can be done in which data are gathered just once, perhaps over a period of days or weeks or months, in order to answer a research question. Such studies are called one-shot or cross-sectional studies.

Example 6.24

Data were collected from stock brokers between April and June of last year to study their concerns in a turbulent stock market. Data with respect to this particular research had not been collected before, nor will they be collected again from them for this research.

What are some questions that could be answered by a cross-sectional study?

Example 6.25

A drug company desirous of investing in research for a new obesity (reduction) pill conducted a survey among obese people to see how many of them would be interested in trying the new pill. This is a one-shot or cross-sectional study to assess the likely demand for the new product.

The purpose of both the studies in the two foregoing examples was to collect data that would be pertinent to find the answer to a research question. Data collection at one point in time was sufficient. Both were cross-sectional designs.

Longitudinal Studies

What are some Qs that can only be answered by a longitudinal study (we all start out as tiny in our grandma's womb) the individuals or these in disease 20/30 s 50/60s

In some cases, however, the researcher might want to study people or phenomena at more than one point in time in order to answer the research question. For instance, the researcher might want to study employees' behavior before and after a change in the top management, so as to know what effects the change accomplished. Here, because data are gathered at two different points in time, the study is not cross-sectional or of the one-shot kind, but is carried longitudinally across a period of time. Such studies, as when data on the dependent variable are gathered at two or more points in time to answer the research question, are called longitudinal studies.

Example 6.26

UPS experienced a shutdown for 15 days during the Teamsters' walkout and their clients shifted their business to other carriers such as FedEx and the U.S. Postal Service. After the termination of the strike, UPS tried to woo their customers back through several strategies and collected data month after month to see what progress they were making in this regard.

business trends summer autumn? coming from college unhappen?

Here, data were collected every month to assess whether UPS had regained the business volume. Since data were collected at various points in time to answer the same research question (have we regained lost ground?), the study is a longitudinal one.

Example 6.27   A marketing manager is interested in tracing the pattern of sales of a particular product in four different regions of the country on a quarterly basis for the next 2 years. Since data are collected several times to answer the same issue (tracing pattern of sales), the study falls under the longitudinal category.

Longitudinal studies take more time and effort and cost more than cross-sectional studies. However, well-planned longitudinal studies could, among other things, help to identify cause-and-effect relationships. For example, one could study the sales volume of a product before and after an advertisement, and provided other environmental changes have not impacted on the results, one could attribute the increase in the sales volume, if any, to the advertisement. If there is no increase in sales, one could conclude that either the advertisement is ineffective or it will take a longer time to take effect.

Experimental designs invariably are longitudinal studies since data are collected both before and after a manipulation. Field studies could also be longitudinal. For example, a study of the comparison data pertaining to the reactions of managers in a company toward working women now and 10 years later will be a longitudinal field study. Most field studies conducted, however, are cross-sectional in nature because of the time, effort, and costs involved in collecting data over several time periods. Longitudinal studies will certainly be necessary if a manager wants to keep track of certain factors (e.g., sales, advertising effectiveness, etc.) over a period of time to assess improvements, or to detect possible causal connections (sales promotions and actual sales data; frequency of drug testing and reduction in drug usage, etc.). Though more expensive, longitudinal studies offer some good insights.

REVIEW OF ELEMENTS OF RESEARCH DESIGN

This concludes the discussions on the basic design issues regarding purpose of the study, type of investigation, extent of researcher interference, study setting, unit of analysis, and the time horizon. The researcher would determine the appropriate decisions to be made in the study design based on the problem definition, the research objectives, the extent of rigor desired, and cost considerations. Sometimes, because of the time and costs involved, a researcher might be constrained to settle for less than the "ideal" research design. For instance, the researcher might have to conduct a cross-sectional instead of a longitudinal study, do a field study rather than an experimental design, choose a smaller rather than a larger sample size, and so on, thus suboptimizing the research design decisions and settling for a lower level of scientific rigor because of resource constraints. This trade-off between rigor and resources will be a deliberate and conscious decision made by the manager/researcher based on the scope of and reasons for the study, and will have to be explicity stated in any written research proposal. Compromises so made also account for why management studies are not entirely scientific, as discussed in Chapter 2.

A rigorous research design that might involve higher costs is essential if the results of the study are critical for making important decisions affecting the organization's survival and/or the well-being of the vast majority of the publics of the system. It is best to think about the research design decision issues even as the theoretical framework is developed. The researcher has to be very clear about each aspect discussed in this chapter before embarking on data collection.

Do Exercises 6.1–6.4 at the end of this chapter

MANAGERIAL IMPLICATIONS

Knowledge about research design issues helps the manager to understand what the researcher is attempting to do. The manager also understands why the reports sometimes indicate data analytic results based on small sample sizes, when a lot of time has been spent in collecting data from several scores of individuals, as in the case of studies involving groups, departments, or branch offices.

One of the important decisions a manager has to make before starting a study pertains to how rigorous the study ought to be. Knowing that more rigorous research designs consume more resources, the manager is in a position to weigh the gravity of the problem experienced and decide what kind of design would yield acceptable results in an efficient manner. For example, the manager might decide that knowledge of which variables are *associated* with employee performance is good enough to enhance performance results and there is no need to ferret out the *cause* therefor. Such a decision would result not only in economy in resources, but also cause the least disruption to the smooth flow of work for employees and preclude the need for collecting data longitudinally. Knowledge of interconnections among various aspects of the research design helps managers to call for the most effective study, after weighing the nature and magnitude of the problem encountered, and the type of solution desired.

 One of the main advantages in fully understanding the difference between causal and correlational studies is that managers do not fall into the trap of making implicit causal assumptions when two variables are only associated with each other. They realize that A could cause B, or B could cause A, or both A and B could covary because of some third variable.

Knowledge of research design details also helps managers to study and intelligently comment on research proposals.

SUMMARY

In this chapter we examined the basic research design issues and the choice points available to the manager/researcher. We discussed the situations in which exploratory, descriptive, hypothesis-testing, and case studies are called for. We examined causal versus correlational studies, and the implications of either for determining the study setting, extent of researcher interference, and time horizon of the study. We noted that the unit of analysis refers to the level at which data are aggregated for analysis, and that the time horizon of studies could be one-shot or longitudinal. Finally, we examined the circumstances in which each design decision would be appropriate.

In the next chapter we will discuss how experimental designs are set up and the ways in which cause-and-effect relationships can be traced.

DISCUSSION QUESTIONS AND POINTS TO PONDER

1. What are the basic research design issues? Describe them in some detail.
2. Why is it important to consider basic design issues before conducting the study and even as early as at the time of formulating the research question?
3. Is a field study totally out of the question if one is trying to establish cause-and-effect relationships?
4. "An exploratory study is just as useful as a predictive study." Discuss this statement.
5. Why is the unit of analysis an integral part of the research design?
6. Discuss the interrelationships among noncontrived setting, the purpose of the study, type of investigation, researcher interference, and time horizon of study.
7. Below are three scenarios. Indicate how the researcher should proceed in each case; that is, determine the following, giving reasons:
   a. The purpose of the study
   b. The type of investigation
   c. The extent of researcher interference
   d. The study setting
   e. The time horizon for the study
   f. The unit of analysis

Scenario A

Ms. Joyce Lynn, the owner of a small business (a women's dress boutique), has invited a consultant to tell her how her business is different from similar small businesses within a 60-mile radius with respect to use of the most modern computer technology, sales volume, profit margin, and staff training.

Scenario B

Mr. Paul Hodge, the owner of several restaurants on the East Coast, is concerned about the wide differences in their profit margins. He would like to try some incentive plans for increasing the efficiency levels of those restaurants that lag behind. But before he actually does this, he would like to be assured that the idea would work. He asks a researcher to help him on this issue.

Scenario C

A manager is intrigued why some people seem to derive joy from work and get energized by it, while others find it troublesome and frustrating.

Exercise 6.1   A foreman thinks that the low efficiency of the machine tool operators is directly linked to the high level of fumes emitted in the workshop. He would like to prove this to his supervisor through a research study.

1. Would this be a causal or a correlational study? Why?
2. Is this an exploratory, descriptive, or hypothesis-testing (analytical or predictive) study? Why?
3. What kind of a study would this be: field study, lab experiment, or field experiment? Why?
4. What would be the unit of analysis? Why?
5. Would this be a cross-sectional or a longitudinal study? Why?

Exercise 6.2   Many were concerned about the operations of the infamous BCCI, the international banking institution. If the government had desired to probe into the details, would this investigation have called for:

1. A causal or correlational study? Why?
2. An exploratory, descriptive, or hypothesis-testing study or case analysis? Why?
3. A field study, lab experiment, or field experiment? Why?
4. A cross-sectional or longitudinal study? Why?

Exercise 6.3   Below is an adapted case of BFI from an issue of *Business Week*. The newly appointed Chief Executive of BFI desires to conduct a study to effect improvements and asks you to work out the research design details. After reading the short case that follows, discuss fully the design decisions that you as a researcher will make to investigate the situation, giving reasons for your choices.

Tossing Out the Trash at BFI

Brown Ferris Industries (BFI), a waste management company, grew rapidly by snapping up local dump sites, collection routes, and recycling businesses across the country and abroad during the 1980s and early 1990s. But while BFI was paying a lot of money for acquiring collection routes, it had not linked these to the company-owned landfills, and this cost BFI dearly. As a consequence, it had to pay outsiders a lot of money to dispose of its trash.

However, BFI's recycling business was booming, since the profits in recycling were high. But in the mid 1990s profits from recycling dropped drastically and BFI finished the fiscal year that ended in September 1996 with a heavy loss. Things have not improved much since.

Exercise 6.4

War on Cancer

Dr. Larry Norton of Memorial Sloan-Kettering Cancer Center predicts that cancer treatment will undergo major changes. Several drugs are being developed to battle cancer without harming healthy tissues. It is a question of discovering which of these drugs does the job best.

Design a study that would help find which drug would do the trick.

EXPERIMENTAL DESIGNS

TOPICS DISCUSSED

LAB AND FIELD EXPERIMENTS

CONTROL

MANIPULATION

CONTROLLING THE CONTAMINATING VARIABLES

- Matching
- Randomization

INTERNAL VALIDITY OF LAB EXPERIMENTS

EXTERNAL VALIDITY

FIELD EXPERIMENTS

TRADE-OFF BETWEEN INTERNAL AND EXTERNAL VALIDITY

FACTORS AFFECTING INTERNAL VALIDITY

- History Effects
- Maturation Effects
- Testing Effects
- Instrumentation Effects
- Selection Effects
- Statistical Regression Effects
- Mortality Effects

INTERNAL VALIDITY IN CASE STUDIES

FACTORS AFFECTING EXTERNAL VALIDITY

TYPES OF EXPERIMENTAL DESIGNS AND INTERNAL VALIDITY

- Quasi-Experimental Designs
- True Experimental Designs
- Ex Post Facto Designs

SIMULATION

ETHICAL ISUES IN EXPERIMENTAL RESEARCH

MANAGERIAL IMPLICATIONS

APPENDIX: FURTHER EXPERIMENTAL DESIGNS

CHAPTER OBJECTIVES

After completing Chapter 7, you should be able to:

1. Distinguish between causal and correlational analysis.
2. Explain the difference between lab and field experiments.
3. Explain the following terms: nuisance variables, manipulation, experimental and control groups, treatment effect, matching, and randomization.
4. Discuss internal and external validity in experimental designs.
5. Discuss the seven possible threats to internal validity in experimental designs.
6. Describe the different types of experimental designs.
7. Discuss the Solomon four-group design and its implications for internal validity.
8. Apply what has been learned to class assignments and exams.

Consider the following three scenarios.

Scenario A   For some time now, there has been the feeling that individual companies and the economy will be better served if executive compensation contracts are entered into, making the CEOs accountable for performance. Currently the top executives are compensated irrespective of their performance, making them permanent corporate fixtures.

A switch to the new mode is likely to irk the chiefs, but is definitely worth a try if it does work. But how can we be sure that it would work?

Scenario B   A study of absenteeism and the steps taken to curb it indicate that companies use the following incentives to reduce it:

14% give bonus days

39% offer cash

39% present recognition awards

4% award prizes

4% pursue other strategies

Asked about their effectiveness,

22% of the companies said they were very effective

66% said they were somewhat effective

12% said they were not at all effective

What does the above information tell us? How do we know what kinds of incentives **cause** people not to absent themselves? What particular incentive(s) did the 22% of companies that found their strategies to be "very effective" offer? Is there a direct causal connection between one or two specific incentives and absenteeism?

Scenario C

The dagger effect of layoffs is that there is a sharp drop in the commitment of workers who are retained, even though they might well understand the logic of the reduction in the workforce.

Does layoff really cause employee commitment to drop off, or is something else operating in this situation?

The answers to the questions raised in Scenarios A, B, and C might be found by using experimental designs in researching the issues.

In the previous chapter we had touched on experimental designs. In this chapter, we will discuss both lab experiments and field experiments in detail. Experimental designs, as we know, are set up to examine possible cause and effect relationships among variables, in contrast to correlational studies, which examine the relationships among variables without necessarily trying to establish if one variable causes another.

To establish that variable X **causes** variable Y, *all three* of the following conditions should be met:

1. Both X and Y should covary [i.e., when one goes up, the other should also simultaneously go up (or down)].
2. X (the presumed causal factor) should precede Y. In other words, there must be a time sequence in which the two occur.
3. No other factor should possibly cause the change in the dependent variable Y.

It may thus be seen that to establish causal relationships between two variables in an organizational setting, several variables that might covary with the dependent variable have to be controlled. This would then allow us to say that variable X and variable X alone causes the dependent variable Y. Useful as it is to know the cause-and-effect relationships, establishing them is not easy, because several other variables that covary with the dependent variable have to be controlled. It is not always possible to control all the covariates while manipulating the causal factor (the independent variable that is causing the dependent variable) in organizational settings, where events flow or occur naturally and normally. It is, however, possible to first isolate the effects of a variable in a tightly controlled artificial setting (the lab setting), and after testing and establishing the cause-and-effect relationship under these tightly controlled conditions, see how generalizable such relationships are to the field setting.

Let us illustrate this with an example. Suppose a manager believes that staffing the accounting department completely with personnel with M.Acc. (Master of Accountancy) degrees will increase its productivity. It is well nigh impossible to transfer all those without the M.Acc. degree currently in the department to other departments and recruit fresh M.Acc. degree holders to take their place. Such a course of action is bound to disrupt the work of the entire organization inasmuch as many new people will have to be trained, work will slow down, employees will get upset, and so on. However, the hypothesis that possession of a M.Acc. degree would *cause* increases in productivity can be tested in an artificially created setting (i.e., not at the regular workplace) in which an accounting job can be given to three groups of people: those with a M.Acc. degree, those without a M.Acc. degree, and a mixed group of those with and without a M.Acc. degree (as is the case in the present work setting). If the first group performs exceedingly well, the second group poorly, and the third group falls somewhere in the middle, there will be evidence to indicate that the M.Acc. degree qualification might indeed *cause* productivity to rise. If such evidence is found, then planned and systematic efforts can be initiated to gradually transfer those without the M.Acc. degree in the accounting department to other departments and recruit others with this degree to this department. It is then possible to see to what extent productivity does, in fact, go up in the department because all the staff members are M.Acc. degree holders.

As we saw earlier, experimental designs fall into two categories: experiments done in an artificial or contrived environment, known as **lab experiments,** and those done in the natural environment in which activities regularly take place, known as the **field experiment.**

THE LAB EXPERIMENT

As stated earlier, when a cause-and-effect relationship between an independent and a dependent variable of interest is to be clearly established, then all other variables that might contaminate or confound the relationship have to be tightly controlled. In other words, the possible effects of other variables on the dependent variable have to be accounted for in some way, so that the actual causal effects of the investigated independent variable on the dependent variable can be determined. It is also necessary to manipulate the independent variable so that the extent of its causal effects can be established. The controls and manipulations are best done in an artificial setting (the laboratory), where the causal effects can be tested. When controls and manipulations are introduced to establish cause-and-effect relationships in an artificial setting, we have laboratory experimental designs, also known as lab experiments.

Because we use the terms *control* and *manipulation,* let us examine what these concepts mean.

CONTROL

When we postulate cause-and-effect relationships between two variables X and Y, it is possible that some other factor, say A, might also influence the dependent variable Y. In such a case, it will not be possible to determine the extent to which Y occurred only because of X, since we do not know how much of the total variation of Y was caused by the presence of the other factor A. For instance, a Human Resource Development manager might arrange for special training to a set of newly recruited secretaries in creating web pages, to prove to the VP (his boss), that such training would *cause* them to function more effectively. However, some of the new secretaries might function more effectively than others, mainly or partly because they have had previous intermittent experience with the web. In this case, the manager cannot prove that the special training alone *caused* greater effectiveness, since the previous intermittent experience of some secretaries with the web is a contaminating factor. If the true effect of the training on learning is to be assessed, then the learners' previous experience has to be controlled. This might be done by not including in the experiment those who already have had some experience with the web. This is what we mean when we say we have to control the contaminating factors, and we will later see how this is done.

MANIPULATION OF THE INDEPENDENT VARIABLE

In order to examine the causal effects of an independent variable on a dependent variable, certain manipulations need to be tried. Manipulation simply means that we *create* different levels of the independent variable to assess the impact on the dependent variable. For example, we may want to test the theory that depth of knowledge of various manufacturing technologies is *caused* by rotating the employees on all the jobs on the production line and in the design department, over a 4-week period. Then we can *manipulate* the independent variable, "rotation of employees," by rotating one group of production workers and exposing them to all the systems during the 4-week period, rotating another group of workers only partially during the 4 weeks (i.e., exposing them to only half of the manufacturing technologies), and leaving the third group to continue to do what they are currently doing, without any special rotation. By measuring the depth of knowledge of these groups both before and after the manipulation (also known as the "treatment"), it would be possible to assess the extent to which the treatment *caused* the effect, after controlling the contaminating factors. If deep knowledge is indeed caused by rotation and exposure, the results would show that the third group had the lowest increase in depth of knowledge, the second group had some significant increase, and the first group had the greatest gains!

Let us look at another example on how causal relationships are established by manipulating the independent variable. Let us say we want to test the effects of lighting on worker production levels among sewing machine operators. To establish cause-and-effect relationship, we must first measure the production levels of all the operators over a 15-day period with the usual amount of light they work with—say 60-watt lamps. We might then want to split the group of 60 operators into three groups of 20 members each, and while allowing one subgroup to continue to work under the same conditions as before (60-watt electric lightbulbs) we might want to manipulate the intensity of the light for the other two sub-groups, by making one group work with 75-watt and the other with 100-watt lightbulbs. After the different groups have worked with these varying degrees of light exposure for 15 days, each group's total production for these 15 days may be analyzed to see if the difference between the preexperimental and the post-experimental productions among the groups is directly related to the intensity of the light to which they have been exposed. If our hypothesis that better lighting increases the production levels is correct, then the subgroup that did not have any change in the lighting (called the control group), should have no increase in production and the other two groups should show increases, with the ones having the most light (100 watts) showing greater increases than those who had the 75-watt lighting.

In this case the independent variable, lighting, has been manipulated by exposing different groups to different degrees of changes in it. This manipulation of the independent variable is also known as the **treatment,** and the results of the treatment are called **treatment effects.**

Let us illustrate how variable X can be both controlled and manipulated in the lab setting through Example 7.1.

Example 7.1

Let us say an entrepreneur—the owner of a toy shop—is rather disappointed with the number of imitation "Ninja turtles" (greatly in demand) produced by his workers, who are paid wages at an hourly rate. He might wonder whether paying them piece rates would increase their production levels. However, before implementing the piece-rate system, he would want to make sure that switching over to the new system would indeed achieve the objective.

In a case like this, the researcher might first want to test the causal relationships in a lab setting, and if the results are encouraging, conduct the experiment later in a field setting. In designing the lab experiment, the researcher should first think of possible factors that would affect the production level of the workers, and then try to control these. Other than piece rates, previous job experience might also influence the rate of production because familiarity with the job makes it easy for people to increase their productivity levels.

In some cases, where the jobs are very strenuous and require muscular strength, gender differences may affect productivity. Let us say that for the type of production job discussed earlier, age, gender, and prior experience of the employees are the factors that would influence the production levels of the employees. The researcher needs to control these three variables. Let us see how this can be done.

Suppose the researcher intends to set up four groups of 15 people each, for the lab experiment—one to be used as the control group, and the other three subjected to three different pay manipulations. Now, the variables that may impact on the cause-and-effect relationship can be controlled in two different ways: either by matching the groups or through randomization. These concepts are explained before we proceed further.

CONTROLLING THE CONTAMINATING EXOGENOUS OR "NUISANCE" VARIABLES

Matching Groups

One way of controlling the contaminating or "nuisance" variables is to match the various groups by picking the confounding characteristics and deliberately spreading them across groups. For instance, if there are 20 women among the 60 members, then each group will be assigned 5 women, so that the effects of gender are distributed across the four groups. Likewise, age and experience factors can be matched across the four groups, such that each group has a similar mix of individuals in terms of gender, age, and experience. Because the suspected contaminating factors are matched across the groups, we may take comfort in saying that variable X alone causes variable Y, if such is the result of the study. But here, we are not sure that we have controlled *all* the nuisance factors, since we may not be aware of them all. A safer bet is to randomize.

Randomization

Another way of controlling the contaminating variables is to assign the 60 members randomly (i.e., with no predetermination) to the four groups. That is, every member would have a known and equal chance of being assigned to any of these four groups. For instance, we might throw the names of all the 60 members into a hat, and draw their names. The first 15 names drawn may be assigned to the first group, the second 15 to the second group, and so on, or the first person drawn might be assigned to the first group, the second person drawn to the second group, and so on. Thus, in randomization, the process by which individuals are drawn (i.e., everybody has a known and equal chance of being drawn) and their assignment to any particular group (each individual could be assigned to any one of the groups set up) are both random. By thus randomly assigning members to the groups we would be distributing the confounding variables among the groups equally. That is, the variables of age, sex, and previous experience—the controlled variables—will have an equal probability of being distributed among the groups. The process of randomization would ideally ensure that each group is comparable to the other, and that all variables, including the effects of age, sex and previous experience are controlled. In other words, each of the groups will have some members who have more experience mingled with those who have less or no experience. All groups will have members of different age and sex composition. Thus randomization would ensure that if these variables do indeed have a contributory or confounding effect, we would have controlled their confounding effects (along with those of other unknown factors) by distributing them across groups. This is achieved because when we manipulate the independent variable of piece rates by having no piece rate system at all for one group (control) and having different piece rates for the other three groups (experimental), we can determine the causal effects of the piece rates on production levels. Any errors or biases caused by age, sex, and previous experience are now distributed

Table 7.1
Cause and Effect Relationship after Randomization

Groups	Treatment	Treatment Effect (% increase in production over pre-piece rate system)
Experimental group 1	$1.00 per piece	10
Experimental group 2	$1.50 per piece	15
Experimental group 3	$2.00 per piece	20
Control group (no treatment)	Old hourly rate	0

equally among all four groups. Any causal effects found would be over and above the effects of the confounding variables.

To make it clear, let us illustrate this with some actual figures as in Table 7.1. Note that because the effects of experience, sex, and age have been controlled in all the four groups by randomly assigning the members to them, and the control group had no increase in productivity, it can be reliably concluded from the result that the percentage increases in production are a result of the piece rate (treatment effects). In other words, piece rates are the cause of the increase in the number of toys produced. We cannot now say that the cause-and-effect relations have been confounded by other "nuisance" variables, because they have been controlled through the process of randomly assigning members to the groups. Here, we have high **internal validity** or confidence in the cause-and-effect relationship.

Advantages of Randomization

The difference between matching and randomization is that in the former case individuals are deliberately and consciously matched to control the differences among group members, whereas in the latter case we expect that the process of randomization would distribute the inequalities among the groups, based on the laws of normal distribution. Thus, we need not be particularly concerned about any known or unknown confounding factors.

In sum, compared to randomization, matching might be less effective, since we may not know all the factors that could possibly contaminate the cause-and-effect relationship in any given situation, and hence fail to match some critical factors across all groups while conducting an experiment. Randomization, however, will take care of this, since *all* the contaminating factors will be spread across all groups. Moreover, even if we know the confounding variables, we may not be able to find a match for all such variables. For instance, if gender is a confounding variable, and if there are only two women in a four-group experimental design, we will not be able to match all the groups with respect to gender. Randomization solves these dilemmas as well. Thus, lab experimental designs involve control of the contaminating variables through the process of either matching or randomization, and the manipulation of the treatment.

INTERNAL VALIDITY

Internal validity refers to the confidence we place in the cause-and-effect relationship. In other words, it addresses the question, "To what extent does the research design permit us to say that the independent variable A **causes** a change in the dependent variable B?" As Kidder and Judd (1986) note, in research with high internal validity, we are relatively better able to argue that the relationship is causal, whereas in studies with low internal validity, causality cannot be inferred at all. In lab experiments where cause-and-effect relationships are substantiated, internal validity can be said to be high.

So far we have talked about establishing cause-and-effect relationships within the lab setting, which is an artificially created and controlled environment. You might yourself have been a subject taking part in one of the lab experiments conducted by the psychology or other departments on campus at some time. You might not have been specifically told what cause-and-effect relationships the experimenter was looking for, but you would have been told what is called a "cover story." That is, you would have been apprised in general terms of some reason for the study and your role in it, without divulging its true purpose. After the end of the experiment you would also have been debriefed and given a full explanation of the experiment, and any questions you might have had would have been answered. This is how lab experiments are usually conducted: Subjects are selected and assigned to different groups through matching or randomization; they are moved to a lab setting; they are given some details of the study and a task to perform; and some kind of questionnaire or other tests are administered both before and after the task is completed. The results of these studies would indicate the cause-and-effect relationship between the variables under investigation.

EXTERNAL VALIDITY OR GENERALIZABILITY OF LAB EXPERIMENTS

To what extent would the results found in the lab setting be transferable or generalizable to the actual organizational or field settings? In other words, if we do find a cause-and-effect relationship after conducting a lab experiment, can we then confidently say that the same cause-and-effect relationship will also hold true in the organizational setting?

Consider the following situation. If in a lab experimental design the groups are given the simple production task of screwing bolts and nuts onto a plastic frame, and the results indicate that the groups who were paid piece rates were more productive than those who were paid hourly rates, to what extent can we then say that this would be true of the sophisticated nature of the jobs performed in organizations? The tasks in organizational settings are far more complex, and there might be several confounding variables that cannot be controlled—for example, experience. Under such circumstances, we cannot be sure that the cause-and-effect relationship found in the lab experiment is necessarily likely to hold true in the field setting. To test the causal relationships in the organizational setting, field experiments are done. These will now be briefly discussed.

THE FIELD EXPERIMENT

A field experiment, as the name implies, is an experiment done in the natural environment in which work goes on as usual, but treatments are given to one or more groups. Thus in the field experiment, even though it may not be possible to control all the nuisance variables because members cannot be either randomly assigned to groups, or matched, the treatment can still be manipulated. Control groups could also be set up in the field experiments. The experimental and control groups in the field experiment could be made up of the people working at several plants within a certain radius, or from the different shifts in the same plant, or in some other way. If there are three different shifts in a production plant, for instance, and the effects of the piece-rate system are to be studied, one of the shifts can be used as the control group, and the two other shifts given two different treatments or the same treatment—that is, different piece rates or the same piece rate. Any cause-and-effect relationship found under these conditions would have wider generalizability to other similar production settings, even though we may not be sure to what extent the piece rates alone were the *cause* of the increase in productivity, because some of the other confounding variables could not be controlled.

EXTERNAL VALIDITY

What we just discussed can be referred to as an issue of external validity versus internal validity. *External validity* refers to the extent of generalizability of the results of a causal study to other settings, people, or events, and *internal validity* refers to the degree of our confidence in the causal effects (i.e., that variable X causes variable Y). Field experiments have more external validity (i.e., the results are more generalizable to other similar organizational settings), but less internal validity (i.e., we cannot be certain of the extent to which variable X alone causes variable Y). Note that in the lab experiment, the reverse is true. The internal validity is high but the external validity is rather low. In other words, in lab experiments we can be sure that variable X causes variable Y because we have been able to keep the other confounding exogenous variables under control, but we have so tightly controlled several variables to establish the cause and effect relationship that we do not know to what extent the results of our study can be generalized, if at all, to field settings. In other words, since the lab setting does not reflect the "real world" setting, we do not know to what extent the lab findings validly represent the realities in the outside world.

TRADE-OFF BETWEEN INTERNAL AND EXTERNAL VALIDITY

There is thus a trade-off between internal validity and external validity. If we want high internal validity, we should be willing to settle for lower external

Which is more likely to be a priority in your D.P.?

validity and vice versa. To ensure both types of validity, researchers usually try first to test the causal relationships in a tightly controlled artificial or lab setting, and once the relationship has been established, they try to test the causal relationship in a field experiment. Lab experimental designs in the management area have thus far been done to assess, among other things, gender differences in leadership styles, managerial aptitudes, and so on. However, gender differences and other factors found in the lab settings are frequently not found in field studies (Osborn & Vicars, 1976). These problems of external validity usually limit the use of lab experiments in the management area. Field experiments are also infrequently undertaken because of the resultant unintended consequences—personnel becoming suspicious, rivalries and jealousies being created among departments, and the like.

FACTORS AFFECTING INTERNAL VALIDITY

Even the best designed lab studies could be influenced by factors that might affect the internal validity of the lab experiment. That is, some confounding factors might still be present that could offer rival explanations as to what is causing the dependent variable. These possible confounding factors pose a *threat to internal validity*. The seven major threats to internal validity are the effects of history, maturation, testing, instrumentation, selection, statistical regression, and mortality and these are explained below with examples.

History Effects

Certain events or factors that would have an impact on the independent variable–dependent variable relationship might unexpectedly occur while the experiment is in progress, and this history of events would confound the cause-and-effect relationship between the two variables, thus affecting the internal validity. For example, let us say that the manager of a Dairy Products Division wants to test the effects of the "buy one, get one free" sales promotion on the sale of the company-owned brand of packaged cheese, for a week. She carefully records the sales of the packaged cheese during the previous 2 weeks to assess the effect of the promotion. However, on the very day that her sales promotion goes into effect, the Dairy Farmer's Association unexpectedly launches a multimedia advertisement on the benefits of consuming dairy products, especially cheese. The sales of all dairy products, including cheese, go up in all the stores, including the one where the experiment had been in progress. Here, because of unexpected advertisement, one cannot be sure how much of the increase in sales of the packaged cheese in question was due to the sales promotion and how much to the advertisement of the Dairy Farmers' Association! The effects of *history* have reduced the internal validity or the faith that can be placed on the conclusion that the sales promotion caused the increase in sales. The history effects in this case are illustrated in Figure 7.1.

To give another example, let us say a bakery is studying the effects of adding to its bread a new ingredient that is expected to enrich it and offer

Figure 7.1

Illustration of history effects in experimental design.

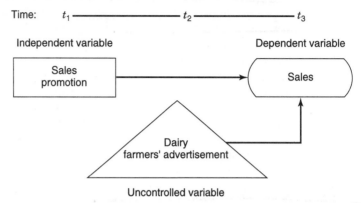

more nutritional value to children under 14 years of age within 30 days, subject to a certain daily intake. At the start of the experiment the bakery takes a measure of the health of 30 children through some medical yardsticks. Thereafter, the children are given the prescribed intakes of bread daily. Unfortunately, on day 20 of the experiment, a flu virus hits the city in epidemic proportions affecting most of the children studied. This unforeseen and uncontrollable effect of history, flu, has contaminated the cause-and-effect relationship study for the bakery.

Maturation Effects

Cause-and-effect inferences can also be contaminated by the effects of the passage of time—another uncontrollable variable. Such contamination is called *maturation effects.* The maturation effects are a function of the processes—both biological and psychological—operating within the respondents as a result of the passage of time. Examples of maturation processes could include *growing older, getting tired, feeling hungry,* and *getting bored.* In other words, there could be a maturation effect on the dependent variable purely because of the passage of time. For instance, let us say that an R & D director contends that increases in the efficiency of workers would result within 3 months' time if advanced technology is introduced in the work setting. If at the end of the 3 months increased efficiency is indeed found, it will be difficult to claim that the advanced technology (and it *alone*) increased the efficiency of workers, because with the passage of time, employees would also have gained experience, resulting in better job performance and therefore in improved efficiency. Thus, the internal validity also gets reduced owing to the effects of maturation inasmuch as it is difficult to pinpoint how much of the increase is attributable to the introduction of the enhanced technology alone. Figure 7.2 illustrates the maturation effects in the above example.

Figure 7.2
Illustration of maturation effects on cause-and-effect relationship.

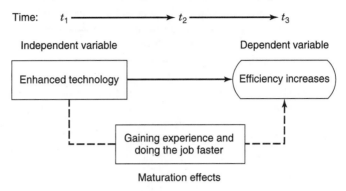

Maturation effects

Testing Effects

Frequently, to test the effects of a treatment, subjects are given what is called a *pretest* (say, a short questionnaire eliciting their feelings and attitudes). That is, first a measure of the dependent variable is taken (the pretest), then the treatment given, and after that a second test, called the *posttest,* administered. The difference between the posttest and the pretest scores is then attributed to the treatment. However, the very fact that respondents were exposed to the pretest might influence their responses on the posttest, which would adversely impact on internal validity.

For example, if a challenging job is expected to cause increases in job satisfaction, and a pretest on job satisfaction is administered asking for employees' level of satisfaction with their current jobs, it might sensitize people to the issue of job satisfaction. When a challenging job is introduced and a further job satisfaction questionnaire administered subsequently, the respondents might now react and respond to the posttest with a different frame of reference than if they had not originally been sensitized to the issue of job satisfaction through the pretest.

This kind of sensitization through previous testing is called the *testing effect,* which also affects the internal validity of experimental designs. In the above case, though increases in job satisfaction can legitimately be measured through pre- and posttests, the pretest could confound the cause-and-effect relationship by sensitizing the respondents to the posttest. Thus, testing effects are another threat to internal validity.

Instrumentation Effects

Instrumentation effects are yet another source of threat to internal validity. These might arise because of a change in the measuring instrument between pretest and posttest, and not because of the treatment's differential impact at the end (Cook & Campbell, 1979a). For instance, an observer who is involved in observing a particular pattern of behaviors in respondents before a treatment might start concentrating on a different set of behaviors after the treatment. The frame of measurement of behaviors (in a sense, the measuring instrument) has now changed and will not reflect the change in behaviors that can be attributed to the treatment. This is also true in the case of physical measuring instruments like the spring balance or other finely calibrated instruments that might lose their accuracy due to loss of tension with constant use, resulting in erroneous final measurement.

In organizations, instrumentation effects in experimental designs are possible when the pretest is done by the experimenter, treatments are given to the experimental groups, and the posttest on measures such as performance is done by different managers. One manager might measure performance by the final units of output, a second manager might take into account the number of rejects as well, and a third manager might also take into consideration the amount of resources expended in getting the job done! Here, there are at least three different measuring instruments, if we treat each manager as a performance measuring instrument.

Thus, instrumentation effects also pose a threat to internal validity in experimental designs.

Selection Bias Effects

The threat to internal validity could also come from improper or unmatched selection of subjects for the experimental and control groups. For example, if a lab experiment is set up to assess the impact of working environment on employees' attitudes toward work, and if one of the experimental conditions is to have a group of subjects work for about 2 hours in a room with some mild stench, an ethical researcher might disclose this condition to prospective subjects, who may decline participation in the study. However, some volunteers might be lured through incentives (say a payment of $70 for the 2 hours of participation in the study). The volunteers so selected may be quite different from the others (inasmuch as they may come from an environment of deprivation) and their responses to the treatment might be quite different. Such bias in the selection of the subjects might contaminate the cause-and-effect relationships and pose a threat to internal validity as well. Hence, newcomers, volunteers, and others who cannot be matched with the control groups would pose a threat to internal validity in certain types of experiments.

Statistical Regression

The effects of statistical regression are brought about when the members chosen for the experimental group have extreme scores on the dependent variable to begin with. For instance, if a manager wants to test if he can increase the "salesmanship" repertoire of the sales personnel through Dale Carnegie–type programs, he should not choose those with extremely low or extremely high abilities for the experiment. This is because we know from the laws of probability that those with very low scores on a variable (in this case, current sales abilities) have a greater probability of showing improvement and scoring closer to the mean on the posttest after being exposed to the treatment. This phenomenon of low scorers

"There's only one way to go"

tending to score closer to the mean is known as "regressing toward the mean" (statistical regression). Likewise, those with very high abilities would also have a greater tendency to regress toward the mean—they will score lower on the posttest than on the pretest. Thus, those who are at either end of the continuum with respect to a variable would not "truly" reflect the cause-and-effect relationship. The phenomenon of statistical regression is thus yet another threat to internal validity.

Mortality

Another confounding factor on the cause-and-effect relationship is the mortality or attrition of the members in the experimental or control group or both, as the experiment progresses. When the group composition changes over time across the groups, comparison between the groups becomes difficult, because those who dropped out of the experiment may confound the results. Again, we would not be able to say how much of the effect observed arises from the treatment, and how much is attributable to the members who dropped out, since those who stayed with the experiment could have reacted differently from those who dropped out. Let us see an example.

Example 7.2

Sometimes it really is "mortality" (death)

A sales manager had heard glowing reports about three different training programs that train salespersons in effective sales strategies. All *three* were of 6 weeks' duration. The manager was curious to know which one would offer the best results for the company. The first program took the trainees daily on field trips and demonstrated effective and ineffective sales strategies through practical experience. The second program trained groups on the same strategies but indoors in a classroom type of setting, lecturing, role playing, and answering question from the participants. The third program used mathematical models and simulations to increase sales effectiveness.

The manager chose eight trainees each for the three different programs and sent them to training. By the end of the fourth week, three trainees from the first group, one from the second group, and two from the third group had dropped out of the training programs due to a variety of reasons including ill health, family exigencies, transportation problems, and a car accident. This attrition from the various groups has now made it impossible to compare the effectiveness of the various programs.

Thus, mortality can also lower the internal validity of an experiment.

IDENTIFYING THREATS TO INTERNAL VALIDITY

Let us examine each of the possible seven threats to internal validity in the context of the following scenario.

An organizational consultant wanted to demonstrate to the president of a company, through an experimental design, that the democratic style of leadership best enhances the morale of employees. She set up three experimental groups and one control group for the purpose and assigned members to each of the groups randomly. The three experimental groups were headed by an autocratic leader, a democratic leader, and a laissez-faire leader, respectively.

The members in the three experimental groups were administered a pretest. Since the control group was not exposed to any treatment, they were not given a pretest. As the experiment progressed, two members in the democratic treatment group got quite excited and started moving around to the other members saying that the participative atmosphere was "great" and "performance was bound to be high in this group." Two members from each of the autocratic and laissez-faire groups left after the first hour saying they had to go and could no longer participate in the experiment. After 2 hours of activities, a posttest was administered to all the participants, including the control group members, on the same lines as the pretest.

History Effects. The action of the two members in the participative group by way of unexpectedly moving around in an excited manner and remarking that participative leadership is "great" and the "performance is bound to be high in this group" might have boosted the morale of all the members in the group. It would be difficult to separate out how much of the increase in morale was due to the participative condition alone and how much to the sudden enthusiasm displayed by the two members.

Maturation. It is doubtful that maturation will have any effects on morale in this situation, since the passage of time, in itself, may not have anything much to do with increase or decrease in morale.

Testing. The pretests are likely to have sensitized the respondents to the posttest. Thus, testing effects would exist. However, if *all* the groups had been given both the pre- and the posttests, the testing effects across all groups would have been taken care of (i.e., nullified) and the posttests of each of the experimental groups could have been compared with that of the control group to detect the effects of the treatment. Unfortunately, the control group was not given the pretest, and thus, this group's posttest scores were not biased by the pretest—a phenomenon that could have occurred in the experimental groups. Hence, it is incorrect, on the face of it, to compare the experimental groups' scores with those of the control group.

Instrumentation. Since the same questionnaire has measured morale both before and after the treatment for all members, we do not expect instrumentation bias.

Selection Bias. Since members have been randomly assigned to all groups, we do not expect selection bias to exist.

Statistical Regression. Though not specifically stated, we can assume that all the members participating in the experiment were selected randomly from a normally distributed population, in which case, the issue of statistical regression contaminating the experiment does not arise.

Mortality. Since members dropped out of two experimental groups, the effects of mortality could affect internal validity.

In effect, three of the seven threats to internal validity do apply in this case. The history, testing, and mortality effects are of concern and hence the internal validity will not be high.

INTERNAL VALIDITY IN CASE STUDIES

If there are several threats to internal validity even in a tightly controlled lab experiment, it should become quite clear why we cannot draw conclusions about causal relationships from **case studies** that describe the events that occurred during a particular time. Unless a well-designed experimental study, randomly assigning members to experimental and control groups and successfully manipulating the treatment, indicates possible causal relationships, it would be impossible to say which factor causes another. For instance, there are several causes attributed to "Slice," the soft drink introduced by Pepsico Inc., not taking off after its initial success. Among the reasons given are (1) a cutback in advertisement for Slice, (2) operating on the mistaken premise that the juice content in Slice would appeal to health-conscious buyers, (3) Pepsico's attempts to milk the brand too quickly, (4) several strategic errors made by Pepsico, (5) underestimation of the time taken to build a brand, and the like. While all the above could provide the basis for developing a theoretical framework for explaining the variance in the sales of a product such as Slice, conclusions about cause-and-effect relationships cannot be determined from anecdotal events.

FACTORS AFFECTING EXTERNAL VALIDITY

Whereas internal validity raises questions about whether it is the treatment alone or some additional extraneous factor that causes the effects, external validity raises issues about the generalizability of the findings to other settings. For instance, the extent to which the experimental situation differs from the setting to which the findings are to be generalized is directly related to the degree of threat it poses to external validity. To illustrate, subjects in a lab experiment might be given a pretest and a posttest. Those findings, however, cannot be generalized to the organizational world, where a pretest followed up by a posttest is rarely administered to employees. Thus the effects of the treatment will not be the same in the field, and external validity suffers a diminution. Another threat is the selection of the subjects. In a lab setting, the types of subjects selected for the experiment could be very different from the types of employees recruited by the organizations. For example, students in a university might be allotted a task that could be manipulated to study the effects on their performance. The findings from this experiment cannot be generalized, however, to the real world of work, where the employees and the nature of the jobs would both be quite different. Thus, subject selection and its interaction with the treatment would also pose a threat to external validity. These are just some of the factors that restrict generalizability. Maximum external validity can be obtained by ensuring that, as far as possible, the lab experimental conditions are as close to and compatible with the real-world situation. It is in this sense that field experiments have greater external validity than lab experiments. That is, the effects of the treatment can be generalized to other settings that are similar to the one where the field experiment was conducted. In Chapter 11, we will discuss generalizability as a function of sampling design.

REVIEW OF FACTORS AFFECTING INTERNAL AND EXTERNAL VALIDITY

In summary, at least seven contaminating factors exist that might affect the internal validity of experimental designs. These are the effects of history, maturation, testing, instrumentation, selection, statistical regression, and mortality. It is, however, possible to reduce the biases by enhancing the level of sophistication of the experimental design. Whereas some of the more sophisticated designs, discussed below, would help increase the internal validity of the experimental results, they could also become expensive and time consuming.

Threats to external validity can be combated by creating experimental conditions that are as close as possible to the situations to which the results of the experiment are to be generalized. For more extensive discussions on validity, see Cook and Campbell (1979b).

The different types of experimental designs and the extent to which internal validity is met in each are discussed next.

TYPES OF EXPERIMENTAL DESIGNS AND INTERNAL VALIDITY

Let us consider some of the commonly used experimental designs and determine the extent to which they guard against the seven factors that could contaminate the internal validity of experimental results. The shorter the time span of the experiments, the less the chances are of encountering history, maturation, and mortality effects. Experiments lasting an hour or two do not usually meet with many of these problems. It is only when experiments are spread over an extended period of say, several months, that the possibility of encountering more of the confounding factors increases.

Quasi-Experimental Designs

Some studies expose an experimental group to a treatment and measure its effects. Such an experimental design is the weakest of all designs, and it does not measure the true cause-and-effect relationship. This is so because there is no comparison between groups, nor any recording of the status of the dependent variable as it was prior to the experimental treatment and how it changed after the treatment. In the absence of such control, the study is of no scientific value in determining cause-and-effect relationships. Hence, such a design is referred to as a quasi-experimental design. The following two are quasi-experimental designs.

Pretest and Posttest Experimental Group Design

An experimental group (without a control group) may be given a pretest, exposed to a treatment, and then given a posttest to measure the effects of the treatment. This can be diagrammed as in Figure 7.3, where O refers to some process of observation or measurement, X represents the exposure of a group to an experimental treatment, and the X and Os in the row are applied to the same specific group. Here, the effects of the treatment can be obtained by measuring the difference between the posttest and the pretest (O_2–O_1). Note, however, that **testing** and **instrumentation effects** might contaminate the internal validity. If the experiment is extended over a period of time, history and maturation effects may also confound the results.

Posttests Only with Experimental and Control Groups

Some experimental designs are set up with an experimental and a control group, the former alone being exposed to a treatment and not the latter. The effects of the treatment are studied by assessing the difference in the outcomes—that is, the posttest scores of the experimental and control groups. This is illustrated in Figure 7.4. Here is a case where the testing effects have been avoided because there is no pretest, only a posttest. Care has to be taken, however, to make sure that the two groups are matched for all the possible contaminating "nuisance" variables. Otherwise, the true effects of the treatment cannot be determined by merely looking at the difference in the posttest scores of the two groups. Randomization would take care of this problem.

There are at least two possible threats to validity in this design. If the two groups are not matched or randomly assigned, **selection biases** could contaminate the results. That is, the differential recruitment of the persons making up the two groups would confound the cause-and-effect relationship. **Mortality**

Figure 7.3
Pretest and posttest experimental group design.

Group	Pretest score	Treatment	Posttest score
Experimental group	O_1	X	O_2

Treatment effect = $(O_2 - O_1)$

Figure 7.4

Posttest only with experimental and control groups.

Group	Treatment	Outcome
Experimental group	X	O_1
Control group		O_2

Treatment effect $= (O_1 - O_2)$

(the dropout of individuals from groups) can also confound the results, and thus pose a threat to internal validity.

True Experimental Designs

Experimental designs, which include both the treatment and control groups and record information both before and after the experimental group is exposed to the treatment, are known as ex post facto experimental designs. These are discussed below.

Pretest and Posttest Experimental and Control Group Designs

This design can be visually depicted as in Figure 7.5. Two groups—one experimental and the other control—are both exposed to the pretest and the posttest. The only difference between the two groups is that the former is exposed to a treatment whereas the latter is not. Measuring the difference between the differences in the post- and pretest scores of the two groups would give the net effects of the treatment. Both groups have been exposed to both the pre- and posttests, and both groups have been randomized; thus we could expect that the history, maturation, testing, and instrumentation effects have been controlled. This is so due to the fact that whatever happened with the experimental group (e.g., maturation, history, testing, and instrumentation) also happened with the control group, and in measuring the net effects (the difference in the differences between the pre- and posttest scores) we have controlled these contaminating factors. Through the process of randomization, we have also controlled the effects of selection biases and statistical regression. **Mortality** could, however, pose a problem in this design. In experiments that take several weeks, as in the

Figure 7.5

Pretest and posttest experimental and control groups.

Group	Pretest	Treatment	Posttest
Experimental group	O_1	X	O_2
Control group	O_3		O_4

Treatment effect $= [(O_2 - O_1) - (O_4 - O_3)]$

case of assessing the impact of training on skill development, or measuring the impact of technology advancement on effectiveness, some of the subjects in the experimental group may drop out before the end of the experiment. It is possible that those who drop out are in some way different from those who stay on until the end and take the posttest. If so, mortality could offer a plausible rival explanation for the difference between O_2 and O_1.

Solomon Four-Group Design

To gain more confidence in internal validity in experimental designs, it is advisable to set up two experimental groups and two control groups for the experiment. One experimental group and one control group can be given both the pretest and the posttest, as shown in Figure 7.6. The other two groups will be given only the posttest. Here the effects of the treatment can be calculated in several different ways, as indicated in the figure. To the extent that we come up with almost the same results in each of the different calculations, we can attribute the effects to the treatment. This increases the internal validity of the results of the experimental design. This design, known as the Solomon four-group design, is perhaps the most comprehensive and the one with the least number of problems with internal validity.

Solomon Four-Group Design and Threats to Internal Validity

Let us examine how the threats to internal validity are taken care of in the Solomon four-group design. It is important to note that subjects have been randomly selected and randomly assigned to groups. This removes the **statistical regression and selection biases.** Group 2, the control group that was exposed to both the pre- and posttest, helps us to see whether or not history, maturation, testing, instrumentation, regression, or mortality threaten internal validity. If

Figure 7.6
Solomon four-group design.

Group	Pretest	Treatment	Posttest
1. Experimental	O_1	X	O_2
2. Control	O_3		O_4
3. Experimental		X	O_5
4. Control			O_6

Treatment effect (E) could be judged by:
$$E = (O_2 - O_1)$$
$$E = (O_2 - O_4)$$
$$E = (O_5 - O_6)$$
$$E = (O_5 - O_3)$$
$$E = [(O_2 - O_1) - (O_4 - O_3)]$$
If all Es are similar, the cause-and-effect relationship is highly valid.

scores O_3 and O_4 (pre- and posttest scores of Group 2) remain the same, then it is established that neither history, nor maturation, nor testing, nor instrumentation, nor statistical regression, nor morality has had an impact. In other words, these have had no impact at all.

Group 3, the experimental group that was not given a pretest, helps to establish whether or not testing effects have affected internal validity in a given experiment. The difference, if any, between O_2 (the posttest score of Group 1, which was exposed to a treatment and also took a pretest) and O_5 (the posttest score of Group 3, which was exposed to a treatment but did not take the pretest), can be attributed to the testing effects. If, however, O_2 and O_5 are equal, then internal validity has not been thwarted by testing effects.

Group 4 (which has had only the posttest score but not the pretest or exposure to any treatment) helps us to see whether or not changes in the posttest scores for our experimental group are a function of the combined effects of history and maturation by comparing O_6 (the posttest score of the control group without the pretest) with O_1 (the pretest score of the experimental group that was exposed to a pretest) and O_3 (the pretest score of the control group that was exposed to a pretest as well). If all three scores are similar, maturation and history effects have not been a problem.

Thus, the Solomon four-group experimental design guarantees the maximum internal validity, ruling out many other rival hypotheses. Where establishing cause-and-effect relationship is critical for the survival of businesses, as for example pharmaceutical companies, which often face lawsuits for questionable products, the Solomon four-group design is eminently useful. However, because of the number of subjects that need to be recruited, the care with which the study has to be designed, the time that needs to be devoted to the experiment, and other reasons, the cost of conducting such an experiment is high. The experimental setup shown in Figure 7.4 with one experimental and one control group, exposing both to the posttest only, is a viable alternative since it has many of the advantages of the Solomon four-group design and can do with just half the number of subjects.

Table 7.2 summarizes the threats to internal validity covered by the different experimental designs. If the subjects have all been randomly assigned to the groups, then selection biases and statistical regression are eliminated in all cases.

Double-Blind Studies

When extreme care and rigor are needed in experimental designs as in the case of discovery of new medicines that could impact on human lives, blind studies are conducted to avoid any bias that might creep in. For example, pharmaceutical companies experimenting with the efficacy of newly developed drugs in the prototype stage ensure that the subjects in the experimental and control groups are kept unaware of who is given the drug, and who the placebo. Such studies are called *blind studies*.

When Aviron tested and announced the Flu-mist vaccine, neither the subjects nor the researchers who administered the vaccine to them were aware of the

Table 7.2

Major Threats to Internal Validity in Different Experimental Designs When Members Are Randomly Selected and Assigned

Types of Experimental Designs	Major Threats to Internal Validity
1. Pretest & posttest with one experimental group only	Testing, history, maturation
2. Posttests only with one experimental and one control group	Maturation
3. Pretest & posttest with one experimental and one control group	Mortality
4. Solomon four-group design	Mortality

"true" versus the "placebo" treatment. The entire process was conducted by an outside testing agency which alone knew who got what treatment. Since both the experimenter and the subjects are blinded, such studies are called **double-blind studies.** Since there is no tampering with the treatment in any way, such experimental studies are the least biased.

As mentioned previously, managers rarely undertake the study of cause-and-effect relationships in organizations using experimental designs because of the inconveniences and disruptions they cause to the system.

Ex Post Facto Designs

Cause-and-effect relationships are sometimes established through what is called the ex post facto design. Here, there is no manipulation of the independent variable in the lab or field setting, but subjects who have already been exposed to a stimulus and those not so exposed are studied. For instance, training programs might have been introduced in an organization 2 years earlier. Some might have already gone through the training while others might not. To study the effects of training on work performance, performance data might now be collected for both groups. Since the study does not immediately follow after the training, but much later, it is an ex post facto design.

More advanced experimental designs such as the completely randomized design, randomized block design, Latin square design, and the factorial design are described in the Appendix to this chapter, for the student interested in these.

SIMULATION

An alternative to lab and field experimentation currently being used in business research is simulation. Simulation uses a model-building technique to determine the effects of changes, and computer-based simulations are becoming popular in business research. A simulation can be thought of as an experiment conducted in a specially created setting that very closely represents the natural environment in which activities are usually carried on. In that sense, the simulation lies somewhere between a lab and a field experiment, insofar as the environment is artificially created but not far different from "reality." Participants are exposed to real-world experiences over a period of time, lasting anywhere from several hours to several weeks, and they can be randomly assigned to different treatment groups. If managerial behavior as a function of a specific treatment is to be studied, subjects will be asked to operate in an environment very much like an office, with desks, chairs, cabinets, telephones, and the like. Members will be randomly assigned the roles of directors, managers, clerks, and so on, and specific stimuli will be presented to them. Thus, while the researcher would retain control over the assignment and manipulation, the subjects would be left free to operate as in a real office. In essence, some factors will be built into or incorporated in the simulated system and others left free to vary (participants' behavior, within the rules of the game). Data on the dependent variable can be obtained through observation, videotaping, audio recording, interviews, or questionnaires.

Causal relationships can be tested since both manipulation and control are possible in simulations. Two types of simulations can be done: one in which the nature and timing of simulated events are totally determined by the researcher (called experimental simulation), and the other (called free simulation) where the course of activities is at least partly governed by the reaction of the participants to the various stimuli as they interact among themselves. **Looking Glass,** the free simulation developed by Lombardo, McCall, and DeVries (1983) to study leadership styles, has been quite popular in the management area.

Cause-and-effect relationships are better established in experimental simulations where the researcher exercises greater control. In simulations involving several weeks, however, there could be a high rate of attrition of members. Experimental and free simulations are both expensive, since creating real-world conditions in an artificial setting and collecting data over extended periods of time involve the deployment of many types of resources. Simulations can be done in specially created settings using subjects, computers, and mathematical models. Steufert, Pogash, and Piasecki (1988), who assessed managerial competence through a 6-hour computer-assisted simulation, are of opinion that simulation technology may be the only viable method to simultaneously study several types of executive styles. Computer-based simulations are frequently used in the accounting and finance areas. For example, the effectiveness of various analytic review procedures in detecting errors in account balances has been tested through simulations (Knechel, 1986). In the finance area, risk management has been studied through simulations. Simulations have also been used to understand the complex relationships in the financing of pension plans and making important investment decisions (Perrier & Kalwarski, 1989). It is possible to vary several variables (workforce demographics, inflation rates, etc.) singly or simultaneously in such models.

Prototypes of machines and instruments are often the result of simulated models. Simulation has also been used by many companies to test the robustness and efficacy of various products. We are also familiar with flight simulators, driving simulators, and even nuclear reactor simulators. Here, the visual patterns presented keep changing in response to the reactions of the individual (the pilot, the driver, or the emergency handler) to the previous stimulus presented, and not in any predetermined order. Entire business operations, from office layout to profitability, can be simulated using different prospective scenarios. With increasing access to sophisticated technology, and the advancement of mathematical models, simulation is becoming an important managerial decision-making tool. It is quite likely that we will see simulation being used as a managerial tool to enhance motivation, leadership, and the like, in the future. Simulation can also be applied as a problem-solving managerial tool in other behavioral and administrative areas. Programmed, computer-based simulation models in behavioral areas could serve managerial decision making very well indeed.

ETHICAL ISSUES IN EXPERIMENTAL DESIGN RESEARCH

It is appropriate at this juncture to briefly discuss a few of the many ethical issues involved in doing research, some of which are particularly relevant to conducting lab experiments. The following practices are considered *unethical:*

- Putting pressure on individuals to participate in experiments through coercion, or applying social pressure.
- Giving menial tasks and asking demeaning questions that diminish their self-respect.
- Deceiving subjects by deliberately misleading them as to the true purpose of the research.
- Exposing participants to physical or mental stress.
- Not allowing subjects to withdraw from the research when they want to.
- Using the research results to disadvantage the participants, or for purposes not to their liking.
- Not explaining the procedures to be followed in the experiment.
- Exposing respondents to hazardous and unsafe environments as we saw earlier in the case of Johns Hopkins University.
- Not debriefing participants fully and accurately after the experiment is over.
- Not preserving the privacy and confidentiality of the information given by the participants.
- Withholding benefits from control groups.

The last item is somewhat controversial as to whether or not it should be an ethical dilemma, especially in organizational research. If three different incentives are offered for three experimental groups and none is offered to the control group, it is a fact that the control group has participated in the experiment with absolutely no benefit. Similarly, if four different experimental groups receive four different levels of training but the control group does not, the other four groups have gained expertise that the control group has been denied. But should this be deemed to become an ethical dilemma *preventing* experimental designs with control groups in organizational research? Perhaps not, for at least three reasons. One is that several others in the system who did not participate in the experiment did not benefit either. Second, even in the experimental groups, some would have benefited more than the others (depending on the extent to which the causal factor is manipulated). Finally, if a cause-and-effect relationship is found, the system would in all probability implement the newfound knowledge sooner or later and everyone would ultimately stand to gain. The assumption that the control group did not benefit from participating in the experiment may not be a sufficient reason not to use lab or field experiments.

Many universities have a "human subjects committee" to protect the right of individuals participating in any type of research activity involving people. The basic function of these committees is to discharge the moral and ethical responsibilities of the university system by studying the procedures outlined in the research proposals and giving their stamp of approval to the study. The human subjects committee might require the investigators to modify their procedures or inform the subjects fully, if occasion demanded it.

MANAGERIAL IMPLICATIONS

Before using experimental designs in research studies, it is essential to consider whether they are necessary at all, and if so, at what level of sophistication. This is because experimental designs call for special efforts and varying degrees of interference with the natural flow of activities. Some questions that need to be addressed in making these decisions, are the following:

1. Is it really necessary to identify causal relationships, or would it suffice if the correlates that account for the variance in the dependent variable were known?

2. If it is important to trace the causal relationships, which of the two, internal validity or external validity, is needed more, or are both needed? If only internal validity is important, a carefully designed lab experiment would be the answer; if generalizability is the more important criterion, then a field experiment would be called for; if both are equally important, then a lab study should be first undertaken, followed by a field experiment, if the results of the former warrant the latter.

3. Is cost an important factor in the study? If so, would a less rather than more sophisticated experimental design do?

These decision points are illustrated in the chart in Figure 7.7.

Though managers may not often be interested in cause-and-effect relationships, a good knowledge of experimental designs could foster some pilot studies to be undertaken to examine if factors such as bonus systems, piece rates, rest pauses, and so on lead to positive outcomes such as better motivation,

Figure 7.7

Decision points for embarking on an experimental design.

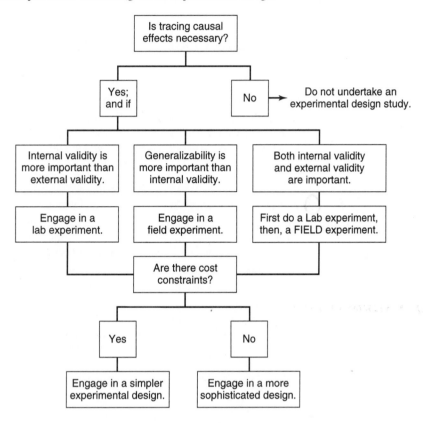

improved job performance, and other favorable working conditions at the workplace. Marketing managers would be able to use experimental designs to study the effects on sales of advertisements, sales promotions, pricing, and the like. Awareness of the usefulness of simulation as a research tool can also result in creative research endeavors in the management area, as it currently does in the manufacturing side of businesses.

SUMMARY

This chapter covered experimental designs, with particular reference to lab and field experiments. We examined how the contaminating variables in detecting the cause-and-effect relationship can be controlled through the processes of matching and randomization. Issues of internal and external validity and the seven factors that could affect internal validity were discussed. Also, some types of experimental designs that can be used to test cause-and-effect relationships and their usefulness in the context of validity and practicality were examined. We also described the ethical issues involved in conducting experimental research and the implications for managers in using experimental designs.

The next chapter discusses how the variables—whether in a field survey or in an experimental design—can be measured.

DISCUSSION QUESTIONS AND POINTS TO PONDER

1. What are the differences between causal and correlational studies?

2. In what ways do lab experiments differ from field experiments?

3. Define the terms *control* and *manipulation*. Describe a possible lab experiment where you would need to control a variable. Include also a possible variable over which you would have no control but which could affect your experiment.

4. Explain the possible ways in which you can control "nuisance" variables.

5. What is internal validity and what are the threats it stands exposed to?

6. Explain the concept of "trade-off between internal validity and external validity."

7. Explain fully how you would demonstrate to machine operators and convince them through research that thorough knowledge of the operating policies and procedures (by reading the manual) would eliminate almost all "on-the-job" accidents.

8. "If a control group is a part of an experimental design, one need not worry about controlling other exogenous variables." Discuss this statement.

9. A researcher wants to set up a lab experiment to test the effects of different kinds of leadership styles on followers' attitudes. The three particular kinds of leadership styles she is interested in are autocratic, democratic, and participative. You are asked to enlist some students to play the part of followers. What cover story would you give the participants?

10. Comment on the following statement: "Because the external validity of lab experiments is not usually high, they are useless for investigating cause and effect relationships in organizations."

11. "Covariance—that is, two variables varying together either positively or negatively—and control are integral aspects of experimental designs." Discuss.

12. "The Solomon four-group design is the answer to all our research questions pertaining to cause-and-effect relations because it guards against all the threats to internal validity." Comment.

13. Below is an adapted note from *Business Week* published some time ago. After reading it, apply what you have learned in this chapter, and design a study after sketching the theoretical framework.

The Vital Role of Self-Esteem

Why do some people earn more than others? Economists focused on the importance of education, basic skills, and work experience—what they called human capital—on increased productivity, and said these were reflected in greater earning power. Researchers also found that self-esteem was instrumental in acquiring human capital.

---

14. Design a study to examine the following situation.

> An organization would like to introduce one of two types of new manufacturing processes to increase the productivity of workers, and both involve heavy investment in expensive technology. The company wants to test the efficacy of each process in one of its small plants.

assign groups to consider the 4 designs in the following Appendix ... come up w/ Q's pertaining to each & have each group present ... findings to class

APPENDIX

FURTHER EXPERMENTAL DESIGNS

In this chapter we discussed different types of experimental designs where groups were subjected to one or more treatments and the effects of the manipulation measured. However, the simultaneous effects of two or more variables on a dependent variable may sometimes be desired to be assessed, and this would call for more complex designs. Among the many advanced experimental designs that are available, we will examine here the completely randomized design, the randomized block design, Latin square design, and the factorial design.

It would be useful to understand some terms before describing the various designs. The term **factor** is used to denote an independent variable—for example, price. The term **level** is used to denote various gradations of the factor—for example, high price, medium price, low price—while making it clear as to what these gradations signify (e.g., high price is anything over $2 per piece; medium is $1–$2 per piece; low price is anything less than $1 per piece). **Treatment** refers to the various levels of the factors. A **blocking factor** is a preexisting variable in a given situation that might have an effect on the dependent variable in addition to the treatment, the impact of which would be important to assess. In effect, a blocking factor is an independent variable that has an effect on the dependent variable, but which preexists in a given situation, as for example, the number of women and men in an organization; or teenagers, middle-aged men, and senior citizens as customers of a store, and so on.

THE COMPLETELY RANDOMIZED DESIGN

Let us say that a bus transportation company manager wants to know the effects of fare reduction by 5, 7, and 10 cents, on the average daily increase in the number of passengers using the bus as a means of transportation. He may take 27 routes that the buses usually ply, and randomly assign nine routes for each of the treatments (i.e., reduction of fares by 5, 7, and 10 cents) for a 2-week period. His experimental design would look as shown in Figure 7.8, where the Os on the left indicate the number of passengers that used the bus for the 2 weeks preceding the treatment; X_1, X_2, and X_3 indicate the three different treatments (fare reductions of 5, 7, and 10 cents per mile), and the Os on the right indicate the number of passengers that used the bus as the transportation mode during the 2 weeks when the fares were reduced. The manager will be able to assess the impact of the three treatments by deducting each of the three Os on the left from its corresponding O on the right. The results of this study would provide the answer to the bus company manager's question.

Figure 7.8

Illustration of a completely randomized design.

Routes	Number of Passengers Before	Treatment	Number of Passengers After
Group 1 of nine routes	O_1	X_1	O_2
Group 2 of nine routes	O_3	X_2	O_4
Group 3 of nine routes	O_5	X_3	O_6

RANDOMIZED BLOCK DESIGN

In the foregoing case, the bus company manager was interested only in the effects of different levels of price reduction on the increase in the number of passengers, in general. He may be more interested however, in targeting the price reduction on the right routes or sectors. For example, it is likely that the reduction in fares will be more welcome to senior citizens and residents of crowded urban areas where driving is stressful, than to car owners living in the suburbs, who may not be equally appreciative of and sensitive to price reduction. Thus, reduction in fares would attract more passengers if targeted to the right groups (i.e., the right blocking factor—the residential areas). In this case, the bus company manager would first identify the routes that would fall into the three blocks—those in suburbs, crowded urban areas, or residential areas of retirees. Thus, the 27 routes would get assigned to one or the other of three blocks and then randomly assigned, within blocks, to the three treatments. The experimental design would now look as in Figure 7.9.

Through the above randomized block design, not only can the direct effect of each treatment (i.e., the main effect of the level, which is the effect of each type of fare reduction) be assessed, but also the joint effects of price and the residential area route (the interaction effect). For example, the general effect of a 5-cent reduction for all routes will be known by the increase in passengers across

Figure 7.9

Illustration of a randomized block design.

Fare Reduction	Blocking Factor: Residential Areas		
	Suburbs	Crowded Urban Areas	Retirement Areas
5c	X_1	X_1	X_1
7c	X_2	X_2	X_2
10c	X_3	X_3	X_3

Note that the Xs above only indicate various levels of the blocking factor and the Os (the number of passengers before and after each treatment at each level) are not shown, though these measures will be taken.

all three residential areas, and the general effect of a 5-cent reduction on those in the suburbs alone will also be known by seeing the effects in the first cell. If the highest average daily number of increased passengers is 75 for a 7-cent decrease for the crowded urban area route, followed by an increase of 30 for the retirees' areas for the 10-cent decrease, and an increase of 5 passengers for a 5-cent reduction for the suburbs, the bus company manager can work out a cost-benefit analysis and decide on the course of action to be taken. Thus, the randomized block design is a more powerful technique, providing more information for decision making. However, the cost of this experimental design will be higher.

LATIN SQUARE DESIGN

Whereas the randomized block design helps the experimenter to minimize the effects of one nuisance variable (variation among the rows) in evaluating the treatment effects, the Latin square design is very useful when two nuisance blocking factors (i.e., variations across both the rows and the columns) are to be controlled. Each treatment appears an equal number of times in any one ordinal position in each row. For instance, in studying the effects of bus fare reduction on passengers, two nuisance factors could be (1) the day of the week: (a) midweek (Tuesday through Thursday), (b) weekend, (c) Monday and Friday, and (2) the (three) residential localities of the passengers. A three by three Latin square design can be created in this case, to which will be randomly assigned the three treatments (5, 7, and 10 cent fare reduction), such that each treatment occurs only once in each row and column intersection. The Latin square design would look as in Figure 7.10. After the experiment is carried out and the net increase in passengers under each treatment calculated, the average treatment effects can be gauged. The price reduction that offers the best advantage can also be assessed.

A problem with the Latin square design is that it presupposes the absence of interaction between the treatments and blocking factors, which may not always be the case. We also need as many cells as there are treatments. Furthermore, it is an uneconomical design compared to some others.

Figure 7.10
Illustration of the Latin square design.

Residential Area	Day of the Week		
	Midweek	Weekend	Monday/Friday
Suburbs	X_1	X_2	X_3
Urban	X_2	X_3	X_1
Retirement	X_3	X_1	X_2

Figure 7.11
Illustration of a 3 × 3 factorial design.

Type of Bus	Bus Fare Reduction Rates		
	5c	7c	10c
Luxury Express	X_1Y_1	X_2Y_1	X_3Y_1
Standard Express	X_2Y_2	X_1Y_2	X_3Y_2
Regular	X_3Y_3	X_2Y_3	X_1Y_3

FACTORIAL DESIGN

Thus far we have discussed experimental designs in the context of examining a cause-and-effect relationship between one independent variable and the dependent variable. The factorial design enables us to test the effects of *two or more manipulations* at the same time on the dependent variable. In other words, two treatments can be simultaneously manipulated and their single and joint (known as main and interaction) effects assessed. For example, the manager of the bus company might be interested in knowing passenger increases if he used three different types of buses (Luxury Express, Standard Express, Regular) and manipulated both the fare reduction and the type of vehicle used, simultaneously. Figure 7.11 illustrates the 3 × 3 factorial design that will be used for the purpose.

Here, two factors are used with three levels of each. The above is completely randomized, since the fares are randomly assigned to one of nine treatment combinations. A wealth of information can be obtained from this design. For example, the bus company manager would know the increase in passengers for each fare reduction, for each type of vehicle, and for the two in combination. Thus, the main effects of the two independent variables as well as the interactions among them can be assessed. For this reason, the factorial design is more efficient than several single-factor randomized designs.

It is also statistically possible to control one or more variables through **covariance analysis.** For example, it may be suspected that even after randomly assigning members to treatments, there is a further "nuisance" factor. It is possible to statistically block such factors while analyzing the data.

Several other complex experimental designs are also available and are treated in books devoted to experimental designs.

MEASUREMENT OF VARIABLES: OPERATIONAL DEFINITION AND SCALES

TOPICS DISCUSSED

MEASUREMENT OF VARIABLES

OPERATIONAL DEFINITION

- Dimensions and Elements of Concepts
- What an Operational Definition Is Not

THE FOUR TYPES OF SCALES

- Nominal
- Ordinal
- Interval
- Ratio

INTERNATIONAL DIMENSIONS OF OPERATIONAL DEFINITION
  AND SCALING

CHAPTER OBJECTIVES

1. After completing Chapter 8, you should be able to operationally define (or operationalize) concepts.
2. You should know the characteristics and power of the four types of scales—nominal, ordinal, interval, and ratio.

Measurement of the variables in the theoretical framework is an integral part of research and an important aspect of research design (see shaded portion in figure on next page). Unless the variables are measured in some way, we will not be able to test our hypotheses and find answers to complex research issues. In this chapter, we will discuss how variables lend themselves to measurement.

HOW VARIABLES ARE MEASURED

Objects that can be physically measured by some calibrated instruments pose no measurement problems. For example, the length and width of a rectangular

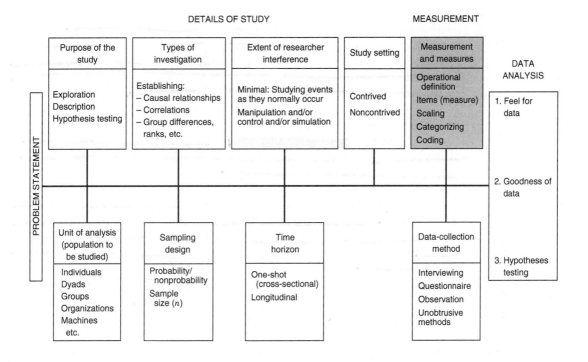

office table can be easily measured with a measuring tape or a ruler. The same is true for measuring the office floor area. Data representing several demographic characteristics of the office personnel are also easily obtained by asking employees simple, straightforward questions, as for example:

- How long have you been working in this organization?
- How long have you been working on this particular assignment?
- What is your job title?
- What is your marital status?

One can also check the company records to obtain or verify certain types of information, as for example, the absenteeism of employees or their objective performance in terms of the number of products produced or the rejects during the course of each month. However, even such objective data might, in some cases, call for careful interpretation while making managerial decisions. For example, the decision to fire a factory worker would depend on whether he was responsible for 10 rejects during a particular day because he was running a high fever (one incident of a day's bad work that was beyond the control of the worker), or if he had 10 days of several instances of rejects over the course of a month because he is just a slipshod worker (10 *incidents of laxity*). Here, the number of incidents and the motivation of the worker are likely to play a part in decision making.

Certain things lend themselves to easy measurement through the use of appropriate measuring instruments, as for example, physiological phenomena pertaining to human beings such as blood pressure, pulse rates, and body temperature, as well as certain physical attributes such as height and weight. But when we get into the realm of people's subjective feelings, attitudes, and perceptions, the measurement of these factors or variables becomes difficult. This is one of the aspects of organizational behavior and management research that adds to the complexity of research studies.

There are at least two types of variables: One lends itself to objective and precise measurement; the other is more nebulous and does not lend itself to accurate measurement because of its subjective nature. However, despite the lack of physical measuring devices to measure the latter type, there are ways of tapping the subjective feelings and perceptions of individuals. One technique is to reduce the abstract notions, or concepts such as motivation, involvement, satisfaction, buyer behavior, stock market exuberance, and the like, to observable behavior and characteristics. In other words, the abstract notions are broken down into observable characteristic behavior. For instance, the concept of thirst is abstract; we cannot see thirst. However, we would expect a thirsty person to drink plenty of fluids. In other words, the expected reaction of people to thirst is to drink fluids. If several people say they are thirsty, then we may determine the thirst levels of each of these individuals by the measure of the quantity of fluids that they drink to quench their thirst. We will thus be able to measure their levels of thirst, even though the concept of thirst itself is abstract and nebulous. Reduction of abstract concepts to render them measurable in a tangible way is called operationalizing the concepts.

OPERATIONAL DEFINITION: DIMENSIONS AND ELEMENTS

Operationalizing, or operationally defining a concept to render it measurable, is done by looking at the behavioral dimensions, facets, or properties denoted by the concept. These are then translated into observable and measurable elements so as to develop an index of measurement of the concept. Operationally defining a concept involves a series of steps. An example will help to illustrate how this is done.

Example 8.1

OPERATIONALIZING THE CONCEPT OF ACHIEVEMENT MOTIVATION

Let us try to operationally define achievement motivation, a concept of interest to educators, managers, and students alike. What behavioral dimensions or facets or characteristics would we expect to find in people with high achievement motivation? They would probably have the following five typical broad characteristics, which we will call *dimensions*.

1. They would be driven by work; that is, they would be working almost round the clock in order to derive the satisfaction of having "achieved and accomplished."

2. Many of them would generally be in no mood to relax and direct their attention to other than work-related activity.

3. Because they want always to be achieving and accomplishing, they would prefer to work on their own rather than with others.

4. With mind and heart set on accomplishment and achievement, they would rather engage in challenging jobs rather than easy, hum-drum ones. However, they would not want to take on excessively challenging jobs because the expectation and probability of accomplishment and achievement in such jobs would not be very high.

5. They would be yearning to know how they are progressing in their jobs as they go along. That is, they would like to get frequent feedback in direct and subtle ways from their superiors, colleagues, and on occasions even their subordinates, to know how they are progressing.

Thus, we would expect those with high achievement motivation to drive themselves hard at work, find it difficult to relax, prefer to work alone, engage in challenging, but not too challenging jobs, and seek feedback. Although breaking the concept into these five dimensions has somewhat reduced its level of abstraction, we have still not operationalized the concept into measurable elements of behavior. This could be done by examining each of the five dimensions and breaking each further into its elements, thus delineating the actual patterns of behavior that would be exhibited. These should somehow be quantitatively measurable so that we can distinguish those who have high motivation from those with less. Let us see how this can be done.

Elements of Dimension 1

It is possible to describe the behavior of a person who is driven by work. Such a person will (1) be at work all the time, (2) be reluctant to take time off from work, and (3) persevere even in the face of some setbacks. These types of behavior would lend themselves to measurement.

For instance, we can count the number of hours employees engage themselves in work-related activities during work hours, beyond working hours at the workplace, and at home where they are likely to pursue their unfinished assignments. Thus, the number of hours put in by them on their work would be an index of the extent to which work "drives" them.

Next, keeping track of how frequently people continue to persevere doing their job despite failures is a reflection of how persevering they are in achieving their goals. A student who drops out of school due to failure to pass the first exam can by no means be deemed to be a highly persevering, achievement-oriented individual. However, a student who, despite getting D grades on three quizzes, toils day and night unceasingly in order to understand and master a course he considers difficult, would exhibit persevering and achievement-oriented behaviors. Achievement-motivated individuals would not usually want to give up on their tasks even when confronted by initial failures. Perseverance would urge them to continue. Hence, a measure of perseverance could be obtained by the number of setbacks people experience on the task and yet continue to work undaunted by failures. For example, an accountant might find that she is unable to balance the books. She spends an hour trying to detect the error, fails to do so, gives up, and leaves the workplace. Another employee in the same position stays patiently on the job, discovers the error, and balances the books spending the entire evening in the process. In this case it is easy to tell which of the two is the more persevering by merely observing them.

Finally, in order to measure the reluctance to take time off, we need only know how frequently people take time off from their jobs, and for what reasons. If an employee is found to have taken 7 days off during the previous 6 months to watch football games, attend an out-of-town circus, and visit friends, we would conclude that the individual would probably not hesitate to take time away from the job. However, if an individual has never been absent even a single day during the past 15 months, and has not missed work even when slightly indisposed, it is evident that he is too dedicated to work to take time off from the job.

Thus, if we can measure how many hours per week individuals spend on work-related activities, how persevering they are in completing their daily tasks, and how frequently and for what reasons they take time off from their jobs, we would have a measure of the extent to which employees are driven by work. This variable, when thus measured, would place individuals on a continuum ranging from those who are least driven by work, to those whose very life is work. This, then, would give some indication of the extent of their achievement motivation.

Figure 8.1 schematically diagrams the dimensions (the several facets or main characteristics) and the elements (representative behaviors) for the concept of achievement motivation. Frequent reference to this figure will help you follow the ensuing discussions.

Elements of Dimension 2

The degree of unwillingness to relax can be measured by asking persons such questions as (1) how often do you think about work while you are away from the workplace? (2) what are your hobbies? and (3) how do you spend your time when you are away from the workplace? Those who are able to relax would indicate that they do not generally think about work or the workplace while at home, spend time on hobbies, engage in leisure-time activities, and spend their waking hours with the family or in other social or cultural activities.

Thus, we can place employees on a continuum ranging from those who relax very well to those who relax very little. This dimension also then becomes measurable.

Elements of Dimension 3

Individuals with high achievement motivation have no patience with ineffective people and are reluctant to work with others. Whereas achievement-motivated persons in the organization may rank very high on these behavioral predispositions,

Figure 8.1

Dimensions (D) and elements (E) of the concept (C) achievement motivation.

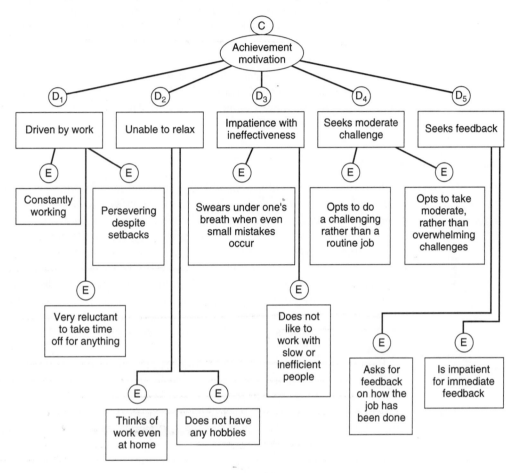

there may be others who are not highly achievement motivated. The latter may not at all mind ineffectiveness in either themselves or others, and may be quite willing to work with almost anybody. Thus impatience with ineffectiveness can also be measured by observing behavior.

Elements of Dimension 4

A measure of how excited people are at seeking challenging jobs can be had by asking employees what kinds of jobs they prefer. A number of different job descriptions can be presented—some jobs entailing stereotyped work of a routine nature, and others calling for gradations of challenges built into them. Employee preferences for different types of jobs could then be placed on a continuum ranging from those who prefer fairly routine jobs to those who prefer jobs with a progressive increase in challenge. Those opting for medium degrees of challenge are likely to be more achievement motivated than those who opt for either lower or higher degrees of challenge. The achievement-oriented individuals tend to be realistic and choose jobs that are reasonably challenging and within reach of accomplishment. The heedless and overconfident persons would perhaps choose the highly challenging jobs where the success is slow in coming, oblivious to whether or not the end results will be achieved. Those who are low in achievement motivation would perhaps choose the more routine type of jobs. Thus, those seeking moderate challenges can also be identified.

Elements of Dimension 5

Those who desire feedback would seek it from their superiors, co-workers, and sometimes even from their subordinates. They would want to know others' opinions on how well they are performing. Feedback, both positive and negative, would indicate to them how much they are achieving and accomplishing. If they receive messages suggesting a need for improvement, they will act on them. Hence, they would be constantly seeking feedback from several sources. By keeping track of how often individuals seek feedback from others during a certain period of time—say, over several months—employees can again be placed on a continuum ranging from those who seek extensive feedback from all sources to those who never seek any feedback from anyone at any time.

Having thus operationalized the concept of achievement motivation by reducing its level of abstraction to observable behaviors, it is possible to develop a good measure to tap the concept of achievement motivation. Its usefulness is that others could use the same measure, thus ensuring replicability. It should, however, be recognized, that any operational definition is likely to (1) exclude some of the important dimensions and elements arising from failure to recognize or conceptualize them, and (2) include certain irrelevant features, mistakenly thought to be relevant. You would recall that we had earlier pointed out that management research cannot be 100% scientific because we do not have the "perfect" measuring instruments.

Operationally defining the concept, nevertheless, is the best way to measure it. However, actually observing and counting the number of times individuals behave in particular ways, even if practical, would be too laborious and time consuming. So, instead of actually observing the behaviors of individuals, we could ask them to report their own behavior patterns by asking them appropriate questions, which they can respond to on some scale that we provide. In Example 8.2 we will look at the type of questions that may be asked to tap achievement motivation.

Example 8.2   Answers to the following questions from respondents would be one way of tapping the level of achievement motivation.

1. To what extent would you say you push yourself to get the job done on time?
2. How difficult do you find it to continue to do your work in the face of initial failures or discouraging results?
3. How often do you neglect personal matters because you are preoccupied with your job?
4. How frequently do you think of your work when you are at home?
5. To what extent do you engage yourself in hobbies?
6. How disappointed would you feel if you did not reach the goals you had set for yourself?
7. How much do you concentrate on achieving your goals?
8. How annoyed do you get when you make mistakes?
9. To what extent would you prefer to work with a friendly but incompetent colleague, rather than a difficult but competent one?
10. To what extent would you prefer to work by yourself rather than with others?
11. To what extent would you prefer a job that is difficult but challenging, to one that is easy and routine?
12. To what extent would you prefer to take on extremely difficult assignments rather than moderately challenging ones?
13. During the past 3 months, how often have you sought feedback from your superiors on how well you are performing your job?
14. How often have you tried to obtain feedback on your performance from your co-workers during the past 3 months?
15. How often during the past 3 months have you checked with your subordinates that what you are doing is not getting in the way of their efficient performance?
16. To what extent would it frustrate you if people did not give you feedback on how you are progressing?

The foregoing illustrates a possible way to measure variables relating to the subjective domain of people's attitudes, feelings, and perceptions by first operationally defining the concept. Operational definition consists in the reduction of the concept from its level of abstraction, by breaking it into its dimensions and elements, as discussed. By tapping the behaviors associated with a concept, we can measure the variable. Of course, the questions will ask for responses on some scale attached to them (such as "very little" to "very much"), which we will discuss in the next chapter.

What an Operational Definition Is Not

Just as important as it is to understand what an operational definition is, equally important is it to remember what it is not. An operational definition does not describe the correlates of the concept. For example, success in performance cannot be a dimension of achievement motivation, even though a motivated person is likely to meet with it in large measure. Thus, achievement motivation and performance and/or success may be highly correlated, but we cannot measure an individual's level of motivation through success and performance. Performance and success could have been made possible as a consequence of achievement motivation, but in and of themselves, the two are not measures of it. To elaborate, a person with high achievement motivation might have failed for some reason, perhaps beyond her control, to perform the job successfully. Thus, if we judge the achievement motivation of this person with performance as the yardstick, we would have measured the wrong concept. Instead of measuring achievement motivation—our variable of interest—we would have measured performance, another variable we had not intended to measure nor were interested in.

Thus, it is clear that operationally defining a concept does not consist of delineating the reasons, antecedents, consequences, or correlates of the concept. Rather, it describes its observable characteristics in order to be able to measure the concept. It is important to remember this because if we either operationalize the concepts incorrectly or confuse them with other concepts, then we will not have valid measures. This means that we will not have "good" data, and our research will not be scientific.

Having seen what an operational definition is, and what it is not, let us now operationally define another concept that is relevant to the classroom: the concept of "learning."

Example 8.3

OPERATIONALIZING THE CONCEPT OF LEARNING
Learning is an important concept in the educational setting. Teachers tend to measure student learning through exams. Students quite often feel, probably rightly, that exams do not really measure learning—at least not the multiple-choice questions that are asked in exams.

How then might we measure the abstract concept called learning? As before, we need to define the concept operationally and break it down to observable and measurable behaviors. In other words, we should delineate the dimensions and elements of the concept of learning. The dimensions of learning may well be as follows:

1. Understanding   2. Retention   3. Application

In other words, we can be reasonably certain that a student in the class is "learning" when the individual (1) understands what is taught in the classroom, (2) retains (i.e., remembers) what is understood, and (3) applies whatever has been understood and remembered.

Terms such as understanding, remembering, and applying are still abstract even though they have helped us to get a better grasp of what learning is all about. It is necessary to break these three dimensions into elements so that we

Figure 8.2
Dimensions (D) and elements (E) of the concept (C) learning.

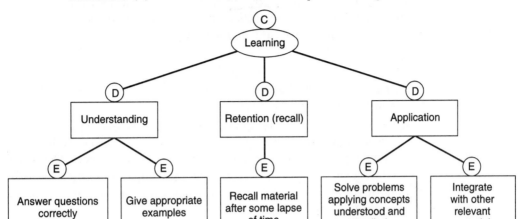

can measure the concept of learning. A schematic diagram of the operational definition of the concept of learning is shown in Figure 8.2. The diagram will facilitate our understanding of the discussion that follows.

A teacher can assess whether students have understood a concept that has been just taught by asking them to explain it and furnishing suitable examples. If they answer correctly, the teacher may assume that the students have understood. By giving a test a week or month later, the teacher can measure for how long they remember what has been taught. By asking them to apply the concepts learned in a new problem situation, the teacher can also measure how much they can put into application what is understood. If they solve the problem successfully using the material taught to them in class, the teacher will be reasonably assured that learning has indeed been achieved. To the extent that they do not successfully apply the concepts taught, learning might not have advanced to the degree expected. Note that in this case, **application** of the relevant concepts subsumes both **understanding** and **retention.** That is, one cannot apply the concepts unless one has understood them *and* retained them in memory. In most multiple-choice questions, understanding and retention are generally tested; the application aspects are often not. Exams, when properly designed, could be an effective instrument for assessing the learning that students acquire during the semester. In other words, it is possible to reliably measure learning when exam questions are well designed to tap the students' understanding, retention, and ability to apply what has been taught.

Again, it is very important to remember that learning is no measure of the effort the teacher expends in explaining, nor that put in by the student to understand, though both of these naturally tend to enhance understanding. Although both may be correlated to learning they do not actually measure it.

A Measure of Student Learning

An exam that measures *learning* in students (i.e., if they have grasped the concept of motivation) would include the following questions (the particular dimensions tapped are shown in parentheses):

1. Define the concept of motivation *(recall)*.
2. State the various theories of motivation and explain them, giving examples *(understanding and recall)*.
3. In the beginning of the semester, the class was split into two debate teams, one to argue for the manager's role as a motivator, and the other that it is outside the province of a manager to motivate the employees. State three important arguments advanced by each group *(understanding* and *recall)*.
4. What is your viewpoint of the manager's role as motivator? *(understanding* and *analysis)*.
5. Describe three different situations in which a manager of a work organization would use equity theory, the expectancy theory, and job design to motivate employees *(application)*.
6. In the San Jose Camp case, how could Bob have been motivated to take interest in the camp's activities? Adequately defend your answer, citing the appropriate theories and why they are superior to some of the other possible solutions *(application,* which subsumes *understanding* and *retention)*.
7. How does motivation relate to leadership? How are both these concepts related to a manager's job? *(understanding, retention, application)*.

Review of Operational Definition

We have thus far examined how to operationally define concepts and to frame and ask questions that are likely to measure the concepts. Operational definitions are necessary to measure abstract concepts such as those that usually fall into the subjective areas of feelings and attitudes. More objective variables such as age or educational level are easily measured through simple straightforward questions and do not have to be operationally defined. Luckily, measures for many concepts that are relevant in the organizational context have already been developed by researchers. While you review the literature in a given area, you might want to particularly note the reference that discusses the instrument used to tap the concept in the study, and read it. The article will tell you when the measure was developed, by whom, and for how long it has been in use. Only a well-developed instrument, which has been operationally defined with care, will be accepted and frequently used by other researchers.

Now do Exercises 8.1 and 8.2.

SCALES

Now that we have learned how to operationalize concepts, we need to measure them in some manner. To this end, we will examine in this chapter the types of scales that can be applied to measure different variables and in the next, we will see how we actually apply them.

A scale is a tool or mechanism by which individuals are distinguished as to how they differ from one another on the variables of interest to our study. The scale or tool could be a gross one in the sense that it would only broadly categorize individuals on certain variables, or it could be a fine-tuned tool that would differentiate individuals on the variables with varying degrees of sophistication.

There are four basic types of scales: nominal, ordinal, interval, and ratio. The degree of sophistication to which the scales are fine-tuned increases progressively as we move from the nominal to the ratio scale. That is, information on the variables can be obtained in greater detail when we employ an interval or a ratio scale than the other two scales. As the calibration or fine-tuning of the scale increases in sophistication, so does the power of the scale. With more powerful scales, increasingly sophisticated data analyses can be performed, which, in turn, means that more meaningful answers can be found to our research questions. However, certain variables lend themselves with greater ease to more powerful scaling than others. Let us now examine each of these four scales.

Nominal Scale

A nominal scale is one that allows the researcher to assign subjects to certain categories or groups. For example, with respect to the variable of gender, respondents can be grouped into two categories—male and female. These two groups can be assigned code numbers 1 and 2. These numbers serve as simple and convenient category labels with no intrinsic value, other than to assign respondents to one of two nonoverlapping or *mutually exclusive* categories. Note that the categories are also *collectively exhaustive*. In other words, there is no third category into which respondents would normally fall. Thus, nominal scales categorize individuals or objects into mutually exclusive and collectively exhaustive groups. The information that can be generated from nominal scaling is to calculate the percentage (or frequency) of males and females in our sample of respondents. For example, if we had interviewed 200 people, and assigned code number 1 to all male respondents and number 2 to all female respondents, then computer analysis of the data at the end of the survey may show that 98 of the respondents are men and 102 are women. This frequency distribution tells us that 49% of the survey's respondents are men and 51% women. Other than this marginal information, such scaling tells us nothing more about the two groups. Thus the nominal scale gives some basic, categorical, gross information.

Example 8.4   Let us take a look at another variable that lends itself to nominal scaling—the nationality of individuals. We could nominally scale this variable in the following mutually exclusive and collectively exhaustive categories.

American	Japanese
Australian	Polish
Chinese	Russian
German	Swiss
Indian	Zambian
✳ Other	

Note that every respondent has to fit into one of the above eleven categories and that the scale will allow computation of the numbers and percentage of respondents that fit into them.

Now respond to Exercise 8.3.

Ordinal Scale

An ordinal scale not only categorizes the variables in such a way as to denote differences among the various categories, it also rank-orders the categories in some meaningful way. With any variable for which the categories are to be ordered according to some preference, the ordinal scale would be used. The preference would be ranked (e.g., from best to worst; first to last) and numbered 1, 2, and so on. For example, respondents might be asked to indicate their preferences by ranking the importance they attach to five distinct characteristics in a job that the researcher might be interested in studying. Such a question might take the following form:

Example 8.5

Rank the following five characteristics in a job in terms of how important they are for you. You should rank the most important item as 1, the next in importance as 2, and so on, until you have ranked each of them 1, 2, 3, 4, or 5.

Job Characteristic   **Ranking of Importance**

The opportunity provided by the job to:

1. Interact with others.   —

2. Use a number of different skills.   —

3. Complete a whole task from beginning to end.   —

4. Serve others.   —

5. Work independently.   —

The ordinal scale helps the researcher to determine the percentage of respondents who consider interaction with others as most important, those who consider using a number of different skills as most important, and so on. Such knowledge might help in designing jobs that would be seen as most enriched by the majority of the employees.

We can now see that the ordinal scale provides more information than the nominal scale. The ordinal scale goes beyond differentiating the categories to providing information on how respondents distinguish them by rank-ordering them. Note, however, that the ordinal scale does not give any indication of the magnitude of the differences among the ranks. For instance, in the job characteristics example, the first-ranked job characteristics might be only marginally preferred over the second-ranked characteristic, whereas the characteristic that is ranked third might be preferred in a much larger degree than the one ranked fourth. Thus, in ordinal scaling, even though differences in the ranking of objects, persons, or events investigated are clearly known, we do not know their magnitude. This deficiency is overcome by interval scaling, which is discussed next.

Now respond to Exercise 8.4.

Interval Scale

An interval scale allows us to perform certain arithmetical operations on the data collected from the respondents. Whereas the nominal scale allows us only to qualitatively distinguish groups by categorizing them into mutually exclusive and collectively exhaustive sets, and the ordinal scale to rank-order the preferences, the interval scale lets us measure the distance between any two points on the scale. This helps us to compute the means and the standard deviations of the responses on the variables. In other words, the interval scale not only groups individuals according to certain categories and taps the order of these groups, it also measures the magnitude of the differences in the preferences among the individuals. If, for instance, employees think that (1) it is more important for them to have a variety of skills in their jobs than to complete a task from beginning to end, and (2) it is more important for them to serve people than to work independently on the job, then the interval scale would indicate whether the first preference is to the same extent, a lesser extent, or a greater extent than the second. This can be done by now changing the scale from the ranking type in Example 8.5 to make it appear as if there were several points on a scale that would represent the extent or magnitude of the importance of each of the five job characteristics. Such a scale could be indicated for the job design example, as follows.

Example 8.6   Indicate the extent to which you agree with the following statements as they relate to your job, by *circling* the appropriate number against each, using the scale given below.

Strongly Disagree 1	Disagree 2	Neither Agree Nor Disagree 3	Agree 4	Strongly Agree 5

The following opportunities offered by the job are very important to me:

a. Interacting with others	1	2	3	4	5
b. Using a number of different skills	1	2	3	4	5
c. Completing a task from beginning to end	1	2	3	4	5
d. Serving others	1	2	3	4	5
e. Working independently	1	2	3	4	5

Let us illustrate how the interval scale establishes the equality of the magnitude of differences in the scale points. Let us suppose that employees circle the numbers 3, 1, 2, 4, and 5 for the five items in Example 8.6. They then indicate to us that the extent of their preference for skill utilization over doing the task from beginning to end is the same as the extent of their preference for serving customers over working independently. That is, the magnitude of difference represented by the space between points 1 and 2 on the scale is the same as the magnitude of difference represented by the space between points 4 and 5, or between any other two points. Any number can be added to or subtracted from the numbers on the scale, still retaining the magnitude of the difference. For instance, if we add 6 to all five points on the scale, the interval scale will have the numbers 7 to 11 (instead of 1 to 5). The magnitude of the difference between 7 and 8 is still the same as the magnitude of the difference between 9 and 10. Thus, the origin, or the starting point, could be any *arbitrary number.* The clinical thermometer is a good example of an interval-scaled instrument; it has an arbitrary origin and the magnitude of the difference between 98.6 degrees (supposed to be the normal body temperature) and 99.6 degrees is the same as the magnitude of the difference between 104 and 105 degrees. Note, however, that one may not be seriously concerned if one's temperature rises from 98.6 to 99.6, but is likely to be so when the temperature goes up from 104 to 105 degrees!

The interval scale, then, taps the differences, the order, and the equality of the magnitude of the differences in the variable. As such, it is a more powerful scale than the nominal and ordinal scales, and has for its measure of central tendency the arithmetic mean. Its measures of dispersion are the range, the standard deviation, and the variance.

> **Now respond to Exercises 8.5 and 8.6.**

Ratio Scale

The ratio scale overcomes the disadvantage of the arbitrary origin point of the interval scale, in that it has an *absolute* (in contrast to an *arbitrary*) zero point, which is a meaningful measurement point. Thus the ratio scale not only measures the magnitude of the differences between points on the scale but also taps the proportions in the differences. It is the most powerful of the four scales because it has a unique zero origin (not an arbitrary origin) and subsumes all the properties of the other three scales. The weighing balance is a good example of a ratio scale. It has an absolute (and not arbitrary) zero origin calibrated on it, which allows us to calculate the ratio of the weights of two individuals. For instance, a person weighing 250 pounds is *twice* as heavy as one who weighs 125 pounds. Note that multiplying or dividing both of these numbers (250 and 125) by any given number will preserve the ratio of 2:1. The measure of central tendency of the ratio scale could be either the arithmetic or the geometric mean and the measure of dispersion could be either the standard deviation, or variance, or the coefficient of variation. Some examples of ratio scales are those pertaining to actual age, income, and the number of organizations individuals have worked for.

The properties of the scales, as fine-tuning is increasingly achieved, are summarized in Figure 8.3. We may also see from the figure how the power of the statistic increases as we move away from the nominal scale (where we group subjects or items under some categories), to the ordinal scale (where we rank-order the

Figure 8.3
Properties of the four scales.

Scale	Difference	Order	Distance	Unique Origin	Measures of Central Tendency	Measures of Dispersion	Some Tests of Significance
Nominal	Yes	No	No	No	Mode	—	X^2
Ordinal	Yes	Yes	No	No	Median	Semi-interquartile range	Rank-order correlations
Interval	Yes	Yes	Yes	No	Arithmetic mean	Standard deviation, variance, coefficient of variation	t, F
Ratio	Yes	Yes	Yes	Yes	Arithmetic or geometric mean	Standard deviation or variance or coefficient of variation	t, F

Note: The interval scale has 1 as an arbitrary starting point. The ratio scale has the natural origin 0, which is meaningful.

categories), to the interval scale (where we tap the magnitude of the differences), to the ratio scale (which allows us to measure the proportion of the differences).

You must have surmised by now that some variables, such as gender, can be measured only on the nominal scale, while others, such as temperature, can be measured on a nominal scale (high/low), or ordinal scale (hot-medium-low), or the interval scale through the thermometer. Whenever it is possible to use a more powerful scale than a less or one, it is wise to do so.

Now respond to Exercise 8.7.

Now that we have looked at the four types of scales, let us see, through the following examples, when and how they would be used.

Example 8.7
USE OF THE NOMINAL SCALE
Nominal scale is always used for obtaining personal data such as gender or department in which one works, where grouping of individuals or objects is useful, as shown below.

1. *Your gender*
   ___ Male
   ___ Female

2. *Your department*
   ___ Production
   ___ Sales
   ___ Accounting
   ___ Finance
   ___ Personnel
   ___ R & D
   ___ Other (specify)

Example 8.8
USE OF THE ORDINAL SCALE
Ordinal scale is used to rank the preferences or usage of various brands of a product by individuals and to rank order individuals, objects, or events, as per the examples below.

1. Rank the following personal computers with respect to their usage in your office, assigning the number 1 to the most used system, 2 to the next most used, and so on. If a particular system is not used at all in your office, put a 0 next to it.

   ___ Apple   ___ Hewlett-Packard
   ___ Compaq   ___ IBM
   ___ Comp USA   ___ Packard Bell
   ___ Dell Computer   ___ Sony
   ___ Gateway   ___ Toshiba
            ___ Other (Specify)

2. Rank the cities listed below in the order that you consider suitable for opening a new plant. The city considered the most suitable will be ranked 1, the next 2, and so on.

___ Cincinnati   ___ Milwaukee

___ Detroit   ___ Pittsburgh

___ Des Moines   ___ St. Louis

___ Houston

Example 8.9

USE OF THE INTERVAL SCALE

Interval scale is used when responses to various items that measure a variable can be tapped on a five-point (or seven-point or any other number of points) scale, which can thereafter be summated across the items. See example below of a Likert scale.

> Using the scale below, please indicate your response to each of the items that follow, by *circling* the number that best describes your feeling.

Strongly Disagree 1	Disagree 2	Neither Agree Nor Disagree 3	Agree 4	Strongly Agree 5
1. My job offers me a chance to test myself and my abilities.	1	2	3	4	5
2. Mastering this job meant a lot to me.	1	2	3	4	5
3. Doing this job well is a reward in itself.	1	2	3	4	5
4. Considering the time spent on the job, I feel thoroughly familiar with my tasks and responsibilities.	1	2	3	4	5

Example 8.10

USE OF THE RATIO SCALE

Ratio scales are usually used in organizational research when exact numbers on objective (as opposed to subjective) factors are called for, as in the following questions:

1. How many other organizations did you work for before joining this system? ___

2. Please indicate the number of children you have in each of the following categories:

   ___ below 3 years of age

   ___ between 3 and 6

   ___ over 6 years but under 12

   ___ 12 years and over

3. How many retail outlets do you operate? ___

The responses to the questions could range from 0 to any reasonable figure.

Review of Scales

The four scales that can be applied to the measurement of variables are the nominal, ordinal, interval, and ratio scales. The nominal scale highlights the differences by classifying objects or persons into groups, and provides the least amount of information on the variable. The ordinal scale provides some additional information by rank-ordering the categories of the nominal scale. The interval scale not only ranks, but also provides us with information on the magnitude of the differences in the variable. The ratio scale indicates not only the magnitude of the differences but also their proportion. Multiplication or division would preserve these ratios. As we move from the nominal to the ratio scale, we obtain progressively increasing precision in quantifying the data, and greater flexibility in using more powerful statistical tests. Hence, whenever possible and appropriate, a more powerful rather than a less powerful scale should be used to measure the variables of interest.

We have discussed both operational definition and scaling. The following two exercises might be interesting to work on.

Do Exercises 8.8. and 8.9.

INTERNATIONAL DIMENSIONS OF OPERATIONAL DEFINITION AND SCALING

Operational Definition

In conducting transnational research, it is important to remember that certain variables have different meanings and connotations in different cultures. For instance, the term "love" is subject to several interpretations in different cultures and has at least 20 different interpretations in some countries. Likewise, the concept "knowledge" is equated with "jnana" in some Eastern cultures and construed as "realization of the Almighty." Thus, it is wise for researchers who hail from a country speaking a different language to recruit the help of local scholars to operationally define certain concepts while engaging in cross-cultural research.

Scaling

Apart from sensitivity to operational definition of concepts in other cultures, the issue of scaling also needs to be addressed in cross-cultural research. Different cultures react differently to issues of scaling. For instance, a 5-point or a 7-point scale may make no difference in the United States, but could in the responses of subjects in other countries (see Sekaran & Martin, 1982; Sekaran & Trafton, 1978). Barry (1969) for instance, found that in some countries, a 7-point scale is more sensitive than a 4-point scale in eliciting unbiased responses.

Thus, in developing instruments for cross-cultural research, one should be careful about both the operational definition and scaling methods used.

SUMMARY

In this chapter, we saw that any concept can be broken down to dimensions and elements for measurement through a set of items. We also examined the four types of scales—nominal, ordinal, interval, and ratio. We could see that knowledge of operationalization of a concept and the type of scales to use for purposes of categorizing, rank ordering, and tapping variables to varying degrees of sophistication, helps managers to undertake small surveys on their own, without much difficulty. We also discussed briefly the nuances in operational definition and scaling in cross-cultural research and were alerted to the dangers of operationalizing certain concepts in other cultures that might have different connotations.

As we shall see in the next chapter, which discusses the development of measures to tap concepts, most instruments have already been developed for organizational research, which would be useful to managers in the work environment.

DISCUSSION QUESTIONS AND POINTS TO PONDER

1. What is meant by operational definition and why is it necessary?
2. Operationally define the following:
   a. Sexual harassment
   b. Diversity-positive environment
   c. Career success
3. Describe the four types of scales.
4. How is the interval scale more sophisticated than the nominal and ordinal scales?
5. Why is the ratio scale considered to be the most powerful of the four scales?

[handwritten margin note: Bring in an example of a scale & discuss what type it is & if the same variable could have been put on another scale]

EXERCISES

Exercise 8.1   Schematically depict the operational definition of the concept of **stress** and develop 10 questions that would measure stress.

Exercise 8.2   Schematically depict the operational definition of the concept of enriched job and develop 12 items to measure it.

Exercise 8.3   Suggest two variables that would be natural candidates for nominal scales, and set up mutually exclusive and collectively exhaustive categories for each.

Exercise 8.4   Develop an ordinal scale for consumer preferences for different brands of beer.

Exercise 8.5   Measure any three variables on an interval scale.

Exercise 8.6   Example 8.2 lists 14 items directed toward tapping achievement motivation. Take items 6 to 9 and item 14, and use an interval scale to measure them. Reword the questions if you wish, without changing their meaning.

Exercise 8.7   Mention one variable for each of the four scales in the context of a market survey, and explain how or why it would fit into the scale.

Exercise 8.8   Attempt to delineate the dimensions and elements of the concept "intangible assets" of an organization.

Exercise 8.9   Try to delineate the dimensions of the concept of waging war in the context of the present political environment.

MEASUREMENT: SCALING, RELIABILITY, VALIDITY

TOPICS DISCUSSED

SCALING TECHNIQUES FREQUENTLY USED

- Rating Scales
  - *Dichotomous Scale*
  - *Category Scale*
  - *Likert Scale*
  - *Semantic Differential Scale*
  - *Numerical Scales*
  - *Itemized Rating Scale*
  - *Fixed or Constant Sum Rating Scale*
  - *Stapel Scale*
  - *Graphic Rating Scale*
  - *Consensus Scale*
- Ranking Scales
  - *Paired Comparisons*
  - *Forced Choice*
  - *Comparative Scale*

GOODNESS OF MEASURES

- Stability
  - *Test–Retest Reliability*
  - *Parallel-Form Reliability*
- Internal Consistency
  - *Split-Half Reliability*
  - *Interitem Consistency Reliability*
- Validity
- Content Validity
  - *Face Validity*
- Criterion-Related Validity
  - *Concurrent Validity*
  - *Predictive Validity*
- Construct Validity

CHAPTER OBJECTIVES

After completing Chapter 9, you should be able to:

1. Know how and when to use the different forms of rating scales and ranking scales.

2. Explain stability and consistency and how they are established.

3. Be conversant with the different forms of validity.

4. Discuss what "goodness" of measures means, and why it is necessary to establish it in research.

Now that we know the four different types of scales that can be used to measure the operationally defined dimensions and elements of a variable, it is necessary to examine the methods of scaling (that is, assigning numbers or symbols) to elicit the attitudinal responses of subjects toward objects, events, or persons. There are two main categories of attitudinal scales (not to be confused with the four different *types of scales*)—the *rating scale* and the *ranking scale*. Rating scales have several response categories and are used to elicit responses with regard to the object, event, or person studied. Ranking scales, on the other hand, make comparisons between or among objects, events, or persons and elicit the preferred choices and ranking among them. Both scales are discussed below.

RATING SCALES

The following rating scales are often used in organizational research:

Dichotomous scale

Category scale

Likert scale

Numerical scales

Semantic differential scale

Itemized rating scale

Fixed or constant sum rating scale

Stapel scale

Graphic rating scale

Consensus scale

Other scales such as the Thurstone Equal Appearing Interval Scale, and the Multidimensional Scale are less frequently used. We will briefly describe each of the above attitudinal scales.

Dichotomous Scale

The dichotomous scale is used to elicit a Yes or No answer, as in the example below. Note that a nominal scale is used to elicit the response.

Example 9.1   *Do you own a car?*   Yes   No

Category Scale

The category scale uses multiple items to elicit a single response as per the following example. This also uses the nominal scale.

Example 9.2   *Where in northern California do you reside?*   __ North Bay
                                                                    __ South Bay
                                                                    __ East Bay
                                                                    __ Peninsula
                                                                    __ Other

Likert Scale   *Append some extra time here*

The Likert scale is designed to examine how strongly subjects agree or disagree with statements on a 5-point scale with the following anchors:

Strongly Disagree	Disagree	Neither Agree Nor Disagree	Agree	Strongly Agree
1	2	3	4	5

The responses over a number of items tapping a particular concept or variable (as per the following example) are then summated for every respondent. This is an interval scale and the differences in the responses between any two points on the scale remain the same.

Example 9.3

> *Using the preceding Likert scale, state the extent to which you agree with each of the following statements:*
>
> *My work is very interesting*   1   2   3   4   5
> *I am not engrossed in my work all day*   1   2   3   4   5
> *Life without my work will be dull*   1   2   3   4   5

Semantic Differential Scale

Several bipolar attributes are identified at the extremes of the scale, and respondents are asked to indicate their attitudes, on what may be called a semantic space, toward a particular individual, object, or event on each of the attributes. The bipolar adjectives used, for instance, would employ such terms as Good–Bad; Strong–Weak; Hot–Cold. The semantic differential scale is used to assess respondents' attitudes toward a particular brand, advertisement, object, or individual. The responses can be plotted to obtain a good idea of their perceptions. This is treated as an interval scale. An example of the semantic differential scale follows.

Example 9.4

Responsive	— — — — — — —	Unresponsive
Beautiful	— — — — — — —	Ugly
Courageous	— — — — — — —	Timid

Numerical Scale

The numerical scale is similar to the semantic differential scale, with the difference that numbers on a 5-point or 7-point scale are provided, with bipolar adjectives at both ends, as illustrated below. This is also an interval scale.

Example 9.5   *How pleased are you with your new real estate agent?*

Extremely								Extremely
Pleased	7	6	5	4	3	2	1	Displeased

Itemized Rating Scale

A 5-point or 7-point scale with anchors, as needed, is provided for each item and the respondent states the appropriate number on the side of each item, or circles the relevant number against each item, as per the examples that follow. The responses to the items are then summated. This uses an interval scale.

Example 9.6 (i)   *Respond to each item using the scale below, and indicate your response number on the line by each item.*

1	2	3	4	5
Very Unlikely	Unlikely	Neither Unlikely Nor Likely	Likely	Very Likely

1. I will be changing my job within the next 12 months.   —
2. I will take on new assignments in the near future.   —
3. It is possible that I will be out of this organization within the next 12 months.   —

Note that the above is a *balanced rating scale* with a *neutral* point.

Example 9.6 (ii)   *Circle the number that is closest to how you feel for the item below.*

Not at All Interested	Somewhat Interested	Moderately Interested	Very Much Interested
1	2	3	4

How would you rate your interest in changing current organizational policies?	1 2 3 4		

This is an *unbalanced rating scale* which does *not* have a neutral point.

The itemized rating scale provides the flexibility to use as many points in the scale as considered necessary (4, 5, 7, 9, or whatever), and it is also possible to use different anchors (e.g., Very Unimportant to Very Important; Extremely Low to Extremely High). When a neutral point is provided, it is a balanced rating scale, and when it is not, it is an unbalanced rating scale.

Research indicates that a 5-point scale is just as good as any, and that an increase from 5 to 7 or 9 points on a rating scale does not improve the reliability of the ratings (Elmore & Beggs, 1975).

The itemized rating scale is frequently used in business research, since it adapts itself to the number of points desired to be used, as well as the nomenclature of the anchors, as is considered necessary to accommodate the needs of the researcher for tapping the variable.

Fixed or Constant Sum Scale

The respondents are here asked to distribute a given number of points across various items as per the example below. This is more in the nature of an ordinal scale.

Example 9.7   *In choosing a toilet soap, indicate the importance you attach to each of the following five aspects by allotting points for each to total 100 in all.*

Fragrance	—
Color	—
Shape	—
Size	—
Texture of lather	—
Total points	100

Stapel Scale

This scale simultaneously measures both the direction and intensity of the attitude toward the items under study. The characteristic of interest to the study is placed at the center and a numerical scale ranging, say, from + 3 to − 3, on either side of the item as illustrated below. This gives an idea of how close or distant the individual response to the stimulus is, as shown in the example below. Since this does not have an absolute zero point, this is an interval scale.

Example 9.8

State how you would rate your supervisor's abilities with respect to each of the characteristics mentioned below, by circling the appropriate number.

+3	+3	+3
+2	+2	+2
+1	+1	+1
Adopting Modern Technology	Product Innovation	Interpersonal Skills
−1	−1	−1
−2	−2	−2
−3	−3	−3

Graphic Rating Scale

A graphical representation helps the respondents to indicate on this scale their answers to a particular question by placing a mark at the appropriate point on the line, as in the following example. This is an ordinal scale, though the following example might appear to make it look like an interval scale.

Example 9.9

On a scale of 1 to 10, how would you rate your supervisor?

```
┌ 10  Excellent
├
├
├
├    5   All right
├
├
├
├
└  1   Very bad
```

Find an example

This scale is easy to respond to. The brief descriptions on the scale points are meant to serve as a guide in locating the rating rather than represent discrete categories. The **faces scale,** which depicts faces ranging from smiling to sad (illustrated in Chapter 10), is also a graphic rating scale. used to obtain responses regarding people's feelings with respect to some aspect—say, how they feel about their jobs.

Consensus Scale

Scales are also developed by consensus, where a panel of judges selects certain items, which in its view measure the relevant concept. The items are chosen particularly based on their pertinence or relevance to the concept. Such a consensus scale is developed after the selected items are examined and tested for their

Note → there are other more complex scales rarely used in industry ex TEA IS & MS

validity and reliability. One such consensus scale is the **Thurstone Equal Appearing Interval Scale,** where a concept is measured by a complex process followed by a panel of judges. Using a pile of cards containing several descriptions of the concept, a panel of judges offers inputs to indicate how close or not the statements are to the concept under study. The scale is then developed based on the consensus reached. However, this scale is rarely used for measuring organizational concepts because of the time necessary to develop it.

Other Scales

There are also some advanced scaling methods such as **multidimensional scaling,** where objects, people, or both, are visually scaled, and a conjoint analysis is performed. This provides a visual image of the relationships in space among the dimensions of a construct.

It is to be noted that usually the Likert or some form of numerical scale is usually the one most frequently used to measure attitudes and behaviors in organizational research.

RANKING SCALES

As already mentioned, **ranking scales** are used to tap preferences between two or among more objects or items (ordinal in nature). However, such ranking may not give definitive clues to some of the answers sought. For instance, let us say there are four product lines and the manager seeks information that would help decide which product line should get the most attention. Let us also assume that 35% of the respondents choose the first product, 25% the second, and 20% choose each of products three and four as of importance to them. The manager cannot then conclude that the first product is the most preferred since 65% of the respondents did not choose that product! Alternative methods used are the *paired comparisons, forced choice,* and the *comparative* scale, which are discussed below.

Paired Comparison

The **paired comparison** scale is used when, among a small number of objects, respondents are asked to choose between two objects at a time. This helps to assess preferences. If, for instance, in the previous example, during the paired comparisons, respondents consistently show a preference for product one over products two, three, and four, the manager reliably understands which product line demands his utmost attention. However, as the number of objects to be compared increases, so does the number of paired comparisons. The paired choices for n objects will be $[(n)(n-1)/2]$. The greater the number of objects or stimuli, the greater the number of paired comparisons presented to the respondents, and the greater the respondent fatigue. Hence paired comparison is a good method if the number of stimuli presented is small.

Forced Choice

The **forced choice** enables respondents to rank objects relative to one another, among the alternatives provided. This is easier for the respondents, particularly if the number of choices to be ranked is limited in number.

Example 9.10   Rank the following magazines that you would like to subscribe to in the order of preference, assigning 1 for the most preferred choice and 5 for the least preferred.

Fortune	—
Playboy	—
Time	—
People	—
Prevention	—

Comparative Scale

The **comparative scale** provides a benchmark or a point of reference to assess attitudes toward the current object, event, or situation under study. An example of the use of comparative scale follows.

Example 9.11   *In a volatile financial environment, compared to stocks, how wise or useful is it to invest in Treasury bonds? Please circle the appropriate response.*

More Useful		About the Same		Less Useful
1	2	3	4	5

In sum, nominal data lend themselves to dichotomous or category scale; ordinal data to any one of the ranking scales—paired comparison, forced choice, or comparative scales; and interval or interval-like data to the other rating scales, as seen from the various examples above. The semantic differential and the numerical scales are, strictly speaking, not interval scales, though they are often treated as such in data analysis.

Rating scales are used to measure most behavioral concepts. Ranking scales are used to make comparisons or rank the variables that have been tapped on a nominal scale.

GOODNESS OF MEASURES

Now that we have seen how to operationally define variables and apply different scaling techniques, it is important to make sure that the instrument that we develop to measure a particular concept is indeed *accurately* measuring the variable, and that in fact, we are *actually* measuring the concept that we set out to measure. This ensures that in operationally defining perceptual and attitudinal variables, we have not overlooked some important dimensions and elements or included some irrelevant ones. The scales developed could often be imperfect, and errors are prone to occur in the measurement of attitudinal variables. The use of better instruments will ensure more accuracy in results, which in turn, will enhance the scientific quality of the research. Hence, in some way, we need to assess the "goodness" of the measures developed. That is, we need to be reasonably sure that the instruments we use in our research do indeed measure the variables they are supposed to, and that they measure them accurately.

Let us now examine how we can ensure that the measures developed are reasonably good. First an item analysis of the responses to the questions tapping the variable is done, and then the reliability and validity of the measures are established, as described below.

Item Analysis

Item analysis is done to see if the items in the instrument belong there or not. Each item is examined for its ability to discriminate between those subjects whose total scores are high, and those with low scores. In item analysis, the means between the high-score group and the low-score group are tested to detect significant differences through the *t*-values (see Module at the end of the book for explanation of *t*-tests). The items with a high *t*-value (test which is able to identify the highly discriminating items in the instrument) are then included in the instrument. Thereafter, tests for the reliability of the instrument are done and the validity of the measure is established.

Very briefly, reliability tests *how consistently* a measuring instrument measures whatever concept it is measuring. Validity tests how well an instrument that is developed measures the *particular concept* it is intended to measure. In other words, validity is concerned with whether we measure the right concept, and reliability with stability and consistency of measurement. Validity and reliability of the measure attest to the scientific rigor that has gone into the research study. These two criteria will now be discussed. The various forms of reliability and validity are depicted in Figure 9.1.

RELIABILITY

look up defenition, from other books

The reliability of a measure indicates the extent to which it is without bias (error free) and hence ensures consistent measurement across time and across the various items in the instrument. In other words, the reliability of a measure is an indication of the stability and consistency with which the instrument measures the concept and helps to assess the "goodness" of a measure.

Stability of Measures

The ability of a measure to remain the same over time—despite uncontrollable testing conditions or the state of the respondents themselves—is indicative of its

Put on exam → just leave boxes blank. ✳

Figure 9.1

Testing Goodness of Measures: Forms of Reliability and Validity.

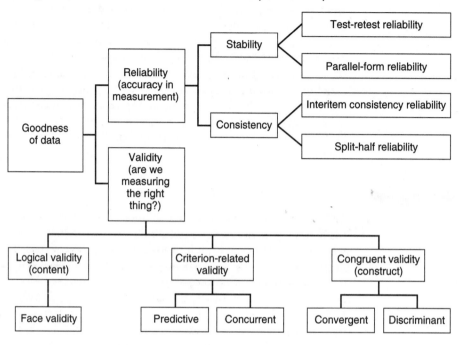

ex?

stability and low vulnerability to changes in the situation. This attests to its "goodness" because the concept is stably measured, no matter when it is done. Two tests of stability are test–retest reliability and parallel-form reliability.

Test–Retest Reliability

The reliability coefficient obtained with a repetition of the same measure on a second occasion is called test–retest reliability. That is, when a questionnaire containing some items that are supposed to measure a concept is administered to a set of respondents now, and again to the same respondents, say several weeks to 6 months later, then the correlation between the scores obtained at the two different times from one and the same set of respondents is called the test–retest coefficient. The higher it is, the better the test–retest reliability, and consequently, the stability of the measure across time.

Parallel-Form Reliability

When responses on two comparable sets of measures tapping the same construct are highly correlated, we have parallel-form reliability. Both forms have similar items and the same response format, the only changes being the wordings and

2 exams of same subjects

the order or sequence of the questions. What we try to establish here is the error variability resulting from wording and ordering of the questions. If two such comparable forms are highly correlated (say 8 and above), we may be fairly certain that the measures are reasonably reliable, with minimal error variance caused by wording, ordering, or other factors.

Internal Consistency of Measures

The internal consistency of measures is indicative of the homogeneity of the items in the measure that tap the construct. In other words, the items should "hang together as a set," and be capable of independently measuring the same concept so that the respondents attach the same overall meaning to each of the items. This can be seen by examining if the items and the subsets of items in the measuring instrument are correlated highly. Consistency can be examined through the inter-item consistency reliability and split-half reliability tests.

Interitem Consistency Reliability

This is a test of the consistency of respondents' answers to all the items in a measure. To the degree that items are independent measures of the same concept, they will be correlated with one another. The most popular test of interitem consistency reliability is the Cronbach's coefficient alpha (Cronbach's alpha; Cronbach, 1946), which is used for multipoint-scaled items, and the Kuder–Richardson formulas (Kuder & Richardson, 1937), used for dichotomous items. The higher the coefficients, the better the measuring instrument.

Split-Half Reliability

Split-half reliability reflects the correlations between two halves of an instrument. The estimates would vary depending on how the items in the measure are split into two halves. Split-half reliabilities could be higher than Cronbach's alpha only in the circumstance of there being more than one underlying response dimension tapped by the measure and when certain other conditions are met as well (for complete details, refer to Campbell, 1976). Hence, in almost all cases, Cronbach's alpha can be considered a perfectly adequate index of the interitem consistency reliability.

It should be noted that the consistency of the judgment of several raters on how they view a phenomenon or interpret some responses is termed *interrater reliability*, and should not be confused with the reliability of a measuring instrument. As we had noted earlier, interrater reliability is especially relevant when the data are obtained through observations, projective tests, or unstructured interviews, all of which are liable to be subjectively interpreted.

It is important to note that reliability is a necessary but not sufficient condition of the test of goodness of a measure. For example, one could very reliably measure a concept establishing high stability and consistency, but it may not be the concept that one had set out to measure. **Validity** ensures the ability of a scale to measure the intended concept. We will now discuss the concept of validity.

VALIDITY

We examined earlier, in Chapter 7, the terms *internal validity* and *external validity* in the context of experimental designs. That is, we were concerned about the issue of the authenticity of the cause-and-effect relationships (internal validity), and their generalizability to the external environment (external validity). We are now going to examine the validity of the measuring instrument itself. That is, when we ask a set of questions (i.e., develop a measuring instrument) with the hope that we are tapping the concept, how can we be reasonably certain that we are indeed measuring the concept we set out to do and not something else? This can be determined by applying certain validity tests.

Several types of validity tests are used to test the goodness of measures and writers use different terms to denote them. For the sake of clarity, we may group validity tests under three broad headings: **content validity, criterion-related validity,** and **construct validity.**

Content Validity

Content validity ensures that the measure includes an adequate and representative set of items that tap the concept. The more the scale items represent the domain or universe of the concept being measured, the greater the content validity. To put it differently, content validity is a function of how well the dimensions and elements of a concept have been delineated.

A panel of judges can attest to the content validity of the instrument. Kidder and Judd (1986) cite the example where a test designed to measure degrees of speech impairment can be considered as having validity if it is so evaluated by a group of expert judges (i.e., professional speech therapists).

Face validity is considered by some as a basic and a very minimum index of content validity. Face validity indicates that the items that are intended to measure a concept, do on the face of it look like they measure the concept. Some researchers do not see it fit to treat face validity as a valid component of content validity.

Criterion-Related Validity

Criterion-related validity is established when the measure differentiates individuals on a criterion it is expected to predict. This can be done by establishing *concurrent validity* or *predictive validity,* as explained below.

Concurrent validity is established when the scale discriminates individuals who are known to be different; that is, they should score differently on the instrument as in the example that follows.

Example 9.12 If a measure of work ethic is developed and administered to a group of welfare recipients, the scale should differentiate those who are enthusiastic about accepting a job and glad of an opportunity to be off welfare, from those who would not want to work even when offered a job. Obviously, those with high work ethic values would not want to be on welfare and would yearn for employment to be on their own. Those who are low on work ethic values, on the other hand, might exploit the opportunity to survive on welfare for as long as possible, deeming work to be a drudgery. If both types of individuals have the same score on the work ethic scale, then the test would *not* be a measure of work ethic, but of something else.

Predictive validity indicates the ability of the measuring instrument to differentiate among individuals with reference to a future criterion. For example, if an aptitude or ability test administered to employees at the time of recruitment is to differentiate individuals on the basis of their future job performance, then those who score low on the test should be poor performers and those with high scores good performers.

Construct Validity

Construct validity testifies to how well the results obtained from the use of the measure fit the theories around which the test is designed. This is assessed through **convergent** and **discriminant** validity, which are explained below.

Convergent validity is established when the scores obtained with two different instruments measuring the same concept are highly correlated.

Discriminant validity is established when, based on theory, two variables are predicted to be uncorrelated, and the scores obtained by measuring them are indeed empirically found to be so.

Validity can thus be established in different ways. Published measures for various concepts usually report the kinds of validity that have been established for the instrument, so that the user or reader can judge the "goodness" of the measure. Table 9.1 summarizes the kinds of validity discussed here.

Some of the ways in which the above forms of validity can be established are through (1) *correlational analysis* (as in the case of establishing concurrent and predictive validity or convergent and discriminant validity), (2) factor analysis, a multivariate technique that would confirm the dimensions of the concept that have been operationally defined, as well as indicate which of the items are most appropriate for each dimension (establishing construct validity), and (3) the multitrait, multimethod matrix of correlations derived from measuring concepts by different forms and different methods, additionally establishing the robustness of the measure.

In sum, the **goodness of measures** is established through the different kinds of validity and reliability depicted in Figure 9.1. The results of any research can only be as good as the measures that tap the concepts in the theoretical framework. We need to use well-validated and reliable measures to ensure that our research is scientific. Fortunately, measures have been developed for many important concepts in organizational research and their psychometric properties (i.e., the reliability and validity) established by the developers. Thus, researchers can use the instruments already reputed to be "good," rather than laboriously develop their own measures. When using these measures, however, researchers

Table 9.1
Types of Validity

Validity	Description
Content validity	Does the measure adequately measure the concept?
Face validity	Do "experts" validate that the instrument measures what its name suggests it measures?
Criterion-related validity	Does the measure differentiate in a manner that helps to predict a criterion variable?
Concurrent validity	Does the measure differentiate in a manner that helps to predict a criterion variable currently?
Predictive validity	Does the measure differentiate individuals in a manner as to help predict a future criterion?
Construct validity	Does the instrument tap the concept as theorized?
Convergent validity	Do two instruments measuring the concept correlate highly?
Discriminant validity	Does the measure have a low correlation with a variable that is supposed to be unrelated to this variable?

should cite the source (i.e., the author and reference) so that the reader can seek more information if necessary.

It is not unusual that two or more equally good measures are developed for the same concept. For example, there are several different instruments for measuring the concept of job satisfaction. One of the most frequently used scales for the purpose, however, is the Job Descriptive Index (JDI) developed by Smith, Kendall, and Hulin (1969). When more than one scale exists for any variable, it is preferable to use the measure that has better reliability and validity and is also more frequently used.

At times, we may also have to adapt an established measure to suit the setting. For example, a scale that is used to measure job performance, job characteristics, or job satisfaction in the manufacturing industry may have to be modified slightly to suit a utility company or a health care organization. The work environment in each case is different and the wordings in the instrument may have to be suitably adapted. However, in doing this, we are tampering with an established scale, and it would be advisable to test it for the adequacy of the validity and reliability afresh.

A sample of a few measures used to tap some frequently researched concepts in the management and marketing areas is provided in the Appendix to this chapter.

SUMMARY

In this chapter, we saw what kinds of attitude rating scales and ranking scales can be used in developing instruments after a concept has been operationally defined. We also discussed how the goodness of measures is established by means of item analysis, and reliability and validity tests. We also noted that the Likert scale and other types of interval-type scales such as the numerical scale, are extensively used in organizational research since they lend themselves to more sophisticated data analysis. Finally, we discussed the goodness of measures in terms of reliability and validity and the various ways in which these can be established.

Knowledge of the different scales and scaling techniques helps managers to administer short surveys by designing questions that use ranking or rating scales, as appropriate. Awareness of the fact that measures are already available for many organizational concepts further facilitates mini-exploratory surveys by managers.

In the next chapter, we will see the different sources and methods of data collection.

DISCUSSION QUESTIONS AND POINTS TO PONDER

1. Briefly describe the difference between attitude rating scales and ranking scales and indicate when the two are used.

2. Why is it important to establish the "goodness" of measures and how is this done?

3. Construct a semantic differential scale to assess the properties of a particular brand of coffee or tea.

4. Whenever possible, it is advisable to use instruments that have already been developed and repeatedly used in published studies, rather than develop our own instruments for our studies. Do you agree? Discuss the reasons for your answer.

5. "A valid instrument is always reliable, but a reliable instrument may not always be valid." Comment on this statement.

EXERCISE

Develop and name the type of measuring instrument you would use to tap the following:

a. Which brands of beer are consumed by how many individuals?

b. Among the three types of exams—multiple choice, essay type, and a mix of both—which is the one preferred most by students.

c. To what extent do individuals agree with your definition of accounting principles.

d. How much people like an existing organizational policy.

e. The age of employees in an organization.

f. The number of employees in each of the 20 departments of a company.

APPENDIX

EXAMPLES OF SOME MEASURES

Some of the measures used in behavioral research can be found in the *Handbook of Organizational Measurement* by Price (1972) and in the *Michigan Organizational Assessment Package* published by the Institute of Survey Research in Ann Arbor, Michigan. Several measures can also be seen in *Psychological Measurement Yearbooks* and in other published books. A sample of measures from the management and marketing areas is provided in this Appendix.

MEASURES FROM MANAGEMENT RESEARCH

Below is a sample of five scales used to measure five variables related to management research.

I. Job Involvement

	Strongly Disagree	Disagree	Neither Agree nor Disagree	Agree	Strongly Agree
1. My job means a lot more to me than just money.	1	2	3	4	5
2. The major satisfaction in my life comes from my job.	1	2	3	4	5
3. I am really interested in my work.	1	2	3	4	5
4. I would probably keep working even if I didn't need the money.	1	2	3	4	5
5. The most important things that happen to me involve my work.	1	2	3	4	5
6. I will stay overtime to finish a job, even if I am not paid for it.	1	2	3	4	5
7. For me, the first few hours at work really fly by.	1	2	3	4	5
8. How much do you actually enjoy performing the daily activities that make up your job?	1	2	3	4	5
9. How much do you look forward to coming to work each day?	1	2	3	4	5

Source: J. K. White and R. R. Ruh (1973). Effects of personal values on the relationship between participation and job attitudes. *Administrative Science Quarterly*, 18, 4, p. 509. Reproduced with permission.

II. Participation in Decision Making

	Strongly Disagree	Disagree	Neither Agree nor Disagree	Agree	Strongly Agree
1. In general, how much say or influence do you have on how you perform your job?	1	2	3	4	5
2. To what extent are you able to decide how to do your job?	1	2	3	4	5
3. In general, how much say or influence do you have on what goes on in your work group?	1	2	3	4	5
4. In general, how much say or influence do you have on decisions that affect your job?	1	2	3	4	5
5. My superiors are receptive and listen to my ideas and suggestions.	1	2	3	4	5

Source: J. K. White and R. R. Ruh (1973). Effects of personal values on the relationship between participation and job attitudes. *Administrative Science Quarterly,* 18, 4, p. 509. Reproduced with permission.

III. Role Conflict

	Very False						Very True
1. I have to do things that should be done differently.	1	2	3	4	5	6	7
2. I work under incompatible policies and guidelines.	1	2	3	4	5	6	7
3. I receive an assignment without the manpower to complete it.	1	2	3	4	5	6	7
4. I have to buck a rule or policy in order to carry out an assignment.	1	2	3	4	5	6	7
5. I work with two or more groups who operate quite differently.	1	2	3	4	5	6	7
6. I receive incompatible requests from two or more people.	1	2	3	4	5	6	7
7. I do things that are apt to be accepted by one person and not accepted by others.	1	2	3	4	5	6	7
8. I receive an assignment without adequate resources and materials to execute it.	1	2	3	4	5	6	7
9. I work on unnecessary things.	1	2	3	4	5	6	7

Source: J. R. Rizzo, R. J. House, and S. I. Lirtzman (1970). Role conflict and ambiguity in complex organizations. *Administrative Science Quarterly,* 15, p. 156. Reproduced with permission.

IV. Career Salience

Strongly Disagree 1	Disagree 2	Slightly Disagree 3	Neutral 4	Slightly Agree 5	Agree 6	Strongly Agree 7

1. My career choice is a good occupational decision for me. ____
2. My career enables me to make significant contributions to society. ____
3. The career I am in fits me and reflects my personality. ____
4. My education and training are not tailored for this career. ____
5. I don't intend changing careers.
6. All the planning and thought I gave for pursuing this career are a waste. ____
7. My career is an integral part of my life. ____

Source: U. Sekaran. (1986) *Dual-Career Families: Contemporary Organizational and Counseling Issues.* San Francisco: Jossey Bass. Reproduced with permission.

V. Least Preferred Coworker Scale (to assess whether employees are primarily people-oriented or task-oriented)

Look at the words at both ends of the line before you put in your "X." Please remember that there are *no right or wrong answers.* Work rapidly; your first answer is likely to be the best. Please do not omit any items, and mark each item only once.

LPC

Think of the person *with whom you can work least well.* He may be someone you work with now, or he may be someone you knew in the past.

He does not have to be the person you like least well, but should be the person with whom you had the most difficulty in getting a job done. Describe this person as he appears to you.

Pleasant	8 7 6 5 4 3 2 1	Unpleasant
Friendly	8 7 6 5 4 3 2 1	Unfriendly
Rejecting	8 7 6 5 4 3 2 1	Accepting
Helpful	8 7 6 5 4 3 2 1	Frustrating
Unenthusiastic	8 7 6 5 4 3 2 1	Enthusiastic
Tense	1 2 3 4 5 6 7 8	Relaxed
Distant	1 2 3 4 5 6 7 8	Close
Cold	1 2 3 4 5 6 7 8	Warm
Cooperative	8 7 6 5 4 3 2 1	Uncooperative
Supportive	8 7 6 5 4 3 2 1	Hostile
Boring	1 2 3 4 5 6 7 8	Interesting
Quarrelsome	1 2 3 4 5 6 7 8	Harmonious
Self-assured	8 7 6 5 4 3 2 1	Hesitant
Efficient	8 7 6 5 4 3 2 1	Inefficient
Gloomy	8 7 6 5 4 3 2 1	Cheerful
Open	8 7 6 5 4 3 2 1	Guarded

Source: Fred E. Fiedler. (1967). *A Theory of Leadership Effectiveness.* New York: McGraw-Hill. Reproduced with permission.

MEASURES FROM MARKETING RESEARCH

Below is a sample of some scales used to measure commonly researched concepts in marketing. Bruner and Hensel have done extensive work since 1992 in documenting and detailing several scores of scales in marketing research. For each scale examined, they have provided the following information:

1. Scale description
2. Scale origin
3. Samples in which the scale was used
4. Reliability of the scale
5. Validity of the scale
6. How the scale was administered
7. Major findings of the studies using the scale.

The interested student should refer to the two volumes of *Marketing Scales Handbook* by G. C. Bruner and P. J. Hensel, published by the American Marketing Association. The first volume covers scales used in articles published in the 1980s, and volume two covers scales used in articles published from 1990 to 1993. The third volume covers the period from 1994 and 1997. Also refer to the web site: http://www.siu.edu:80/departments/coba/marketing/osr

I. Index of Consumer Sentiment Toward Marketing

1. Listed below are seven statements pertaining to each of the four marketing areas. There is also a fifth section labeled "Marketing in General." It contains four statements.

   For each statement, please "X" the box which best describes how strongly you agree or disagree with each statement. For example, if you strongly agree the quality of most products today is as good as can be expected then "X" the Agree Strongly box. On the other hand, if you strongly disagree the quality of most products today is as good as can be expected, then "X" the Disagree Strongly box. Remember to "X" one box for each statement.

PRODUCT QUALITY	Strongly Disagree	Somewhat Disagree	Neither Agree nor Disagree	Somewhat Agree	Strongly Agree
The quality of most products I buy today is as good as can be expected.	☐1	☐2	☐3	☐4	☐5
I am satisfied with most of the products I buy.	☐1	☐2	☐3	☐4	☐5
Most products I buy wear out too quickly.	☐1	☐2	☐3	☐4	☐5
Products are not made as well as they used to be.	☐1	☐2	☐3	☐4	☐5
Too many of the products I buy are defective in some way.	☐1	☐2	☐3	☐4	☐5

The companies that make products I buy don't care enough about how well they perform.	☐1	☐2	☐3	☐4	☐5
The quality of products I buy has consistently improved over the years.	☐1	☐2	☐3	☐4	☐5

PRICE OF PRODUCTS	Strongly Disagree	Somewhat Disagree	Neither Agree nor Disagree	Somewhat Agree	Strongly Agree
Most products I buy are overpriced.	☐1	☐2	☐3	☐4	☐5
Businesses could charge lower prices and still be profitable.	☐1	☐2	☐3	☐4	☐5
Most prices are reasonable considering the high cost of doing business.	☐1	☐2	☐3	☐4	☐5
Competition between companies keeps prices reasonable.	☐1	☐2	☐3	☐4	☐5
Companies are unjustified in charging the prices they charge.	☐1	☐2	☐3	☐4	☐5
Most prices are fair.	☐1	☐2	☐3	☐4	☐5
In general, I am satisfied with the prices I pay.	☐1	☐2	☐3	☐4	☐5

ADVERTISING FOR PRODUCTS	Strongly Disagree	Somewhat Disagree	Neither Agree nor Disagree	Somewhat Agree	Strongly Agree
Most advertising provides consumers with essential information.	☐1	☐2	☐3	☐4	☐5
Most advertising is very annoying.	☐1	☐2	☐3	☐4	☐5
Most advertising makes false claims.	☐1	☐2	☐3	☐4	☐5
If most advertising was eliminated, consumers could be better off.	☐1	☐2	☐3	☐4	☐5
I enjoy most ads.	☐1	☐2	☐3	☐4	☐5
Advertising should be more closely regulated.	☐1	☐2	☐3	☐4	☐5
Most advertising is intended to deceive rather than to inform consumers.	☐1	☐2	☐3	☐4	☐5

RETAILING OR SELLING	Strongly Disagree	Somewhat Disagree	Neither Agree nor Disagree	Somewhat Agree	Strongly Agree
Most retail stores serve their customers well.	☐1	☐2	☐3	☐4	☐5
Because of the way retailers treat me, most of my shopping is unpleasant.	☐1	☐2	☐3	☐4	☐5

I find most retail salespeople to be very helpful.	□1	□2	□3	□4	□5
Most retail stores provide an adequate selection of merchandise.	□1	□2	□3	□4	□5
In general, most middlemen make excessive profits.	□1	□2	□3	□4	□5
When I need assistance in a store, I am usually not able to get it.	□1	□2	□3	□4	□5
Most retailers provide adequate service.	□1	□2	□3	□4	□5

MARKETING IN GENERAL	Strongly Disagree	Somewhat Disagree	Neither Agree nor Disagree	Somewhat Agree	Strongly Agree
Most businesses operate on the philosophy that the consumer is always right.	□1	□2	□3	□4	□5
Despite what is frequently said, "let the buyer beware" is the guiding philosophy of most businesses.	□1	□2	□3	□4	□5
Most businesses seldom shirk their responsibility to the consumer.	□1	□2	□3	□4	□5
Most businesses are more interested in making profits than in serving consumers.	□1	□2	□3	□4	□5

2. Now, I'd like to know how satisfied you are, in general, with each of these four marketing areas. Please 'X' the one box which best describes your overall satisfaction with each marketing area.

	Very Satisfied	Somewhat Satisfied	Neither Satisfied nor Dissatisfied	Somewhat Dissatisfied	Very Dissatisfied
The *quality* of most of the products available to buy.	□1	□2	□3	□4	□5
The *prices* of most products.	□1	□2	□3	□4	□5
Most of the *advertising* you read, see, and hear.	□1	□2	□3	□4	□5
The *selling conditions* at most of the stores at which you buy products.	□1	□2	□3	□4	□5

3. Listed below are four questions which ask about how often you have had problems with the products you buy, the prices you pay, the advertising you read, see, and hear, and the stores at which you shop.

After each statement, there are five numbers from 1 to 5. The higher the number means you have experienced the problem more often. The lower the number means you have experienced the problem less often.

For each question, please "X" the box which comes closest to how often the problem occurs. Remember to "X" one box for each question.

	Very Seldom				Very Often
How *often* do you have problems with or complaints about the *products* you buy?	□1	□2	□3	□4	□5
How *often* do you have problems with or complaints about the *prices* you pay?	□1	□2	□3	□4	□5
How *often* do you have problems with or complaints about *advertising?*	□1	□2	□3	□4	□5
How *often* do you have problems with or complaints about the *stores* at which you buy products?	□1	□2	□3	□4	□5

Source: J. F. Gaski and M. J. Etzel. (1986). The index of consumer sentiment toward marketing. *Journal of Marketing,* 50, 71–81. Reproduced with permission of American Marketing Association.

II. SERVQUAL-P Battery (to assess the quality of service rendered)

Reliability

1. Provides the service as promised.
2. Is dependable in handling customers' service problems.
3. Performs the service right the first time.
4. All _____'s employees are well-trained and knowledgeable.

Responsiveness

5. Employees of _____ give you prompt service.
6. Employees of _____ are always willing to help you.
7. Employees of _____ are always ready to respond to your requests.
8. _____gives customers individual attention.

Personalization

9. Everyone at _____ is polite and courteous.
10. The _____ employees display personal warmth in their behavior.
11. All the persons working at _____ are friendly and pleasant.
12. The _____ employees take the time to know you personally.

Tangibles

13. _____ has modern-looking equipment.

14. _____'s physical facilities are visually appealing.

15. _____'s employees have neat and professional appearance.

16. Materials associated with the service (such as pamphlets or statements) are visually appealing at _____.

Source: B. Mittal and W. M. Lassar. (1996). The role of personalization in service encounters. *Journal of Retailing*, 72, 95–109. Reproduced with permission of Jai Press, Inc.

III. Role Ambiguity (Salesperson)

Very False						Very True
1	2	3	4	5	6	7

1. I feel certain about how much authority I have in my selling position. ____

2. I have clearly planned goals for my selling job. ____

3. I am sure I divide my time properly while performing my selling tasks. ____

4. I know my responsibilities in my selling position. ____

5. I know exactly what is expected of me in my selling position. ____

6. I receive lucid explanations of what I have to do in my sales job. ____

A modified version of Rizzo, House, and Lirtzman's (1970) Role ambiguity in complex organizations scale published in *Administrative Science Quarterly*, 15, p. 156

DATA COLLECTION METHODS

TOPICS DISCUSSED

SOURCES OF DATA

- Focus Groups
- Panels
- Unobtrusive Sources

DATA COLLECTION METHODS

- Interviewing
  - *Unstructured and Structured interviews*
  - *Tips for Interviewing*
  - *Face-to-Face and Telephone Interviews*
  - *Computer-Assisted Interviews*
- Questionnaires and Questionnaire Design
  - *Personally Administered Questionnaires and Mail Questionnaires*
  - *Principles of Wording*
  - *Principles of Measurement*
  - *General Appearance of the Questionnaire*
  - *Electronic Questionnaire Design and Surveys*
- Observational Studies
  - *Participant and Nonparticipant Observation*
  - *Structured and Unstructured Observation*
- Projective Tests

MULTIMETHODS AND MULTISOURCES OF DATA COLLECTION

SETTING WHEREFROM DATA ARE COLLECTED

INTERNATIONAL DIMENSIONS OF SURVEYS

MANAGERIAL ADVANTAGE

ETHICS IN DATA COLLECTION

CHAPTER OBJECTIVES

After completing Chapter 10, you should:

1. Know the difference between primary and secondary data and their sources.

2. Be conversant with the various data collection methods.

3. Know the advantages and disadvantages of each method.

4. Make logical decisions as to the appropriate data collection methods(s) for specific studies.

5. Demonstrate your skills in interviewing others to collect data.

6. Design questionnaires to tap different variables.

7. Evaluate questionnaires, distinguishing the "good" and "bad" questions therein.

8. Identify and minimize the biases in various data collection methods.

9. Discuss the advantages of multisources and multimethods of data collection.

10. Apply what you have learned to class assignments and projects.

11. Understand the issues related to cross-cultural research.

Having examined how variables are measured, we will now discuss the various sources of data and the ways in which data can be gathered for purposes of analysis, testing hypotheses, and answering the research questions. The source of the information and the manner in which data are collected could well make a big difference to the rigor and effectiveness of the research project.

We will first examine the sources of data and then discuss the data collection methods.

SOURCES OF DATA

Data can be obtained from primary or secondary sources. Primary data refer to information obtained firsthand by the researcher on the variables of interest for the specific purpose of the study. Secondary data refer to information gathered from sources already existing, as we saw in Chapter 4 while discussing literature survey.

Some examples of sources of *primary data* are individuals, focus groups, panels of respondents specifically set up by the researcher and from whom opinions may be sought on specific issues from time to time, or some unobtrusive sources such as a trash can. The Internet could also serve as a primary data source when questionnaires are administered over it.

Data can also be obtained from *secondary sources,* as for example, company records or archives, government publications, industry analyses offered by the media, web sites, the Internet, and so on. In some cases, the environment or particular settings and events may themselves be sources of data, as for example, studying the layout of a plant.

We will first examine the four main primary sources of data—individuals, focus groups, panels, and unobtrusive methods—and then discuss the secondary sources.

PRIMARY SOURCES OF DATA

Apart from the individuals who provide information when interviewed, administered questionnaires, or observed—discussed at length under Data Collection Methods in this chapter—another rich source of primary data is focus groups.

Focus Groups

Focus groups consist typically of 8 to 10 members with a moderator leading the discussions for about 2 hours on a particular topic, concept, or product. Members are generally chosen on the basis of their expertise in the topic on which information is sought. For example, computer specialists may be selected to form a focus group to discuss matters related to computers and computing, and women with children may compose the focus group to identify how organizations can help working mothers.

The focus sessions are aimed at obtaining respondents' impressions, interpretations, and opinions, as the members talk about the event, concept, product, or service. The moderator plays a vital role in steering the discussions in a manner that would draw out the information sought, and keeping the members on track.

Focus group discussions on a specific topic at a particular location and at a specified time provide the opportunity for a flexible, free-flowing format for the members. The unstructured and spontaneous responses are expected to reflect the genuine opinions, ideas, and feelings of the members about the topic under discussion. Focus groups are relatively inexpensive and can provide fairly dependable data within a short time frame.

Role of the Moderator

The selection of and role played by the moderator are critical. The moderator introduces the topic, observes, and takes notes and/or tapes the discussions. The moderator never becomes an integral part of the discussions, but merely steers the group persuasively to obtain all the relevant information, and helps the group members to get through any impasse that might occur. The moderator also ensures that all members participate in the discussion and that no member dominates the group. Someone from the research team may also observe the proceedings through a one-way mirror, listening to the verbal statements and noticing the nonverbal cues of the members.

The Nature of Data Obtained Through Focus Groups

It should be noted that though data obtained through these homogeneous group members are the least expensive of the various data collection methods, and also lend themselves for quick analysis, the content analysis of the data so obtained provides only *qualitative* and not *quantitative* information. Also, since the members are not selected scientifically to reflect the opinions of the population at large (see the next chapter on sampling for more details on this), their opinions cannot be considered to be truly representative. However, when exploratory information is collected as a basis for further scientific research, focus groups serve an important function. Consider for example, the value of focus groups in exploring the concept of "Intellectual Property." When animated discussions take place, there is a serendipitous flow of new ideas among the group members who discuss the nuances of each thought process. Researchers are thereby helped to obtain valuable insights from the snowballing effects of the discussions.

In sum, focus groups are used for (1) exploratory studies, (2) making generalizations based on the information generated by them, and (3) conducting sample surveys. Focus groups have been credited with enlightening investigators as to why certain products are not doing well, why certain advertising strategies are effective, why specific management techniques do not work, and the like.

Videoconferencing

If regional variations in responses are expected, several focus groups could be formed including trained moderators at different locations. This process is easily facilitated through videoconferencing. By zooming in on a particular member the nonverbal cues and gestures of that individual can be captured, as and when desired. This also obviates the need for an observer looking through a one-way mirror.

With the great strides in technological advancement, and with the facility for communication with the moderator by relaying instant messages, videoconferencing as a means of gathering information from different groups in distant locations is indeed a promising prospect for the future.

It should be noted that online focus groups are also common. E-mail, web sites, and Internet chat rooms facilitate focus group sessions as well.

Panels

Panels, like focus groups, are another source of primary information for research purposes. Whereas focus groups meet for a one-time group session, panels (of members) meet more than once. In cases where the effects of certain interventions or changes are to be studied over a period of time, panel studies are very useful. Individuals are randomly chosen to serve as panel members for a research study. For instance, if the effects of a proposed advertisement for a certain brand of coffee are to be assessed quickly, the panel members can be exposed to the advertisement and their intentions of purchasing that brand assessed. This can be taken as the response that could be expected of consumers if, in fact, they had been exposed to the advertisement. A few months later, the product manager might think of introducing a change in the flavor of the same product and explore its effects on this panel. Thus, a continuing set of "experts" serves as the sample base or the sounding board for assessing the effects of change. Such expert members compose the panel, and research that uses them is called a *panel study*.

The Nielsen television index is based on the television viewing patterns of a panel. The index is designed to provide estimates of the size and nature of the audience for individual television programs. The data are gathered through audimeter instruments hooked to television sets in approximately 1,200 cooperating households. The audimeters are connected to a central computer, which records when the set is turned on and spotlights what channel is tuned. From these data, Nielsen develops estimates of the number and percentage of all TV households viewing a given TV show.

Other panels used in marketing research include the National Purchase Diary Panel, the National Family Opinion Panel, and the Consumer Mail Panel.

Static and Dynamic Panels

Panels can be either *static* (i.e., the same members serve on the panel over extended periods of time) or *dynamic* (i.e., the panel members change from time to time as various phases of the study are in progress). The main advantage of the static panel is that it offers a good and sensitive measurement of the changes that take place between two points in time—a much better alternative than using two different groups at two different times. The disadvantage, however, is that the panel members could become so sensitized to the changes as a result of the endless continuous interviews that their opinions might no longer be representative of what the others in the population might hold. Members could also drop out of the panel from time to time for various reasons, thus raising issues of bias due to mortality. The advantages and disadvantages of the dynamic panel are the reverse of the ones discussed for the static panel.

In sum, a panel is a source of direct information. Panels could be static or dynamic, and are typically used when several aspects of a product are to be studied from time to time.

Unobtrusive Measures

Trace measures, or *unobtrusive measures* as they are also called, originate from a primary source that does not involve people. One example is the wear and tear of journals in a university library, which offers a good indication of their popularity, frequency of use, or both. The number of different brands of soft drink cans found in trash bags also provides a measure of their consumption levels. Signatures on checks exposed to ultraviolet rays could indicate the extent of forgery and frauds; actuarial records are good sources for collecting data on the births, marriages, and deaths in a community; company records disclose a lot of personal information about employees, the level of company efficiency, and other data as well. Thus these unobtrusive sources of data and their use are also important in research.

SECONDARY SOURCES

Secondary data are indispensable for most organizational research. As discussed in Chapter 4, secondary data refer to information gathered by someone other than the researcher conducting the current study. Such data can be internal or external to the organization and accessed through the Internet or perusal of recorded or published information.

Secondary data can be used, among other things, for forecasting sales by constructing models based on past sales figures, and through extrapolation.

There are several sources of secondary data, including books and periodicals, government publications of economic indicators, census data, Statistical Abstracts, data bases (as discussed in Chapter 4), the media, annual reports of companies, etc. Case studies, and other archival records—sources of secondary data—provide a lot of information for research and problem solving. Such data are, as we have seen, mostly qualitative in nature. Also included in secondary sources are schedules maintained for or by key personnel in organizations, the desk calendar of executives, and speeches delivered by them. Much of such internal data, though, could be proprietary and not accessible to all.

Financial databases readily available for research are also secondary data sources. The Compustat Database contains information on thousands of companies organized by industry, and information on global companies is also available through Compustat.

The advantage of seeking secondary data sources is savings in time and costs of acquiring information. However, secondary data as the sole source of information has the drawback of becoming obsolete, and not meeting the specific needs of the particular situation or setting. Hence, it is important to refer to sources that offer current and up-to-date information.

Having examined the various sources of data, let us now look into the data collection methods.

DATA COLLECTION METHODS

Data collection methods are an integral part of research design as shown in the shaded portion in the figure. There are several data collection methods, each with its own advantages and disadvantages. Problems researched with the use of appropriate methods greatly enhance the value of the research.

Data can be collected in a variety of ways, in different settings—field or lab—and from different sources, as we have just discussed. Data collection methods include *interviews*—face-to-face interviews, telephone interviews, computer-assisted interviews, and interviews through the electronic media; *questionnaires* that are either personally administered, sent through the mail, or electronically administered; *observation* of individuals and events with or without videotaping or audio recording; and a variety of other *motivational techniques* such as projective tests.

Interviewing, administering questionnaires, and observing people and phenomena are the three main data collection methods in survey research. Projective tests and other motivational techniques are also sometimes used to tap variables. In such cases, respondents are usually asked to write a story, complete a sentence, or offer their reactions to ambiguous cues such as inkblots or unlabeled pictures. It is assumed that the respondents project into the responses their own thoughts, feelings, attitudes, and expectations, all of which can be interpreted by trained psychologists.

DETAILS OF STUDY   MEASUREMENT

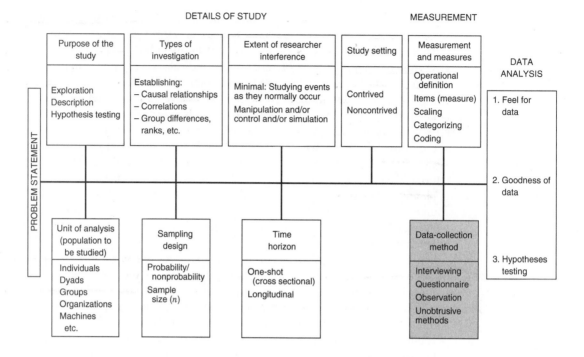

Although interviewing has the advantage of flexibility in terms of adapting, adopting, and changing the questions as the researcher proceeds with the interviews, questionnaires have the advantage of obtaining data more efficiently in terms of researcher time, energy, and costs. Unobtrusive methods of data collection such as its extraction from company records have the advantage of accuracy. For instance, attendance records will probably give a truer and more reliable picture of the absenteeism of employees than information elicited directly from the respondents. Projective tests are usually administered by researchers who have had training in administering them and interpreting the results. Though some management research has been done using projective techniques, they are more frequently used in marketing research.

Modern technology is increasingly playing a key role in shaping data collection methods. Computer-assisted surveys, which help both interviewing as well as preparing and administering questionnaires electronically, are on the increase. Computer-assisted telephone interviewing (CATI), interactive electronic telephonic surveys, as well as administering questionnaires through electronic mail (e-mail), are now being used to facilitate data gathering.

Some of the software available for questionnaire design, response data entry, data analysis, and web and e-mail surveys are SumQuest or SQ Survey Software, Professional Quest, and Perseus.

The choice of data collection methods depends on the facilities available, the degree of accuracy required, the expertise of the researcher, the time span of the study, and other costs and resources associated with and available for data gathering.

We will now examine the various data collection methods under Parts I, II, and III.

PART I: *INTERVIEWING*

One method of collecting data is to interview respondents to obtain information on the issues of interest. Interviews could be unstructured or structured, and conducted either face to face or by telephone or online.

The unstructured and structured interviews are discussed first. Some important factors to be borne in mind while interviewing will then be detailed; the advantages and disadvantages of face-to-face interviewing and telephone interviews enumerated thereafter; and finally, computer-assisted interviews described.

UNSTRUCTURED AND STRUCTURED INTERVIEWS

Unstructured Interviews

Unstructured interviews are so labeled because the interviewer does not enter the interview setting with a planned sequence of questions to be asked of the respondent. The objective of the unstructured interview is to bring some preliminary issues to the surface so that the researcher can determine what variables need further in-depth investigation. In Chapter 4, in the discussion of the "Broad Problem Area," we saw several situations where the manager might entertain a vague idea of certain changes taking place in the situation without knowing what exactly they are. Such situations call for unstructured interviews with the people concerned. In order to understand the situation in its totality, the researcher will interview employees at several levels. In the initial stages, only broad, open-ended questions would be asked, and the replies to them would inform the researcher of the perceptions of the individuals. The type and nature of the questions asked of the individuals might vary according to the job level and type of work done by them. For instance, top and middle-level managers might be asked more direct questions about their perceptions of the problem and the situation. Employees at lower levels may have to be approached differently.

Clerical and other employees at lower hierarchical levels may be asked broad, open-ended questions about their jobs and the work environment during the unstructured interviews. Supervisors may be asked broad questions relating to their department, the employees under their supervision, and the organization. The following question, for instance, may be put to them during the unstructured interview stage:

> *"Tell me something about your unit and department, and perhaps even the organization as a whole, in terms of work, employees, and whatever else you think is important."*

Such a question might elicit an elaborate response from some people; others may just say that everything is fine. Following the leads from the more vocal persons is easy, especially when the interviewer listens carefully to the important messages that they might convey in a very casual manner while responding to a general, global question. As managers and researchers, we should train ourselves to develop these listening skills and identify the critical topics that are touched on. However, when some respondents give a monosyllabic, crisp, short reply that is not informative, the interviewer will have to ask questions that would call for details and cannot be answered in one or two words. Such questions might be phrased as the one below:

"I would like to know something about your job. Please describe to me in detail the things you do on your job on a typical day, from eight in the morning to four in the afternoon."

Several questions might then be asked as a follow-up to the answer. Some examples of such follow-up questions include:

"Compared to other units in this organization, what are the strengths and weaknesses of your unit?"

"If you would like to have a problem solved in your unit, or a bottleneck eliminated, or something attended to that blocks your effectiveness, what would that be?"

If the respondent answers that everything is fine and she has no problems, the interviewer could say: *"That is great! Tell me what contributes to this effectiveness of your unit, because most other organizations usually experience several difficulties."* Such a questioning technique usually brings the respondent's defenses down and makes him or her more amenable to sharing information. Typical of the revised responses to the original question would be something like, "Well, it is not that we never have a problem, sometimes, there is delay in getting the jobs done, crash jobs have some defective items, …" Encouraging the respondent to talk about both the good things and those not-so-good in the unit can elicit a lot of information. Whereas some respondents do not need much encouragement to speak, others do, and they have to be questioned broadly. Some respondents may show reluctance to be interviewed, and subtly or overtly refuse to cooperate. The wishes of such people must be respected and the interviewer should pleasantly terminate such interviews.

Employees at the shop-floor level, and other nonmanagerial and nonsupervisory employees, might be asked very broad questions relating to their jobs, work environment, satisfactions and dissatisfactions at the workplace, and the like—for example:

What do you like about working here?

If you were to tell me what aspects of your job you like and what you do not, what would they be?

Tell me something about the reward systems in this place.

If you were offered a similar job elsewhere, how willing would you be to take it and why?

If I were to seek employment here and request you to describe your unit to me as a newcomer, what would you say?

After conducting a sufficient number of such unstructured interviews with employees at several levels and studying the data obtained, the researcher would know the variables that need greater focus and call for more in-depth information.

This sets the stage for the interviewer to conduct further structured interviews, for which the variables would have been identified.

Structured Interviews

Structured interviews are those conducted when it is known at the outset what information is needed. The interviewer has a list of predetermined questions to be asked of the respondents either personally, through the telephone, or through the medium of a PC. The questions are likely to focus on factors that had surfaced during the unstructured interviews and are considered relevant to the problem. As the respondents express their views, the researcher would note them down. The same questions will be asked of everybody in the same manner. Sometimes, however, based on the exigencies of the situation, the experienced researcher might take a lead from a respondent's answer and ask other relevant questions not on the interview protocol. Through this process, new factors might be identified, resulting in a deeper understanding. However, to be able to recognize a probable response, the interviewer must comprehend the purpose and goal of each question. This is particularly important when a team of trained interviewers conducts the survey.

Visual aids such as pictures, line drawings, cards, and other materials are also sometimes used in conducting interviews. The appropriate visuals are shown to the interviewees, who then indicate their responses to the questions posed. Marketing research, for example, benefits from such techniques in order to capture the likes and dislikes of customers to different types of packaging, forms of advertising, and so on. Visual aids, including painting and drawing, are particularly useful when children are the focus of marketing research. Visual aids also come in handy while endeavoring to elicit certain thoughts and ideas that are difficult to express or awkward to articulate.

When a sufficient number of structured interviews has been conducted and adequate information obtained to understand and describe the important factors operating in the situation, the researcher would stop the interviews. The information would then be tabulated and the data analyzed. This would help the researcher to accomplish the task set out to be done, as for example, to describe the phenomena, or quantify them, or identify the specific problem and evolve a theory of the factors that influence the problem or find answers to the research question. Much qualitative research is done in this manner.

Training Interviewers

When several long interviews are to be conducted, it is often not feasible for one individual to conduct all the interviews. A team of trained interviewers then becomes necessary. Interviewers have to be thoroughly briefed about the research and trained in how to start an interview, how to proceed with the questions, how to motivate respondents to answer, what to look for in the answers, and how to close an interview. They also need to be instructed about taking notes and coding the interview responses. The tips for interviewing, discussed later, should become a part of their repertoire for interviewing.

Good planning, proper training, offering clear guidelines to interviewers, and supervising their work all help in profitably utilizing the interviewing technique as a viable data collection mechanism. Personal interviews provide rich data when respondents spontaneously offer information, in the sense that their answers do not typically fall within a constricted range of responses, as in a questionnaire. However, personal interviews are expensive in terms of time, training costs, and resource consumption.

Review of Unstructured and Structured Interviews

The main purpose of the unstructured interview is to explore and probe into the several factors in the situation that might be central to the broad problem area. During this process it might become evident that the problem, as identified by the client, is but a symptom of a more serious and deep-rooted problem. Conducting unstructured interviews with many people in the organization could result in the identification of several critical factors in the situation. These would then be pursued further during the structured interviews for eliciting more in-depth information on them. This will help identify the critical problem as well as solve it. In applied research, a tentative theory of the factors contributing to the problem is often conceptualized on the basis of the information obtained from the unstructured and structured interviews.

Some Tips to Follow in Interviewing

The information obtained during the interviews should be as free as possible of bias. Bias refers to errors or inaccuracies in the data collected. Biases could be introduced by the interviewer, the interviewee, or the situation. The **interviewer** could bias the data if proper trust and rapport are not established with the interviewee, or when the responses are either misinterpreted or distorted, or when the interviewer unintentionally encourages or discourages certain types of responses through gestures and facial expressions.

Listening attentively to the interviewee, evincing keen interest in what the respondent has to say, exercising tact in questioning, repeating and/or clarifying the questions posed, and paraphrasing some of the answers to ensure their thorough understanding, go a long way in keeping alive the interest of the respondent throughout the interview. Recording the responses accurately is equally important.

Interviewees can bias the data when they do not come out with their true opinions but provide information that they think is what the interviewer expects of them or would like to hear. Also, if they do not understand the questions, they may feel diffident or hesitant to seek clarification. They may then answer questions without knowing their import, and thus introduce biases.

Some interviewees may be turned off because of personal likes and dislikes, or the dress of the interviewer, or the manner in which the questions are put. They may, therefore, not provide truthful answers, but instead, deliberately offer incorrect responses. Some respondents may also answer questions in a socially acceptable manner rather than indicate their true sentiments.

Biases could be **situational** as well, in terms of (1) nonparticipants, (2) trust levels and rapport established, and (3) the physical setting of the interview. *Nonparticipation,* either because of unwillingness or the inability of the interviewee to participate in the study, can bias data inasmuch as the responses of the participants may be different from those of the nonparticipants (which implies that a biased, rather than a representative set of responses is likely to result). Bias also occurs when different interviewers establish *different levels of trust and rapport* with their interviewees, thus eliciting answers of varying degrees of openness. The actual *setting* itself in which the interview is conducted might sometimes introduce biases. Some individuals, for instance, may not feel quite at ease when interviewed at the workplace and therefore not respond frankly and honestly.

In door-to-door or telephone interviews, when the respondent cannot be reached due to unavailability at that time, callbacks and further contacts should be attempted so that the sample does not become biased (discussed in the next chapter on Sampling). The interviewer can also reduce bias by being consistent with the questioning mode as each person is interviewed, by not distorting or falsifying the information received, and by not influencing the responses of the subjects in any manner.

The above biases can be minimized in several ways. The following strategies will be useful for the purpose.

Establishing Credibility and Rapport, and Motivating Individuals to Respond

The projection of professionalism, enthusiasm, and confidence is important for the interviewer. A manager hiring outside researchers would be interested in assessing their abilities and personality predispositions. Researchers must establish rapport with and gain the confidence and approval of the hiring client before they can even start their work in the organization. Knowledge, skills, ability, confidence, articulateness, and enthusiasm are therefore qualities a researcher must demonstrate in order to establish credibility with the hiring organization and its members.

To obtain honest information from the respondents, the researcher/interviewer should be able to establish rapport and trust with them. In other words, the researcher should be able to make the respondent sufficiently at ease to give informative and truthful answers without fear of adverse consequences. To this end, the researcher should state the purpose of the interview and assure complete confidentiality about the source of the responses. Establishing rapport with the respondents may not be easy, especially when interviewing employees at lower levels. They are likely to be suspicious of the intentions of the researchers; they may believe that the researchers are on the management's "side," and therefore likely to propose reduction of the labor force, increase in the workload, and so on. Thus, it is important to ensure that everyone concerned is aware of the researchers' purpose as being one of merely understanding the true state of affairs in the organization. The respondents must be tactfully made to understand that the researchers do not intend to take sides; they are not there to harm the staff, and will provide the results of research to the organization only in aggregates, without disclosing the identity of the individuals. This would encourage the respondents to feel secure about responding.

true ?

The researcher can establish rapport by being pleasant, sincere, sensitive, and nonevaluative. Evincing a genuine interest in the responses and allaying any anxieties, fears, suspicions, and tensions sensed in the situation will help respondents to feel more comfortable with the researchers. If the respondent is told about the purpose of the study and how he or she was chosen to be one of those interviewed, there would be better communication between the parties. Researchers can motivate respondents to offer honest and truthful answers by explaining to them that their contribution would indeed help, and that they themselves may stand to gain from such a survey, in the sense that the quality of life at work for most of them could improve significantly.

Certain other strategies in how questions are posed also help participants to offer less biased responses. These are discussed below.

The Questioning Technique

Funneling

In the beginning of an unstructured interview, it is advisable to ask open-ended questions to get a broad idea and form some impressions about the situation. For example a question that could be asked, would be:

"What are some of your feelings about working for this organization?"

From the responses to this broad question, further questions that are progressively more focused may be asked as the researcher processes the interviewees' responses and notes some possible key issues relevant to the situation. This transition from broad to narrow themes is called the funneling technique.

Unbiased Questions

It is important to ask questions in a way that would ensure the least bias in the response. For example, "Tell me how you experience your job" is a better question than, "Boy, the work you do must be really boring; let me hear how you experience it." The latter question is "loaded" in terms of the interviewer's own perceptions of the job. A loaded question might influence the types of answers received from the respondent. Bias could be also introduced by emphasizing certain words, by tone and voice inflections, and through inappropriate suggestions.

Clarifying Issues

To make sure that the researcher understands issues as the respondent intends to represent them, it is advisable to restate or rephrase important information given by the respondent. For instance, if the interviewee says, "There is an unfair promotion policy in this organization; seniority does not count at all. It is the juniors who always get promoted," the researcher might interject, "So you are saying that juniors always get promoted over the heads of even capable seniors." Rephrasing in this way clarifies the issue of whether or not the respondent considers ability important. If certain things that are being said are not clear, the researcher should seek clarification. For example, if the respondent happened to say, "The facilities here are really poor; we often have to continue working even when we are dying of thirst," the researcher might ask if there is no water fountain or drinking water available in the building. The respondent's reply to this might well indicate that there is a water fountain across the hall, but the respondent would have liked one on his side of the work area as well.

Helping the Respondent to Think Through Issues

If the respondent is not able to verbalize her perceptions, or replies, "I don't know," the researcher should ask the question in a simpler way or rephrase it. For instance, if a respondent is unable to specify what aspects of the job he dislikes, the researcher might ask the question in a simpler way. For example, the respondent might be asked which task he would prefer to do: serve a customer or do some filing work. If the answer is "serve the customer," the researcher might use another aspect of the respondent's job and ask the paired-choice question again. In this way, the respondent can sort out which aspects of the job he likes better than others.

Taking Notes

When conducting interviews, it is important that the researcher makes written notes as the interviews are taking place, or as soon as the interview is terminated. The interviewer should not rely on memory, because information recalled from memory is imprecise and often likely to be incorrect. Furthermore, if more than one interview is scheduled for the day, the amount of information received increases, as do possible sources of error in recalling from memory as to who said what. Information based solely on recall introduces bias into the research.

The interviews can be recorded on tape if the respondent has no objection. However, taped interviews might bias the respondents' answers because they know that their voices are being recorded, and their anonymity is not preserved in full. Hence, even if the respondents do not object to being taped, there could be some bias in their responses. Before recording or videotaping interviews, one should be reasonably certain that such a method of obtaining data is not likely to bias the information received. Any audio or videotaping should always be done only after obtaining the respondent's permission.

Review of Tips to Follow in Interviewing

Establishing credibility as able researchers with the client system and the organizational members is important for the success of the research project. Researchers need to establish rapport with the respondents and motivate them to give responses relatively free from bias by allaying whatever suspicions, fears, anxieties, and concerns they may have about the research and its consequences. This can be accomplished by being sincere, pleasant, and nonevaluative. While interviewing, the researcher has to ask broad questions initially and then narrow them down to specific areas, ask questions in an unbiased way, offer clarifications when needed, and help respondents to think through difficult issues. The responses should be transcribed immediately and not be trusted to memory and later recall.

Having looked at unstructured and structured interviews and learned something about how to conduct the interviews, we can now discuss face-to-face and telephone interviews.

Face-to-Face and Telephone Interviews

Interviews can be conducted either face to face or over the telephone. They could also be computer-assisted. Although most unstructured interviews in organizational research are conducted face to face, structured interviews could be either face to face or through the medium of the telephone, depending on the level of complexity of the issues involved, the likely duration of the interview, the convenience of both parties, and the geographical area covered by the survey. Telephone interviews are best suited when information from a large number of respondents spread over a wide geographic area is to be obtained quickly, and the likely duration of each interview is, say, 10 minutes or less. Many market surveys, for instance, are conducted through structured telephone interviews. In addition, computer-assisted telephone interviews (CATI) are also possible, and easy to manage.

Face-to-face interviews and telephone interviews have other advantages and disadvantages. These will now be briefly discussed.

Face-to-Face Interviews

Advantages. The main advantage of face-to-face or direct interviews is that the researcher can adapt the questions as necessary, clarify doubts, and ensure that the responses are properly understood, by repeating or rephrasing the questions. The researcher can also pick up nonverbal cues from the respondent. Any discomfort, stress, or problems that the respondent experiences can be detected through frowns, nervous tapping, and other body language unconsciously exhibited by her. This would be impossible to detect in a telephone interview.

Disadvantages. The main disadvantages of face-to-face interviews are the geographical limitations they may impose on the surveys and the vast resources needed if such surveys need to be done nationally or internationally. The costs of training interviewers to minimize interviewer biases (e.g., differences in questioning methods, interpretation of responses) are also high. Another drawback is that respondents might feel uneasy about the anonymity of their responses when they interact face to face with the interviewer.

Telephone Interviews

Advantages. The main advantage of telephone interviewing, from the researcher's point of view, is that a number of different people can be reached (if need be, across the country or even internationally) in a relatively short period of time. From the respondents' standpoint it would eliminate any discomfort that some of them might feel in facing the interviewer. It is also possible that most of them would feel less uncomfortable disclosing personal information over the phone than face to face.

Disadvantages. A main disadvantage of telephone interviewing is that the respondent could unilaterally terminate the interview without warning or explanation, by hanging up the phone. Caller ID might further aggravate the situation. This is understandable, given the numerous telemarketing calls people are bombarded with on a daily basis. To minimize this type of a nonresponse problem, it would be advisable to call the interviewee ahead of time to request participation in the survey, giving an approximate idea of how long the interview would last, and setting up a mutually convenient time. Interviewees usually tend to appreciate this courtesy and are more likely to cooperate. It is a good policy not to prolong the interview beyond the time originally stated. As mentioned earlier, another disadvantage of the telephone interview is that the researcher will not be able to see the respondent to read the nonverbal communication.

Interviewing is a useful data collection method, especially during the exploratory stages of research. Where a large number of interviews are conducted with a number of different interviewers, it is important to train the interviewers with care in order to minimize interviewer biases manifested in such ways as voice inflections, differences in wordings, and interpretation. Good training decreases interviewer biases.

Additional Sources of Bias in Interview Data

We have already discussed several sources of bias in data collection. Biased data will be obtained when respondents are interviewed while they are extremely busy or are not in good humor. Responses to issues such as strikes, layoffs, or the like could also be biased. The personality of the interviewer, the introductory sentence, inflection of the voice, and such other aspects could introduce additional biases. Awareness of the many sources of bias will enable interviewers to obtain relatively valid information.

Sampling biases, which include inability to contact persons whose telephone numbers have changed, could also affect the quality of the research data. Likewise, people with unlisted numbers who are not contacted could also bias the sample (discussed in the next chapter), and hence, the data obtained. With the introduction of caller ID, it is possible for telephone interviews to be ridden with complexity.

Computer-Assisted Interviewing

With computer-assisted interviews (CAI), thanks to modern technology, questions are flashed onto the computer screen and interviewers can enter the answers of the respondents directly into the computer. The accuracy of data collection is considerably enhanced since the software can be programmed to flag the "offbase" or "out-of-range" responses. CAI software also prevents interviewers from asking the wrong questions or in the wrong sequence since the questions are automatically flashed to the respondent in an ordered sequence. This would, to some extent, eliminate interviewer-induced biases.

CATI and CAPI

There are two types of computer-assisted interview programs: CATI (computer-assisted telephone interviewing) and CAPI (computer-assisted personal interviewing).

CATI, used in research organizations, is useful inasmuch as responses to surveys can be obtained from people all over the world since the PC is networked into the telephone system. The PC monitor prompts the questions with the help of software and the respondent provides the answers. The computer selects the telephone number, dials, and places the responses in a file. The data are analyzed later. Computerized, voice-activated telephone interviews are also possible for short surveys. Data can also be gathered during field surveys through handheld computers that record and analyze responses.

CAPI involves big investments in hardware and software. CAPI has an advantage in that it can be self-administered; that is, respondents can use their own computers to run the program by themselves once they receive the software and enter their responses, thereby reducing errors in recording. However, not everyone is comfortable using a personal computer and some may not have access to it.

The **voice recording system** assists CATI programs by recording interviewees' responses. Courtesy, ethics, as well as legal requirements would require that the respondent's permission to record be obtained before the **voice capture system** (VCS) is activated. The VCS allows the computer to capture the respondents' answers, which are recorded in a digital mode and stored in a data file. They can be played back later, for example, to listen to customers by region, industry, or any combination of different sets of factors.

In sum, the advantages of computer-assisted interviews can be stated simply as quick and more accurate information gathering, plus faster and easier analysis of data. The field costs are low and automatic tabulation of results is possible. It is more efficient in terms of costs and time, once the initial heavy investment in equipment and software has been made. However, to be really cost-effective, large surveys should be done frequently enough to warrant the heavy front-end investment and programming costs.

Computer-Aided Survey Services

Several research organizations offer their services to companies who engage in occasional data gathering. For instance, the National Computer Network provides computer survey services for conducting marketing studies. Some of the advantages of using these services are that (1) the researcher can start analyzing the data even as the field survey is in progress, since results can be transmitted to clients through modem in raw or tabulated form; (2) data can be automatically "cleaned up" and errors, if any, fixed even as they are being collected; (3) biases due to ordering questions in a particular way (known as the ordering effects) can be eliminated since meaningful random start patterns can be incorporated into the questioning process; (4) skip patterns (e.g., if the answer to this question is NO, skip to question #19) can be programmed into the process; and (5) questions can be customized to incorporate the respondents' terminology of concepts into subsequent questions.

Computer surveys can be conducted either by mailing the disks to respondents or through online surveys, with the respondents' personal computers being hooked up to computer networks. Survey System provided by Creative Reasearch Systems and Interview System provided by Compaq Co. are two of the several computer survey systems available in the market.

Advantages of Software Packages

Field notes taken by interviewers as they collect data generally have to be transcribed, hand-coded, hand-tabulated, and so on—all of which are tedious and time consuming. Computers vastly ease the interviewers' job with regard to these activities. Automatic indexing of the data can be done with special programs. The two modes in operation are (1) **indexing** such that specific responses are coded in a particular way; and (2) **retrieval** of data with a fast search speed—covering 10,000 pages in less than 5 seconds. Text-oriented database management retrieval program allows the user to go through the text, inserting marks that link related units of text. The associative links formed are analytical categories specified by the researcher. Once the links are created, the program allows the user to activate them by opening multiple windows on the screen.

We thus see that computers make a big impact on data collection. With greater technological advancement and a reduction of hardware and software costs, computer-assisted interviews promise to become a primary method of data collection in the future.

Review of Interviewing

Interviews are one method of obtaining data; they can be either unstructured or structured, and can be conducted face to face, over the telephone, or through the medium of the PC. Unstructured interviews are usually conducted to obtain definite ideas about what is, and is not, important and relevant to particular problem situations. Structured interviews give more in-depth information about specific variables of interest. To minimize bias in responses, the interviewer must establish rapport with the respondents and ask unbiased questions. The face-to-face interview and that conducted over the telephone have their advantages and disadvantages, and both have their use in different circumstances. Computer-assisted interviewing, which entails heavy initial investment, is an asset for interviewing and for the analyses of qualitative, spontaneous responses. Computer interactive interviews show promise to become an increasingly important mode of data collection in the future. Next, we will see how data can be gathered through questionnaires.

PART II: QUESTIONNAIRES

A questionnaire is a preformulated written set of questions to which respondents record their answers, usually within rather closely defined alternatives. Questionnaires are an efficient data collection mechanism when the researcher knows exactly what is required and how to measure the variables of interest. Questionnaires can be administered personally, mailed to the respondents, or electronically distributed.

Personally Administered Questionnaires

When the survey is confined to a local area, and the organization is willing and able to assemble groups of employees to respond to the questionnaries at the workplace, a good way to collect data is to personally administer the questionnaires. The main advantage of this is that the researcher or a member of the research team can collect all the completed responses within a short period of time. Any doubts that the respondents might have on any question could be clarified on the spot. The researcher is also afforded the opportunity to introduce the research topic and motivate the respondents to offer their frank answers. Administering questionnaires to large numbers of individuals at the same time is less expensive and consumes less time than interviewing; it does not also require as much skill to administer the questionnaire as to conduct interviews. Wherever possible, questionnaires are best administered personally to groups of people because of these advantages. However, organizations are often unable or disinclined to allow work hours to be spent on data collection, and other ways of getting the questionnaries back after completion may have to be found. In such cases, employees may be given blank questionnaires to be collected from them personally on completion after a few days, or mailed back by a certain date in self-addressed, stamped envelopes provided to them for the purpose. Scanner sheets (the answer sheets that are usually provided for answering multiple-choice questions in exams) are usually sent with the questionnaire, so that respondents can circle their answers to each question on the sheet, which can then be directly entered into the computer as data, without someone having to code and then manually enter them in the computer. Disks containing the questions can also be sent to respondents who have, and can use, personal computers.

Mail Questionnaires

The main advantage of mail questionnaires is that a wide geographical area can be covered in the survey. They are mailed to the respondents, who can complete them at their convenience, in their homes, and at their own pace. However, the return rates of mail questionnaires are typically low. A 30% response rate is considered acceptable. Another disadvantage of the mail questionnaire is that any doubts the respondents might have cannot be clarified. Also, with very low return rates it is difficult to establish the representativeness of the sample because those responding to the survey may not at all represent the population they are supposed to. However, some effective techniques can be employed for improving the rates of response to mail questionnaires. Sending follow-up letters, enclosing some small monetary amounts as incentives with the questionnaire, providing the respondent with self-addressed, stamped return envelopes, and keeping the questionnaire brief do indeed help.

Mail questionnaires are also expected to meet with a better response rate when respondents are notified in advance about the forthcoming survey, and a reputed research organization administers them with its own introductory cover letter.

The choice of using the questionnaire as a data gathering method might be restricted if the researcher has to reach subjects with very little education. Adding pictures to the questionnaires, if feasible, might be of help in such cases. For most organizational research, however, after the variables for the research have been identified and the measures therefor found or developed, the questionnaire is a convenient data collection mechanism. Field studies, comparative surveys, and experimental designs often use questionnaires to measure the variables of interest. Because questionnaires are in common use in surveys, it is necessary to know how to design them effectively. A set of guidelines for questionnaire construction follows.

GUIDELINES FOR QUESTIONNAIRE DESIGN

Sound questionnaire design principles should focus on three areas. The first relates to the wording of the questions. The second refers to planning of issues of how the variables will be categorized, scaled, and coded after receipt of the responses. The third pertains to the general appearance of the questionnaire. All three are important issues in questionnaire design because they can minimize

Figure 10.1
Principles of Questionnaire Design.

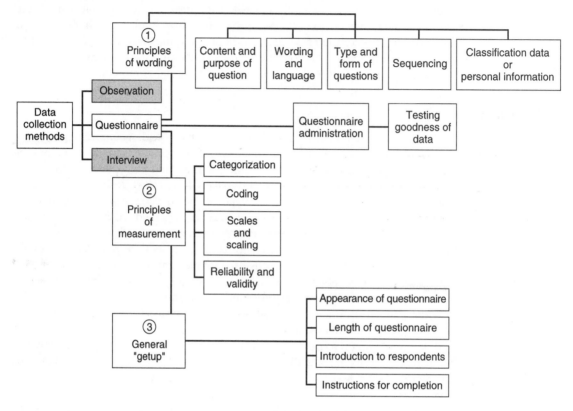

biases in research. These issues are discussed below. The important aspects are schematically depicted in Figure 10.1.

Principles of Wording

The principles of wording refer to such factors as (1) the appropriateness of the content of the questions, (2) how questions are worded and the level of sophistication of the language used, (3) the type and form of questions asked, (4) the sequencing of the questions, and (5) the personal data sought from the respondents. Each of these is explained below.

Content and Purpose of the Questions

The nature of the variable tapped—subjective feelings or objective facts—will determine what kinds of questions will be asked. If the variables tapped are of a subjective nature (e.g., satisfaction, involvement), where respondents' beliefs, perceptions, and attitudes are to be measured, the questions should tap the dimensions and elements of the concept. Where objective variables such as age and educational levels of respondents are tapped, a single direct question—preferably one that has an ordinal scaled set of categories—would be appropriate. Thus the purpose of each question should be carefully considered so that the variables are adequately measured and yet no superfluous questions are asked.

Language and Wording of the Questionnaire

The language of the questionnaire should approximate the level of understanding of the respondents. The choice of words would depend on their educational level, the usage of terms and idioms in the culture, and the frames of reference of the respondents. For instance, even when English is the spoken or official language in two cultures, certain words may be alien to one culture. Terms such as "working here is a *drag*," and "she is a *compulsive* worker," may not be interpreted the same way in different cultures. Some blue-collar workers may not understand terminology such as "organizational structure." Thus it is essential to word the questions in a way that could be understood by the respondent. If some questions are either not understood or are interpreted differently by the respondent, the researcher will obtain the wrong answers to the questions, and responses will thus be biased. Hence, the questions asked, the language used, and the wording should be appropriate to tap respondents' attitudes, perceptions, and feelings.

Type and Form of Questions

Type of question refers to whether the question will be open-ended or closed. Form refers to positively and negatively worded questions.

Open-Ended versus Closed Questions.
Open-ended questions allow respondents to answer them in any way they choose. An example of an open-ended question is asking the respondent to state five things that are interesting and challenging in the job. Another example is asking what the respondents like about their supervisors or their work environment. A third example is to invite their comments on the investment portfolio of the firm.

A closed question, in contrast, would ask the respondents to make choices among a set of alternatives given by the researcher. For instance, instead of asking the respondent to state any *five* aspects of the job that she finds interesting and challenging, the researcher might list 10 or 15 aspects that might seem interesting or challenging in jobs and ask the respondents to rank the first five among these in the order of their preference. All items in a questionnaire using a nominal, ordinal, or Likert or ratio scale are considered closed.

Closed questions help the respondents to make quick decisions to choose among the several alternatives before them. They also help the researcher to code the information easily for subsequent analysis. Care has to be taken to ensure that the alternatives are mutually exclusive and collectively exhaustive. If there are overlapping categories, or if all possible alternatives are not given (i.e., the categories are not exhaustive), the respondents might get confused and the advantage of their being enabled to make a quick decision is thus lost.

Some respondents may find even well-delineated categories in a closed question rather confining and might avail of the opportunity to make additional comments. This is the reason that many questionnaires end with a final open-ended question that invites respondents to comment on topics that might not have been covered fully or adequately. The responses to such open-ended questions have to be edited and categorized for subsequent data analysis.

Positively and Negatively Worded Questions. Instead of phrasing all questions positively, it is advisable to include some negatively worded questions as well, so the tendency in respondents to mechanically circle the points toward one end of the scale is minimized. For example, let us say that a set of six questions is used to tap the variable "perceived success" on a 5-point scale, with 1 being "very low" and 5 being "very high" on the scale. A respondent who is not particularly interested in completing the questionnaire is more likely to stay involved and remain alert while answering the questions when positively and negatively worded questions are interspersed in it. For instance, if the respondent had circled 5 for a positively worded question such as, *"I feel I have been able to accomplish a number of different things in my job,"* he cannot circle number 5 again to the negatively worded question, *"I do not feel I am very effective in my job."* The respondent is now shaken out of any likely tendency to mechanically respond to one end of the scale. In case this does still happen, the researcher has an opportunity to detect such biases. A good questionnaire should therefore include both positively and negatively worded questions. The use of double negatives and excessive use of the words *not* and *only* should be avoided in the negatively worded questions because they tend to confuse respondents. For instance, it is better to say, *"Coming to work is no great fun"* than to say *"Not coming to work is greater fun than coming to work."* Likewise, it is better to say *"The rich need no help"* than to say *"Only the rich do not need help."*

Double-Barreled Questions. A question that lends itself to different possible responses to its subparts is called a double-barreled question. Such questions should be avoided and two or more separate questions asked instead. For example, the question *"Do you think there is a good market for the product and that it will sell well?"* could bring a "yes" response to the first part (i.e., there is a good market for the product) and a "no" response to the latter part (i.e., it will not sell well for various other reasons). In this case, it would be better to ask two questions: (1) *"Do you think there is a good market for the product?"* and (2) *"Do you think the product will sell well?"* The answers might be "yes" to both, "no" to both, "yes" to the first and "no" to the second, or "yes" to the second and "no" to the first. If we combined the two questions and asked a double-barreled question, we would confuse the respondents and obtain ambiguous responses. Hence, double-barreled questions should be eliminated.

Ambiguous Questions. Even questions that are not double-barreled might be ambiguously worded and the respondent may not be sure what exactly they mean.

An example of such a question is *"To what extent would you say you are happy?"* Respondents might find it difficult to decide whether the question refers to their state of feelings at the workplace, or at home, or in general. Because it is an organizational survey, she might presume that the question relates to the workplace. Yet the researcher might have intended to inquire about the general, overall degree of satisfaction that the individual experiences in everyday life—a very global feeling not specific to the workplace alone. Thus, responses to ambiguous questions have built-in bias inasmuch as different respondents might interpret such items in the questionnaire differently. The result would be a mixed bag of ambiguous responses that do not accurately provide the correct answer to the question.

Recall-Dependent Questions. Some questions might require respondents to recall experiences from the past that are hazy in their memory. Answers to such questions might have bias. For instance, if an employee who has had 30 years' service in the organization is asked to state when he first started working in a particular department and for how long, he may not be able to give the correct answers and may be way off in his responses. A better source for obtaining that information would be the personnel records.

Leading Questions. Questions should not be phrased in such a way that they lead the respondents to give the responses that the researcher would like or want them to give. An example of such a question is: *"Don't you think that in these days of escalating costs of living, employees should be given good pay raises?"* By asking such a question, we are signaling and pressuring respondents to say "yes." Tagging the question to rising living costs makes it difficult for most respondents (unless they are the top bosses in charge of budget and finances) to say, "No; not unless their productivity increases too!" Another way of asking the question about pay raises to elicit less biased responses would be: *"To what extent do you agree that employees should be given higher pay raises?"* If respondents think that the employees do not deserve a higher pay raise at all, their response would be "Strongly Disagree"; if they think that respondents should be definitely given a high pay raise, they would respond to the "Strongly Agree" end of the scale, and the in-between points would be chosen depending on the strength of their agreement or disagreement. In this case, the question is not framed in a suggestive manner as in the previous instance.

Loaded Questions. Another type of bias in questions occurs when they are phrased in an emotionally charged manner. An example of such a loaded question is asking employees: *"To what extent do you think management is likely to be vindictive if the Union decides to go on strike?"* The words "strike" and "vindictive" are emotionally charged terms, polarizing management and unions, Hence, asking a question such as the above would elicit strongly emotional and highly biased responses. If the purpose of the question is twofold, that is, to find (1) the extent to which employees are in favor of strike and (2) the extent to which they fear adverse reactions if they do go on strike, then these are the two specific questions that need to be asked. It may turn out that the employees are not strongly in favor of a strike and they also do not believe that management would retaliate if they did go on strike!

Social Desirability. Questions should not be worded such that they elicit socially desirable responses, For instance, a question such as *"Do you think that older people should be laid off?"* would elicit a response of "no," mainly because society would frown on a person who would say that elderly people should be fired even if they are capable of performing their jobs satisfactorily. Hence, irrespective of the true feelings of the respondent, a socially desirable answer would be provided. If the purpose of the question is to gauge the extent to which organizations are seen as obligated to retain those above 65 years of age, a differently worded question with less pressure toward social desirability would be: *"There are advantages and disadvantages to retaining senior citizens in the workforce. To what extent do you think companies should continue to keep the elderly on their payroll?"*

Sometimes certain items that tap social desirability are deliberately introduced at various points in the questionnaire and an index of each individual's social desirability tendency is calculated therefrom. This index is then applied to all other responses given by the individual in order to adjust for social desirability biases (Crowne & Marlowe, 1980; Edwards, 1957).

Length of Questions. Finally, simple, short questions are preferable to long ones. As a rule of thumb, a question or a statement in the questionnaire should not exceed 20 words, or exceed one full line in print (Horst, 1968; Oppenheim, 1986).

Sequencing of Questions

The sequence of questions in the questionnaire should be such that the respondent is led from questions of a general nature to those that are more specific, and from questions that are relatively easy to answer to those that are progressively more difficult. This funnel approach, as it is called (Festinger & Katz, 1966), facilitates the easy and smooth progress of the respondent through the items in the questionnaire. The progression from general to specific questions might mean that the respondent is first asked questions of a global nature that pertain to the organization, and then is asked more incisive questions regarding the specific job, department, and the like. Easy questions might relate to issues that do not involve much thinking; the more difficult ones might call for more thought, judgment, and decision making in providing the answers.

In determining the sequence of questions, it is advisable not to place contiguously a positively worded and a negatively worded question tapping the same element or dimension of a concept. For instance, placing two questions such as the following, one immediately after the other, is not only awkward but might also seem insulting to the respondent.

1. *I have opportunities to interact with my colleagues during work hours.*
2. *I have few opportunities to interact with my colleagues during work hours.*

First, there is no need to ask the very same question in a positive and a negative way. Second, if for some reason this is deemed necessary (e.g., to check the consistency of the responses), the two questions should be placed in different parts of the questionnaire, as far apart as possible.

The way questions are sequenced could also introduce certain biases, frequently referred to as the ordering effects. Though randomly placing the questions in the questionnaire would reduce any systematic biases in the response, it is very rarely done, because of subsequent confusion while categorizing, coding, and analyzing the responses.

In sum, the language and wording of the questionnaire focus on such issues as the type and form of questions asked (i.e., open-ended and closed questions, and positively and negatively worded questions), as well as avoiding double-barreled questions, ambiguous questions, leading questions, loaded questions, questions prone to tap socially desirable answers, and those involving distant recall. Questions should also not be unduly long. Using the funnel approach helps respondents to progress through the questionnaire with ease and comfort.

Classification Data or Personal Information

Classification data, also known as personal information or demographic questions, elicit such information as age, educational level, marital status, and income. Unless absolutely necessary, it is best not to ask for the name of the respondent. If, however, the questionnaire has to be identified with the respondents for any reason, then the questionnaire could be numbered and connected by the researcher to the respondent's name, in a separately maintained, private document. This procedure should be clearly explained to the respondent. The reason for using the numerical system in questionnaires is to ensure the anonymity of the respondent, should the questionnaires fall into the hands of someone in the organization.

Whether questions seeking personal information should appear in the beginning or at the end of the questionnaire is a matter of choice for the researcher. Some researchers ask for personal data at the end rather than the beginning of the questionnaire (Oppenheim, 1986). Their reasoning may be that by the time the respondent reaches the end of the questionnaire he or she would have been convinced of the legitimacy and genuineness of the questions framed by the researcher, and hence, would be more inclined and amenable to share personal information. Researchers who prefer to elicit most of the personal information at the very beginning may opine that once respondents have shared some of their personal history, they may have psychologically identified themselves with the questionnaire, and may feel a commitment to respond. Thus whether one asks for this information in the beginning or at the end of the questionnaire is a matter of individual choice. However, questions seeking details of income, or other highly sensitive information—if at all deemed necessary—are best placed at the very end of the questionnaire.

Even so, it would be a wise policy to ask for such information by providing a range of response options, rather than seeking exact figures. For example, the variables can be tapped as shown below:

Example 10.1

Age (years)	Annual Income
☐ Under 20	☐ Less than $20,000
☐ 20–30	☐ $20,000–30,000
☐ 31–40	☐ $30,001–40,000
☐ 41–50	☐ $40,001–50,000
☐ 51–60	☐ $50,001–70,000
☐ Over 60	☐ $70,001–90,000
	☐ Over $90,000

In organizational surveys, it is advisable to gather certain demographic data such as age, sex, educational level, job level, department, and number of years in the organization, even if the theoretical framework does not necessitate or include these variables. Such data will help to describe the sample characteristics in the report written after data analysis. However, when there are only a few respondents in a department, then questions likely to reveal their identity might render them futile, objectionable, and threatening to employees. For instance, if there is only one female in a department, then she would refrain from responding to the question on gender, because it would establish the source of the data; this apprehension is understandable.

To sum up, certain principles of wording need to be followed while designing a questionnaire. The questions asked must be appropriate for tapping the variable. The language and wording used should be such that it is meaningful to the employees. The form and type of questions should be geared to minimize respondent biases. The sequencing of the questions should facilitate the smooth progress of the responses from the start to the finish. The personal data should be gathered with due regard to the sensitivity of the respondents' feelings, and with respect for privacy.

PRINCIPLES OF MEASUREMENT

Just as there are guidelines to be followed to ensure that the wording of the questionnaire is appropriate to minimize bias, so also are there some principles of measurement to be followed to ensure that the data collected are appropriate to test our hypotheses. These refer to the scales and scaling techniques used in measuring concepts, as well as the assessment of reliability and validity of the measures used, which were all discussed in Chapter 9.

As we have seen, appropriate scales have to be used depending on the type of data that need to be obtained. The different scaling mechanisms that help us to anchor our scales appropriately should be properly used. Wherever possible, the interval and ratio scales should be used in preference to nominal or ordinal scales. Once data are obtained, the "goodness of data" is assessed through tests of validity and reliability. *Validity* establishes how well a technique, instrument, or process measures a particular concept, and *reliability* indicates how stably and consistently the instrument taps the variable. Finally, the data have to be obtained in a manner that makes for easy categorization and coding, both of which are discussed later.

GENERAL APPEARANCE OR "GETUP" OF THE QUESTIONNAIRE

Not only is it important to address issues of wording and measurement in questionnaire design, but it is also necessary to pay attention to how the questionnaire looks. An attractive and neat questionnaire with appropriate introduction, instructions, and well-arrayed set of questions and response alternatives will make it easier for the respondents to answer them. A good introduction, well-organized instructions, and neat alignment of the questions are all important. These elements are briefly discussed with examples.

A Good Introduction

A proper introduction that clearly discloses the identity of the researcher and conveys the purpose of the survey is absolutely necessary. It is also essential to establish some rapport with the respondents and motivate them to respond to the questions in the questionnaire wholeheartedly and enthusiastically. Assurance of confidentiality of the information provided by them will allow for less biased answers. The introduction section should end on a courteous note, thanking the respondent for taking the time to respond to the survey. The following is an example of an appropriate introduction.

Example 10.2

Department of Management
Southern Illinois University at Carbondale
Carbondale, Illinois 62901

Date

Dear Participant,

This questionnaire is designed to study aspects of life at work. The information you provide will help us better understand the quality of our work life. Because *you* are the one who can give us a correct picture of how *you* experience your work life, I request you to respond to the questions frankly and honestly.

Your response will be kept *strictly confidential*. Only members of the research team will have access to the information you give. In order to ensure the utmost privacy, we have provided an identification number for each participant. This number will be used by us only for follow-up procedures. The numbers, names, or the completed questionnaires will not be made available to anyone other than the research team. A summary of the results will be mailed to you after the data are analyzed.

Thank you very much for your time and cooperation. I greatly appreciate your organization's and your help in furthering this research endeavor.

Cordially,
(Sd)
Anita Sigler, Ph.D.
Professor

Organizing Questions, Giving Instructions and Guidance, and Good Alignment

Organizing the questions logically and neatly in appropriate sections and providing instructions on how to complete the items in each section will help the respondents to answer them without difficulty. Questions should also be neatly aligned in a way that allows the respondent to complete the task of reading and answering the questionnaire expending the least time and effort and without straining the eyes.

A specimen of the portion of a questionnaire incorporating the above points follows.

Example 10.3   SECTION TWO: ABOUT WORK LIFE

> The questions below ask about how you experience your work life. Think in terms of your everyday experiences and accomplishments on the job and put the most appropriate response number for you on the side of each item, using the scale below.

Strongly Agree	Agree	Slightly Agree	Neutral	Slightly Disagree	Disagree	Strongly Disagree
1	2	3	4	5	6	7

1. I do my work best when my job assignments are fairly difficult. ____
2. When I have a choice, I try to work in a group instead of by myself. ____
3. In my work assignments, I try to be my own boss. ____
4. I seek an active role in the leadership of a group. ____
5. I try very hard to improve on my past performance at work. ____
6. I pay a good deal of attention to the feelings of others at work. ____
7. I go my own way at work, regardless of the opinions of others. ____
8. I avoid trying to influence those around me to see things my way. ____
9. I take moderate risks, sticking my neck out to get ahead at work. ____
10. I prefer to do my own work, letting others do theirs. ____
11. I disregard rules and regulations that hamper my personal freedom. ____

Personal Data

Demographic or personal data could be organized as in the example that follows. Note the ordinal scaling of the age variable.

Example 10.4   SECTION ONE: ABOUT YOURSELF

> Please *circle* the numbers representing the most appropriate responses for you in respect of the following items.

1. Your Age (years)

1 Under 20
2 20–35
3 36–50
4 51–65
5 Over 65

2. Your Highest
Completed Level
of Education

1 Elementary school
2 High school
3 College degree
4 Graduate degree
5 Other (specify)

3. Your Gender

1 Female
2 Male

4. Your Marital Status

1 Married
2 Single
3 Widowed
4 Divorced or
   separated
5 Other (specify)

5. Number of
Preschool Children
(under 5 Years of Age)

1 None
2 One
3 Two
4 Three or more

6. Age of the Eldest
Child in Your
Care (years)

1 Under 5
2 5–12
3 13–19
4 Over 19
5 Not applicable

7. Number of Years
Worked in the
Organizations

1 Less than 1
2 1–2
3 3–5
4 6–10
5 Over 10

8. Number of Other
Organizations Worked
for Before Joining
This Organization

1 None
2 One
3 Two
4 Three
5 Four or more

9. Present Work Shift

1 First
2 Second
3 Third

10. Job Status

1 Top management
2 Middle management
3 First-level supervisor
4 Nonmanagerial

Information on Income and Other Sensitive Personal Data

Though demographic information can be sought either at the beginning or at the end of the questionnaire, information of a very private and personal nature such as income, state of health, and so on, if at all considered necessary for the survey, should be asked at the end of the questionnaire, rather than the beginning. Also, such questions should be justified by explaining how this information might contribute to knowledge and problem solving, so that respondents do not perceive them to be of an intrusive or prying nature (see example below). Postponing such questions to the end would help reduce respondent bias if the individual is vexed by the personal nature of the question.

Example 10.5 Because many people believe that income is a significant factor in explaining the type of career decisions individuals make, the following two questions are very important for this research. Like all other items in this questionnaire, the responses to these two questions will be kept confidential. Please *circle* the most appropriate number that describes your position.

Roughly, *my total yearly* income before taxes and other deductions is:	Roughly, the *total yearly income* before taxes and other deductions of *my immediate family—including* my own job income, income from other sources, and the income of my spouse—is:
1 Less than $36,000	1 Less than $36,000
2 $36,001–50,000	2 $36,001–50,000
3 $50,001–70,000	3 $50,001–70,000
4 $70,001–90,000	4 $70,001–90,000
5 Over $90,000	5 $90,001–120,000
	6 $120,001–150,000
	7 Over $150,000

Open-Ended Question at the End

The questionnaire could include an open-ended question at the end allowing respondents to comment on any aspect they choose. It would end with an expression of sincere thanks to respondents. The last part of the questionnaire could look like the following.

Example 10.6 *The questions in the survey may not be all-embracing and comprehensive and may not therefore have afforded you an opportunity to report some things you may want to say about your job, organization, or yourself. Please make any additional comments needed, in the space provided.*

How did you feel about completing this questionnaire?
Check the face in the following diagram that reflects your feelings.

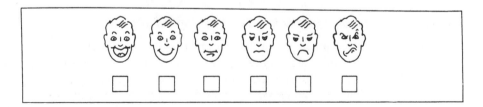

Concluding the Questionnaire

The questionnaire should end on a courteous note, reminding the respondent to check that all the items have been completed, as per the example below.

Example 10.7   *I sincerely appreciate your time and cooperation. Please check to make sure that you have not skipped any questions inadvertently, and then drop the questionnaire in the locked box, clearly marked for the purpose, at the entrance of your department.*

Thank you!

Review of Questionnaire Design

We have devoted a lot of attention to questionnaire design because questionnaires are the most common method of collecting data. The principles of questionnaire design relate to how the questions are worded and measured, and how the entire questionnaire is organized. To minimize respondent biases and measurement errors, all the principles discussed have to be followed carefully.

Questionnaires are most useful as a data collection method especially when large numbers of people are to be reached in different geographical regions. They are a popular method of collecting data because researchers can obtain information fairly easily, and the questionnaire responses are easily coded. When well-validated instruments are used, the findings of the study benefit the scientific community since the results can be replicated and additions to the theory base made.

There are several ways of administering questionnaires. Questionnaires can be personally administered to respondents, inserted in magazines, periodicals, or newspapers, mailed to respondents, or electronically distributed through e-mail—both via the Internet and Intranet. Software is also available to frame subsequent questions based on the subject's response to the preceding question. Companies' web sites can also elicit survey responses, for example, reactions to customer service, product utility, and the like. Global research is now vastly facilitated by the electronic system.

Pretesting of Structured Questions

Whether it is a structured interview where the questions are posed to the respondent in a predetermined order, or a questionnaire that is used in a survey, it is important to pretest the instrument to ensure that the questions are understood by the respondents (i.e., there is no ambiguity in the questions) and that there are no problems with the wording or measurement. Pretesting involves the use of a small number of respondents to test the appropriateness of the questions and their comprehension. This helps to rectify any inadequacies, in time, before administering the instrument orally or through a questionnaire to respondents, and thus reduce biases.

It would be good to debrief the results of the pretest and obtain additional information from the small group of participants (who would serve the role of a focus group) on their general reactions to the questionnaire and how they felt about completing the instrument.

ELECTRONIC QUESTIONNAIRE DESIGN AND SURVEYS

Online questionnaire surveys are easily designed and administered when microcomputers are hooked up to computer networks. Data disks can also be mailed to respondents, who may use their own personal computers for responding to the questions. These will, of course, be helpful only when the respondents know how to use the computer and feel comfortable responding in this manner.

As stated earlier, CAPPA, which facilitates the preparation and administration of questionnaires, is particularly useful for marketing research. The CAPPA system includes 10 programs enabling the user to design a sophisticated computerized questionnaire, computerize the data collection process, and analyze the data collected. More reliable data are likely to result since the respondent can go back and forth and easily change a response, and various on- and off-screen stimuli are provided to sustain respondents' interest.

A program is designed into the CAPPA system that checks for syntactical or logical errors in the coding. Even as the survey is in progress, descriptive summaries of the cumulative data can be obtained either on the screen or in printed form. After data collection is complete, a data-editing program identifies missing or out-of-range data (e.g., a 6 in response to a question on a 5-point scale). The researcher can set the parameters for either deleting the missing responses where there are too many, or computing the mean on other responses and substituting this figure for the missing response. CAPPA also includes data analytic programs such as cross-tabs, ANOVA, multiple regression, and others (discussed later in the book). Randomization of questions and the weighting of respondents to ensure more representative results (in cases where the sample either overrepresents or underrepresents certain population groups—discussed later, in the chapter on Sampling) are some of the attractive features of CAPPA.

Several programs are developed to administer questionnaires electronically. As disks are inexpensive, mailing them across the country is no problem either. The PC medium nonresponse rates may not be any higher than those of the mail questionnaire response. With increase of computer literacy, we can expect electronic questionnaire administration to take on an increasing role in the future.

SPSS (Statistical Package for the Social Sciences) has several software programs for research purposes including (1) SPSS Data Entry Builder for creating surveys that can be administered over the web, phone, or mail; (2) SPSS Data Entry Enterprise Server for entering the responses; and (3) SPSS 11.0 for data analysis and charts.

The advantages and disadvantages of personal or face-to-face interviews, telephone interviews, personally administered questionnaires, mail questionnaires, and questionnaires distributed through the electronic system are tabulated in Table 10.1.

It should be pointed out that information obtained from respondents either through interviews or questionnaires, being self-report data, could be biased. That is the reason why data should be collected from different sources and by different methods, as discussed later.

PART III: OTHER METHODS OF DATA COLLECTION

Observational Surveys

Whereas interviews and questionnaires elicit responses from the subjects, it is possible to gather data without asking questions of respondents. People can be

Table 10.1

Advantages and Disadvantages of Interviews and Questionnaires

Mode of Data Collection	Advantages	Disadvantages
Personal or Face-to-Face Interviews	Can establish rapport and motivate respondents. Can clarify the questions, clear doubts, add new questions. Can read nonverbal cues. Can use visual aids to clarify points. Rich data can be obtained. CAPI can be used and responses entered in a portable computer.	Takes personal time. Costs more when a wide geographic region is covered. Respondents may be concerned about confidentiality of information given. Interviewers need to be trained. Can introduce interviewer biases. Respondents can terminate the interview at any time.
Telephone Interviews	Less costly and speedier than personal interviews. Can reach a wide geographic area. Greater anonymity than personal interviews. Can be done using CATI.	Nonverbal cues cannot be read. Interviews will have to be kept short. Obsolete telephone numbers could be contacted, and unlisted ones omitted from the sample.
Personally Administered Questionnaire	Can establish rapport and motivate respondent. Doubts can be clarified. Less expensive when administered to groups of respondents. Almost 100% response rate ensured. Anonymity of respondent is high.	Organizations may be reluctant to give up company time for the survey with groups of employees assembled for the purpose.
Mail Questionnaires	Anonymity is high. Wide geographic regions can be reached. Token gifts can be enclosed to seek compliance. Respondent can take more time to respond at convenience. Can be administered electronically, if desired.	Response rate is almost always low. A 30% rate is quite acceptable. Cannot clarify questions. Follow-up procedures for nonresponses are necessary.
Electronic Quesionnaires	Easy to administer. Can reach globally. Very inexpensive. Fast delivery. Respondents can answer at their convenience like the mail questionnaire.	Computer literacy is a must. Respondents must have access to the facility. Respondent must be willing to complete the survey.

observed in their natural work environment or in the lab setting, and their activities and behaviors or other items of interest can be noted and recorded.

Apart from the activities performed by the individuals under study, their movements, work habits, the statements made and meetings conducted by them, their facial expressions of joy, anger, and other emotions, and body language can be observed. Other environmental factors such as layout, work-flow patterns, the closeness of the seating arrangement, and the like, can also be noted. Children can be observed as to their interests and attention span with various stimuli, such as their involvement with different toys. Such observation would help toy manufacturers, child educators, day-care administrators, and others deeply involved in or responsible for children's development, to design and model ideas based on children's interests, which are more easily observed than traced in any other manner.

The researcher can play one of two roles while gathering field observational data—that of a nonparticipant-observer or participant-observer.

Nonparticipant-Observer

The researcher may collect the needed data in that capacity without becoming an integral part of the organizational system. For example, the researcher might sit in the corner of an office and watch and record how the manager spends her time. Observation of all the activities of managers, over a period of several days, will allow the researcher to make some generalizations on how managers typically spend their time. By merely observing the activities, recording them systematically, and tabulating them, the researcher is able to come up with some findings. This, however, renders it necessary that observers are physically present at the workplace for extended periods of time and makes observational studies time consuming.

Participant-Observer

The researcher may also play the role of the participant-observer. Here, the researcher enters the organization or the research setting, and becomes a part of the work team. For instance, if a researcher wants to study group dynamics in work organizations, then she may join the organization as an employee and observe the dynamics in groups while being a part of the work organization and work groups. Much anthropological research is conducted in this manner, where researchers become a part of the alien culture, which they are interested in studying in depth.

Structured versus Unstructured Observational Studies

Structured Observational Studies

As we have seen, observational studies could be of either the nonparticipant-observer or the participant-observer type. Both of these, again, could be either structured or unstructured. Where the observer has a predetermined set of categories of activities or phenomena planned to be studied, it is a *structured observational study*. Formats for recording the observations can be specifically designed and tailored to each study to suit the goal of that research.

Usually, such matters that pertain to the feature of interest, such as the duration and frequency of the event, as well as certain activities that precede and follow it, are recorded. Environmental conditions and any changes in setting are also noted, if considered relevant. Task-relevant behaviors of the actors, their perceived emotions, verbal and nonverbal communication, and such, are recorded. Observations that are recorded in worksheets or field notes are then systematically analyzed, with minimal personal inferences made by the investigator. Categories can then be developed for further analysis, as described in Chapter 12 on Data Analysis.

Unstructured Observational Studies

At the beginning of a study, it is possible that the observer has no definite ideas of the particular aspects that need focus. Observing events as they take place may also be a part of the plan as in many qualitative studies. In such cases, the observer will record practically everything that is observed. Such a study will be an unstructured observational study.

Unstructured observational studies are claimed to be the hallmark of qualitative research. The investigator might entertain a set of tentative hypotheses that might serve as a guide as to who, when, where, and how the individual will observe. Once the needed information is observed and recorded over a period of time, patterns can be traced, and inductive discovery can then pave the way for subsequent theory building and hypotheses testing.

Advantages and Disadvantages of Observational Studies

There are some specific advantages and disadvantages to gathering data through observation as listed below.

Advantages of Observational Studies

The following are among the advantages of observational studies.

1. The data obtained through observation of events as they normally occur are generally more reliable and free from respondent bias.
2. In observational studies, it is easier to note the effects of environmental influences on specific outcomes. For example, the weather (hot, cold, rainy), the day of the week (midweek as opposed to Monday or Friday), and such other factors that might have a bearing on, for example, the sales of a product, traffic patterns, absenteeism, and the like, can be noted and meaningful patterns might emerge from this type of data.
3. It is easier to observe certain groups of individuals—for example, very young children and extremely busy executives—from whom it may be otherwise difficult to obtain information.

The above three advantages are perhaps unique to observational studies.

Drawbacks of Observational Studies

The following drawbacks of observational studies have also to be noted.

1. It is necessary for the observer to be *physically* present (unless a camera or another mechanical system can capture the events of interest), often for prolonged periods of time.
2. This method of collecting data is not only slow, but also tedious and expensive.
3. Because of the long periods for which subjects are observed, observer fatigue could easily set in, which might bias the recorded data.
4. Though moods, feelings, and attitudes can be guessed by observing facial expressions and other nonverbal behaviors, the cognitive thought processes of individuals cannot be captured.
5. Observers have to be trained in what and how to observe, and ways to avoid observer bias.

Biases in Observational Studies

Data observed from the researcher's point of view are likely to be prone to observer biases. There could be recording errors, memory lapses, and errors in interpreting activities, behaviors, events, and nonverbal cues. Moreover, where several observers are involved, interobserver reliability has to be established before the data can be accepted. Observation of the happenings day in and day out, over extended periods of time, could afflict the observers with ennui and introduce biases in the recording of the observations. To minimize observer bias, observers are usually given training on how to observe and what to record. Good observational studies would also establish interobserver reliability. This could also be established during the training of the observers when videotaped stimuli could be used to determine interobserver reliability. A simple formula can be used for the purpose—dividing the number of agreements among the trainees by the number of agreements and disagreements—thus establishing the reliability coefficient.

Respondent bias could also be a threat to the validity of the results of observational studies, because those who are observed may behave differently during the period of the study, especially if the observations are confined to a short period of time. However, in studies of longer duration, the employees become more relaxed as the study progresses and tend to behave normally. For these reasons, researchers doing observational studies discount the data recorded in the first few days, if they seem to be quite different from what is observed later.

Summary of Observational Studies

Observational studies have a formulated research purpose and are systematically planned. Such studies can be structured or unstructured, with the investigator being a participant or nonparticipant in the study setting. All phenomena of interest are systematically recorded and quality control can be exercised by eliminating biases. Observational studies can provide rich data and insights into the nature of the phenomena observed. They have offered much understanding of interpersonal and group dynamics. Interestingly, observational data can also be quantified through tabulations.

Data Collection Through Mechanical Observation

There are situations where machines can provide data by recording the events of interest as they occur, without a researcher being physically present. Nielsen ratings is an oft-cited example in this regard. Other examples include collection of details of products sold by types or brands tracked through optical scanners and bar codes at the checkout stand, and tracking systems keeping a record of how many individuals utilize a facility or visit a web site. Films and electronic recording devices such as video cameras can also be used to record data. Such mechanically observed data are error-free. ?

Projective Methods

Certain ideas and thoughts that cannot be easily verbalized or that remain at the unconscious levels in the respondents' minds can usually be brought to the surface through motivational research. This is typically done by trained professionals who apply different probing techniques in order to bring to the surface deep-rooted ideas and thoughts in the respondents. Familiar techniques for gathering such data are word associations, sentence completion, thematic apperception tests (TAT), inkblot tests, and the like.

Word association techniques, such as asking the respondent to quickly associate a word—say, *work*—with the first thing that comes to mind, are often used to get at the true attitudes and feelings. The reply would be an indication of what work means to the individual. Similarly, *sentence completion* would have the respondent quickly complete a sentence, such as "Work is—." One respondent might say, "Work is a lot of fun," whereas another might say "Work is drudgery." These responses may provide some insights into individuals' feelings and attitudes toward work.

Thematic Apperception Tests (TAT) call for the respondent to weave a story around a picture that is shown. Several need patterns and personality characteristics of employees could be traced through these tests. *Inkblot tests,* another form of motivational research, use colored inkblots that are interpreted by the respondents, who explain what they see in the various patterns and colors.

Although these types of projective tests are useful for tapping attitudes and feelings that are difficult to obtain otherwise, they cannot be resorted to by researchers who are not trained to conduct motivational research.

Consumer preferences, buying attitudes and behaviors, product development, and other marketing research strategies make substantial use of in-depth probing. TAT and inkblot tests are on their way out in marketing research since advertisers and others now use the sentence completion tests and word association tests more frequently. Sketch drawings, collages from magazine pictures, filling in the balloon captions of cartoon characters, and other strategies are also being followed to see how individuals associate different products, brands, advertisements, and so on, in their minds. Agencies frequently ask subjects to sketch "typical" users of various brands and narrate stories about them. The messages conveyed through the unsophisticated drawings are said to be very powerful, helping the development of different marketing strategies.

The idea behind motivational research is that "emotionality" ("I identify with it" feeling) rather than "rationality" ("it is good for me" thought), which is what keeps a product or practice alive, is captured. Emotions are powerful motivators of actions, and knowledge of what motivates individuals to act is very useful. The failure of attempts to trade in the "New Coke" for "Classic Coke" is an oft-cited example of the emotional aspect. Emotionality is clearly at the nonrational, subconscious level, lending itself to capture by projective techniques alone.

MULTIMETHODS OF DATA COLLECTION

Because almost all data collection methods have some biases associated with them, collecting data through multimethods and from multiple sources lends rigor to research. For instance, if the responses collected through interviews, questionnaires, and observation are strongly correlated with one another, then we will have more confidence about the goodness of the collected data. If the same question fetches discrepant answers in the questionnaire and during the interview, then an air of uncertainty emerges and we would be inclined to discard both data as being biased.

Likewise, if data obtained from several sources bear a great degree of similarity, we would have stronger conviction in the goodness of the data. For example, if an employee rates his performance as 4 on a 5-point scale, and his supervisor gives him a similar rating, we may be inclined to consider him a better than average worker. On the contrary, if he gives himself a 5 on the 5-point scale and his supervisor gives him a rating of 2, then we will not know to what extent there is a bias and from which source. Therefore, high correlations among data obtained on the same variable from different sources and through different data collection methods lend more credibility to the research instrument and to the data obtained through these instruments. Good research entails collection of data from multiple sources and through multiple data collection methods. Such research, though, would be more costly and time consuming.

Review of the Advantages and Disadvantages of Different Data Collection Methods and When to Use Each

Having discussed the various data collection methods, we will now briefly recount the advantages and disadvantages of the three most commonly used data collection methods—interviews, questionnaires, and observation—and examine when each method can be most profitably used.

Face-to-face interviews provide rich data, offer the opportunity to establish rapport with the interviewees, and help to explore and understand complex issues. Many ideas ordinarily difficult to articulate can also be brought to the sur-

See
p251

face and discussed during such interviews. On the negative side, face-to-face interviews have the potential for introducing interviewer bias and can be expensive if a large number of subjects are involved. Where several interviewers become necessary, adequate training becomes a necessary first step.

Face-to-face interviews are best suited at the exploratory stages of research when the researcher tries to get a handle on concepts or the situational factors.

Telephone interviews help to contact subjects dispersed over various geographic regions and obtain immediate responses from them. This is an efficient way of collecting data when one has specific questions to ask, needs the responses quickly, and has the sample spread over a wide geographic area. On the negative side, the interviewer cannot observe the nonverbal responses of the respondents, and the interviewee can block a call.

Telephone interviews are best suited for asking structured questions where responses need to be obtained quickly from a sample that is geographically spread.

Personally administering questionnaires to groups of individuals helps to (1) establish rapport with the respondents while introducing the survey, (2) provide clarifications sought by the respondents on the spot, and (3) collect the questionnaires immediately after they are completed. In that sense, there is a 100% response rate. On the negative side, administering questionnaires personally is expensive, especially if the sample is geographically dispersed.

Personally administered questionnaires are best suited when data are collected from organizations that are located in close proximity to one another and groups of respondents can be conveniently assembled in the company's conference (or other) rooms.

Mail questionnaires are advantageous when responses to many questions have to be obtained from a sample that is geographically dispersed, or it is difficult or not possible to conduct telephone interviews without much expense. On the negative side, mailed questionnaires usually have a low response rate and one cannot be sure if the data obtained are biased since the nonrespondents may be different from those who did respond.

The mailed questionnaire survey is best suited (and perhaps the only alternative open to the researcher) when information is to be obtained on a substantial scale through structured questions, at a reasonable cost, from a sample that is widely dispersed geographically.

Observational studies help to comprehend complex issues through direct observation (either as a participant or a nonparticipant-observer) and then, if possible, asking questions to seek clarifications on certain issues. The data obtained are rich and uncontaminated by self-report biases. On the negative side, they are expensive, since long periods of observation (usually encompassing several weeks or even months) are required, and observer bias may well be present in the data.

Because of the costs involved, very few observational studies are done in business. Henry Mintzberg's study of managerial work is one of the best known published works that used an observational data collection method. Observational studies are best suited for research requiring non–self-report descriptive data; that is, when behaviors are to be understood without directly asking the respondents themselves. Observational studies can also capture "in-the-stores buying behaviors."

SETTING FROM WHICH DATA ARE GATHERED

Data can be collected in any one of the aforementioned ways in the natural environment of the workplace. Data may also be collected in artificial lab settings where variables are controlled and manipulated, or they can be gathered in the homes of the respondents, on the street, in malls, or in a setting where a LAN (Local Area Network) system is available. It is not unusual to find marketers conducting what are known as intercept interviews in malls and fairs, to obtain vast marketing information.

INTERNATIONAL DIMENSIONS OF SURVEYS

We have so far discussed instrument development for eliciting responses from subjects within a country. With the globalization of business operations, managers often need to compare the business effectiveness of their subsidiaries in different countries. Researchers engaged in cross-cultural research also endeavor to trace the similarities and differences in the behavioral and attitudinal responses of employees at various levels in different cultures. When data are collected through questionnaires and occasionally through interviews, one should pay attention to the measuring instruments and how data are collected, in addition to being sensitive to cultural differences in the use of certain terms. Surveys should also be tailored to the different cultures as discussed below.

Special Issues in Instrumentations for Cross-Cultural Research

Certain special issues need to be addressed while designing instruments for collecting data from different countries. Since different languages are spoken in different countries, it is important to ensure that the translation of the instrument to the local language matches accurately to the original language. For this purpose, the instrument should be first translated by a local expert. Supposing a comparative survey is to be done between Japan and the United States, and the researcher is a U.S. national, then the instrument has first to be translated from English to Japanese. Then, another bilinguist should translate it back to English. This back translation, as it is called, ensures vocabulary equivalence (i.e., that the words used have the same meaning). Idiomatic equivalence could also become an issue where some idioms unique to one language just do not lend themselves for translation to another language. Conceptual equivalence, where the meanings of certain words could differ in different cultures, is yet another issue to which attention has to be paid. As stated earlier, the meaning of the concept "love" may differ in different cultures. All these issues can be taken care of through good back translation by persons who are facile with the relevant languages and are also knowledgeable about the customs and usages in the concerned cultures.

The following examples culled from Business Week show the pitfalls in cross-cultural advertising and emphasize the need for back translation of messages for idiomatic and conceptual equivalence. Not only is the meaning lost in some advertisement messages while literally translating the English words into the native languages, but in some cases they actually become offensive. Here are some examples:

1. GM took a step back when it tried to market the NOVA in Central and South America. In Spanish, "No va" means "it doesn't go."

2. Pepsi's "Come Alive With the Pepsi Generation," when translated into Chinese, means "Pepsi brings Your Ancestors From the Grave."

3. Frank Perdue's chicken slogan, "It takes a strong man to make a tender chicken" translates in Spanish to, "It takes an aroused man to make a chicken affectionate."

4. When American Airlines wanted to advertise its new leather first-class seats to Mexico, its "Fly in Leather" campaign would have literally translated to "Fly Naked" in Spanish.

5. The "Got Milk?" in Spanish would translate to "Are you lactating?"

Issues in Data Collection

At least three issues are important for cross-cultural data collection—response equivalence, timing of data collection, and the status of the individual collecting the data. Response equivalence is ensured by adopting uniform data collection procedures in the different cultures. Identical methods of introducing the study, the researcher, task instructions, and closing remarks, in personally administered questionnaires, would provide equivalence in motivation, goal orientation, and response attitudes. Timing of data collected across cultures is also critical for cross-cultural comparison. Data collection should be completed within acceptable time frames in the different countries—say within 3 to 4 months. If too much time elapses in collecting data in the different countries, much might change during the time interval in either country or all the countries.

As pointed out as early as 1969 by Mitchell, in interview surveys, the egalitarian oriented interviewing style used in the West may not be appropriate in societies that have well-defined status and authority structures. Also, when a foreigner comes to collect data, the responses might be biased for fear of portraying the country to a "foreigner" in an "adverse light" (Sekaran, 1983). The researcher has to be sensitive to these cultural nuances while engaging in cross-cultural research. It is worthwhile collaborating with a local researcher while developing and administering the research instrument, particularly when the language and customs of the respondents are different from those of the researcher.

MANAGERIAL ADVANTAGE

As a manager, you will perhaps engage consultants to do research and may not be collecting data yourself through interviews, questionnaires, or observation. However, during those instances, when you will perforce have to obtain work-related information through interviews with clients, employees, or others, you will know how to phrase unbiased questions to elicit the right types of useful responses. Moreover, you, as the sponsor of research, will be able to decide at what level of sophistication you want data to be collected, based on the complexity and gravity of the situation. Moreover, as a constant participant-observer of all that goes around you at the workplace, you will be able to understand the dynamics operating in the situation. Also, as a manager, you will be able to differentiate between good and bad questions used in surveys with sensitivity to cultural variations, not only in scaling but also in developing the entire survey instrument, and in collecting data, as discussed in this chapter.

ETHICS IN DATA COLLECTION

Several ethical issues should be addressed while collecting data. As previously noted, these pertain to those who sponsor the research, those who collect the data, and those who offer them. The sponsors should ask for the study to be done to better the purpose of the organization, and not for any other self-serving reason. They should respect the confidentiality of the data obtained by the researcher, and not ask for the individual or group responses to be disclosed to them, or ask to see the questionnaires. They should have an open mind in accepting the results and recommendations in the report presented by the researchers.

Ethics and the Researcher

1. Treating the information given by the respondent as strictly confidential and guarding his or her privacy is one of the primary responsibilities of the researcher. If the vice president or some other top executive desires to take a look at the completed questionnaires, the obligatory need to preserve the confidentiality of the documents should then be pointed out. They should be reminded that prior understanding of this had already been reached with them before starting the survey.

   Also, report on data for a subgroup of say, less than 10 individuals, should be dealt with tactfully to preserve the confidentiality of the group members. The data can be combined with others, or treated in another unidentifiable manner. It is difficult to sanitize reports to protect sources and still preserve the richness of detail of the study. An acceptable alternative has to be found, since preserving confidentiality is the fundamental goal.

2. The researcher should not misrepresent the nature of the study to subjects, especially in lab experiments. The purpose of the research must be explained to them.

3. Personal or seemingly intrusive information should not be solicited, and if it is absolutely necessary for the project, it should be tapped with high sensitivity to the respondent, offering specific reasons therefor.

4. Whatever be the nature of data collection method, the self-esteem and self-respect of the subjects should never be violated.

5. No one should be forced to respond to the survey and if someone does not want to avail of the opportunity to participate, the individual's desire should be respected. Informed consent of the subjects should be the goal of the

researcher. This holds true even when data are collected through mechanical means, such as recording interviews, videotaping, and the like.

6. Nonparticipant-observers should be as nonintrusive as possible. In qualitative studies, personal values could easily bias the data. It is necessary for the researcher to make explicit his or her assumptions, expectations, and biases, so that informed decisions regarding the quality of the data can be made by the manager.

7. In lab studies, the subjects should be debriefed with full disclosure of the reason for the experiment after they have particpated in the study.

8. Subjects should never be exposed to situations where they could be subject to physical or mental harm. The researcher should take personal responsibility for their safety.

9. There should be absolutely no misrepresentation or distortion in reporting the data collected during the study.

Ethical Behaviors of Respondents

1. The subject, once having exercised the choice to participate in a study, should cooperate fully in the tasks ahead, such as responding to a survey or taking part in an experiment.

2. The respondent also has an obligation to be truthful and honest in the responses. Misrepresentation or giving information, knowing it to be untrue, should be avoided.

SUMMARY

In this chapter we examined various sources of data and several data collection methods. We discussed the advantages and disadvantages as well as the biases inherent in each data collection method. We also examined the impact of technology on data collection. Because of the inherent biases in each of the data collection methods, the collection of data from multiple sources and through multiple methods was recommended. The final decision would, of course, be governed by considerations of cost, and the degree of rigor that the given research goal would call for. We also pointed out some issues in cross-cultural research such as back translation and alerted the reader to the pitfalls while collecting data in a different culture.

In the next chapter we will discuss sampling designs and how data can be collected from samples to make the results generalizable to the population under study.

DISCUSSION QUESTIONS AND POINTS TO PONDER

1. Describe the different data sources, explaining their usefulness and disadvantages.

2. As a manager, you have invited a research team to come in, study, and offer suggestions on how to improve the performance of your staff. What steps would you take to allay their apprehensions even before the research team sets foot in your department?

3. What is bias, and how can it be reduced during interviews?

4. Explain the principles of wording, stating how these are important in questionnaire design, citing examples not in the book.

5. What are projective techniques and how can they be profitably used?

6. How are multiple methods of data collection and from multiple sources related to the reliability and validity of the measures?

7. "Every data collection method has its own built-in biases. Therefore, resorting to multimethods of data collection is only going to compound the biases." How would you critique this statement?

8. "One way to deal with discrepancies found in the data obtained from multiple sources is to average the figures and take the mean as the value of the variable." What is your reaction to this?

9. How has the advancement in technology helped data gathering?

10. How will you use the data from observational study to reach scientific conclusions?

11. The fewer the biases in measurement and in data collection procedures, the more scientific the research. Comment on this statement.

EXERCISES

Exercise 10.1   A production manager wants to assess the reactions of the blue-collar workers in his department (including foremen) to the introduction of computer-integrated manufacturing (CIM) systems. He is particularly interested to know how they would perceive the effects of CIM on:

a. their future jobs

b. additional training that they will have to receive

c. future job advancement.

Design a questionnaire for the production manager.

Exercise 10.2   Seek permission from a professor to sit in two sessions of his or her class, and do an unstructured, nonparticipant-observer study. Give your conclusions on the data, and include in the short report your observation sheets and tabulations.

Exercise 10.3   First conduct an unstructured and later a structured *interview,* with any professor not known to you, to learn about his or her values and strategy in teaching courses. Write up the results, and include the formats you used for both stages of the research.

Exercise 10.4   The president of Serakan Co. suspects that most of the 500 male and female employees of the organization are somewhat alienated from work. He is also of the view that those who are more involved (less alienated) are also the ones who experience greater satisfaction with their work lives.

Design a questionnaire the president could use to test his hypothesis.

Exercise 10.5   Design an interview schedule to assess the "intellectual capital" as perceived by employees in an organization—the dimensions and elements for which you had earlier developed.

Add infos & examples concerning manufacturing
- potatoes
- widgets
- assembly lines
(not always people)

TOPICS DISCUSSED

POPULATION, ELEMENT, POPULATION FRAME, SAMPLE, SUBJECT, SAMPLING

REASONS FOR SAMPLING

REPRESENTATIVENESS OF THE SAMPLE

PROBABILITY SAMPLING

- Simple Random Sampling
- Systematic Sampling
- Stratified Random Sampling: Proportionate and Disproportionate
- Cluster Sampling: Single-Stage and Multistage Clusters
- Area Sampling
- Double Sampling

NONPROBABILITY SAMPLING

- Convenience Sampling
- Judgment Sampling
- Quota Sampling

SAMPLING IN CROSS-CULTURAL RESEARCH

ISSUES OF PRECISION AND CONFIDENCE IN DETERMINING SAMPLE SIZE

PRECISION AND CONFIDENCE: TRADE-OFFS

SAMPLE DATA AND HYPOTHESIS TESTING

SAMPLE SIZE

EFFICIENCY IN SAMPLING

SAMPLING IN QUALITATIVE STUDIES

MANAGERIAL RELEVANCE

examples of when each is used is given @ back of chapter
↳ add more from another perspective

CHAPTER OBJECTIVES

After completing Chapter 11, you should be able to:

1. Define sampling, sample, population, element, subject, and population frame.
2. Describe and discuss the different sampling designs.

3. Identify the use of appropriate sampling designs for different research purposes.

4. Explain why sample data are used to test hypotheses.

5. Discuss precision and confidence.

6. Estimate sample size.

7. Discuss the factors to be taken into consideration for determining sample size.

8. Discuss efficiency in sampling.

9. Discuss generalizability in the context of sampling designs.

10. Apply the material learned in this chapter to class assignments and projects.

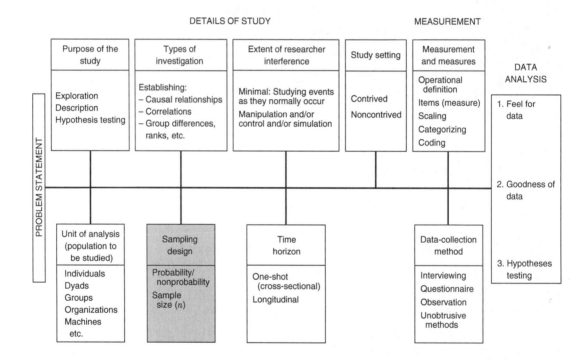

Surveys are useful and powerful in finding answers to research questions through data collection and subsequent analyses, but they can do more harm than good if the population is not correctly targeted. That is, if data are not collected from the people, events, or objects that can provide the correct answers to solve the problem, the survey would be in vain. The process of selecting the right individuals, objects, or events for study is known as *sampling* (shaded portion in the figure), which we will examine in some detail in this chapter.

POPULATION, ELEMENT, POPULATION FRAME, SAMPLE, AND SUBJECT

In learning how representative data (i.e., as reflected in the universe) can be collected, a few terms as described below, have to be first understood.

Population

Population refers to the entire group of people, events, or things of interest that the researcher wishes to investigate. For instance, if the CEO of a computer firm wants to know the kinds of advertising strategies adopted by computer firms in the Silicon Valley, then all computer firms situated there will be the population. If a banker is interested in investigating the savings habits of blue-collar workers in the mining industry in the United States, then all blue-collar workers in that industry throughout the country will form the population. If an organizational consultant is interested in studying the effects of a 4 day workweek on the white-collar workers in a telephone company in Southern Illinois, then all white-collar workers in that company will make up the population. If regulators want to know how patients in nursing homes run by Beverly Enterprises are cared for, then all the patients in all the nursing homes run by them will form the population. If, however, the regulators are interested only in one particular nursing home in Michigan run by Beverly Enterprises, then only the patients in that specific nursing home will form the population.

Element

An element is a single member of the population. If 1,000 blue-collar workers in a particular organization happen to be the population of interest to a researcher, each blue-collar worker therein is an element. If 500 pieces of machinery are to be approved after inspecting a few, there would be 500 elements in this population. Incidentally, the census is a count of all elements in the human population.

Population Frame

The population frame is a listing of all the elements in the population from which the sample is drawn. The payroll of an organization would serve as the population frame if its members are to be studied. Likewise, the university registry containing a listing of all students, faculty, administrators, and support staff in the university during a particular academic year or semester could serve as the population frame for a study of the university population. A roster of class students could be the population frame for the study of students in a class. The telephone directory is also frequently used as a population frame for some types of studies, even though it has an inherent bias inasmuch as some numbers are unlisted and certain others may have become obsolete.

Although the population frame is useful in providing a listing of each element in the population, it may not always be a current, updated document. For instance, the names of members who have recently left the organization or dropped out of the university, as well as members who have only recently joined the organization or the university may not appear in the organization's payroll or the university registers on a given day. The most recently installed or disconnected telephones will not, likewise, be included in the current telephone directory. Hence, though the population frame may be available in many cases, it may not always be entirely correct or complete. However, the researcher might recognize this problem and not be too concerned about it, because a few additions and deletions in the telephone directory might not make any significant difference to the study. Even if she is concerned about it, and spends time and effort trying to obtain an updated population frame, there is no guarantee that the new population frame has an accurate listing of *all* the elements either, for the reasons already discussed.

Sample

A sample is a subset of the population. It comprises some members selected from it. In other words, some, but not all, elements of the population would form the sample. If 200 members are drawn from a population of 1,000 blue-collar workers, these 200 members form the sample for the study. That is, from a study of these 200 members, the researcher would draw conclusions about the entire population of the 1,000 blue-collar workers. Likewise, if there are 145 in-patients in a hospital and 40 of them are to be surveyed by the hospital administrator to assess their level of satisfaction with the treatment received, then these 40 members will be the sample.

A sample is thus a subgroup or subset of the population. By studying the sample, the researcher should be able to draw conclusions that would be generalizable to the population of interest.

Subject

A subject is a single member of the sample, just as an element is a single member of the population. If 200 members from the total population of 1,000 blue-collar workers formed the sample for the study, then each blue-collar worker in the sample is a subject. As another example, if a sample of 50 machines from a total of 500 machines is to be inspected, then every one of the 50 machines is a subject, just as every single machine in the total population of 500 machines is an element.

SAMPLING

Sampling is the *process* of selecting a sufficient number of elements from the population, so that a study of the sample and an understanding of its properties or characteristics would make it possible for us to generalize such properties or characteristics to the population elements. The characteristics of the population such as μ (the population mean), σ (the population standard deviation), and σ^2 (the population variance) are referred to as its *parameters*. The central tendencies, the dispersions, and other statistics in the sample of interest to the research are treated as approximations of the central tendencies, dispersions, and other parameters of the population. As such, all conclusions drawn about the sample under study are generalized to the population. In other words, the sample statistics—$\bar{X}$ (the sample mean), S (standard deviation), and S^2 (the variation in the sample)—are used as estimates of the population parameters μ, σ, and σ^2. Figure 11.1 shows the relationship between the sample and the population.

Reasons for Sampling

The reasons for using a sample, rather than collecting data from the entire population, are self-evident. In research investigations involving several hundreds and even thousands of elements, it would be practically impossible to collect data from, or test, or examine every element. Even if it were possible, it would be prohibitive in terms of time, cost, and other human resources. Study of a sample rather than the entire population is also sometimes likely to produce more reliable results. This is mostly because fatigue is reduced and fewer errors will therefore result in collecting data, especially when a large number of elements is involved. In a few cases, it would also be impossible to use the entire population to gain knowledge about, or test something. Consider, for instance, the case of electric bulbs. In testing the life of a batch of bulbs, if we were to burn every bulb produced, there would be none left to sell! This is known as destructive sampling.

Representativeness of Samples

The need for choosing the right sample for a research investigation cannot be overemphasized. We know that rarely will the sample be the exact replica of the population from which it is drawn. For instance, very few sample means ($\bar{X}$) are likely to be exactly equal to the population means (μ). Nor is the standard devi-

Figure 11.1
The Relationship between Sample and Population.

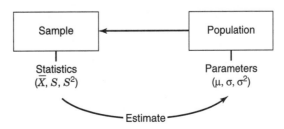

ation of the sample *(S)* likely to be the same as the standard deviation of the population (σ). However, if we choose the sample in a scientific way, we can be reasonably sure that the sample statistic (e.g., $\overline{X}$, *S*, or S^2) is fairly close to the population parameter (i.e., μ, σ, or $σ^2$). To put it differently, it is possible to choose the sample in such a way that it is representative of the population. There is always the slight probability, however, that sample values might fall outside the population parameters.

NORMALITY OF DISTRIBUTIONS

many

Attributes or characteristics of the population are generally normally distributed. For instance, when attributes such as height and weight are considered, most people will be clustered around the mean, leaving only a small number at the extremes who are either very tall or very short, very heavy or very light, and so on, as indicated in Figure 11.2. If we are to estimate the population characteristics from those represented in a sample with reasonable accuracy, the sample has to be so chosen that the distribution of the characteristics of interest follows the same pattern of normal distribution in the sample as it does in the population. From the central limit theorem, we know that the sampling distribution of the sample mean is normally distributed. As the sample size *n* increases, the means of the random samples taken from practically any population approach a normal distribution with mean μ and standard deviation σ. In sum, irrespective of whether or not the attributes of the population are normally distributed, if we take a sufficiently *large number of* samples and *choose* them with care, we will have a sampling distribution of the means that has normality. This is the reason that the two important issues in sampling are the sample size *(n)* and the sampling design, as discussed later.

When the properties of the population are not overrepresented or underrepresented in the sample, we will have a representative sample. When a sample consists of elements in the population that have extremely high values on the variable we are studying, the sample mean $\overline{X}$ will be far higher than the population mean μ. If, in contrast, the sample subjects consist of elements in the pop-

Figure 11.2
Normal Distribution in a Population.

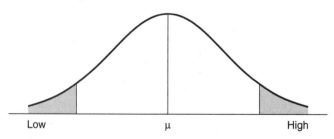

| Low | μ | High |

ulation with extremely low values on the variable of interest, the sample mean $\bar{X}$ will be much lower than the true population mean μ. If our sampling design and sample size are right, however, the sample mean $\bar{X}$ will be within close range of the true population mean μ. Thus, through appropriate sampling designs, we can ensure that the sample subjects are not chosen from the extremes, but are truly representative of the properties of the population. The more representative of the population the sample is, the more generalizable are the findings of the research. Recall that generalizability is one of the hallmarks of scientific research, as we saw in Chapter 2.

Though in view of our concern about generalizability we may be particular about choosing representative samples for most research, some cases may not call for such concern for generalizability. For instance, at the exploratory stages of fact finding, we may be interested only in "getting a handle" on the situation, and therefore limit the interview to only the most conveniently available people. The same is true when time is of the essence, and urgency in getting information overrides in priority a high level of accuracy. For instance, a film agency might want to find out quickly the impact on the viewers of a newly released film exhibited the previous evening. The interviewer might question the first 20 people leaving the theater after seeing the film and obtain their reactions. On the basis of their replies, she may form an opinion as to the likely success of the film. As another example, a restaurant manager might want to find the reactions of customers to a new item added to the menu to determine whether or not it has been a popular and worthwhile addition. For this purpose, the first 15 people who partook of the special item might be interviewed, and their reactions obtained. In such cases, having instant information may be more gainful than obtaining the most representative facts. It should, however, be noted that the results of such convenience samples are not reliable and can never be generalized to the population. We will now discuss the different types of sampling designs, bearing in mind the following points in the determination of the choice.

1. What is the relevant target population of focus to the study?
2. What exactly are the parameters we are interested in investigating?
3. What kind of a sampling frame is available?
4. What is the sample size needed?
5. What costs are attached to the sampling design?
6. How much time is available to collect the data from the sample?

PROBABILITY AND NONPROBABILITY SAMPLING

There are two major types of sampling designs: probability and nonprobability sampling. In probability sampling, the elements in the population have some known chance or probability of being selected as sample subjects. In nonprobability sampling, the elements do not have a known or predetermined chance of being selected as subjects. Probability sampling designs are used when the representativeness of the sample is of importance in the interests of wider generalizability. When time or other factors, rather than generalizability, become critical, nonprobability sampling is generally used.

Each of these two major designs has different sampling strategies. Depending on the extent of generalizability desired, the demands of time and other resources, and the purpose of the study, different types of probability and nonprobability sampling designs are chosen. These are discussed next.

PROBABILITY SAMPLING

When elements in the population have a known chance of being chosen as subjects in the sample, we resort to a probability sampling design. Probability sampling can be either unrestricted (simple random sampling) or restricted (complex probability sampling) in nature.

Unrestricted or Simple Random Sampling

In the unrestricted probability sampling design, more commonly known as simple random sampling, every element in the population has a *known and equal* chance of being selected as a subject. Let us say there are 1,000 elements in the population, and we need a sample of 100. Suppose we were to drop pieces of paper in a hat, each bearing the name of one of the elements, and draw 100 of those from the hat with our eyes closed. We know that the first piece drawn will have a 1/1,000 chance of being drawn, the next one a 1/999 chance of being drawn, and so on. In other words, we know that the probability of any one of them being chosen is 1 in the number of the population, and we also know that each single element in the hat has the same or equal probability of being chosen. We certainly know that computers can generate random numbers and one does not have to go through the tedious process of pulling out names from a hat!

When we thus draw the elements from the population, it is most likely that the distribution patterns of the characteristics we are interested in investigating in the population are also likewise distributed in the subjects we draw for our sample. This sampling design, known as *simple random sampling,* has the least bias and offers the most generalizability. However, this sampling process could become cumbersome and expensive; in addition an entirely updated listing of the population may not always be available. For these and other reasons, other probability sampling designs are often chosen instead.

Restricted or Complex Probability Sampling

As an alternative to the simple random sampling design, several complex probability sampling (restricted probability) designs can be used. These probability sampling procedures offer a viable, and sometimes more efficient alternative to the unrestricted design we just discussed. Efficiency is improved in that more information can be obtained for a given sample size using some of the complex probability sampling procedures than the simple random sampling design. The five most common complex probability sampling designs—systematic sampling, stratified random sampling, cluster sampling, area sampling, and double sampling—will now be discussed.

Systematic Sampling

The systematic sampling design involves drawing every nth element in the population starting with a randomly chosen element between 1 and n. The procedure is exemplified below.

Example 11.1

If we want a sample of 35 households from a total population of 260 houses in a particular locality, then we could sample every seventh house starting from a random number from 1 to 7. Let us say that the random number is 7, then houses numbered 7, 14, 21, 28, and so on, would be sampled until the 35 houses are selected.

The one problem to be borne in mind in the systematic sampling design is the probability of a systematic bias creeping into the sample. In the above example, for instance, let us say that every seventh house happens to be a corner house. If the focus of the research study conducted by the construction industry is to control "noise pollution" experienced by residents through the use of appropriate filtering materials, then the residents of corner houses may not be exposed to as much noise as the houses that are in between. Information on noise levels gathered from corner house dwellers might therefore bias the researcher's data. The likelihood of drawing incorrect conclusions from such data is thus high. In view of the scope for such systematic bias, the researcher must consider the plans carefully and make sure that the systematic sampling design is appropriate for the study, before deciding on it.

For market surveys, consumer attitude surveys, and the like, the systematic sampling design is often used, and the telephone directory frequently serves as the population frame for this sampling design.

Stratified Random Sampling

While sampling helps to estimate population parameters, there may be identifiable subgroups of elements within the population that may be expected to have different parameters on a variable of interest to the researcher. For example, to the Human Resources Management Director interested in assessing the extent of training that the employees in the system feel they need, the entire organization will form the population for study. But the extent, quality, and intensity of training desired by middle-level managers, lower-level managers, first-line supervisors, computer analysts, clerical workers, and so on will be different for each group. Knowledge of the kinds of differences in needs that exist for the different groups will help the director to develop useful and meaningful training programs for each group in the organization. Data will therefore have to be collected

[handwritten margin notes: ★ proper @ all levels of population ★ potatoes ★ Find Def in another Book]

in a manner that would help the assessment of needs at each subgroup level in the population. The unit of analysis then would be at the group level and the stratified random sampling process will come in handy.

Stratified random sampling, as its name implies, involves a process of stratification or segregation, followed by random selection of subjects from each stratum. The population is first divided into mutually exclusive groups that are relevant, appropriate, and meaningful in the context of the study. For instance, if the president of a company is concerned about low motivational levels or high absenteeism rates among the employees, it makes sense to stratify the population of organizational members according to their job levels. When the data are collected and the analysis is done, we may find that contrary to expectations, it is the middle-level managers that are not motivated. This information will help the president to focus on action at the right level and devise better methods to motivate this group. Tracing the differences in the parameters of the subgroups within a population would not have been possible without the stratified random sampling procedure. If either the simple random sampling or the systematic sampling procedure were used in a case like this, then the high motivation at some job levels and the low motivation at other levels would have canceled each other out, thus masking the real problems that exist at a particular level or levels.

Stratification also helps when research questions such as the following are to be answered:

1. Are the machinists more accident prone than clerical workers?
2. Are Hispanics more loyal to the organization than Native Americans?

Stratifying customers on the basis of life stages, income levels, and the like to study buying patterns and stratifying companies according to size, industry, profits, and so forth to study stock market reactions are all common examples of the use of stratification as a sampling design technique.

Stratification is an efficient research sampling design; that is, it provides more information with a given sample size. Stratification should follow the lines appropriate to the research question. If we study consumer preferences for a product, stratification of the population could be by geographical areas, market segments, consumers' age, consumers' gender, or various combinations of these. If an organization contemplates budget cuts, the effects of these cuts on employee attitudes can be studied with stratification by department, function, or region. Stratification ensures homogeneity within each stratum (i.e., very few differences or dispersions on the variable of interest within each stratum), but heterogeneity (variability) between strata. In other words, there will be more between group differences than within-group differences.

Proportionate and Disproportionate Stratified Random Sampling. Once the population has been stratified in some meaningful way, a sample of members from each stratum can be drawn using either a simple random sampling or a systematic sampling procedure. The subjects drawn from each stratum can be either proportionate or disproportionate to the number of elements in the stratum. For instance, if an organization employs 10 top managers, 30 middle managers, 50 lower-level managers, 100 supervisors, 500 clerks, and 20 secretaries, and a stratified sample of about 140 people is needed for some specific survey, the researcher might decide to include in the sample 20% of members from each stratum. That is, members represented in the sample from each stratum will be proportionate to the total number of elements in the respective strata. This would mean that 2 from the top, 6 from the middle, and 10 from the lower levels of management will be included in the sample. In addition, 20 supervisors, 100 clerks, and 4 secretaries will be represented in the sample, as shown in the third column of Table 11.1. This type of sampling is called a proportionate stratified random sampling design.

In situations like the one above, researchers might sometimes be concerned that information from only 2 members at the top and 6 from the middle levels would not truly reflect how all members at those levels would respond. Therefore, a researcher might decide instead, to use a disproportionate stratified random sampling procedure. The number of subjects from each stratum will now be altered, while keeping the sample size unchanged. Such a sampling design is illustrated in the far right-hand column in Table 11.1. The idea here is that the 60 clerks might be considered adequate to represent the population of 500 clerks; 7 out of 10 managers at the top level would also be considered representative of the top managers, and likewise 15 out of the 30 managers at the middle level. This redistribution of the numbers in the strata would be considered more appropriate and representative for the study than the previous proportionate sampling design.

Disproportionate sampling decisions are made either when some stratum or strata are too small or too large, or when there is more variability suspected within a particular stratum. As an example, the educational levels among supervisors, which may be considered as influencing perceptions, may range from elementary school to master's degrees. Here, more people will be sampled at the supervisory level. Disproportionate sampling is also sometimes done when it is easier, simpler, and less expensive to collect data from one or more strata than from others.

Table 11.1
Proportionate and Disproportionate Stratified Random Sampling

		Number of Subjects in the Sample	
Job Level	Number of Elements	Proportionate Sampling (20% of the elements)	Disproportionate Sampling
Top management	10	2	7
Middle-level management	30	6	15
Lower-level management	50	10	20
Supervisors	100	20	30
Clerks	500	100	60
Secretaries	20	4	10
Total	710	142	142

In summary, stratified random sampling involves stratifying the elements along meaningful levels and taking proportionate or disproportionate samples from the strata. This sampling design is more efficient than the simple random sampling design because, for the same sample size, each important segment of the population is better represented, and more valuable and differentiated information is obtained with respect to each group.

Cluster Sampling

Groups or chunks of elements that, ideally, would have heterogeneity among the members within each group are chosen for study in cluster sampling. This is in contrast to choosing some elements from the population as in simple random sampling, or stratifying and then choosing members from the strata as in stratified random sampling, or choosing every nth element in the population as in systematic sampling. When several groups with intragroup heterogeneity and intergroup homogeneity are found, then a random sampling of the clusters or groups can ideally be done and information gathered from each of the members in the randomly chosen clusters. Ad hoc organizational committees drawn from various departments to offer inputs to the company president to enable him to make decisions on product development, budget allocations, marketing strategies, and the like, are good examples of different clusters. Each of these clusters or groups contains a heterogeneous collection of members with different interests, orientations, values, philosophy, and vested interests, drawn from different departments to offer a variety of perspectives. Drawing on their individual and combined insights, the president is able to make final decisions on strategic moves for the company. Cluster samples offer more heterogeneity within groups and more homogeneity among groups—the reverse of what we find in stratified random sampling, where there is homogeneity within each group and heterogeneity across groups.

The unit costs of cluster sampling are much lower than those of other probability sampling designs of simple or stratified random sampling or systematic sampling. However, cluster sampling exposes itself to greater biases and is the least generalizable of all the probability sampling designs, because most naturally occurring clusters in the organizational context do not contain heterogeneous elements. In other words, the conditions of intracluster heterogeneity and intercluster homogeneity are often not met.

For these reasons, cluster sampling technique is not very common in organizational research. Further, as in the case of the committee example cited above, duplication of members in several clusters is also possible. Moreover, for marketing research activities, naturally occurring clusters, such as clusters of residents, buyers, students, or shops, do not have much heterogeneity among the elements. As stated earlier, there is more intracluster homogeneity than heterogeneity in such clusters. Hence, cluster sampling, though less costly, does not offer much efficiency in terms of precision or confidence in the results. However, cluster sampling offers convenience. For example it is easier to inspect an assortment of units packed inside, say, four boxes (i.e., all the elements in the four clusters) than to open 30 boxes in a shipment in order to inspect a few units from each at random.

Single-Stage and Multistage Cluster Sampling. We have thus far discussed single-stage cluster sampling, which involves the division of the population into convenient clusters, randomly choosing the required number of clusters as sample subjects, and investigating all the elements in each of the randomly chosen clusters. Cluster sampling can also be done in several stages and is then known as multistage cluster sampling. For instance, if we were to do a national survey of the average monthly bank deposits, cluster sampling would first be used to select the urban, semiurban, and rural geographical locations for study. At the next stage, particular areas in each of these locations would be chosen. At the third stage, banks within each area would be chosen. In other words, multistage cluster sampling involves a probability sampling of the primary sampling units; from each of these primary units, a probability sample of the secondary sampling units is then drawn; a third level of probability sampling is done from each of these secondary units, and so on, until we have reached the final stage of breakdown for the sample units, when we will sample every member in those units.

Area Sampling

The area sampling design constitutes geographical clusters. That is, when the research pertains to populations within identifiable geographical areas such as counties, city blocks, or particular boundaries within a locality, area sampling can be done. Thus, area sampling is a form of cluster sampling within an area. Sampling the needs of consumers before opening a 24-hour convenience store in a particular part of town would involve area sampling. Location plans for retail stores, advertisements focused specifically on local populations, and TV and radio programs beamed at specific areas could all use an area sampling design to gather information on the interests, attitudes, predispositions, and behaviors of the local area people.

Area sampling is less expensive than most other probability sampling designs, and it is not dependent on a population frame. A city map showing the blocks of the city would be adequate information to allow a researcher to take a sample of the blocks and obtain data from the residents therein.

Double Sampling

This plan is resorted to when further information is needed from a subset of the group from which some information has already been collected for the same study. A sampling design where initially a sample is used in a study to collect some preliminary information of interest, and later a subsample of this primary sample is used to examine the matter in more detail, is called double sampling. For example, a structured interview might indicate that a subgroup of the respondents has more insight into the problems of the organization. These respondents might be interviewed again and asked additional questions. This research would have adopted a double sampling procedure.

Review of Probability Sampling Designs

There are two basic probability sampling plans: the unrestricted or simple random sampling, and the restricted or complex probability sampling plans. In the simple random sampling design, every element in the population has a known and equal chance of being selected as a subject. The complex probability plan consists of five different sampling designs. Of these five, the cluster sampling design is probably the least expensive as well as the least dependable, but is used when no list of the population elements is available. The stratified random sampling design is probably the most efficient, in the sense that for the same number of sample subjects, it offers precise and detailed information. The systematic sampling design has the built-in hazard of possible systematic bias. Area sampling is a popular form of cluster sampling, and double sampling is resorted to when information in addition to that already obtained by using a primary sample has to be collected using a subgroup of the sample.

NONPROBABILITY SAMPLING

In nonprobability sampling designs, the elements in the population do not have any probabilities attached to their being chosen as sample subjects. This means that the findings from the study of the sample cannot be confidently generalized to the population. As stated earlier, however, researchers may at times be less concerned about generalizability than obtaining some preliminary information in a quick and inexpensive way. They would then resort to nonprobability sampling. Sometimes nonprobability sampling could be the only way to obtain data, as discussed later.

Some of the nonprobability sampling plans are more dependable than others and could offer some important leads to potentially useful information with regard to the population. The nonprobability sampling designs, which fit into the broad categories of convenience sampling and purposive sampling, are discussed next.

Convenience Sampling

As its name implies, convenience sampling refers to the collection of information from members of the population who are conveniently available to provide it. One would expect that the "Pepsi Challenge" contest was administered on a convenience sampling basis. Such a contest, with the purpose of determining whether people prefer one product to another, might be held at a shopping mall visited by many shoppers. Those inclined to take the test might form the sample for the study of how many people prefer Pepsi over Coke or product X to product Y. Such a sample is a convenience sample.

Consider another example. A convenience sample of five officers who attended the competitor's showcase demonstration at the county fair the previous evening offered the vice president of the company information on the "new" products of the competitor and their pricing strategies, which helped the VP to formulate some ideas on the next steps to be taken by the company.

Convenience sampling is most often used during the exploratory phase of a research project and is perhaps the best way of getting some basic information quickly and efficiently.

Purposive Sampling

Instead of obtaining information from those who are most readily or conveniently available, it might sometimes become necessary to obtain information from specific target groups. The sampling here is confined to specific types of people who can provide the desired information, either because they are the only ones who have it, or conform to some criteria set by the researcher. This type of sampling design is called purposive sampling, and the two major types of purposive sampling—judgment sampling and quota sampling—will now be explained.

Judgment Sampling

Judgment sampling involves the choice of subjects who are most advantageously placed or in the best position to provide the information required. For instance, if a researcher wants to find out what it takes for women managers to make it to the top, the only people who can give firsthand information are the women who have risen to the positions of presidents, vice presidents, and important top-level executives in work organizations. They could reasonably be expected to have expert knowledge by virtue of having gone through the experiences and processes themselves, and might perhaps be able to provide good data or information to the researcher. Thus, the judgment sampling design is used when a limited number or category of people have the information that is sought. In such cases, any type of probability sampling across a cross-section of the entire population is purposeless and not useful.

Judgment sampling may curtail the generalizability of the findings, due to the fact that we are using a sample of experts who are conveniently available to us. However, it is the only viable sampling method for obtaining the type of information that is required from very specific pockets of people who alone possess the needed facts and can give the information sought. In organizational settings, and particularly for market research, opinion leaders who are very knowledgeable are included in the sample. Enlightened opinions, views, and knowledge constitute a rich data source.

Judgment sampling calls for special efforts to locate and gain access to the individuals who do have the requisite information. As already stated this sampling design may be the only useful one for answering certain types of research questions.

Quota Sampling

Quota sampling, a second type of purposive sampling, ensures that certain groups are adequately represented in the study through the assignment of a quota. Generally, the quota fixed for each subgroup is based on the total numbers of each group in the population. However, since this is a nonprobability sampling plan, the results are not generalizable to the population.

Quota sampling can be considered as a form of proportionate stratified sampling, in which a predetermined proportion of people are sampled from different groups, but on a convenience basis. For instance, it may be surmised that the work attitude of blue-collar workers in an organization is quite different from that of white-collar workers. If there are 60% blue-collar workers and 40% white-collar workers in this organization, and if a total of 30 people are to be interviewed to find the answer to the research question, then a quota of 18 blue-collar workers and 12 white-collar workers will form the sample, because these numbers represent 60% and 40% of the sample size. The first 18 conveniently available blue-collar workers and 12 white-collar workers will be sampled according to this quota. Needless to say, the sample may not be totally representative of the population; hence the generalizability of the findings will be restricted. However, the convenience it offers in terms of effort, cost, and time makes quota sampling attractive for some research efforts. Quota sampling also becomes a necessity when a subset of the population is underrepresented in the organization—for example, minority groups, foremen, and so on. In other words, quota sampling ensures that all the subgroups in the population are adequately represented in the sample. Quota samples are basically stratified samples from which subjects are selected nonrandomly.

In a workplace (and society) that is becoming increasingly heterogeneous because of the changing demographics, quota sampling can be expected to be used more frequently in the future. For example, quota sampling can be used to have some idea of the buying predispositions of various ethnic groups, for getting a feel of how employees from different nationalities perceive the organizational culture, and so on.

Although quota sampling is not generalizable like stratified random sampling, it does offer some information, based on which further investigation, if necessary, can proceed. That is, it is possible that the first stage of research will use the nonprobability design of quota sampling, and once some useful information has been obtained, a probability design will follow. The converse is also entirely possible. A probability sampling design might indicate new areas for research, and nonprobability sampling designs might be used to explore their feasibility.

Review of Nonprobability Sampling Designs

There are two main types of nonprobability sampling designs: convenience sampling and purposive sampling. Convenience sampling is the least reliable of all sampling designs in terms of generalizability, but sometimes it may be the only

✫✫ add examples of how / when to use different sampling for quantitative data ⟹ widget, parts, assembly line, plants etc.

NONPROBABILITY SAMPLING   **279**

viable alternative when quick and timely information is needed, or for exploratory research purposes. Purposive sampling plans fall into two categories: judgment and quota sampling designs. Judgment sampling, though restricted in generalizability, may sometimes be the best sampling design choice, especially when there is a limited population that can supply the information needed. Quota sampling is often used on considerations of cost and time and the need to adequately represent minority elements in the population. Although the generalizability of all nonprobability sampling designs is very restricted, they have certain advantages and are sometimes the only viable alternative for the researcher.

Table 11.2 summarizes the probability and nonprobability sampling designs discussed thus far, and their advantages and disadvantages. Figure 11.3 offers some decision choice points as to which design might be useful for specific research goals.

Examples of When Certain Sampling Designs Would Be Appropriate

✫ give scenarios to students & let them

1. Simple Random Sampling

This sampling design is best when the generalizability of the findings to the whole population is the main objective of the study. Consider the following two examples.

Example 11.2   The human resources director of a company with 82 people on its payroll has been asked by the vice president to consider formulating an implementable flextime policy. The director feels that such a policy is not necessary since everyone seems happy with the 9 to 5 hours, and no one has complained. Formulating such a policy now, in the opinion of the director, runs the risk of creating domestic problems for the staff and scheduling problems for the company. She wants, however, to resort to a simple random sampling procedure to do an initial survey, and with the results, convince the V.P. that there is no need for flextime, and urge him to drop the matter. Since simple random sampling offers the greatest generalizability of the results to the entire population, and the V.P. needs to be convinced, it is important to resort to this sampling design.

Example 11.3   The regional director of sales operations of a medium-sized company having 20 retail stores in each of its four geographical regions of operation, wants to know what types of sales gimmicks worked best for the company overall during the past year. This is to help formulate some general policies for the company *as a whole* and prioritize sales promotion strategies for the coming year.

Instead of studying each of the 80 stores, some *dependable* (i.e., *representative* and *generalizable*) information can be had, based on the study of a few stores drawn through a simple random sampling procedure. That is, each one of the 80 stores would have an equal chance of being included in the sample, and the results of the study would be the most generalizable.

Table 11.2
Probability and Nonprobability Sampling Designs

Sampling Design	Description	Advantages	Disadvantages
Probability Sampling			
1. Simple random sampling	All elements in the population are considered and each element has an equal chance of being chosen as the subject.	High generalizability of findings.	Not as efficient as stratified sampling.
2. Systematic sampling	Every *n*th element in the population is chosen starting from a random point in the population frame.	Easy to use if population frame is available.	Systematic biases are possible.
3. Stratified random sampling (Str.R.S.) Proportionate Str.R.S.	Population is first divided into meaningful segments; thereafter subjects are drawn in proportion to their original numbers in the population.	Most efficient among all probability designs. All groups are adequately sampled and comparisons among groups are possible.	Stratification *must* be meaningful. More time-consuming than simple random sampling or systematic sampling.
Disproportionate Str.R.S.	Based on criteria other than their original population numbers.		Population frame for *each* stratum is essential.
4. Cluster sampling	Groups that have heterogeneous members are first identified; then some are chosen at random; all the members in each of the randomly chosen groups are studied.	In geographic clusters, costs of data collection are low.	The least reliable and efficient among all probability sampling designs since subsets of clusters are more homogeneous than heterogeneous.
5. Area sampling	Cluster sampling within a particular area or locality.	Cost-effective. Useful for decisions relating to a particular location.	Takes time to collect data from an area.
6. Double sampling	The same sample or a subset of the sample is studied twice.	Offers more detailed information on the topic of study.	Original biases, if any, will be carried over. Individuals may not be happy responding a second time.
Nonprobability Sampling			
7. Convenience sampling	The most easily accessible members are chosen as subjects.	Quick, convenient, less expensive.	Not generalizable at all.
8. Judgment sampling	Subjects selected on the basis of their expertise in the subject investigated.	Sometimes, the only meaningful way to investigate.	Generalizability is questionable; not generalizable to entire population.
9. Quota sampling	Subjects are conveniently chosen from targeted groups according to some predetermined number or quota.	Very useful where minority participation in a study is critical.	Not easily generalizable.

Figure 11.3
Choice Points in Sampling Design.

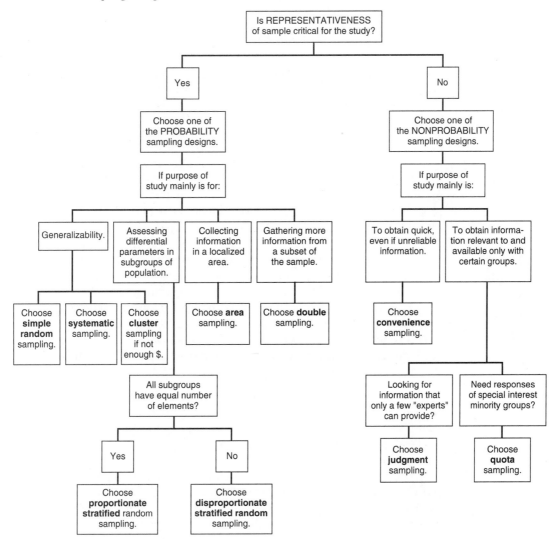

A simple random sampling procedure is recommended in this case since the policy is to be formulated for the company as a whole. This implies that the most representative information has to be obtained that can be generalized to the entire company. This is best accomplished through this design.

It has to be noted that in some cases, where *cost* is a primary consideration (i.e., resources are limited), and the number of elements in the population is very large and/or geographically dispersed, the simple random sampling design may not be the most desirable, because it could become quite expensive. Thus, both the criticality of generalizability and considerations of cost come into play in the choice of this sampling design.

2. Stratified Random Sampling

This sampling design, which is the most efficient, is a good choice when differentiated information is needed regarding various strata within the population, which are known to differ in their parameters. See Examples 11.4 and 11.5 below.

Example 11.4

The director of human resources of a manufacturing firm wants to offer stress management seminars to the personnel who experience high levels of stress. He conjectures that three groups are most prone to stress: the workmen who constantly handle dangerous chemicals, the foremen who are held responsible for production quotas, and the counselors who, day in and day out, listen to the problems of the employees, internalize them, and offer them counsel, with no idea of how much they have really helped the clients.

To get a feel for the experienced level of stress within each of the three groups and the rest of the firm, the director would stratify the sample into four distinct categories: (1) the workmen handling the dangerous chemicals, (2) the foremen, (3) the counselors, and (4) all the rest. He would then choose a *disproportionate random sampling* procedure [since group (3) can be expected to be very small, and groups (2) and (1) are much smaller than group (4)].

This is the only sampling design that would allow the designing of stress management seminars in a meaningful way, targeted at the right groups.

Example 11.5

If in Example 11.3 the regional director had wanted to know which sales promotion gimmick offered the best results for *each* of the geographical areas, so that different sales promotion strategies (according to regional preferences) could be developed, then first the 80 stores would be stratified on the basis of the geographical region, and then a representative sample of stores would be drawn from each of the geographical regions (strata) through a simple random sampling procedure. In this case, since each of the regions has 20 stores, a proportionate stratified random sampling process (say, five stores from each region) would be appropriate. If, however, the northern region had only 3 stores, the southern had 15, and the eastern and western regions had 24 and 38 stores, respectively, then a *disproportionate stratified random sampling* procedure would be the right choice, with all three stores in the northern region being studied, because of the small number of elements in that population.

If the sample size is retained at 20, then the north, south, east, and west regions will probably have samples respectively of three, four, five and eight.

It is interesting to note that sometimes when stratified random sampling might seem logical, it might not really be necessary. For example, when test-marketing results show that Cubans, Puerto Ricans, and Mexicans perceive and consume a particular product the same way, there is no need to segment the market and study each of the three groups using a stratified sampling procedure.

3. Systematic Sampling

If the population frame is large, and a listing of the elements is conveniently available at one place (as in the telephone directory, company payroll, chamber of commerce listings, etc.), then a systematic sampling procedure will offer the advantages of ease and quickness in developing the sample, as illustrated in the following two examples.

Example 11.6   An administrator wants to assess the reactions of employees to a new and improved health benefits scheme that requires a modest increase in the premiums to be paid by the employees for their families. The administrator can assess the enthusiasm for the new scheme by using a systematic sampling design. The company's records will provide the population frame, and every *n*th employee can be sampled. A stratified plan is not called for here since the policy is for the entire company.

Example 11.7   If customers' interest in a highly sophisticated telephone is to be gauged by an entrepreneur, a systematic sampling procedure with the telephone directory as the population frame will be the easiest and quickest way to obtain the information, while still ensuring representativeness of the population studied.

Note: Systematic sampling will be inadvisable where systematic biases can be anticipated to be present. For example, systematic sampling from the personnel directory of a company (especially when it has an equal number of employees in each department), which lists the names of the individuals department-wise, with the head of the department listed first, and the secretary listed next, has inherent biases. The possibility of systematic biases creeping into the data cannot be ruled out in this case, since the selection process may end up picking each of the heads of the department or the departmental secretaries as the sample subjects. The results from such a sample will clearly be biased and not generalizable, despite the use of a probability sampling procedure. Systematic sampling will have to be scrupulously avoided in cases where known systematic biases are possible.

4. Cluster Sampling

This sampling design would be most useful when a heterogeneous group is to be studied at one time. Two examples are offered below.

Example 11.8   A human resources director is interested in knowing why staff resign. Cluster sampling design will be useful in this case for conducting exit interviews of all members completing their final papers in the human resources department on the same day (cluster), before resigning. The clusters chosen for interviews will be based on a simple random sampling of the various clusters of personnel resigning on different days.

The interviews would help to understand the reasons for turnover of a heterogeneous group of individuals (i.e., from various departments), and the study could be conducted at a low cost.

Example 11.9   A financial analyst desires to study the lending practices of pawnbrokers in Santa Clara County, California. All the pawnbrokers in each city would form a cluster. By randomly sampling the clusters, the analyst would be able to draw conclusions on the lending practices.

5. Area Sampling

Area sampling is best suited when the goal of the research is confined to a particular locality or area as per the example below.

Example 11.10   A telephone company wants to install a public telephone outlet in a locality where crime is most rampant, so that victims can have access to a telephone. Studying the crime statistics and interviewing the residents in a particular area will help to choose the right location for installation of the phone.

6. Double Sampling

This design provides added information at minimal additional expenditure. See the example below.

Example 11.11   In Example 11.8 (exit interview example), some individuals (i.e., a subset of the original cluster sample) might have indicated that they were resigning because of philosophical differences with the company's policies. The researcher might want to do an in-depth interview with these individuals to obtain further information regarding the nature of the policies disliked, the actual philosophical differences, and why these particular issues were central to the individuals' value systems. Such additional detailed information from the target group through the double sampling design could help the company to look for ways of retaining employees in the future.

7. Convenience Sampling

This nonprobability design, which is not generalizable at all, is used at times to obtain some "quick" information to get a "feel" for the phenomenon or variables of interest. See example below.

Example 11.12   The accounts executive has established a new accounting system that maximally utilizes computer technology. Before making further changes, he would like to get a feel for how the accounting clerks react to the new system without making it seem that he has doubts about their acceptability. He may then "casually" talk to the first five accounting personnel that walk into his office, trying to gauge their reactions.

   Note: Convenience sampling should be resorted to in the interests of expediency, with the full knowledge that the results are not generalizable at all.

8. Judgment Sampling: One Type of Purposive Sampling

Judgment sampling design is used where the collection of "specialized informed inputs" on the topic area researched is vital, and the use of any other sampling designs would not offer opportunities to obtain the specialized information, as per the example that follows.

Example 11.13   A pharmaceutical company wants to trace the effects of a new drug on patients with specific health problems (muscular dystrophy, sickle cell anemia, rheumatoid arthritis, etc.). It then contacts such individuals and, with the group of voluntarily consenting patients, tests the drug. This is a judgment sample because data are collected from appropriate special groups.

9. Quota Sampling: A Second Type of Purposive Sampling

This sampling design allows for the inclusion of *all* groups in the system researched. Thus groups who are small in numbers are not neglected, as per the example below.

Example 11.14   A company is considering operating an on-site kindergarten facility. But before taking further steps, it wants to get the reactions of four groups to the idea: (1) Employees who are parents of kindergarten-age children, and where both are working outside of the home, (2) employees who are parents of kindergarten-age children, but where one of them is *not* working outside of the home, (3) single parents with kindergarten-age children, and (4) all those without children of kindergarten age. If the four groups are expected to represent 60%, 7%, 23%, and 10% respectively, in the population of 420 employees in the company, then a quota sampling will be appropriate to represent the four groups.

 Note: The last group should also be included in the sample since there is a possibility that they may perceive this as a facility that favors only the parents of kindergarten children, and therefore resent the idea. It is easy to see that resorting to quota sampling would be important in a case such as this.

 In effect, as can be seen from the discussions on sampling designs thus far, *decisions on which design to use* depend on many factors, including the following:

1. Extent of prior knowledge in the area of research undertaken.
2. The main objective of the study—generalizability, efficiency, knowing more about subgroups within a population, obtaining some quick (even if unreliable) information, etc.
3. Cost considerations—is exactitude and generalizability worth the extra investment of time, cost, and other resources in resorting to a more, rather than less sophisticated sampling design? Even if it is, is suboptimization because of cost or time constraints called for? (See also Figure 11.3.)

The advantages and disadvantages of the different probability and nonprobability sampling designs are tabulated in Table 11.2.

In sum, choosing the appropriate sampling plan is one of the important research design decisions the researcher has to make. The choice of a specific design will depend broadly on the goal of research, the characteristics of the population, and considerations of cost.

SAMPLING IN CROSS-CULTURAL RESEARCH

While engaging in cross-cultural research, it is appropriate here to point out that, as in instrument development and data collection, one has to be sensitive to the issue of selecting **matched samples** in the different countries while conducting cross-cultural research. The nature and types of organizations studied, whether subjects are from rural or urban areas, and the types of sampling designs used, should all be similar in the different countries to enable true comparisons.

ISSUES OF PRECISION AND CONFIDENCE IN DETERMINING SAMPLE SIZE

Having discussed the various probability and nonprobability sampling designs, we now need to focus attention on the second aspect of the sampling design issue—the sample size. Suppose we select 30 people from a population of 3,000 through a simple random sampling procedure. Will we be able to generalize our findings to the population with confidence, since we have chosen a probability design that has the most generalizability? What is the sample size that would be required to make reasonably precise generalizations with confidence? What do precision and confidence mean? These issues will be considered now.

A reliable and valid sample should enable us to generalize the findings from the sample to the population under investigation. In other words, the sample statistics should be reliable estimates and reflect the population parameters as closely as possible within a narrow margin of error. No sample statistic ($\overline{X}$, for instance) is going to be *exactly* the same as the population parameter (μ), no matter how sophisticated the probability sampling design is. Remember that the very reason for a probability design is to increase the probability that the sample statistics will be as close as possible to the population parameters! Though the point estimate $\overline{X}$ may not accurately reflect the population mean μ, an interval estimate can be made within which μ will lie, with probabilities attached—that is, at particular confidence levels. The issues of confidence interval and confidence level are addressed in the following discussions on precision and confidence.

Precision

Precision refers to how close our estimate is to the true population characteristic. Usually, we would estimate the population parameter to fall within a range, based on the sample estimate. For example, let us say that from a study of a simple random sample of 50 of the total 300 employees in a workshop, we find that the average daily production rate per person is 50 pieces of a particular product ($\bar{X}$ = 50). We might then (by doing certain calculations, as we shall see later) be able to say that the *true* average daily production of the product (μ) would lie anywhere between 40 and 60 for the population of employees in the workshop. In saying this, we offer an interval estimate, within which we expect the true population mean production to be (μ = 50 ± 10). The narrower this interval, the greater the precision. For instance, if we are able to estimate that the population mean would fall anywhere between 45 and 55 pieces of production (μ = 50 ± 5) rather than 40 and 60 (μ = 50 ± 10), then we would have more precision. That is, we would now estimate the mean to lie within a narrower range, which in turn means that we estimate with greater exactitude or precision.

Precision is a function of the range of variability in the sampling distribution of the sample mean. That is, if we take a number of different samples from a population, and take the mean of each of these, we will usually find that they are all different, are normally distributed, and have a dispersion associated with them. The smaller this dispersion or variability, the greater the probability that the sample mean will be closer to the population mean. We need not necessarily take several different samples to estimate this variability. Even if we take only one sample of 30 subjects from the population, we will still be able to estimate the variability of the sampling distribution of the sample mean. This variability is called the standard error, denoted by $S_{\bar{X}}$. The standard error is calculated by the following formula:

$$S_{\bar{X}} = \frac{S}{\sqrt{n}}$$

where S is the standard deviation of the sample, n is the sample size, and $S_{\bar{X}}$ indicates the standard error or the extent of precision offered by the sample.

Note that the standard error varies inversely with the square root of the sample size. Hence, if we want to reduce the standard error given a particular standard deviation in the sample, we need to increase the sample size. Another noteworthy point is that the smaller the variation in the population, the smaller the standard error, which in turn implies that the sample size need not be large. Thus, low variability in the population requires a smaller sample size.

In sum, the closer we want our sample results to reflect the population characteristics, the greater will be the precision we would aim at. The greater the precision required, the larger is the sample size needed, especially when the variability in the population itself is large.

Confidence

Whereas precision denotes how close we estimate the population parameter based on the sample statistic, confidence denotes how *certain* we are that our estimates will really hold true for the population. In the previous example of production rate, we know we are more precise when we estimate the true mean production (μ) to fall somewhere between 45 and 55 pieces, than somewhere between 40 and 60. However, we may have more confidence in the latter estimation than in the former. After all, anyone can say with 100% certainty or confidence that the mean production (μ) will fall anywhere between zero and infinity! Other things being equal, the narrower the range, the lower the confidence. In other words, there is a trade-off between precision and confidence for any given sample size, as we shall see later in this chapter.

In essence, confidence reflects the level of certainty with which we can state that our estimates of the population parameters, based on our sample statistics, will hold true. The level of confidence can range from 0 to 100%. A 95% confidence is the conventionally accepted level for most business research, most commonly expressed by denoting the significance level as $p \leq .05$. In other words, we say that at least 95 times out of 100, our estimate will reflect the true population characteristic.

SAMPLE DATA, PRECISION, AND CONFIDENCE IN ESTIMATION

Precision and confidence are important issues in sampling because when we use sample data to draw inferences about the population, we hope to be fairly "on target," and have some idea of the extent of possible error. Because a point estimate provides no measure of possible error, we do an interval estimation to ensure a *relatively accurate* estimation of the population parameter. Statistics that have the same distribution as the sampling distribution of the mean are used in this procedure, usually a z or a t statistic.

For example, we may want to estimate the mean dollar value of purchases made by customers when they shop at department stores. From a sample of 64 customers sampled through a systematic sampling design procedure, we may find that the sample mean $\bar{X} = 105$, and the sample standard deviation $S = 10$. $\bar{X}$, the sample mean, is a point estimate of μ, the population mean. We could construct a confidence interval around $\bar{X}$ to estimate the range within which μ would fall. The standard error $S_{\bar{X}}$ and the percentage or level of confidence we require will determine the width of the interval, which can be represented by the following formula, where K is the t statistic for the level of confidence desired.

$$\mu = X \pm KS_{\bar{X}}$$

We already know that:

$$S_{\bar{X}} = \frac{S}{\sqrt{n}}$$

Here,

$$S_{\bar{X}} = \frac{10}{\sqrt{64}} = 1.25$$

From the table of critical values for t in any statistics book (see Table II, columns 5, 6, and 9, at the end of this book), we know that:

For 90% confidence level, the K value is 1.645.

For 95% confidence level, the K value is 1.96.

For 99% confidence level, the K value is 2.576.

If we desire a 90% confidence level in the above case, then $\mu = 105 \pm 1.645\ (1.25)$ (i.e., $\mu = 105 \pm 2.056$). μ would thus fall between 102.944 and 107.056. These results indicate that using a sample size of 64, we could state with 90% confidence that the true population mean value of purchases for all customers would fall between $102.94 and $107.06. If we now want to be 99% confident of our results without increasing the sample size, we would necessarily have to sacrifice precision, as may be seen from the following calculation: $\mu = 105 \pm 2.576\ (1.25)$. The value of μ now falls between 101.78 and 108.22. In other words, the width of the interval has increased and we are now less precise in estimating the population mean, though we are a lot more confident about our estimation. It is not difficult to see that if we want to maintain our original precision while increasing the confidence, or maintain the confidence level while increasing precision, or we want to increase both the confidence and the precision, we need a larger sample size.

In sum, the sample size, n, is a function of:

1. the variability in the population
2. precision or accuracy needed
3. confidence level desired
4. type of sampling plan used—for example, sample random sampling versus startified random sampling

TRADE-OFF BETWEEN CONFIDENCE AND PRECISION

We have noted that if we want more precision, or more confidence, or both, the sample size needs to be increased—unless, of course, there is very little variability in the population itself. However, if the sample size (n) cannot be increased, for whatever reason—say, we cannot afford the costs of increased sampling—then, with the same n, the only way to maintain the same level of precision would be by forsaking the confidence with which we can predict our estimates. That is, we reduce the confidence level or the certainty of our estimate. This trade-off between precision and confidence is illustrated in Figures 11.4a and b. Figure 11.4a indicates that 50% of the time the true mean will fall within the narrow range indicated in the figure, the .25 in each tail representing the 25% nonconfidence, or the probability of making errors, in our estimation on either side. Figure 11.4b indicates that 99% of the time we would expect the true mean μ to fall within the much wider range indicated in the figure and there is only a .005% chance that we would be making an error in this estimation. That is, in Figure 11.4a, we have more precision but less confidence (our confidence level is only 50%). In Figure 11.4b, we have high confidence (99%), but then we are far from being precise—that is, our estimate falls within a broad interval range.

It thus becomes necessary for researchers to consider at least four aspects while making decisions on the sample size needed to do the research: (1) How much precision is really needed in estimating the population characteristics of interest—that is, what is the *margin* of allowable error? (2) How much confidence is really needed—that is, how much *chance* can we take of making errors in estimating the population parameters? (3) To what extent is there *variability* in the population on the characteristics investigated? (4) What is the *cost–benefit* analysis of increasing the sample size?

SAMPLE DATA AND HYPOTHESIS TESTING

So far we have discussed sample data as a means of estimating the population parameters, but sample data can also be used to test hypotheses about population values rather than simply to estimate population values. The procedure for this testing incorporates the same information as in interval estimation, but the goals behind the two methods are somewhat different.

Referring to the earlier example of the average dollar value purchases of customers in a department store, instead of trying to estimate the average purchase value of the store's customers with a certain degree of accuracy, let us say that we now wish to determine wheather or not customers expend the same average amount in purchases at Department Store A as in Department Store B. From Chapter 5, we know that we would first set the null hypothesis, which would state that there would be no difference in the dollar values expended by customers shopping at the two different stores. This would be expressed as:

$$H_O: \mu_A - \mu_B = 0$$

The alternate hypothesis of differences would be stated nondirectionally (since we have no idea whether customers buy more at Store A or Store B) as:

$$H_A: \mu_A - \mu_B \neq 0$$

If we take a sample of 20 customers from each of the two stores and find that the mean dollar value purchases of customers in Store A is 105 with a standard

Figure 11.4
Illustration of the Trade-off between Precision and Confidence. (a) More Precision but Less Confidence. (b) More Confidence but Less Precision.

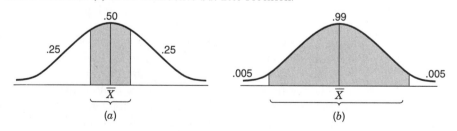

deviation of 10, and the corresponding figures for Store B are 100 and 15, respectively, we see that:

$$X_A - X_B = 105 - 100 = 5$$

whereas our null hypothesis had postulated no difference (difference = 0). Should we then conclude that our alternate hypothesis is to be accepted? We cannot say! To determine this we must first find the probability or likelihood of the two group means having a difference of 5 in the context of the null hypothesis of a difference of 0. This can be done by converting the difference in the sample means to a t statistic and seeing what the probability is of finding a t of that value. The t distribution has known probabilities attached to it [see Table II (t-table) in the Appendix at the end of the book]. Looking at the t distribution table, we find that with two samples of 20 each [the degrees of freedom become ($n1 + n2$) − 2 = 38] for the t value to be significant at the .05 level, the critical value should be around 2.021 (see t table column 6 against v 40). We need to use the 2-tailed test since we do not know whether the difference between Store A and Store B will be positive or negative. For even a 90% probability, it should be at least 1.684 (see the number to the left of 2.021). The t statistic can be calculated for testing our hypothesis as follows:

$$t = \frac{\left(\overline{X}_1 - \overline{X}_2\right) - \left(\mu_1 - \mu_2\right)}{S_{\overline{X}1} - S_{\overline{X}2}}$$

$$S_{\overline{X}1} - S_{\overline{X}2} = \sqrt{\frac{n_1 s_1^2 + n_2 s_2^2}{(n_1 + n_2 - 2)}\left(\frac{1}{n_1} + \frac{1}{n_2}\right)}$$

$$= \sqrt{\frac{\left(20 \times 10^2\right) + \left(20 \times 15^2\right)}{20 + 20 - 2}\left(\frac{1}{20} + \frac{1}{20}\right)}$$

$$t = \frac{\left(\overline{X}_A - \overline{X}_B\right) - \left(\mu_A - \mu_B\right)}{4.136}$$

We already know that

$$\overline{X}_A - \overline{X}_B = 5 \text{ (the difference in the means of the two stores)}$$

and

$$\mu_A - \mu_B = 0 \text{ (from our null hypothesis)}$$

Then

$$t = \frac{5 - 0}{4.136} = 1.209$$

This *t* value of 1.209 is much below the value of 2.021 [for 40 degrees of free-dom for a two population *t*-test, the closest to the actual 38 *df* {(20+20)–2}] required for the conventional 95% probability, and even for the 90% probability, which requires a value of 1.684. We can thus say that the difference of 5 that we found between the two stores is not significantly different from 0. The conclusion, then, is that there is no significant difference between how much customers buy (dollars expended) at Department Store A and Department Store B. We will thus accept the null hypothesis and reject the alternative.

Sample data can thus be used not only for estimating the population parameters, but also for testing hypotheses about population values, population correlations, and so forth, as we will see more fully in Chapter 13.

DETERMINING THE SAMPLE SIZE

Now that we are aware of the fact that the sample size is governed by the extent of precision and confidence desired, how do we determine the sample size required for our research? The procedure can be illustrated through an example.

Suppose a manager wants to be 95% confident that the expected monthly withdrawals in a bank will be within a confidence interval of ± $500. Let us say that a study of a sample of clients indicates that the average withdrawals made by them have a standard deviation of $3,500. What would be the sample size needed in this case?

We noted earlier that the population mean can be estimated by using the formula:

$$\mu = \bar{X} \pm K \, S_{\bar{x}}$$

Since the confidence level needed here is 95%, the applicable *K* value is 1.96 (*t* table). The interval estimate of ± $500 will have to encompass a dispersion of (1.96 × standard error). That is,

$$500 = 1.96 \times S_{\bar{x}}$$
$$S_{\bar{x}} = 500/1.96 = 255.10$$

We already know that

$$S_{\bar{X}} = \frac{S}{\sqrt{n}}$$

$$255.10 = \frac{3500}{\sqrt{n}}$$

$$n = 188$$

The sample size needed in the above was 188. Let us say that this bank has a total clientele of only 185. This means we cannot sample 188 clients. We can in this case apply the correction formula and see what sample size would be needed to have the same level of precision and confidence given the fact that we have a total of only 185 clients. The correction formula is as follows:

$$S_{\bar{X}} = \frac{S}{\sqrt{n}} \times \sqrt{\frac{N-n}{N-1}}$$

where N is the total number of elements in the population, n is the sample size to be estimated, $S_{\bar{X}}$ is the standard error of estimate of the mean, and S is the standard deviation of the sample mean.

Applying the correlation formula, we find that

$$255.10 = \frac{3500}{\sqrt{n}} \times \sqrt{\frac{185-n}{184}}$$

$$n = 94$$

We would now sample 94 of the total 185 clients.

To understand the impact of precision and/or confidence on the sample size, let us try changing the confidence level required in the bank withdrawal exercise which needed a sample size of 188 for a confidence level of 95%. Let us say that the bank manager now wants to be 99% sure that the expected monthly withdrawals will be within the interval of ±$500. What will be the sample size now needed?

$S_{\bar{x}}$ *will now be*

$$\frac{500}{2.576} = 194.099$$

$$194.099 = \frac{3500}{\sqrt{n}}$$

$$n = 325$$

The sample has now to be increased 1.73 times (from 188 to 325) to increase the confidence level from 95% to 99%!

Try calculating the sample size if the precision has to be narrowed down from $500 to $300 for a 95% and a 99% confidence level! Your answers should show the sample sizes needed as 523 and 902, respectively. These results dramatically highlight the costs of increased precision, confidence, or both. It is hence a good idea to think through how much precision and confidence one really needs, before determining the sample size for the research project.

So far we have discussed sample size in the context of precision and confidence with respect to one variable only. However, in research, the theoretical framework has several variables of interest, and the question arises how one should come up with a sample size when all the factors are taken into account. Krejcie and Morgan (1970) greatly simplified size decision by providing a table that ensures a good decision model. Table 11.3 provides that generalized scientific guideline for sample size decisions. The interested student is advised to read Krejcie and Morgan (1970) as well as Cohen (1969) for decisions on sample size.

In research => Be able to justify
you decision based on past precedure
+ outside expertise

Table 11.3
Sample Size for a Given Population Size

N	S	N	S	N	S
10	10	220	140	1200	291
15	14	230	144	1300	297
20	19	240	148	1400	302
25	24	250	152	1500	306
30	28	260	155	1600	310
35	32	270	159	1700	313
40	36	280	162	1800	317
45	40	290	165	1900	320
50	44	300	169	2000	322
55	48	320	175	2200	327
60	52	340	181	2400	331
65	56	360	186	2600	335
70	59	380	191	2800	338
75	63	400	196	3000	341
80	66	420	201	3500	346
85	70	440	205	4000	351
90	73	460	210	4500	354
95	76	480	214	5000	357
100	80	500	217	6000	361
110	86	550	226	7000	364
120	92	600	234	8000	367
130	97	650	242	9000	368
140	103	700	248	10000	370
150	108	750	254	15000	375
160	113	800	260	20000	377
170	118	850	265	30000	379
180	123	900	269	40000	380
190	127	950	274	50000	381
200	132	1000	278	75000	382
210	136	1100	285	1000000	384

IMPORTANCE OF SAMPLING DESIGN AND SAMPLE SIZE

It is now possible to see how both sampling design and the sample size are important to establish the representativeness of the sample for generalizability. If the appropriate sampling design is not used, a large sample size will not, in itself, allow the findings to be generalized to the population. Likewise, unless the sample size is adequate for the desired level of precision and confidence, no sampling design, however sophisticated, can be useful to the researcher in meeting the objectives of the study. Hence, sampling decisions should consider both the sampling design and the sample size. Too large a sample size, however (say, over 500) could also become a problem inasmuch as we would be prone to committing Type II errors. That is, we would accept the findings of our research, when in fact we should reject them. In other words, with too large a sample size, even weak relationships (say a correlation of .10 between two variables) might reach significance levels, and we would be inclined to believe that these significant relationships found in the sample are indeed true of the population, when in reality they may not be. Thus, neither too large nor too small sample sizes help research projects.

Another point to consider, even with the appropriate sample size, is whether statistical significance is more relevant than practical significance. For instance, a correlation of .25 may be statistically significant, but since this explains only about 6% of the variance ($.25^2$), how meaningful is it in terms of practical utility?

Roscoe (1975) proposes the following rules of thumb for determining sample size:

1. Sample sizes larger than 30 and less than 500 are appropriate for most research.

2. Where samples are to be broken into subsamples; (male/females, juniors/seniors, etc.), a minimum sample size of 30 for each category is necessary.

3. In multivariate research (including multiple regression analyses), the sample size should be several times (preferably 10 times or more) as large as the number of variables in the study.

4. For simple experimental research with tight experimental controls (matched pairs, etc.), successful research is possible with samples as small as 10 to 20 in size.

EFFICIENCY IN SAMPLING

Efficiency in sampling is attained when for a given level of precision (standard error), the sample size could be reduced, or for a given sample size (n), the level of precision could be increased. Some probability sampling designs are more efficient than others. The simple random sampling procedure is not always the most efficient plan to adopt; some other probability sampling designs are often more efficient. A stratified random sampling plan is often the most efficient, and a disproportionate stratified random sampling design has been shown to be more efficient than a proportionate sampling design in many cases. Cluster sampling is less efficient than simple random sampling because there is generally more homogeneity among the subjects in the clusters than is found in the elements in the population. Multistage cluster sampling is more efficient than single-stage cluster sampling when there is more heterogeneity found in the earlier stages. There is often a trade-off between time and cost efficiencies (as achieved in nonprobability sampling designs) and precision efficiencies (as achieved in many probability sampling plans). The choice of a sampling plan thus depends on the objectives of the research, as well as on the extent and nature of efficiency desired.

It depends on population, resources & desired outcomes

SAMPLING AS RELATED TO QUALITATIVE STUDIES

In qualitative studies, only small samples of individuals, groups, or events are invariably chosen, in view of the in-depth nature of the study. Obviously, it is not possible to engage in intensive examination of all the factors—central and peripheral—with a sample of, say, 300. That will entail huge costs and energy expenditure.

For the above reason, qualitative studies use small samples, which means that the generalizability of the findings is very restricted. Data analytic procedures will be mostly of the nonparametric type (explained in Chapter 12), and as noted, external validity will be low. In qualitative studies, it is possible to use any of the sampling designs discussed in this chapter, but if the purpose of the study is merely to explore and try to understand phenomena, a convenience sample is almost always used.

Review of Sample Size Decisions

We can summarize the factors affecting decisions on sample size as (1) the extent of precision desired (the confidence interval); (2) the acceptable risk in predicting that level of precision (confidence level); (3) the amount of variability in the population itself; (4) the cost and time constraints; and, in some cases, (5) the size of the population itself.

As a rule of thumb, sample sizes between 30 and 500 could be effective depending on the type of sampling design used and the research question investigated. Qualitative studies typically use small sample sizes because of their intensive nature. When qualitative studies are undertaken for exploratory purposes, the sampling design will be convenience sampling.

MANAGERIAL RELEVANCE

Awareness of sampling designs and sample size helps managers to understand why a particular method of sampling is used by researchers. It also facilitates understanding of the cost implications of different designs, and the trade-off between precision and confidence vis-á-vis the costs. This enables managers to understand the risk they take in implementing changes based on the results of the research study. While reading journal articles, this knowledge also helps managers to assess the generalizability of the findings and analyze the implications of trying out the recommendations made therein in their own system.

SUMMARY

Sampling design decisions are important aspects of research design and include both the sampling plan to be used and the sample size that will be needed. Probability sampling plans lend themselves to generalizability and nonprobability sampling designs, though not generalizable, and offer convenience and timely information. Some probability plans are more efficient than others. Though nonprobability sampling plans have limitations in terms of generalizability, they are often the only designs available for certain types of investigation, as in the case of exploratory research, or where information is needed quickly, or is available with only certain special groups.

The sample size is determined by the level of precision and confidence desired in estimating the population parameters, as well as the variability in the population itself. Cost considerations could also play a part. The generalizability of the findings from a study of the sample to the population is dependent on its representativeness—that is, the sophistication of the sampling design used, and the sample size. Sample data are used for both estimating population parameters and hypothesis testing.

Care should be taken not to overgeneralize the results of any study to populations that are *not* represented by the sample. This is a problem common in some research studies.

In the next two chapters, we will see how the data gathered from a sample of respondents in the population are analyzed to test the hypotheses generated and find answers to the research questions.

DISCUSSION QUESTIONS AND POINTS TO PONDER

1. Identify the relevant population for the following research foci, and suggest the appropriate sampling design to investigate the issues, explaining *why* they are appropriate. Wherever necessary, identify the population frame as well.

   a. A gun manufacturing firm would like to know the types of guns possessed by various age groups in Washington, D.C.

   b. A hospital administrator wants to find out if the single parents working in the hospital have a higher rate of absenteeism than parents who are not single.

   c. A researcher would like to assess the extent of pilferage in the materials storage warehouses of manufacturing firms on the East Coast.

   d. The director of human resources wants to investigate the relationship between drug abuse and dysfunctional behavior of blue-collar workers in a particular plant.

2. a. Explain why cluster sampling is a probability sampling design.

   b. What are the advantages and disadvantages of cluster sampling?

   c. Describe a situation where you would consider the use of cluster sampling.

3. a. Explain what precision and confidence are and how they influence sample size.

   b. Discuss what is meant by the statement: There is a trade-off between precision and confidence under certain conditions.

4. The use of a convenience sample used in organizational research is correct because all members share the same organizational stimuli and go through almost the same kinds of experience in their organizational life. Comment.

5. Use of a sample of 5,000 is not necessarily better than one of 500. How would you react to this statement?

6. Nonprobability sampling designs ought to be preferred to probability sampling designs in some cases. Explain with an example.

7. Because there seems to be a trade-off between accuracy and confidence for any given sample size, accuracy should be always considered more important than precision. Explain with reasons why you would or would not agree.

8. Overgeneralizations give rise to much confusion and other problems for researchers who try to replicate the findings. Explain what is meant by this.

9. Double sampling is probably the least used of all sampling designs in organizational research. Do you agree? Provide reasons for your answer.

10. Why do you think the sampling design should feature in a research proposal?

 EXERCISES

For the situations presented in Exercises 11.1 to 11.6 below, indicate what would be the relevant population and the most appropriate sampling design. Make sure you discuss the reasons for your answers.

Exercise 11.1

A medical inspector desires to estimate the overall average monthly occupancy rates of the cancer wards in 80 different hospitals that are evenly located in the northwestern, southeastern, central, and southern suburbs of New York City.

Exercise 11.2

The director of University Women's Professional Advancement (UWPA), appointed by the president of Southern Illinois University at Carbondale to enhance the status of women on campus some 2 years ago, was listening to a speech made by the president of the Women's Caucus. It suddenly occurred to the director that it would be a great idea to get the opinion of members of this vocal group on how effective they perceived UWPA to be in enhancing the status of women on campus. She thought she could ask a few quick questions as the audience left the meeting room. What should be her sampling design and how should she proceed?

Exercise 11.3

A magazine article suggested that "Consumers 35 to 44 will soon be the nation's biggest spenders, so advertisers must learn how to appeal to this over-the-thrill crowd." If this suggestion appeals to an apparel manufacturer, what should the sampling design be to assess the tastes of this group?

Exercise 11.4

Carbondale is a university town with about 24,000 students—a number of whom come from various parts of the world. For instance, there are about 200 Indian and 600 Malaysian students—about half of each category being women—and a further 1,000 students from over 55 other countries attend Southern Illinois University at Carbondale.

Martha Ellenden, a talented and adventurous seamstress, desires to open a tailoring shop (so rare these days!) in Carbondale, close to the University Mall, where she lives. She has a good sewing machine and would start her business immediately if she knew there would be adequate demand for her services. To assess the market potential, Martha would like to talk to a few women to estimate how many clients she might attract. While the American women buy ready-made clothes from the University Mall, she knows that the international women, particularly the Indians and the Malays, prefer to buy plain material from the Mall and either stitch their own blouses or get them stitched at their native homes. How should Martha go about selecting a sample of 45 individuals to estimate the potential demand?

Exercise 11.5   The McArthur Co. produces special vacuum cleaners for conveniently cleaning the inside of cars. About a thousand of these are produced every month with stamped serial number and stored serially in a stockroom. Once a month an inspector does a quality control check on 50 of these. When he certifies them as to quality, the units are released from the stockroom for sale. The production and sales managers, however, are not satisfied with the quality control check since, quite often, many of the units sold are returned by customers because of various types of defects. What would be the most useful sampling plan to test the 50 units?

Exercise 11.6   A consultant had administered a questionnaire to some 285 employees using a simple random sampling procedure. As she looked at the responses, she suspected that two questions might not have been clear to the respondents. She would like to know if her suspicion is well-founded.

Exercise 11.7   In an article in the *Wall Street Journal* titled "Kellogg to Study Work of Salaried Staff, Setting Stage for Possible Job Cutbacks," it was stated that Kellogg's earnings remained under heavy competitive pressure and its cereal market continued to slip. It was also stated that Kellogg was seeking to regain its lost momentum through the first three strategies listed below, to which the last two are added.

1. Increasing production efficiencies.
2. Developing new products.
3. Increasing product promotion through advertising effectiveness.
4. Tapping creative ideas from organizational members at different levels.
5. Assessing perceptions of organizational health and vitality.

Discuss in as much detail as possible the sampling design you would use for each of the five strategies above. Give reasons for your choice.

Exercise 11.8   Care for elderly relatives is a concern for many working parents. If you were to do a scientific study of this, what kind of a sampling design would you use? Discuss your response with reasons for the choice of the population and sample.

Exercise 11.9   Enacting a death penalty moratorium is definitely worthwhile since DNA evidence has proved the innocence of several individuals on death row. Supporters of the moratorium in California demand an independent study of the manner of execution of the death penalty by the State, and if there are racial or geographical disparities in its application. Design a sampling model for such a study.

DATA ANALYSIS AND INTERPRETATION

TOPICS DISCUSSED

GETTING DATA READY FOR ANALYSIS

- Editing Data
- Handling Blank Responses
- Coding
- Categorizing
- Entering Data

DATA ANALYSIS

- Basic Objectives in Data Analysis
- Feel for the Data
- Testing Goodness of Data
- Hypothesis Testing

DATA ANALYSIS AND INTERPRETATION

- Use of Several Data-Analytic Techniques
- Descriptive Statistics
- Inferential Statistics

SOME SOFTWARE PACKAGES USEFUL FOR DATA ANALYSIS

USE OF EXPERT SYSTEMS IN SELECTING THE APPROPRIATE
STATISTICAL TESTS

CHAPTER OBJECTIVES

After completing Chapter 12 you should be able to:

1. Edit questionnaire and interview responses.
2. Handle blank responses.
3. Set up the coding key for the data set and code the data.
4. Categorize data.
5. Create a data file.
6. Use SPSS or Excel or SAS or other software program for data entry and data analysis.
7. Get a "feel" for the data.
8. Test the goodness of data.
9. Interpret the computer results of tests of various hypotheses.

After data have been collected from a representative sample of the population, the next step is to analyze them to test the research hypotheses. Data analysis is now routinely done with software programs such as SPSS, SAS, STATPAK, SYSTAT, Excel, and the like. All are user-friendly and interactive and have the capability to seamlessly interface with different databases. Excellent graphs and charts can also be produced through most of these software programs. Some of the charts generated from Excel's Chart Wizard may be seen in the next chapter.

However, before we start analyzing the data to test hypotheses, some preliminary steps need to be completed. These help to ensure that the data are reasonably good and of assured quality for further analysis. Figure 12.1 identifies the four steps in data analysis: (1) getting data ready for analysis, (2) getting a feel for the data, (3) testing the goodness of data, and (4) testing the hypotheses. We will now examine each of these steps.

GETTING DATA READY FOR ANALYSIS

After data are obtained through questionnaires, interviews, observation, or through secondary sources, they need to be edited. The blank responses, if any, have to be handled in some way, the data coded, and a categorization scheme has to be set up. The data will then have to be keyed in, and some software program used to analyze them. Each of these stages of data preparation is discussed below.

Figure 12.1
Flow diagram of data analysis process.

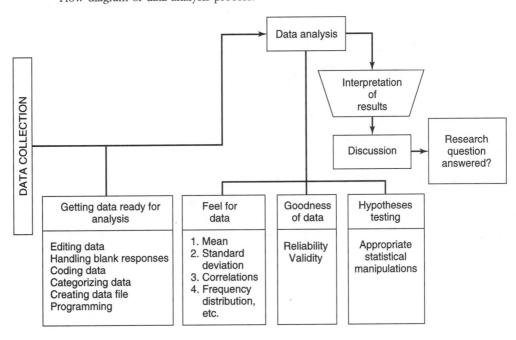

Editing Data

Data have to be edited, especially when they relate to responses to open-ended questions of interviews and questionnaires, or unstructured observations. In other words, information that may have been noted down by the interviewer, observer, or researcher in a hurry must be clearly deciphered so that it may be coded systematically in its entirety. Lack of clarity at this stage will result later in confusion. In an earlier chapter, it was recommended that such editing should be done preferably the very same day the data are collected so that the respondents may be contacted for any further information or clarification, as needed. The edited data should be identifiable through the use of a different color pencil or ink so that the original information is still available in case of further doubts later.

Incoming mailed questionnaire data have to be checked for incompleteness and inconsistencies, if any, by designated members of the research staff. Inconsistencies that can be logically corrected should be rectified and edited at this stage. For instance, the respondent might have inadvertently not answered the question on a questionnaire asking whether or not she is married. Against the column asking for the number of years married, she might have responded 12 years; in the number of children column, she might have marked 2, and for ages of children, she might have answered 8 and 4. The latter three responses would indicate that the respondent is in all probability married. The unfilled response to the marital status question could then be edited by the researcher to read "yes." It is, however, possible that the respondent deliberately omitted responding to the item because she is either a widow or has lately been separated or widowed, or for some other reason. If such were to be the case, we would be introducing a bias in the data by editing the data to read "yes." Hence, whenever possible, it would be better to follow up with the respondent and get the correct data while editing. The example we gave is a clear case for editing, but some others may not be so simple, or omissions could be left unnoticed and not rectified. There may be other biases that could affect the goodness of the data, over which the researcher has no control. The validity and the replicability of the study could thus be impaired.

As indicated in Chapter 10 under "Data Collection Methods," much of the editing is automatically taken care of in the case of computer-assisted telephone interviews and electronically administered questionnaires, even as the respondent is answering the questions.

Handling Blank Responses

Not all respondents answer every item in the questionnaire. Answers may have been left blank because the respondent did not understand the question, did not know the answer, was not willing to answer, or was simply indifferent to the need to respond to the entire questionnaire. In the last situation, the respondent is likely to have left many of the items blank. If a substantial number of questions—say, 25% of the items in the questionnaire—have been left unanswered, it may be a good idea to throw out the questionnaire and not include it in the data set for analysis. In this event, it is important to mention the number of returned but unused responses due to excessive missing data in the final report submitted to the sponsor of the study. If, however, only two or three items are left blank in a questionnaire with, say, 30 or more items, we need to decide how these blank responses are to be handled.

One way to handle a blank response to an interval-scaled item with a mid-point would be to assign the midpoint in the scale as the response to that particular item. An alternative way is to allow the computer to ignore the blank responses when the analyses are done. This, of course, will reduce the sample size whenever that variable is involved in the analyses. A third way is to assign to the item the mean value of the responses of all those who have responded to that particular item. A fourth is to give the item the mean of the responses of this particular respondent to all other questions measuring this variable. A fifth way of dealing with it is to give the missing response a random number within the range for that scale. It should also be noted that SPSS uses linear interpolation from adjacent points as also a linear trend to replace missing data. Thus, there are at least seven different ways of handling missing data.

As may be seen, there are several ways of handling blank responses; a common approach, however, is either to give the midpoint in the scale as the value or to ignore the particular item during the analysis. The computer can be programmed to handle missing and "don't know" responses in the manner we decide to deal with them. The best way to handle missing data to enhance the validity of the study, especially if the sample size is big, is to omit the case where the datum relating to a particular analysis is missing. If however, many of the respondents have answered "don't know" to a particular item or items, further investigation may well be worthwhile. The question might not have been clear or some organizational aspect could have precluded them from answering, which then might need further probing.

Coding

The next step is to code the responses. In Chapter 10, we discussed the convenience of using scanner sheets for collecting questionnaire data; such sheets facilitate the entry of the responses directly into the computer without manual keying in of the data. However, if for whatever reason this cannot be done, then it is perhaps better to use a coding sheet first to transcribe the data from the questionnaire and then key in the data. This method, in contrast to flipping through each questionnaire for each item, avoids confusion, especially when there are many questions and a large number of questionnaires as well. The easiest way to illustrate a coding scheme is through an example. Let us take the correct answer to Exercise 10.4 in Chapter 10—the questionnaire design exercise to test the job involvement–job satisfaction hypothesis in the Serakan Co. case—and see how it can be coded.

Coding the Serakan Co. Data

In the Serakan Co. questionnaire, we have 5 demographic variables and 16 items measuring involvement and satisfaction as shown in Table 12.1.

Table 12.1
Coding of Serakan Co. Questionnaire

1. **Age (years)**	2. **Education**	3. **Job Level**	4. **Sex**
[1] Under 25	[1] High school	[1] Manager	[1] M
[2] 25–35	[2] Some college	[2] Supervisor	[2] F
[3] 36–45	[3] Bachelor's degree	[3] Clerk	5. **Work Shift**
[4] 46–55	[4] Master's degree	[4] Secretary	[1] First
[5] Over 55	[5] Doctoral degree	[5] Technician	[2] Second
	[6] Other (specify)	[6] Other (specify)	[3] Third

5a.   **Employment Status**
[1] Part time
[2] Full time

Here are some questions that ask you to tell us how you experience your work life in general. Please <u>circle</u> the appropriate number on the scales below.

To what extent would you agree with the following statements, on a scale of 1 to 7, 1 denoting very low agreement, and 7 denoting very high agreement?

6. The major happiness of my life comes from my job.	1	2	3	4	5	6	7
7. Time at work flies by quickly.	1	2	3	4	5	6	7
8. I live, eat, and breathe my job.	1	2	3	4	5	6	7
9. My work is fascinating.	1	2	3	4	5	6	7
10. My work gives me a sense of accomplishment.	1	2	3	4	5	6	7
11. My supervisor praises good work.	1	2	3	4	5	6	7
12. The opportunities for advancement are very good here.	1	2	3	4	5	6	7
13. My coworkers are very stimulating.	1	2	3	4	5	6	7
14. People can live comfortably with their pay in this organization.	1	2	3	4	5	6	7
15. I get a lot of cooperation at the workplace.	1	2	3	4	5	6	7
16. My supervisor is not very capable.	1	2	3	4	5	6	7
17. Most things in life are more important than work.	1	2	3	4	5	6	7
18. Working here is a drag.	1	2	3	4	5	6	7
19. The promotion policies here are very unfair.	1	2	3	4	5	6	7
20. My pay is barely adequate to take care of my expenses.	1	2	3	4	5	6	7
21. My work is not the most important part of my life.	1	2	3	4	5	6	7

The responses to the demographic variables can be coded from 1 to 5 for age, and 1 to 6 for the variables of education and job level, depending on which box in the columns was checked by the respondent. Sex can be coded as 1 or 2 depending on whether the response was from a male or a female. Work shift can be coded 1 to 3, and employment status as either 1 or 2.

It is easy to see that when some thought is given to coding at the time of designing the questionnaire, coding can become simple. For example, since numbers were given within the boxes for all the above items (instead of simply putting a box for marking the appropriate one), it would be easy to transfer them to the code sheet, or directly key in the data.

Items numbered 6 to 21 on the questionnaire can be coded by using the actual number circled by the respondents. If, for instance, 3 had been circled for the first question, then the response will be coded as 3; if 4 was circled, we would code it as 4, and so on.

It is possible to key in the data directly from the questionnaires, but that would need flipping through several questionnaires, page by page, resulting in possible errors and omissions of items. Transfer of the data first onto a code sheet would thus help.

Human errors can occur while coding. At least 10% of the coded questionnaires should therefore be checked for coding accuracy. Their selection may follow a systematic sampling procedure. That is, every nth form coded could be verified for accuracy. If many errors are found in the sample, all items may have to be checked.

Categorization

At this point it is useful to set up a scheme for categorizing the variables such that the several items measuring a concept are all grouped together. Responses to some of the negatively worded questions have also to be reversed so that all answers are in the same direction. Note that with respect to negatively worded questions, a response of 7 on a 7-point scale, with 7 denoting "strongly agree," really means "strongly disagree," which actually is a 1 on the 7-point scale. Thus the item has to be reversed so as to be in the same direction as the positively worded questions. This can be done on the computer through a Transform and RECODE statement. In the Serakan Co. data, items 16 to 21 will have to be recoded such that scores of 7 are read as 1; 6 as 2; 5 as 3; 3 as 5; 2 as 6; and 1 as 7.

If the questions measuring a concept are not contiguous but scattered over various parts of the questionnaire, care has to be taken to include all the items without any omission or wrong inclusion.

Entering Data

If questionnaire data are not collected on scanner answer sheets, which can be directly entered into the computer as a data file, the raw data will have to be manually keyed into the computer. Raw data can be entered through any software program. For instance, the SPSS Data Editor, which looks like a spreadsheet, can enter, edit, and view the contents of the data file. Each row of the editor represents a case, and each column represents a variable. All missing values will appear with a period (dot) in the cell. It is possible to add, change, or delete values easily after the data have been entered.

It is also easy to compute the new variables that have been categorized earlier, using the Compute dialog box, which opens when the Transform icon is chosen. Once the missing values, the recodes, and the computing of new variables are taken care of, the data are ready for analysis.

DATA ANALYSIS

In the rest of this chapter, we will elaborate on the various statistical tests and the interpretation of the results of the analyses, using the SPSS Version 11.0 for Windows—a menu-driven software program. In the Appendix to this chapter, we also show the results of data analysis, using Excel. Use of these two programs is illustrated mainly because they are easily available in business settings. It should be noted that any other software program can be used as well, and they would produce similar results, which will be interpreted in the same manner.

Basic Objectives in Data Analysis

In data analysis we have three objectives: getting a feel for the data, testing the goodness of data, and testing the hypotheses developed for the research. The feel for the data will give preliminary ideas of how good the scales are, how well the coding and entering of data have been done, and so on. Suppose an item tapped on a 7-point scale has been improperly coded and/or entered as 8; this will be highlighted by the maximum values on the descriptive statistics and the error can be rectified. The second objective—testing the goodness of data—can be accomplished by submitting the data for factor analysis, obtaining the Cronbach's alpha or the split-half reliability of the measures, and so on. The third objective—hypotheses testing—is achieved by choosing the appropriate menus of the software programs, to test each of the hypotheses using the relevant statistical test. The results of these tests will determine whether or not the hypotheses are substantiated. We will now discuss data analysis with respect to each of these three objectives in detail.

Feel for the Data

We can acquire a feel for the data by checking the central tendency and the dispersion. The mean, the range, the standard deviation, and the variance in the data will give the researcher a good idea of how the respondents have reacted to the items in the questionnaire and how good the items and measures are. If the response to each individual item in a scale does not have a good spread (range) and shows very little variability, then the researcher would suspect that the particular question was probably not properly worded and respondents did not quite understand the intent of the question. Biases, if any, could also be detected if the respondents have tended to respond similarly to all items—that is, stuck to only certain points on the scale. The maximum and minimum scores, mean, standard deviation, variance, and other statistics can be easily obtained, and these will indicate whether the responses range satisfactorily over the scale. Remember that if there is no variability in the data, then no variance can be explained! Researchers go to great lengths obtaining the central tendency, the range, the dispersion, and other statistics for every single item measuring the dependent and independent variables, especially when the measures for a concept are newly developed.

A frequency distribution of the nominal variables of interest should be obtained. Visual displays thereof through histograms/bar charts, and so on, can also be provided through programs that generate charts. In addition to the frequency distributions and the means and standard deviations, it is good to know how the dependent and independent variables in the study are related to each other. For this purpose, an intercorrelation matrix of these variables should also be obtained.

It is always prudent to obtain (1) the frequency distributions for the demographic variables, (2) the mean, standard deviation, range, and variance on the other dependent and independent variables, and (3) an intercorrelation matrix of the variables, irrespective of whether or not the hypotheses are directly related to these analyses. These statistics give a *feel for the data*. In other words, examination of the measure of central tendency, and how clustered or dispersed the variables are, gives a good idea of how well the questions were framed for tapping the concept. The correlation matrix will give an indication of how closely related or unrelated the variables under investigation are. If the correlation between two variables happens to be high—say, over .75—we would start to wonder whether they are really two different concepts, or whether they are measuring the same concept. If two variables that are theoretically stated to be related do not seem to be significantly correlated to each other in our sample, we would begin to wonder if we have measured the concepts validity and reliably. Recall our discussions on convergent and discriminant validity in Chapter 10.

Establishing the goodness of data lends credibility to all subsequent analyses and findings. Hence, getting a feel for the data becomes the necessary first step in all data analysis. Based on this initial feel, further detailed analyses may be done to test the goodness of the data.

Testing Goodness of Data

The reliability and validity of the measures can now be tested.

Reliability

As discussed in Chapter 9, the reliability of a measure is established by testing for both consistency and stability. Consistency indicates how well the items measuring a concept hang together as a set. **Cronbach's alpha** is a reliability coefficient that indicates how well the items in a set are positively correlated to one another. Cronbach's alpha is computed in terms of the average intercorrelations among the items measuring the concept. The closer Cronbach's alpha is to 1, the higher the internal consistency reliability.

Another measure of consistency reliability used in specific situations is the **split-half reliability coefficient.** Since this reflects the correlations between two halves of a set of items, the coefficients obtained will *vary* depending on how the scale is split. Sometimes split-half reliability is obtained to test for consistency when more than one scale, dimension, or factor, is assessed. The items across each of the dimensions or factors are split, based on some predetermined logic (Campbell, 1976). In almost every case, Cronbach's alpha is an adequate test of internal consistency reliability. You will see later in this chapter how Cronbach's alpha is obtained through computer analysis.

As discussed in Chapter 9, the stability of a measure can be assessed through **parallel form reliability** and **test–retest reliability.** When a high correlation between two similar forms of a measure (see Chapter 9) is obtained, parallel form reliability is established. Test–retest reliability can be established by computing the correlation between the same tests administered at two different time periods.

Validity

Factorial validity can be established by submitting the data for factor analysis. The results of factor analysis (a multivariate technique) will confirm whether or not the theorized dimensions emerge. Recall from Chapter 8 that measures are developed by first delineating the dimensions so as to operationalize the concept. Factor analysis would reveal whether the dimensions are indeed tapped by the items in the measure, as theorized. **Criterion-related validity** can be established by testing for the power of the measure to differentiate individuals who are known to be different (refer to discussions regarding concurrent and predictive validity in Chapter 9). **Convergent validity** can be established when there is high degree of correlation between two different sources responding to the same measure (e.g., both supervisors and subordinates respond similarly to a *perceived reward system* measure administered to them). **Discriminant validity** can be established when two distinctly different concepts are not correlated to each other (as, for example, courage and honesty; leadership and motivation; attitudes and behavior). Convergent and discriminant validity can be established through the multitrait multimethod matrix, a full discussion of which is beyond the scope of this book. The student interested in knowing more about factor analysis and the multitrait multimethod matrix can refer to books on those subjects. When well-validated measures are used, there is no need, of course, to establish their validity again for each study. The reliability of the items can, however, be tested.

Hypothesis Testing

Once the data are ready for analysis, (i.e., out-of-range/missing responses, etc., are cleaned up, and the goodness of the measures is established), the researcher is ready to test the hypotheses already developed for the study. In the Module at the end of the book, the statistical tests that would be appropriate for different hypotheses and for data obtained on different scales are discussed. We will now examine the results of analyses of data obtained from a company, and how they are interpreted.

DATA ANALYSIS AND INTERPRETATION

Data analysis and interpretation of results may be most meaningfully explained by referring to a business research project. After a very brief description of the background of the company in which the research was carried out and the sample, we will discuss the analysis done to obtain a feel for the data, establish reliability, and test each hypothesis. We will also discuss how the results are interpreted.

RESEARCH DONE IN EXCELSIOR ENTERPRISES

* Find an in-class example & run it through "analysis"

Excelsior Enterprises is a medium-sized company, manufacturing and selling instruments and supplies needed by the health care industry, including blood pressure instruments, surgical instruments, dental accessories, and so on. The company, with a total of 360 employees working three shifts, is doing reasonably well but could do far better if it did not experience employee turnover at almost all levels and in all the departments. The president of the company called in a research team to study the situation and to make recommendations on the turnover problem.

Since access to those who had left the company would be difficult, the research team suggested to the president that they would talk to the current employees, and based on their inputs and a literature survey, try to get at the factors influencing employees' *intentions to stay with, or leave,* the company. Since past research has shown that intention to leave (ITL) is an excellent predictor of actual turnover, the president concurred.

The team first conducted an unstructured interview with about 50 employees at various levels and from different departments. Their broad statement was: "We are here to find out how you experience your work life. Tell us whatever you consider is important for you in your job, as issues relate to your work, the environment, the organization, supervision, and whatever else you think is relevant. If we get a good handle on the issues involved, we may be able to make appropriate recommendations to management to enhance the quality of your work life. We would just like to talk to you now, and administer a questionnaire later."

Each interview typically lasted about 45 minutes, and notes on the responses were written down by the team members. When the responses were tabulated, it became clear that the issues most frequently brought up by the respondents in one form or another, related to three main areas: the *job* (employees said the jobs were dull or too complex; there was lack of freedom to do the job as one wanted to, etc.), *perceived inequities* (remarks such as "other companies pay more for the kind of jobs we do"; "compared to the work we do, we are not adequately paid"; etc.); and *burnout* (comments such as "there is so much work to be done that by the end of the day we are physically and emotionally exhausted"; "we feel the frequent need to take time off because of exhaustion"; etc.).

A literature survey confirmed that these variables were good predictors of intention to leave and subsequent turnover. In addition, *job satisfaction* was also found to be a useful predictor. A theoretical framework was developed based on the interviews and the literature survey, and five hypotheses (stated later) were developed.

Next, a questionnaire was designed incorporating well-validated and reliable measures for the four independent variables of job characteristics, perceived inequity, burnout, and job satisfaction, and the dependent variable of intention to leave. Demographic variables such as age, education, gender, tenure, job title, department, and work shift were also included in the questionnaire. The questionnaire was administered personally to 174 employees who were chosen on a disproportionate stratified random sampling basis. The responses were entered into the computer. Thereafter, the data were submitted for analysis to test the following hypotheses, which were formulated by the researchers:

1. Men will perceive less equity than women (or women will perceive more equity than men).

2. The job satisfaction of individuals will vary depending on the shift they work.

3. Employees' intentions on leave (ITL) will vary according to their job title. In other words, there will be significant differences in the ITL of top managers, middle level managers, supervisors, and the clerical and blue-collar employees.

4. There will be a relationship between the shifts that people work (first, second, and third shift) and the part-time versus full-time status of employees. In other words, these two factors will not be independent.

5. The four independent variables of job characteristics, distributive justice, burnout, and job satisfaction will significantly explain the variance in intention to leave.

In may be pertinent to point out here that the five hypotheses derived from the theoretical framework are particularly relevant for finding answers to the turnover issue in direct and indirect ways. For example, if men perceived more inequity (as could be conjectured from the interview data), it would be important to set right their (mis)perceptions so that they are less inclined to leave (if indeed a positive correlation between perceived inequities and ITL is found). If work shift has an influence on job satisfaction (irrespective of its influence on ITL), the matter will have to be further examined since job satisfaction is also an important outcome variable for the organization. If employees at particular levels have greater intentions of leaving, further information has to be gathered as to what can be done for these groups. If there is a pattern to the part-time/full-time employees working for particular shifts, this might offer some suggestions for further investigation, such as: "Do part-time employees in the night shift have some special needs that are not addressed currently?" The results of testing the last hypothesis will certainly offer insights into how much of the variance in ITL will be explained by the four independent variables, and what corrective action, if any, needs to be taken.

The researcher submitted the data for computer analysis using the SPSS Version 11.0 for Windows software program. We will now proceed to discuss the results of these analyses and their interpretation. In particular, we will examine the following:

1. The establishment of Cronbach's alpha for the measures.

2. The frequency distribution of the variables.

3. Descriptive statistics such as the mean and standard deviation.

4. The Pearson correlation matrix.

5. The results of hypotheses testing.

Some Preliminary Steps

It is useful to know that the SPSS Student Version 11.0 for Windows comes with an online tutorial, which can be very helpful. To have some idea of how the Main Menu in SPSS Version 11.0 is set up, the main bar lists several items, two of which are used frequently during data analysis—the TRANSFORM and the STATISTICS menus. The Transform menu makes changes to selected variables and computes new variables, and the Statistics menu is used to perform any selected statistical procedure. By clicking on *Recode* in the pull-down menu from Transform, new values can be assigned to a variable, and by clicking on *Compute* and doing what is indicated in the same menu, a new variable can be computed. Missing values can be assigned a number by clicking on *Data* in the menu bar, then clicking on the *Define variable* dialog box, and thereafter on Missing Values, and following through. Once these preliminaries are taken care of, the reliability of measures can be checked.

Checking the Reliability of Measures: Cronbach's Alpha

The interitem consistency reliability or the Cronbach's alpha reliability coefficients of the five independent and dependent variables were obtained. They were all above .80. A sample of the result obtained for Cronbach's alpha test for the dependent variable, Intention to Leave, together with instructions on how it is obtained is, shown in Output 12.1.

The result indicates that the Cronbach's alpha for the six-item Intention to Leave measure is .82. The closer the reliability coefficient gets to 1.0, the better. In general, reliabilities less than .60 are considered to be poor, those in the .70 range, acceptable, and those over .80 good. Cronbach's alpha for the other four independent variables ranged from .81 to .85. Thus, the internal consistency reliability of the measures used in this study can be considered to be good.

It is important to note that all the negatively worded items in the questionnaire should first be reversed before the items are submitted for reliability tests. Unless all the items measuring a variable are in the same direction, the reliabilities obtained will be incorrect.

good consumer of research

Output 12.1
Reliability Analysis

1. From the menus, choose:
   Analyze
     Scale
       Reliability Analysis...
2. Select the variables constituting the scale.
3. Choose Model *Alpha*.

Reliability Output

Reliability Coefficients   6 items
Alpha = .8172   Standardized item alpha = .8168

Obtaining Descriptive Statistics: Frequency Distributions

Frequency distributions were obtained for all the personal data or classification variables. The frequencies for the number of individuals in the various departments for this sample are shown in Output 12.2. It may be seen therefrom that the greatest number of individuals in the sample came from the Production Department (28.1%), followed by the Sales Department (25.3%). Only three individuals (1.7%) came from Public Relations, and five individuals each from the Finance, Maintenance, and Accounting Departments (2.9% from each). The low numbers in the sample in some of the departments are a function of the total population (very few members) in those departments.

From the frequencies obtained for the other variables (results not shown here) it was found that 86% of the respondents are men and 14% women; about 68% worked the first shift, 19% the second shift, and 13% the third shift. Sixteen percent of the respondents worked part time and 84% full time. About 8% had elementary school education, 28% a high school diploma, 23% a bachelor's degree, 30% a master's degree, and 11% had doctoral degrees. About 21% of the respondents had

Output 12.2
Frequencies

From the menus, choose:
    Analyze
        Descriptive Statistics
            Frequencies...
                (Select the relevant variables)
        Choose needed:
            Statistics...
            Charts...
            Format (for the order in which the results are to be displayed)

Frequencies Output

Respondent's Department

	Frequency	Percent	Valid Percent	Cumulative Percent
Marketing	13	7.5	7.5	7.5
Production	49	28.1	28.1	35.6
Sales	44	25.3	25.3	60.9
Finance	5	2.9	2.9	63.8
Servicing	34	19.5	19.5	83.3
Maintenance	5	2.9	2.9	86.2
Personnel	16	9.2	9.2	95.4
Public Relations	3	1.7	1.7	97.1
Accounting	5	2.9	2.9	100.0
Total	174	100.0	100.0	100.0

worked for the organization for less than a year, 20% 1 to 3 years, 20% 4 to 6 years, the balance 39% over 6 years, including 8% who had worked for over 20 years.

We thus have a profile of the employees in this organization, which is useful to describe the sample in the Methods Section of the Written Report (see next chapter). The frequencies can also be visually displayed as bar charts, histograms, or pie charts by clicking on *Statistics* in the menu, then *Summarize,* then *Frequencies,* and *Charts* in the Frequencies dialog box and then selecting the needed chart.

Descriptive Statistics: Measures of Central Tendencies and Dispersion

Descriptive statistics such as maximum, minimum, means, standard deviations, and variance were obtained for the interval-scaled independent and dependent variables. The results are shown in Computer Output 12.3.

It may be mentioned that all variables excepting ITL were tapped on a 5-point scale. ITL was measured on a 4-point scale. From the results, it may be seen that the **mean** on perceived equity (termed distributive justice) is rather low (2.38 on a 5-point scale), as was the mean on experienced burnout (2.67). Job satisfaction is about average (3.12 on a 5-point scale), and the job is perceived as somewhat enriched (3.47). The mean of 2.21 on a 4-point scale for ITL indicates that most of the respondents are neither bent on leaving nor staying. The minimum of 1 indicates that there are some who do not intend to leave at all, and the maximum of 4 indicates that some are seriously considering leaving.

Output 12.3
Descriptive Statistics: Central Tendencies and Dispersions

From the menus, choose:
    Analyze
        Descriptive Statistics
            Descriptives...
                (Select the variables)
                Options...
                (Choose the relevant statistics needed)

Descriptives Output

Descriptive Statistics

	N	Minimum	Maximum	Mean	Std Deviation	Variance
Dist Justice	173	1.00	5.00	2.379	.756	.570
Burnout	173	1.00	4.33	2.671	.521	.271
Job Sat	170	1.61	4.28	3.117	.507	.257
Job Char	167	2.31	4.69	3.474	.518	.268
ITL	174	1.00	4.00	2.212	.673	.453

The **variance** for burnout, job satisfaction, and the job characteristics is not high. The variance for ITL and perceived equity (distributive justice) is only slightly more, indicating that most respondents are very close to the mean on all the variables.

In sum, the perceived equity is rather low, not much burnout experienced, the job is perceived to be fairly enriched, there is average job satisfaction, and there is neither a strong intention to stay with the organization nor to leave it.

Inferential Statistics: Pearson Correlation

The Pearson correlation matrix obtained for the five interval-scaled variables is shown in Output 12.4. From the results, we see that the intention to leave is, as would be expected, significantly, negatively correlated to perceived distributive justice (equity), job satisfaction, and enriched job. That is, the intention to leave is low if equitable treatment and job satisfaction are experienced, and the job is enriched. However, when individuals experience burnout (physical and emotional exhaustion), their intention to leave also increases (positive correlation of .33). Job satisfaction is also positively correlated to perceived equity, and enriched job. It is negatively correlated to burnout and ITL. The correlations are all in the expected direction.

The Pearson correlation coefficient is appropriate for interval- and ratio-scaled variables, and the Spearman Rank or the Kendall's Tau coefficients are appropriate when variables are measured on an ordinal scale. Any bivariate correlation can be obtained by clicking the relevant menu, identifying the variables, and seeking the appropriate parametric or nonparametric statistics.

It is important to note that no correlation exceeded .59 for this sample. If correlations were higher (say, .75 and above), we might have had to suspect whether or not the correlated variables are two different and distinct variables and would have doubted the validity of the measures.

Hypothesis Testing

Five hypotheses were generated for this study as stated earlier. These call for the use of a *t*-test (for hypothesis 1), an ANOVA (for hypotheses 2 and 3), a chi-square test (for hypothesis 4), and a multiple regression analysis (for hypothesis 5). The results of these tests and their interpretation are discussed below.

Hypothesis 1: Use of t-Test. Hypothesis 1 can be stated in the null and alternate as follows:

$H1_0$: There will be no difference between men and women in their perceived inequities.

$$\text{Statistically expressed: } H1_0 \text{ is: } \mu_W = \mu_M$$

where μ_W is the equity perceived by women and μ_M the equity perceived by men.

Output 12.4
Pearson Correlations Matrix

From the menus, choose:
Analyze
  Correlate
    Bivariate...
      (Select relevant variables)
    Option...
      Select:
        a. Type of correlation coefficient: select relevant one (e.g. *Pearson, Kendall's Tau, Spearman*)
        b. Test of significance—*two tailed, one-tailed.*

Correlations

		Dist Justice	Burnout	Job Sat	Job Char	ITL
Pearson Correlation	Dist Justice	1.000	−.374**	.588**	.169*	−.357**
	Burnout	−.374**	1.000	−.474**	−.299**	.328**
	Job Sat	.588**	−.474**	1.000	.328**	−.535**
	Job Char	.169*	−.299**	.328**	1.000	−.274**
	ITL	−.357**	.328**	−.535**	−.274**	1.000
Significance (2-tailed)	Dist Justice		.000	.000	.015	.000
	Burnout	.000		.000	.000	.000
	Job Sat	.000	.000		.000	.000
	Job Char	.015	.000	.000		.000
	ITL	.000	.000	.000	.000	
N	Dist Justice	172	173	169	166	173
	Burnout	172	173	169	166	173
	Job Sat	169	169	173	163	167
	Job Char	166	166	163	173	167
	ITL	173	173	167	167	172

* Correlation at .01 (2 tailed).
** Correlation at .0001 (2-tailed).

$H1_A$: Women will perceive more equity than men (or men will perceive less equity than women).

Statistically expressed: $H1_A$ is: $\mu_W > \mu_M$

A *t*-test will indicate if the perceived differences are significantly different for women than for men. The results of the *t*-test done are shown in Output 12.5. As may be seen, the difference in the means of 2.43 and 2.34 with standard deviations of .75 and .76 for the women and men on perceived equity (or distributive justice) is not significant (see table showing *t*-test for Equality of Means). Thus, **hypothesis 1 is not substantiated.**

Output 12.5
t-Test for Differences between Two Groups

(Independent Samples Test)
Choose:

    Analyze

        Compare Means

            Independent-Samples t Test…

                Select a. single grouping variable and click Define groups to specify the two codes to be compared.

                Options…

                    (Specify Confidence level required – .05, .01, etc.)

t Test Output

Group Statistics

			N	Mean	Std Deviation	Std Error Mean
Dist Justice	Treatment	Male	149	2.43	.75	.052
		Female	25	2.34	.76	.154

Independent Samples Test

		Levene's Test for Equality of Variance		t-test for Equality of Means					95% Confidence Interval of the Mean	
		F	Significance	t	df	Significance (2-tailed)	Mean Difference	Std. Error Difference	Lower	Upper
Dist Justice	Equal variance assumed	1.31	.352	.74	171	.461	.03	.10	.30	.91
	Equal variance not assumed		.67	29	.506	.03	.09	.29	.89	

Hypothesis 2: Use of ANOVA. The second hypothesis can be stated in the null and alternate as follows:

$H2_0$: The job satisfaction of individuals will be the same irrespective of the shift they work (1, 2, or 3).

                    Statistically expressed, $H2_0$ is: $\mu_1 = \mu_2 = \mu_3$

where μ_1, μ_2 and μ_3 signify the means on the job satisfaction of employees working in shifts 1, 2, and 3, respectively.

$H2_A$: The job satisfaction of individuals will *not* be the same (will vary) depending on which shift they work.

                    Statistically expressed, $H2_A$ is: $\mu_1 \neq \mu_2 \neq \mu_3$

Output 12.6
ANOVA

Choose:
Analyze
Compare Means
One-Way ANOVA…
(Select the dependent variable/s and one independent factor variable)

Oneway ANOVA Output

ANOVA

		Sums of Squares	df	Mean Square	F	Sig.
Job Sat	Between Groups	1.659	2	.831	3.327	.038
	Within Groups	39.645	159	.249		
	Total	41.304	161			

For post hoc test to determine in which of the multiple groups the differences lie (as discussed in the text), click on:
Post Hoc…
(Select from among the many tests such as Bonferroni, Scheffe, Tukey, Duncan, as appropriate.)

Since there are more than two groups (three different shifts) and job satisfaction is measured on an interval scale, ANOVA is appropriate to test this hypothesis. The results of ANOVA, testing this hypothesis, are shown in Output 12.6.

The *df* in the third column refers to the degrees of freedom, and each source of variation has associated degrees of freedom. For the between-groups variance, $df = (K - 1)$, where K is the total number of groups or levels. Because there were three shifts, we have $(3 - 1) = 2$ *df*. The *df* for the within-groups sum of squares equals $(N - K)$, where N is the total number of respondents and K is the total number of groups. If there were no missing responses, $(N - K)$ should be $(174 - 3) = 171$. However, in this case, there were 12 missing responses, and hence the associated *df* is $(162 - 3) = 159$.

The mean square for each source of variation (column 5 of the results) is derived by dividing the sum of squares by its associated *df*. Finally, the *F* value itself equals the explained mean square divided by the residual mean square.

$$F = \frac{\text{MS explained}}{\text{MS residual}}$$

In this case, $F = 3.327$ (.831/.249). This *F* value is significant at the .04 level. This implies that **hypothesis 2 is substantiated.** That is, there are significant differences in the mean satisfaction levels of workers in the three shifts, and the null hypothesis can be rejected.

The *F* test used here is called the overall or omnibus F test. To determine among which groups the true differences lie, other tests need to be done, as discussed in Chapter 9. The **Duncan Multiple Range Test** was performed for the purpose (Output not shown). The results showed that the mean job satisfaction for the three groups was 3.15 for the first shift, 2.91 for the second shift, and 3.23 for the third shift. The second shift with the low job satisfaction is the one that is significantly different from groups 1 and 3 at the $p \leq .05$ level.

Hypothesis 3: Use of ANOVA. Hypothesis 3 can be stated in the null and the alternate as follows:

$H3_0$: There will be no difference in the intention to leave of employees at the five different job levels.

Statistically expressed, $H3_0$ is: $\mu_1 = \mu_2 = \mu_3 = \mu_4 = \mu_5$

where the five μ's represent the five means on ITL of employees at the five different job levels.

$H3_A$: The ITL of members at the five different job levels will not be the same

Statistically expressed, $H3_A$ is: $\mu_1 \neq \mu_2 \neq \mu_3 \neq \mu_4 \neq \mu_5$

The results of this ANOVA test shown in Output 12.7 do not indicate any significant differences in the intention to leave among the five groups (F = 1.25; p = .29). Thus, **hypothesis 3 was not substantiated.**

Hypothesis 4: Use of Chi-Square Test. Hypothesis 4 can be stated in the null and alternate as follows:

$H4_0$: Shifts worked and employment status (part-time vs. full-time) will be independent (i.e., will not be related).

$H4_A$: There will be a relationship between the shifts that people work and their part-time vs. full-time status.

Since both variables are nominal, a chi-square (χ^2) test was done, the results of which are shown in Output 12.8. The cross-tabulation *count* indicates that, of

Output 12.7
ANOVA with ITL as the Dependent Variable

One-way ANOVA Output

ANOVA

		Sums of Squares	df	Mean Square	F	Sig.
ITL	Between Groups	2.312	4	.578	1.254	.288
	Within Groups	75.143	163	.461		
	Total	77.455	167			

Output 12.8
Chi-square Test

Choose:
  Analyze
    Descriptive Statistics
      Crosstabs…
        (Enter variables in the Rows and Columns boxes)
          Statistics…
            Select *Chi-square*

Crosstabs Output

Employment Status * Shift Cross-tabulation

Employment Status	Shift			Total
	First	Second	Third	
Full Time	103	25	18	146
Part Time	16	8	4	28
Total	119	33	22	174

Chi-Square Tests

	Value	df	Asymp. Sig (2-sided)
Pearson Chi-square	2.312	2	.314
Likelihood ratio	2.163	2	.339
Linear-by-linear Association	1.103	1	.294
N of valid cases	174		

the full-time employees, 103 work the first shift, 25 work the second shift, and 18 the third shift. Of the part-time employees, 16 work the first shift, 8 the second shift, and 4 the third shift.

It may be seen that the χ^2 value of 2.31, with two degrees of freedom, is not significant. In other words, the part-time/full-time status and the shifts worked are not related. Hence **hypothesis 4 has not been substantiated.**

Hypothesis 5: Use of Multiple Regression Analysis. The last hypothesis can be stated in the null and alternate as follows:

$H5_0$: The four independent variables will *not* significantly explain the variance in intention to leave.

$H5_A$: The four independent variables will significantly explain the variance in intention to leave.

To test this hypothesis, multiple regression analysis was done. The results of regressing the four independent variables against Intention to Leave can be seen in Output 12.9.

The first table in the Output lists the four independent variables that are entered into the regression model and **R** (.548) is the correlation of the four independent variables with the dependent variable, after all the intercorrelations among the four independent variables are taken into account.

In the *Model Summary* table, The **R Square** (.30), which is the explained variance, is actually the square of the multiple R $(.548)^2$ The *ANOVA* table shows that the F value of 16.72 is significant at the .0001 level. In the *df* (degree of freedom) in the same table, the first number represents the number of independent variables (4), the second number (156) is the total number of complete responses for all the variables in the equation *(N)*, minus the number of independent variables *(K)* minus 1. $(N - K - 1)$ [(161 − 4 − 1) = 156]. The F statistic produced (F = 16.72) is significant at the .0001 level.

What the results mean is that 30% of the variance (*R*-square) in Intention to Leave has been significantly explained by the four independent variables. Thus, **hypothesis 5 is substantiated.**

The next table titled *Coefficients* helps us to see which among the four independent variables influences most the variance in ITL (i.e., is the most important). If we look at the column **Beta** under *Standardized Coefficients,* we see that the highest number in the beta is −.37 for job satisfaction, which is significant at the .0001 level. It may also be seen that this is the only independent variable that is significant. The negative beta weight indicates that if ITL is to be reduced, it is necessary to enhance the job satisfaction of employees.

Overall Interpretation and Recommendations to the President

Of the five hypothesis tested, two were substantiated and three were not. From the results of the multiple regression analysis, it is clear that job satisfaction is the most influential factor in explaining employees' intentions to stay with the organization. Whatever is done to increase job satisfaction will therefore help employees to think less about leaving and induce them to stay.

It is also clear from the results that ITL does not differ with job level. That is, employees at all levels feel neither too strongly inclined to stay with the organization nor to leave it. Hence, if retention of employees is a top priority for the president, it is important to pay attention to employees at all levels and formulate policies and practices that help enhance the job satisfaction of all of them. Also, since job satisfaction is found to be significantly lower for employees working the evening shift, further interviews with them might shed some light on the factors that make them dissatisfied. Corrective action can then be taken.

It is informative to find that the perceived equity, though not significantly different for men and women as originally hypothesized, is nevertheless rather low for all (see Output 12.3). The Pearson correlation matrix (Output 12.4) indicates that perceived equity (or distributive justice) is positively correlated

Output 12.9
Multiple Regression Analysis

Choose:
  Analyze
    Regression
      Linear...
        (Enter dependent and independent variables)

Regression Output

Model Summary[3,4]

| | | Variables | | | | Adjusted R | Std. Error of the |
		Entered	Removed	R	R Square	Square	Estimate
Model	1	Job Char Dist Just Burnout Job Sat.[1,2]		.548	.300	.282	.578

[1] Indep.vars: (constant) Job Char, Dist Just, Burnout, Job Sat
[2] All requested variables entered.
[3] Dependent Variable: ITL
[4] Method: Enter

ANOVA[2]

			Sum of Squares	df	Mean Square	F	Significance
Model	1	Regression	22.366	4	5.591	16.717	.000[1]
		Residual	52.180	156	.335		
		Total	74.546	160			

[1] Indep.Vars: (constant) Job Char, Dist Justice, Burnout, Job Sat
[2] Dependent Variable: ITL

Coefficients[1]

| | | Unstandardized Coefficients | | Standardized Coefficients | | |
Model		B	Std. Error	Beta	t	Sig
1	(Constant)	4.048	.603		6.713	.000
	Job Char	−.112	.095	−.084	−1.173	.243
	Dist Justice	−.115	.078	−.121	−1.461	.146
	Burnout	.143	.103	.109	1.393	.166
	Job Sat	−.498	.121	−.371	−4.121	.000

[1] Dependent Variable: INTENTION TO LEAVE

to job satisfaction and negatively correlated to ITL. The president will therefore be well advised to rectify inequities, in the system, if they do really exist, or clear misperceptions of inequities, if this were to be actually the case.

Increasing job satisfaction will no doubt help to reduce employees' intention to quit, but the fact that only 30% of the variance in Intention to Leave was significantly explained by the *four* independent variables considered in this study still leaves 70% unexplained. In other words, there are other additional variables that are important in explaining ITL that have not been considered in this study. So further research might be necessary to explain more of the variance in ITL, if the president desires to pursue the matter further.

We have now seen how different hypotheses can be tested by applying the appropriate statistical tests in data analysis. Based on the interpretation of the results, the research report is then written, making necessary recommendations and discussing the pros and cons of each, together with cost/benefit analysis. Limitations to the study are also specifically stated so that the reader is made aware of the biases that might have crept into the study. This also gives a professional touch to the study, attesting to its scientific orientation.

Overview

SOME SOFTWARE PACKAGES USEFUL FOR DATA ANALYSIS

SPSS Software Packages

As stated in an earlier chapter, SPSS has software programs that can create surveys (questionnaire design) through the *SPSS Data Entry Builder,* collect data over the Internet or Intranet through the *SPSS Data Entry Enterprises Server,* enter the collected data through the SPSS Data Entry Station, and SPSS 11.0 to analyze the data collected.

Various Other Software Programs

Go to the Internet and explore

http://www.asc.org.uk/Register/ShowPackage.asp?ID=162

and the subsequent IDs it indicates. You will see a variety of software programs with a wide range of capabilities. A few of these are listed below.

Package	Main Purposes/Capabilities
1. Askia	Questionnaire design, question libraries, data management, data analysis, charts and graphs
2. ATLAS.ti	Questionnaire design, sampling, e-mail surveys, modeling, interactive graphics
3. Bellview CATI	Questionnaire design, data entry form design, data editing
4. Brand2hand	Questionnaire design, sampling, web-based questionnaires, web interviewing, data editing, data transformation and recoding, statistical analysis, including multivariate analysis. Charts and graphs for presentation can be produced.

USE OF EXPERT SYSTEMS IN CHOOSING THE APPROPRIATE STATISTICAL TESTS

As we know, the Expert System employs unique programming techniques to model the decisions that experts make. A considerable body of knowledge fed into the system and some good software and hardware help the individual using it to make sound decisions about the problem that he or she is concerned about solving. In sum, an Expert System can be thought of as an "advisor," clarifying or resolving problematic issues that are confusing to the individual.

Expert Systems relating to data analysis help the preplexed researcher to choose the most appropriate statistical procedure for testing different types of hypothesis. The *Statistical Navigator* is an Expert System that recommends one or more statistical procedures after seeking information on the **goals** (i.e., the purpose of the analysis—say, to understand the relationship between two variables), and the **data** (i.e., categories, scales).

The *Statistical Navigator* is a useful guide for those who are not well versed in statistics but want to ensure that they use the appropriate statistical techniques.

Incidentally, Expert Systems can also be used for making decisions with respect to various aspects of the research design—**nature of study, time horizon, type of study, study setting, unit of analysis, sampling designs, data collection methods,** and the like.

Other applications of Expert Systems for business decisions using available data include *Auditor* (for decisions on allowing for bad debts), and *Tax Advisor* (this helps audit firms to advise clients on estate planning). As suggested by Luconi, Malone, and Morton (1986), Expert Systems can be used for making decisions with respect to operational control (accounts receivable, inventory control, cash management, production scheduling), management control (budget analysis, forecasting, variance analysis, budget preparation), and strategic planning (warehouse and factory location, mergers and acquisitions, new product planning). Thus, there is infinite scope for developing and using expert systems to aid managerial problem solving and decision making.

SUMMARY

In this chapter we covered the procedure for analyzing data once they are collected. We saw the steps necessary to get the data ready for analysis—editing, coding, and categorizing. Through the example of the research on Excelsior Enterprises, we observed the various statistical analyses and tests used to examine different hypotheses to answer the research question. We also learned how the computer results are interpreted. An important point to note is that data analysis should be based on testing hypotheses that have been already formulated. It would be incorrect to change our original hypotheses to suit the results of data analyses. It is, however, acceptable to develop inductive hypotheses and later test them through further research. We also looked at some of the newly emerging software programs that help with questionnaire design and administration, data gathering, and analysis.

The Appendix to this chapter illustrates the use of Excel in data analysis demonstrated by Professors Barclay and York. In the next chapter we will learn how to write a research report after the data are analyzed and the results interpreted.

DISCUSSION QUESTIONS AND POINTS TO PONDER

1. What kinds of biases do you think could be minimized or avoided during the data analysis stage of research?

2. When we collect data on the effects of treatment in experimental designs, which statistical test would be most appropriate to test the treatment effects?

3. A tax consultant wonders whether he should be more selective about the class of clients he serves so as to maximize his income. He usually deals with four categories of clients: the very rich, rich, upper middle class, and middle class. He has records of each and every client served, the taxes paid by them, and how much he has charged them. Since many particulars in respect of the clients vary (number of dependents, business deductibles, etc.), irrespective of the category they belong to, he would like an appropriate analysis to be done to see which among the four categories of clientele he should choose to continue to serve in the future.

   What kind of analysis should be done in the above case and why?

4. Below are Tables 12A to 12D, summarizing the results of data analyses of research conducted in a sales organization that operates in 50 different cities of the country, and employs a total sales force of about 500. The number of salesman sampled for the study was 150.

   You are to:

   a. Interpret the information contained in each of the tables in as much detail as possible.

   b. Summarize the results for the CEO of the company.

   c. Make recommendations based on your interpretation of the results.

Table 12A
Means, Standard Deviations, Minimum, and Maximum

Variable	Mean	Std. Deviation	Minimum	Maximum
Sales (in 1000s of $)	75.1	8.6	45.2	97.3
No. of salesmen	25	6	5	50
Population (in 100s)	5.1	0.8	2.78	7.12
Per capita income (in 1000s)	20.3	20.1	10.1	75.9
Advertisement (in 1000s of $)	10.3	5.2	6.1	15.7

Table 12B
Correlations Among the Variables

	Sales	Salesmen	Population	Income	Advertisement
Sales	1.0				
No. of salesmen	.76	1.0			
Population	.62	.06	1.0		
Income	.56	.21	.11	1.0	
Ad. expenditure	.68	.16	.36	.23	1.0

All figures above .15 are significant at $p = .05$.
All figures above .35 are significant at $p \leq .001$.

Table 12C
Results of Oneway ANOVA: Sales by Level of Education

Source of Variation	Sums of Squares	dF	Mean Squares	F	Significance of F
Between groups	50.7	4	12.7	3.6	.01
Within groups	501.8	145	3.5		
Total	552.5	150			

Table 12D
Results of Regression Analysis

Multiple R	.65924
R square	.43459
Adjusted R square	.35225
Standard error	.41173
df	(5,144)
F	5.278
Sig	.000

Variable	Beta	t	Sig t
Training of salesmen	.28	2.768	.0092
No. of salesmen	.34	3.55	.00001
Population	.09	0.97	.467
Per capita income	.12	1.200	.089
Advertisement	.47	4.54	.00001

APPENDIX

DATA ANALYSIS USING EXCEL

BY LIZABETH A. BARCLAY AND KENNETH M. YORK, SCHOOL OF BUSINESS ADMINISTRATION, OAKLAND UNIVERSITY, ROCHESTER, MICHIGAN

ANALYSIS OF THE ACCOUNTING CHAIR DATA SET USING EXCEL

Background Information

This was exploratory research done to obtain a feel for the role of Accounting Department chairs before launching a longitudinal study of Burnout in the same population.

The environment of higher education is undergoing change. Universities are seeking new sources of revenue, course delivery is changing, and professors and department chairs are increasingly being asked to engage in activities not traditional to the university job. Universities expect chairs to engage in fund-raising and friend-making at an increasingly intense level. At the same time, chairs are still expected to engage in traditional adminstrative duties as well as conduct research and teach classes.

The researchers designed a questionnaire tapping demographic information on gender, educational level, tenure status, budget, job title, and accreditation status of the chair's business school. The survey also asked for the number of full-time and part-time faculty in the department, and whether they had the terminal degree. The chair's perceptions of time availability, working relationships, and salary comparisons were also obtained. The questionnaire was mailed to 684 current Accounting Department Chairs. Accounting Chairs were selected because that position has entailed traditional chair duties as well as external relationship building to a greater extent than other chair positions.

Two hundred and eight questionnaires were returned (response rate = 31%). Data were entered into an Excel spreadsheet and analyzed using the Data Analysis procedures found under the Tools Menu.

This study tested the following hypotheses:

1. The more faculty with a Ph.D. degree in the department, the higher the chair's compensation vis-à-vis other business school chairs.

2. The proportion of AACSB International (Association to Advance Collegiate Schools of Business) Accredited schools responding to the survey will be higher than the proportion of AACSB International *Accounting* Accredited Schools responding.

3. Male chairs will have a higher number of research articles than female chairs.

4. There will be a relationship between years spent as chair and scores on the Working Relationships Scale.

5. Soft dollars, budget discretion, and the one-item Hours in the Day Scale will significantly predict chairs' number of publications.

ANALYSIS USING EXCEL

A discussion of the results of these analyses using Excel and their interpretation follows. Statistical analysis using a spreadsheet like Excel is different from using a statistical package like SPSS. With Excel, the data and the analysis are both visible to the researcher, whereas SPSS has a separate data file, and at any given time, both the data set and the output cannot be simultaneously displayed.

The data analyses included the following:

1. The establishment of Cronbach's alpha for the relevant scales.

2. The frequency distribution for several of the measures.

3. Measures of Central Tendency and Dispersion.

4. Pearson correlation matrix.

5. Hypothesis testing.

A sample output for each of the preceding, with brief interpretations, follows.

1. Reliability of Chair Time Scale: Cronbach's Alpha

The Alpha coefficient for the "Chair Time Scale" is shown in Output A1. Because the Excel Analysis ToolPak does not directly compute Cronbach's Alpha, the researchers calculated it using a formula; the Data Analysis Tool Correlation was used to calculate the item intercorrelations. The results indicate that Cronbach's Alpha for the 5-item scale is only .53 as shown in Output A1. Therefore, the reliability of this scale would be considered poor. The researchers should consider not using these items as a scale because of the poor reliability.

2. Frequency Distribution

Output A2 shows the frequency distribution obtained for the item "At the end of your current term as chair, which is most appealing to you?" This item assesses which type of career options a current chair might choose. In Excel, frequencies can be generated using the Data Analysis option. After the frequencies are obtained, the Chart Wizard can be used to generate a bar chart.

The results show that most of the current accounting chairs wish to "return to faculty status" (48.0%), followed by those who want to "remain as chair" (33.8%).

Output A1
Reliability

What is the reliability of the Chair Time Scale?

Chair Time Scale (5 Item Scale)

Item16	Item17	Item18	Item19	Item28
3	3	5	3	4
4	4	2	2	2
3	3	2	3	2
1	1	5	3	2
4	4	5	4	3
3	3	5	2	4
4	4	3	3	4
4	4	3	2	2
4	4	3	3	1
3	3	1	1	1
5	4	2	2	2
4	4	3	3	2
2	5	5	5	5
5	4	4	4	3
3	2	3	2	5
5	5	5	2	5
4	3	3	2	2
5	5	3	1	2
3	4	5	3	4
4	4	2	4	5

	Item16	Item17	Item18	Item19	Item28
Item16	1				
Item17	0.2948972	1			
Item18	0.09371693	0.07286597	1		
Item19	0.19300626	0.20885849	0.24420821	1	
Item28	0.23347981	0.19689588	0.13370632	0.14034298	1

$$\text{Cronbach's Alpha} = \frac{N*\text{mean\_inter-item\_correlation}}{[1+\text{mean inter-item\_correlation}*(N-1)]}$$

N = 5
mean_interitem_correlation = 0.18119781
Cronbach's Alpha = 0.53

Steps:
1. From the Tools Menu, select Data Analysis, Correlation.
2. In the Correlation dialog box:
   Enter the Input Range as A7:E213
   Check Grouped by Columns
   Check Labels in first row
   Enter the Output Range as G7
3. Calculate the mean inter-item correlation
   Calculate the average correlation in the matrix created in step 2
   Do not include the correlation of each item with itself, which are all 1
4. Create a formula to calculate Cronbach's Alpha using the mean inter-item correlation and the number of items in the scale.

Output A2
Frequency Distribution

What is the frequency distribution for Appeal?

Item4: At the end of your current term as Chair, which is most appealing to you?
Appeal

Appeal		Bin Range	Bin	Frequency	
2					
1	Return to Faculty		1 Return to Fac	98	48.04%
1	Remain as Chair		2 Remain as Ch	69	33.82%
2	Become chair other university		3 Become chair	2	0.98%
6	Seek higher admin position		4 Seek higher a	8	3.92%
5	Seek higher admin position elsewhere		5 Seek higher a	11	5.39%
2	Retire		6 Retire	13	6.37%
1	Other		7 Other	3	1.47%
2			More	0	
1					
3					
2	**Steps:**				
2	1. From the Tools Menu, select Data Analysis, Histogram.				
1	2. In the Histogram dialog box:				
2	Enter Input Range as A8:A211				
1	Enter Bin Range as E9:E15				
5	Uncheck Labels				
2	Enter Output Range as F8				
6	Click OK				
1	3. Copy cells D9 to D15 into cells F9 to F15.				
1	4. Select column F, then from the Format menu select Autofit selection.				
1	5. On the menu bar, select Chart Wizard.				
1	6. Write formulas to calculate frequency percent:				
1	In cell H9 enter =g9/sum($G$9:$G$15)				
2	Copy the formula in cell H9 to cells H10 to H15				
2	Select cells H9 to H15, then from the Format menu, Cells, Percentage, 2 decimal places				
1	7. For Chart Type, select Column, click Next.				
6	8. For Source Data, enter Data Range as F9:G15, check Series in Columns.				
2	9. For Chart Options, under Titles tab:				
1	Enter Chart Title as Most Appealing After Current Term				
1	Enter Value (Y) axis as Frequency				
2	10. For Chart Options, under Legend tab, uncheck Show legend.				
6	11. For Chart Options, under Data labels tab check Show value, click Next.				
1	12. For Chart Location, select As object in worksheet, click Finish.				
1	13. Resize chart to make all variable labels readable.				

Only 3.9% of chairs aspire to "a higher administrative position" at his/her current school, while 5.4% would like such a position at a different school.

3. Measures of Central Tendency and Dispersion

The results in Output A3 were obtained using the Data Analysis Tool in Excel which calculates such statistics as the mean, standard deviation, skewness, and kurtosis. The "Descriptive Statistics" option under the Data Analysis menu is selected to obtain these measures. Output A3 shows these descriptive statistics for the amount of time (hours per week) spent by the chairs on administrative tasks, teaching, research, and external activities.

The results indicate that the chairs spend most of their time each week on administrative activities, but the variance is large. The mean number of hours spent on teaching, research, and external contact activities are 14.0, 5.6, and 6.8 respectively, with a variance of 51.2, 24.3, and 23.3 hours.

Output A3
Measures of Central Tendency and Dispersion

What is the central tendency and dispersion of hours spent on university-related activities?

Hours Admin	Hours Teaching	Hours Research	Hours External
30	20		1
20	15	5	10
15	25	5	5
20	10	10	
30	20	3	3
15	15	10	20
20	20	15	5
15	15	5	
25	6		10
20	8	8	
3	12	1	4
30	5		5
20	30		3
30	5	5	5
30	15	3	20
30	10	2	
40	10	1	2
20	5	10	15
2	10		1
10	20	10	2
25	15	15	5
20	18	0	25
4	30	0	6
30	6	3	5
30	10		5
20	10	8	5
20	12	4	4
22	10	0	8
40	15	0	
30	12	8	5
30	4		
25	10	2	3

Statistic	Admin	Teaching	Research	External
Mean	21.78536585	13.97087379	5.57431694	6.764171123
Standard Error	0.715453459	0.498394896	0.36436018	0.35318566
Median	20	12	5	5
Mode	20	10	5	5
Standard Deviation	10.2437346	7.153312466	4.92897315	4.829685282
Sample Variance	104.9340985	51.16987923	24.29477632	23.3258993
Kurtosis	0.251951604	0.154998111	1.48395353	3.548399112
Skewness	0.33122651	0.738147106	1.294646362	1.61631887
Range	58	35	20	29
Minimum	2	0	0	1
Maximum	60	35	20	30
Sum	4466	2878	1020.1	1264.9
Count	205	206	183	187

Steps:
1. From the Tools Menu, select Data Analysis, Descriptive Statistics, click OK.
2. In the Descriptive Statistics dialog box:
   Enter the Input Range as A7:D213
   Check Grouped by columns
   Check Labels in first row
   Enter Output Range as F7
   Check Summary Statistics
   Click OK

3. Select columns F to M, then from the Format menu, select Column, Autofit selection, to make the output easier to read.

Not all of the respondents answered each item as evidenced by the reported sample sizes (labeled Count). This *may* mean that some chairs do not engage in any research or external activities.

4. Pearson Correlation

Output A4 shows the intercorrelations among four variables. The Pearson Correlation matrix shown in Output A4 was obtained through the Data Analysis Tool Correlation, in the Tools Menu.

Excel does not give the number of cases for each correlation, nor does it give the probability value for each correlation. To determine statistical significance you must first determine the critical value in the Pearson Correlation Table for a correlation at 121 degrees of freedom (df = number of pairs −2) at the .05 level for a two-tailed test. In this case, the critical value is .178. If the obtained correlation is equal to or greater than the critical value, it is significant. For example, the correlation between the number of faculty with Ph.D.'s and the number of faculty without Ph.D.'s is .03, which is less than the critical value of .178; therefore, the correlation is not statistically significant.

5. Hypothesis Testing

Five hypotheses were generated in this research. These call for the use of a Pearson Correlation (for Hypothesis 1), a Chi-Square (for Hypothesis 2), a *t*-Test (for Hypothesis 3), an ANOVA (for Hypothesis 4), and multiple regression

---

Output A4
Pearson Correlation

What is the correlation between number of Phd, None-Phd, and Part-Time Faculty and chair compensation?

Faculty Phd	Faculty No Phd	Faculty Part-time	Salary Compare
3	3	1	2
4	2	0	2
3	1	1	2
6	2	1	2
7	16	1	2
11	1	2	1
1	5	2	2
11	1	3	2
2	12	14	1
3	2	1	3
3	5	2	2
15	4	9	1
13	2	12	1
6	5	8	2
12	3	1	2
10	5	2	2
14	2	5	2
6	2	2	2

	Phd	No Phd	Part-time	Compare
Phd	1			
No Phd	0.03170196	1		
Part-time	0.386862738	0.106430919	1	
Compare	-0.302635056	0.071494112	-0.049511688	1

df=N-2   121

Steps:
1. From the Tools Menu, select Data Analysis, Correlation, then click OK.
2. In the Correlation dialog box:
      Enter the Input Range as A7:D130
      Click Grouped by columns
      Check Labels in first row
      Enter the Output Range as F7
      Click OK
3. Write a formula to calculate the degrees of freedom for the correlations:
      In cell F13 enter =count(A8:A130)-2

(for Hypothesis 5). The results of these tests and their interpretation are discussed below.

Hypothesis 1: Pearson Correlation

Hypothesis 1 can be stated in the null and alternate form as follows:

$H1_O$: There will be no relationship between the number of Ph.D. faculty in a department and chair compensation relative to other business school chairs.

$H1_A$: There will be a relationship between the number of Ph.D. faculty in a department and the chair compensation relative to other business school chairs.

From the results in Output A4, we can see that the greater the number of Ph.D. faculty, the higher the chair's compensation vis-à-vis other business school chairs. In this study, the respondents indicated that his/her salary was higher than other chairs by picking "1"; therefore, the correlation is a negative –.30. At 121 degrees of freedom and a probability level of .05, the correlation must be .178 or greater to be statistically significant; therefore the null hypothesis is rejected. Thus, hypothesis 1 is substantiated.

Hypothesis 2: Use of Chi-Square Test

Hypothesis 2 can be stated in the null and alternative as:

$H2_O$: The percentage of AACSB International accredited schools responding to the survey will be no different than the percentage of AACSB International Accounting Accredited schools responding.

$H2_A$: The percentage of AACSB International accredited schools responding to the survey will be different than the percentage of AACSB International Accounting Accredited schools responding.

The results shown in Output A5 indicate that of the 205 schools responding, 109 hold AACSB accreditation, while 48 hold the AACSB Accounting Accreditation. The chi-square value of 38.4 with 1 degree of freedom is significant, with $p < .05$. Therefore, Hypothesis 2 is substantiated.

Hypothesis 3: Use of *t*-Test

Hypothesis 3 can be stated in the null and alternative as follows:

$H3_O$: There will be no difference between men and women in the number of research articles reported.

$H3_A$: There will be a difference between male and female chairs in the number of research articles reported.

The results of this *t*-test are shown in Output A6. The *t*-test used is for two samples assuming unequal variance. The *t* value of –0.1517 is not significant, so

Output A5
Chi Square

Is the proportion of AACSB accredited schools different from the proportion of AACSB Accounting Accredited schools?

					AACSB	ACC		Total	
Accredited		Accredited		Yes	109	48		157	
AACSB	Yes	ACC	Yes	No	96	157		253	
	2		2						
	2		2	Total	205	205		410	
	1	1	1	1	%Yes	53.17%	23.41%		
	2		2						
	1	1	1	1			64113760250		
	2		2				1669275025		
	1	1	2		Chi Square		38.40814682		
	2		2		df		1		
	2		2		p-value (2-tail)		5.73923E-10		

$$\text{Chi Square} = \frac{N(AD - BC)^2}{(A+B)(C+D)(A+C)(B+D)}$$

			A	B
			C	D

Steps:
1. Write a formula to identify Yes responses on Accredited AACSB:
    In cell B8 enter formula =if(A8=1,1,"")
    Copy formula in cell B8 to cells B9 to B212
2. Write a formula to identify Yes responses on Accredited ACC:
    In cell D8 enter formula =if(C8=1,1,"")
    Copy formula in cell D8 to cells D9 to D212
3. Write formulas to count the number of responses:
    In cell A214 enter formula =count(A8:A212)
    In cell B214 enter formula =count(B8:B212)
    In cell B215 enter formula =A214-B214
    In cell C214 enter formula =count(C8:C212)
    In cell D214 enter formula =count(D8:D212)
    In cell D215 enter formula =C214-D214
4. Create a 2X2 table to store the results of step 3:
    In cell G7 enter formula +B214
    In cell G8 enter formula +B215
    In cell H7 enter formula +D214
    In cell H7 enter formula +D215
5. Write formulas to calculate the total number of observations for each variable:
    In cell G10 enter formula =sum(G7:G8)
    In cell H10 enter formula =sum(H7:H8)
    In cell J7 enter formula =sum(G7:H7)
    In cell J8 enter formula =sum(G8:H8)
    In cell J10 enter formula =sum(G7:H8)
6. Write formulas to calculate the percentage of Yes for each variable:
    In cell G11 enter formula =G7/G10
    In cell H11 enter formula =H7/H10
7. Write a formula to calculate the chi square
    In cell H13 enter formula =J10*(G7*H8-H7*G8)^2
    In cell H14 enter formula =(G7+H7)*(G8+H8)*(G7+G8)*(H7+H8)
    In cell H15 enter formula =H13/H14
8. Write a formula to calculate the degrees of freedom for the chi square:
    In cell H16 enter formula =(COUNT(G7:H7)-1)*(COUNT(G7:G8)-1)
9. Write a formula to calculate the probability value of the chi square with 1 degree of freedom:
    In cell H17 enter formula =CHIDIST(H15,1)

the null hypothesis is accepted. Thus, this hypothesis is *not* substantiated. Although women have more publications on average (1.125 versus 1.049) there is no *significant* difference between males and females in the number of research articles.

Hypothesis 4: Use of ANOVA

The fourth hypothesis can be stated in the null and alternate forms as follows:

Output A6
t-Test

Is there a difference in scholarly activity by gender?

	Publications	
Gender	Research	
1	0	
1	0	
1	3	
1	0	
1	0	
1	1	
1	4	
1	0	
1	0	
1	2	
1	0	
1	0	
1	2	
1	1	
1	0	
1	0	
1	0	
1	2	
1	0	
1	0	
1	4	
1	0	
1	0	
1	2	
1	2	
1	11	

t-Test: Two-Sample Assuming Unequal Variances

	Variable 1	Variable 2
Mean	1.048543689	1.125
Variance	4.027032172	5.157608696
Observations	103	24
Hypothesized Mean Difference	0	
df	32	
t Stat	-0.151704475	
P(T<=t) one-tail	0.440186215	
t Critical one-tail	1.693888407	
P(T<=t) two-tail	0.88037243	
t Critical two-tail	2.036931619	

Steps:
1. Sort the data by gender:
   Select cells A7 to B134
   From the Data menu, select Sort, check Header row, select sort by Gender, check ascending
   Click OK
2. From the Tools menu, select Data Analysis, t-Test: Two Sample Assuming Unequal Variances, click OK
   From the t-Test menu enter Input Variable 1 Range as B8:B110
   Enter Input Variable 2 Range as B111:B134
   Uncheck Labels
   Enter Alpha as 0.05
   Enter Output Range as D7
3. Reformat output to make it easier to read:
   Select columns E to G, and from the Format menu, select Column, Autofit selection

H4$_O$: Scores on the Working Relationships scale will be the same irrespective of the number of years a person has served as chair.

H4$_A$: Working relationships scale scores will vary depending on the number of years an individual has served as chair.

Because there are more than two groups (service as chair was categorized as 1–2 years, 3–6 years, and 7 or more years) and the working relationship scale is interval in nature, an ANOVA is the appropriate test.

The Excel results can be seen in Output A7. The F-Ratio of 5.028, with 2 and 200 degrees of freedom is statistically significant at $p = .007$. That is, there are significant differences in perceived working relationships based on length of time in office. This hypothesis has been substantiated.

Hypothesis 5: Use of Multiple Regression Analysis

The last hypothesis can be stated in the null and alternate forms as:

H5$_O$: The three independent variables of soft money, budget discretion, and hours in the day will not significantly predict the number of research publications by the chair.

H5$_A$: The three independent variables will significantly predict the number of research publications by the chair.

Output A7
ANOVA

Is there an effect of years spent as chair on working relationships?

Years as Chair

1 to 2	3 to 6	7 or more
23	27	19
21	20	24
26	20	27
23	28	23
26	23	28
23	17	20
24	20	28
18	28	25
20	13	28
21	22	21
23	17	25
26	19	23
20	25	23
22	25	24
20	21	24
22	25	28
22	28	26
20	22	26
16	14	21
23	27	23
28	21	21
29	24	22
16	18	24
	23	13
	20	24
	22	21

Anova: Single Factor

SUMMARY

Groups	Count	Sum	Average	Variance
1 to 2	58	1285	22.15517241	10.23865699
3 to 6	92	2043	22.20652174	12.62720975
7 or more	53	1267	23.90566038	10.97169811

ANOVA

Source of Variation	SS	df	MS	F	P-value	F crit
Between Groups	115.8167934	2	57.90839671	5.02849945	0.00740089	3.041051855
Within Groups	2303.207837	200	11.51603919			
Total	2419.024631	202				

Steps:

1. From the Tools menu, select Data Analysis. ANOVA: Single Factor
2. In the ANOVA: Single Factor dialog box:
   Enter Input range as A7:C99
   Check grouped by columns
   Check Labels in first row
   Set Alpha at 0.05
   Enter Output range as E7
   Click OK
3. Make the ANOVA output easier to read:
   Select columns E to K
   From the Format menu, select Columns, Width, and enter 15

To test this hypothesis, multiple regression analysis was done. The results of regressing the three independent variables against number of research publications can be seen in Output A8. The Multiple R (.3557) is the multiple correlation among the three independent variables and the dependent variable, and the R Square (.1265) is the variance in the dependent variable accounted by the three independent variables. The F-Ratio of 4.59 at 3 and 95 degrees of freedom is statistically significant at the .005 level.

In effect, this hypothesis is substantiated with 12.7 percent of the variance in the number of research publications explained by the three independent variables. However, it should be noted that the variance explained is small, and other variables should be explored in this context.

To determine which variables in the regression equation are significant predictors of the number of research publications by the chair, Excel provides the unstandardized regression coefficients, and a t-statistic and associated probability value for these regression coefficients. For the regression analysis shown in Output A8, both discretionary budget money and soft money are significant predictors of number of research publications by the chair, but the hours-in-the-day scale is not. Excel does not provide standardized regression coefficients (Beta weights).

Overall Interpretation

This was an exploratory study. The authors hoped to learn something about the chair job before starting a longitudinal study on burnout in the chair position. They have learned that one of their scales is not a reliable scale and should be substituted with a better scale. They have learned that chairs with more Ph.D. faculty think they are more highly paid than other business school chairs. Some of the anticipated gender differences in research publications were not substantiated by the results. The time spent as chair of the department also does not seem to be related to working relationships within the department and the school. The variables examined to predict the number of research publications explained only a small part of the variance. Other variables have to be examined in this connection. Some of the measures will have to be refined before launching the next phase of the research effort.

We would like to thank Gadis Dillon and Lizabeth A. Barclay for agreeing to let us use their database to illustrate statistical analysis using Excel. Aspects of this study were presented at the 1997 Meeting of the Midwestern Psychological Association.

Dillon, G. J. & Barclay, L. A. (1997). *Burnout and turnover in academic chairs: The changing educational and professional environment.* Paper presented at the Meeting of the Midwestern Psychological Association.

Output A8
Multiple Regression

Does the amount of discretionary funds and soft dollars in the budget and reported time in the day predict the number of publications by chairs?

Publications Research	Budget Discretionary	Budget Soft $	Hours in Day Scale
0	3	3	5
0	3	2	4
3	2	1	4
0	1	3	5
4	4	4	4
4	2	4	5
2	5	1	5
10	1	3	3
0	3	3	5
0	3	3	4
1	4	4	4
1	5	5	5
1	2	4	1
0	4	2	4
2	1	1	3
2	1	3	5
0	1	1	3
1	1	1	4
4	4	1	4
4	3	1	5
2	3	4	4
2	5	2	5
0	1	5	3
4	2	2	5
0	5	1	5
3	1	1	2
0	4	3	3

SUMMARY OUTPUT

Regression Statistics	
Multiple R	0.35574565
R Square	0.126554967
Adjusted R Square	0.098972492
Standard Error	2.227442955
Observations	99

ANOVA

	df	SS	MS	F	Significance F
Regression	3	68.29366229	22.7645541	4.588238509	0.001481077
Residual	95	471.3427014	4.961502119		
Total	98	539.6963696			

	Coefficients	Standard Error	t Stat	P-value	Lower 95%	Upper 95%	Lower 95.0%	Upper 95.0%
Intercept	1.34327428	1.19364365	1.125156199	0.265273224	-1.026406277	3.712954857	-1.026406277	3.712954857
Discretionary	-0.488309725	0.192187438	-2.540799392	0.012680353	-0.869849756	-0.106769694	-0.869849756	-0.106769694
Soft $	0.651560803	0.181497895	3.589068313	0.000525667	0.291242182	1.011879423	0.291242182	1.011879423
Day Scale	-0.019754994	0.272594701	-0.072470204	0.942380076	-0.56092351	0.521413522	-0.56092351	0.521413522

Steps:
1. From the Tools menu, select Data Analysis, Regression
2. In the Regression dialog box:
   Enter Input Y range as A7:A106
   Enter Input X range as B7:D106
   Check Labels
   Enter Output range as F7
   Click OK
3. Make the output easier to read:
   Select columns F to N
   From the Format menu, select Column, Width, and enter 15

CHAPTER

13

THE RESEARCH REPORT

TOPICS DISCUSSED

THE RESEARCH PROPOSAL

THE WRITTEN REPORT

- Purpose
- Different Types of Reports
- Audience
- Characteristics of a Good Report

CONTENTS OF THE RESEARCH REPORT

- Title of the Report
- Table of Contents
- Copy of Authorization Letter
- Executive Summary or Synopsis
- The Introductory Section
- Method Section
- Results Section
- Discussion Section
- Recommendations and Implementation
- Summary
- Acknowledgments
- References
- Appendix

ORAL PRESENTATION

- Content
- Visual Aids
- Presentation
- Handling Questions

CHAPTER OBJECTIVES

After completing this chapter, you should:

1. Be able to draw up a research proposal.

2. Know what the contents of a research report are.

3. Tailor the report format to meet the needs of different types of research (basic and applied), different research goals that need reports of varying lengths, and different audiences.

4. Be able to write a good:

    Executive summary or synopsis

    Introductory section

    Methods section

    Data analysis section

    Interpretation of the results, using tables and pictorial representations, wherever appropriate.

5. Give your recommendations and suggestions for implementation, as necessary.

6. Write the summary and acknowledgment.

7. Provide the appropriate references.

8. Include appropriate materials in the appendix.

9. Critique research reports and published studies.

10. Know the components of and make a good oral presentation.

THE RESEARCH PROPOSAL

Before any research study is undertaken, there should be an agreement between the person who authorizes the study and the researcher as to the problem to be investigated, the methodology to be used, the duration of the study, and its cost. This ensures that there are no misunderstandings or frustrations later for both parties. This is usually accomplished through the **research proposal,** which the researcher submits and gets approved by the sponsor, who issues a letter of authorization to proceed with the study.

The research proposal drawn up by the investigator is the result of a planned, organized, and careful effort, and basically contains the following:

1. The broad goals of the study.

2. The specific problem to be investigated.

3. Details of the procedures to be followed.

4. The research design offering details on:
    a. The sampling design
    b. Data collection methods
    c. Data analysis.

5. Time frame of the study, including information on when the written report will be handed over to the sponsors.

6. The budget, detailing the costs with reference to specific items of expenditure.

Such a proposal containing the above features is presented to the manager, who might seek clarification on some points, want the proposal to be modified in certain respects, or accept it in toto. A model of a simple research proposal to study the frequent turnover of newly recruited employees is presented below.

Model 13.1   RESEARCH PROPOSAL TO STUDY RETENTION OF NEW EMPLOYEES

Purpose of the Study

To find a solution to the recurring problem of 40% employee turnover within the first 3 years of their recruitment, and more specifically to:

a. Draw up a profile of the employees who quit;

b. Assess if there are any special needs of the new recruits that require to be met; and

c. Determine the reasons for employees leaving the organization in the first 3 years.

The Research Design (i.e., Details of the Study)

Sample: Sixty percent of the 80 individuals who have joined the company within the last 3 years will constitute the sample. These 48 individuals will be chosen through a simple random sampling design, that is, in a manner where each of the 80 individuals will have an equal chance of being selected for the study. This will ensure the accuracy and precision of the results.

Survey Instruments. First, we will administer a questionnaire to the sample of 48 employees, and thereafter interview each of them for about 10 minutes. The questionnaire can be found in Appendix A to this proposal.

Data Collection. The questionnaire will be given to the employees to be completed by them in their homes and returned anonymously to the box set up for the purpose within the specified date. They will all be reminded 2 days before the due date to return their questionnaire, if not already done.

The 10-minute individual interviews will be conducted during office hours in the Conference Hall of the organization at a prearranged time convenient to the interviewees.

Data Analysis. Once the data are collected, the information will be coded and appropriate data analytic techniques used to determine the likely reasons for some employees leaving the organization within 3 years of their joining.

Report. A written report will be submitted within 2 months of the commencement of the study, followed by an oral presentation.

Time Frame. The schedule in Appendix B shows the sequence of activities and the time line for each.

Budget. The budget for this project is in Appendix C.

Once the proposal is accepted, the researcher conducts the research, going through the appropriate steps discussed in the research design process. Soon after the data are analyzed and conclusions drawn from the findings, the investigator is ready to present the results of the research study and make suitable recommendations. This usually takes the form of a written report and is quite often followed up by an oral presentation.

THE REPORT

It is important that the results of the study and the recommendations to solve the problem are effectively communicated to the sponsor, so that the suggestions made are accepted and implemented. Otherwise, all the effort hitherto expended on the investigation would be in vain. Writing the report concisely, convincingly, and with clarity is perhaps as important, if not more, than conducting a perfect research study. Hence, a well-thought-out written report and oral presentation are critical.

The contents and organization of both modes of communication—the written report and the oral presentation—depend on the purpose of the research study, and the audience to which it is targeted. The relevant aspects of the written report and oral presentation are discussed in this chapter.

THE WRITTEN REPORT

The written report enables the manager to weigh the facts and arguments presented therein, and implement the acceptable recommendations, with a view to closing the gap between the existing state of affairs and the desired state. To achieve its goal, the written report has to focus on the issues discussed below.

The Written Report and Its Purpose

Reports could aim at different purposes and hence the form of the written report would vary according to the situation. It is important to identify the **purpose** of the report, so that it can be tailored accordingly. If the purpose is simply to offer *details on some specific areas of interest* requested by a manager, the report can be very narrowly focused and provide the desired information to the manager in a brief format, as in Example 13.1. If, on the other hand, the report is intended to *"sell an idea"* to management, then it has to be more detailed and convincing as to how the proposed idea is an improvement and should be adopted. Here the emphasis would be directed on presenting all the relevant information backed by the necessary data, to persuade the reader to "buy into the idea." An example of the purpose of such a report and its contents can be seen in Example 13.2. A different form of report will be prescribed in some cases, where a manager asks for *several alternative solutions or recommendations* to rectify a problem in a given situation. Here the researcher provides the requested information and the manager chooses from among the alternatives and makes the final decision. In this case, a more detailed report surveying past studies, the methodology used for the present study, different perspectives generated from interviews and current data analyses, and alternative solutions based on the conclusions drawn therefrom will have to be provided. How each alternative helps to improve the problem situation would also have to be discussed. The advantage and disadvantages of each of the proposed solutions, together with a cost-benefit analysis in terms of dollars and/or other resources, will also have to be presented to help the manager make the decision. A situation as in Example 13.3 would warrant this kind of a report. Such a report can also be found in Report 3 of the Appendix to this chapter.

Yet another type of report might require the researcher to *identify the problem and provide the final solution* as well. That is, the researcher might be called in to study a situation, determine the nature of the problem, and offer a report of the findings and recommendations. Such a report has to be very comprehensive, following the format of a full-fledged study, as detailed later in this chapter. A fifth kind of research report is the very scholarly publication presenting the *findings of a basic study* that one usually finds published in academic journals.

Example 13.1   A SIMPLE DESCRIPTIVE REPORT

If a study is undertaken to *understand in detail* certain factors of interest in a given situation (variations in production levels, composition of employees, and the like), then a report describing the phenomena of interest, in the manner desired, is all that is called for. For instance, let us say a human resources manager wants to know how many employees have been recruited during the past 18 months in the organization, their gender composition, educational level, and the average proportion of days that these individuals had absented themselves since recruitment. A simple report giving the desired information would suffice.

In this report, a statement of the **purpose** of the study will be first given (e.g., it was desired that a profile of the employees recruited during the past 18 months in the company, and an idea of their rate of absenteeism be provided. This report offers those details). The **methods** or **procedures** adopted to collect the data would then be given (e.g., the payroll of the company and the personal files of the employees were examined). Finally, a narration of the actual **results,** reinforced by visual tabular and graphical forms of representation of the data, will be provided. Frequency distributions, cross-tabulations, and other data will be presented in a tabular form, and pictorial illustrations will include bar charts (for gender), pie charts (to indicate the proportions of individuals at various educational levels), and so on. This section will summarize the data and may look like the following.

A total of 27 employees were recruited during the past 18 months, of whom 45% are women and 55% are men. Twenty percent have a masters degree, 68% a bachelor's degree, and 12% a high school diploma. The average proportion of days that these employees remained absent during the past 18 months is 6.

These details provide the information required by the manager. It may, however, be a good idea to provide a further gender-wise breakdown of the mean proportion of days of absence of the employees in an appendix, even though this information might not have been specifically requested. If considered relevant, a similar breakdown can also be furnished for people at different job levels.

A short simple report of the type discussed above is provided in Report 1 in the Appendix to this chapter.

Example 13.2   DETAILS OF A REPORT TO "SELL" AN IDEA

The objective of a report may be to *sell an idea to top management.* For example, the Information Systems (IS) manager might want to suggest to the top executives that an **executive information system (EIS)** would greatly enhance the effectiveness of top executives by virtue of the speed and timeliness of the electronic information delivery system. With up-to-the minute information available at the fingertips of executives—something that the current paper reporting system lacks—informed decisions could be made with much confidence. When the executives realize that they can perform their information-intensive activities with ease and speed, and at the same time enhance the quality of their decisions, they will readily buy into the idea. But then the research report for this purpose will have a different thrust and focus in greater detail on the following:

1. Explanation in clear and simple terms of what an EIS is, and how it will be a powerful executive tool for effective decision making.
2. How it would save time (e.g., by giving immediate access to the specific information the executive needs, without the frustrating experience of shuffling papers and ending up with not finding what is needed).
3. How it would have an advantage over and be better than the current system (e.g., since all information is updated two times daily, the EIS will provide executives all the current data needed—marvelously enhancing the quality of the decisions made).
4. How it would boost savings in resources in the long run (backed by a detailed cost-benefit analysis). For instance, compare the costs of training executives in using the system and updating information on a daily basis, versus the benefits of savings accrued through more informed and timely decisions, as in the case of the establishment of a viable "just-in-time" inventory system, with resultant substantial savings to the organization.
5. Illustration of examples from past company history (within the past 2 months, if possible) of how an EIS system would have helped the executives to make more informed decisions in those instances, and how it could have saved the system money/resources.
6. A final forceful and convincing recommendation to adopt EIS as a way of organizational decision making.

A specimen of the type of report discussed above relating to recommending sabbaticals for managers is provided in Report 2 in the Appendix to this chapter.

Example 13.3 A SITUATION WHERE A COMPREHENSIVE REPORT, OFFERING ALTERNATIVE SOLUTIONS, IS NEEDED

The president of a tire company wants several recommendations to be made on planning for the future growth of the company, taking into consideration the manufacturing, marketing, accounting, and financial perspectives. In this case, only a broad objective is stated: corporate growth. There may currently be several impediments that retard growth. One has to carefully examine the situation to determine the obstacles to expansion and how these may be overcome through strategic planning from production, marketing, management, financial, and accounting perspectives. Identification of the problems or impediments in the situation would call for intensive interviews, literature review, industry analysis, formulation of a theoretical perspective, generation of several hypotheses to come up with different alternative solutions, data gathering, data analyses, and then exploration of alternative ways of attaining corporate growth through different strategies. To enable the president to evaluate the alternatives proposed, the pros and cons of implementing each of the alternative solutions, and a statement of the costs and benefits attached to each, would follow.

This report will be more elaborate than the previous two, detailing each of the steps in the study, emphasizing the results of data analysis, and furnishing a strong basis for the various recommendations. The alternatives generated and the pros and cons of each in a report such as this, are likely to follow the format of Report 3 in the Appendix. Report 4 in the Appendix relates to basic research of an issue that was examined by a researcher.

As we can see, the contents and format of a report will depend on the purpose of the study and the needs of the sponsors to whom it is submitted.

The Written Report and Its Audience

The organization of a report, its length, focus on details, data presentation, and illustrations will in part, be a function of the audience for whom it is intended. The letter of transmittal of the report would clearly indicate to whom the report is being sent. An Executive Summary placed at the beginning would offer busy executives just the right amount of vital details—in less than three pages. This will help the busy managers to quickly grasp the essentials of the study and its findings, and turn to the pages that offer more detailed information on aspects that are of special interest to them.

Some managers are distracted by data presented in the form of tables and feel more comfortable with graphs and charts, while others want to see "facts and figures" (Williams, 1990). Both tables and figures are visual forms of representation and need to be presented in reports. Which of these are to be prominently highlighted in the report and which relegated to an appendix is a function of the awareness of the idiosyncracies of the ultimate user of the report. If a report were to be handled by different executives, with different orientations, it should be packaged such that they know where to find the information that meets their preferred mode of information processing. For example, in addition to mentioning about market share in the text, it can be illustrated through a pie chart, and the raw data also presented in a tabular form.

The length, organization, and presentation modes of the report will, among other things, depend at least in part on the target audience. Some businesses might also prescribe their own format for report writing. In all cases, a good report is a function of the knowledge of whom it is intended for and its exact purpose. As we have seen, some reports may have to be long and detailed, and others brief and specific.

Sometimes, the findings of a study could be unpalatable to the executive (e.g., that the organizational policies are outdated and the system is very bureaucratic), or could reflect poorly on management, tending to make them react defensively (e.g., the system has an ineffective top-down approach). In such cases, tact should be exercised in presenting the conclusions without compromising on the actual findings. That is, while there is no need to suppress the unpalatable findings, they can be presented in a nonjudgmental, non–fault-finding or finger-pointing manner, using objective data and facts that forcefully lead to, and convince the managers of the correctness of the conclusions drawn. If this is not done, the report will be read defensively, the recommendations will not be accepted, and the problem will remain unsolved.

Tact and diplomacy combined with honesty and objectivity are essential in report writing and presentation. While this is true for both internal and external research teams, the task of the internal team of writing the research report in such cases becomes even more difficult. Being a part of the very system on which such findings are reported, the internal team might be perceived as challenging the authority of the hierarchy. Although, as a result, chances exist of being intimidated by power and authority, the internal research team, while being polite, should package its findings in a professional, unbiased, and tactful manner, thereby preserving the integrity of the findings and the process.

As an example of such a presentation, if the system has outmoded policies (or is highly bureaucratic), the report can be formatted thus. After presenting the data to support the facts, it might say that these policies (and the system) were perhaps appropriate at the time they were formulated, but the current goals of the present management, coupled with the passage of time, call for a change. It can also highlight the fact that the present system is receptive to changes and changing the policies (or the structure of the organization) will not, therefore, pose difficult problems. A similar appropriate strategy can be followed to change the top-down approach to a bottom-up management style.

Characteristics of a Well-Written Report

Despite the fact that report writing is a function of the purpose of the study and the type of audience to which it is presented, and accordingly has to be tailored to meet both, certain basic features are integral to all written reports. Clarity, conciseness, coherence, the right emphasis on important aspects, meaningful organization of paragraphs, smooth transition from one topic to the next, apt choice of words, and specificity are all important features of a good report. The report should, to the extent possible, be free of technical or statistical jargon unless it happens to be of a technical or statistical nature. Care should also be taken to eliminate grammatical and spelling errors.

Any assumptions made by the researcher should be clearly stated in the report, and facts, rather than opinions, provided. The report should be organized in a manner that enhances the meaningful and smooth flow of materials, as the reader progresses through it. The importance of the appearance of the report and its readability cannot be overemphasized.

Appropriate headings and subheadings help organize the report in a logical manner and allow the reader to follow the transitions easily. A double-spaced, typed report with wide margins on all sides enables the reader to make notes/comments while perusing the contents.

Contents of the Research Report

It is obvious that the research report should bear *a title* that indicates in a succinct manner what the study is about. It should have at the beginning a *table of contents,* the *research proposal,* a copy of the *authorization* to conduct the study, and an *executive summary* (in the case of applied research) or a *synopsis* (in the case of basic research).

All reports should have an introductory section detailing the purpose of the study, giving some background of what it relates to, and stating the problem studied, setting the stage for what the reader could expect in the rest of the report. The body of the report would contain details regarding the framework of the study, hypotheses, if any, sampling design, data collection methods, analysis of data, and the results obtained. The final part of the report would present the findings and draw conclusions. If recommendations have been called for, they would be included, with a cost–benefit analysis provided with respect to each. Such information would clarify the net advantages of implementing each of the recommendations. The details provided in the report should be such as to convince the reader of the thoroughness of the study, and induce confidence in accepting the results and the recommendations made. Every professional report would also point out the limitations of the study (for example, in sampling, data collection, and the like).

Good descriptions and lucid explanations, smooth and easy flow of materials, recommendations that flow logically from the results of data analysis, and an explicit statement of any limitations to the study, provide scientific authenticity to the report. The transmittal letter is best written with a personal touch, wherever appropriate.

In sum, a rigorous, well-conducted study loses all its value when it is not properly presented in writing. To be considered useful, a report should provide a good rationale for the study, clearly present the problem studied, present the results of data analyses fully and adequately, and interpret the data in a manner that is easily understood by the reader. The conclusion drawn from the findings should indicate a clear solution to the problem.

The report can be organized in parts, sections, or chapters and should be tailored to meet the needs of the situation. Good, crisp, and clear writing, figures, charts, and tables that succinctly support or highlight the salient issues, and attractive packaging are some of the essential characteristics of a good report. The writing style should be simple, interesting, precise, and comprehensible. Unbiased and objective presentation of the findings and specific reference to the limitations of the study lend credibility to the research work. Tact and diplomacy are required in presenting unpalatable findings without distortion, and in an objective, nonthreatening, and useful manner that does not offend the sponsor. The format and style of reporting should be tailored to the audience and meet the purpose of the study.

The report would end with a summary and acknowledgment of the help received from various individuals and sources. A list of references cited in the report would then follow. Appendices, if any, would be attached to the report.

A report on the factors influencing the upward mobility of women in accounting firms can be found in Report 4 of the Appendix to this chapter. We will now discuss the different parts of the report.

INTEGRAL PARTS OF THE REPORT

The Title Page

The title of the report should succinctly indicate what the study is all about. Examples of some good report titles are:

1. A Study of Customer Satisfaction with the Pizza Hut at Sunshine City, Illinois
2. Factors Influencing the Burnout of Nurses in Monroe Hospital
3. Antecedents and Consequences of White-Collar Employees' Resistance to Mechanization in Service Industries
4. Factors Affecting the Upward Mobility of Women in Accounting Firms
5. A Study of Portfolio Balancing and Risk Management in Investment Firms

The first two projects will relate to applied research, whereas the last three will be in the realm of basic research.

In addition to the title of the project, the title page will indicate the name of the sponsor of the study, the names of the researchers and their affiliations, and the date of the final report.

Table of Contents

The table of contents with page references usually lists the important headings and subheadings in the report. A separate list of tables and figures should also be listed in the table of contents.

The Research Proposal and the Authorization Letter

A copy of the letter of authorization from the sponsor of the study approving the investigation and detailing its scope will be attached at the beginning of the report along with the research proposal. The authorization makes clear to the reader that the goals of the study have had the full blessings of the organization.

The Executive Summary or Synopsis

The executive summary (or synopsis) is a brief account of the research study that provides an overview, and highlights the following important information related to it: the problem statement, sampling design, data collection methods used, results of data analysis, findings, and recommendations, with suggestions for their implementation. The executive summary (or synopsis) will be brief—usually three pages or less in length.

An example of a synopsis of the study of customer satisfaction with the Pizza Hut in Sunshine City follows.

Example 13.4　SYNOPSIS OF PIZZA HUT STUDY

Introduction and Relevant Details

At the request of the manager of Pizza Hut in Sunshine City, a survey was conducted to assess customer satisfaction. The sample comprised 240 customers who were administered a short questionnaire during a period of 2 months from July 15 to September 14. Each day, four customers who walked into the Pizza Hut at 12:00 noon, 3:00 P.M., 6:00 P.M., and 9:00 P.M. were requested to respond to a short questionnaire on site, after they had eaten the pizza. The questionnaire, requiring less than 3 minutes for completion, asked respondents to give information on their gender and age, and to indicate on a 5-point scale the extent of their satisfaction with (1) the flavor and texture of the pizza, (2) its taste, (3) nutritional value, (4) price, (5) the quality of service, and (6) the ambiance of the eating place. An open-ended question also asked them to offer additional comments they might desire to make. Customers dropped off their responses in a locked box with a slit at the top, kept near the exit.

Results of Data Analysis

Analysis of the data indicated that of the 240 respondents, about 60% were men and 40% women. Most of them were over 25 years of age. Customers expressed greatest satisfaction with the taste of the pizza (a mean of 4.5 on a 5-point scale), followed by its flavor and texture (mean of 4). They were neither pleased nor displeased with the price or the quality of service (3 on a 5-point scale). They were not particularly happy, however, with the ambiance or the nutritional value (mean of 2.5 for each). The comments offered in the open-ended question indicated that some 25 individuals felt that the amount of cheese in the pizza might increase their cholesterol level to the detriment of their health.

Conclusions and Recommendations

These results indicate that customers do like the pizza and have no specific complaints about the price or the service. Should the manager be concerned about the displeasure of the customers with the ambiance or the nutritional value, he could handle it fairly easily. It is possible, for instance, to improve the ambiance with flowers and hanging baskets of plants. Candlelights on the tables in the evenings would also contribute to the improvement.

As for dissatisfaction with the nutritional value, information about the use of only low-fat cheese in the pizza as a health safeguard can be disseminated through the menu card and advertisements. The option of pizza with nonfat cheese may also be offered to the customers.

If enhancement of the level of customer satisfaction is desired, a short training program could be introduced for the waiters for this purpose, and their service thereafter supervised until the "service with a smile" motto is internalized by them.

The Introductory Section

The introductory section starts with a statement of the problem under investigation. The research objective, together with background information of why and how the study was initiated, will also be stated. In the case of basic research the introductory section will offer an idea of the topic that is researched, and why it is important to study it. The arguments would focus on the relevancy, timeliness, and appropriateness of the research, in the context of current factors and trends in society and/or organizations.

The research objective and the problem statement to be studied are clearly set forth in this section.

The Body of the Report

In this part, the details of the interviews conducted, the literature survey, the theoretical framework, and the hypotheses are furnished. The design details such as sampling and data collection methods, as well as the nature and type of study, the time horizon, the field setting, and the unit of analysis, will be described.

The details of the types of data analyses done to test the hypotheses, and the findings therefrom, will be provided next. Tabular and pictorial depictions of the results of data analysis will find a place here. A few of the various ways in which data can be pictorially presented in written reports and oral presentations are illustrated in Figure 13.1.

The Final Part of the Report

The final part of the report will contain the conclusions drawn from the findings. In most cases (depending on the scope of the project), a list of recommendations for implementation will follow. Frequently, a cost–benefit analysis will also be provided. Any limitations to the study, as for example, flaws in sampling due to circumstances beyond one's control, will find a place herein. A brief summation paragraph will also be provided at the end.

Acknowledgments

Help received from others is next acknowledged. Usually, the people who assisted in the study by collecting the questionnaires, acting as liaison persons, helping in data analysis, and so on, are recognized and thanked. The organization is thanked for the facilities provided, and its members for responding to the survey.

Figure 13.1
Pictorial representation of data.

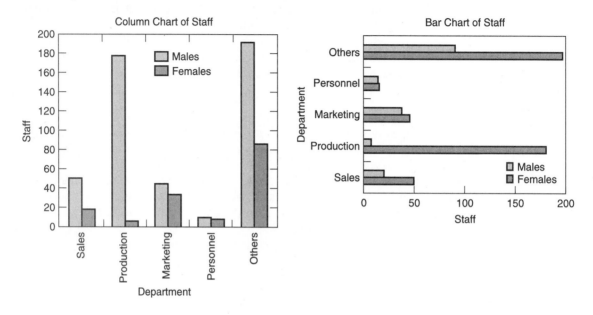

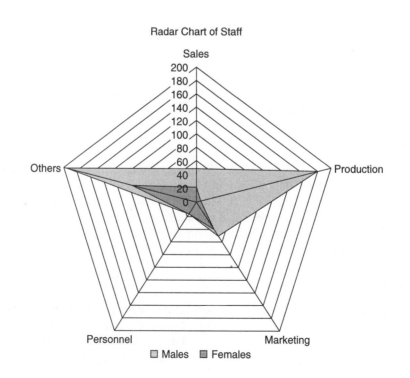

Figure 13.1 (continued)

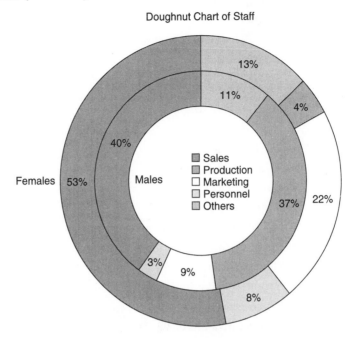

Doughnut Chart of Staff

It should now be easy to see, given the variety of information covered in the report, why it is important to have appropriate headings and subheadings throughout. This assists the reader to progress through the report smoothly, easily, and quickly, while wide margins on all sides help the reader to jot down points or make notes, wherever considered necessary, as one goes through the report.

References

Immediately after the acknowledgments, starting on a fresh page, a list of the references cited in the literature review and at other places in the report will be given. The format of the references has been discussed and illustrated in Section 3 of the Appendix to Chapter 4. Footnotes, if any in the text, are referenced either separately at the end of the report, or at the bottom of the page where the footnote occurs.

Appendix

The appendix, which comes last, is the appropriate place for the organization chart, newspaper clippings or other materials that substantiate the text of the report, detailed verbatim narration of interviews with members, and whatever else would help the reader follow the text. It should also contain a copy of the questionnaire administered to the respondents. If there are several appendices, they could be referenced as Appendix A, Appendix B, and so on, and appropriately labeled.

The above will make clear that the Table of Contents (mentioned earlier) following the title page and the letter of transmittal, would look somewhat as indicated below, with some possible variations.

Table of Contents

Research Proposal

Letter of Authorization

Introduction

- Problem Studied
- Background Information
- Research Goals

Preliminary Details

- Unstructured and Structured Interviews
- Literature Survey
- Theoretical Framework
- Hypotheses Formulated

Research Design

- Type and Nature of the Study
- Sampling Design
- Data Collection Methods
- Data Analytic Techniques Used

Results of Data Analysis

- Hypothesis Substantiated/Unsubstantiated

Conclusions

Recommendations

Limitations of Study

Acknowledgments

References

Tables

Graphs

Appendices

ORAL PRESENTATION

Usually organizations (and instructors in classes) require about a 20-minute oral presentation of the research project, followed by a question and answer session.

The oral presentation calls for considerable planning. Imagine a study that spanned over several months having to be presented in 20 minutes to a live audience! Those who have not read the report at all, or at best only superficially, have to be convinced that the recommendations made therein would indeed prove to be beneficial to the organization. All this will have to be effectively accomplished in the matter of a few minutes.

The challenge exists to present the important aspects of the study so as to hold the interest of the audience, while still providing statistical and quantitative information, which may drive many in it to ennui. Different stimuli (overheads, slides, charts, pictorial and tabular depiction, etc.) have to be creatively provided to the audience to consistently sustain their interest throughout the presentation. To make all this possible, time and effort have to be expended in planning, organizing, and rehearsing the presentation.

Slides, overheads, charts, graphs, handouts—all in large, bold print, and preferably in multicolors—help the presenter to sustain the interest of the audience. They also help the presenter discuss and explain the research project coherently, without *reading* from prepared notes.

Factors irrelevant to the written report, such as dress, mannerisms, gestures, voice modulation, and the like, take on added importance in oral presentations. Speaking audibly, clearly, without distracting mannerisms, and at the right speed for the audience to comprehend is vital for holding their attention. Varying the length of the sentences, establishing eye contact, tone variations, voice modulation, and the rate of flow of information make all the difference to audience receptivity. Use of 3 × 5 cards for orderly presentation helps smooth transitions during the presentation. Thus, the contents of the presentation and the style of delivery should both be planned in detail.

Deciding on the Content

Because a lot of material has to be covered in perhaps a 20-minute presentation, it becomes necessary to decide on the points to be focused on and the importance to be given to each. Remembering that the listener absorbs only a small proportion of all that he or she has heard, it is important to determine what the presenter would like the listener to walk away with, and then organize the presentation accordingly.

Obviously, the problem investigated, the results found, the conclusions drawn, the recommendations made, and the ways in which they can be implemented are of vital interest to organizational members, and need to be emphasized during the presentation. The design aspects of the study, details of the sample, data collection methods, details of data analysis, and the like, can be mentioned in passing to be picked up at the question and answer session by the interested members.

However, depending on the type of audience, it may become necessary to put more stress on the data analytic aspects. For example, if the presentation is made to a group of statisticians in the company, or in a research methods class, the data analyses and results will receive more time than if the project is presented to a group of managers whose main interest lies in the solution of the problem and implementation of the recommendations. Thus, the time and attention devoted to the various components of the study will require adjustment, depending on the audience.

Visual Aids

Graphs, charts, and tables help to drive home the points one wishes to make much faster and more effectively, true to the adage that a picture is worth a thousand words. Visual aids provide a captivating sensory stimulus that sustains the attention of the audience. Modern PowerPoint technology makes it possible for color graphics to be produced on personal computers and projected onto the screen. Slides, transparencies, flip charts, the chalkboard, and handout materials also help the audience to easily follow the points of the speaker's focus. The selection of specific visual modes of presentation will depend, among other things, on the size of the room, the availability of a good screen for projection, and the cost constraints of developing sophisticated visuals. All visuals should be produced with an eye on easy visibility from the far end of the presentation hall. Large, easily readable visuals that are properly labeled in big size bold letters help the audience to focus on the presentation. Visuals that present side-by-side comparisons of the existing and would-be state of affairs via graphs or pie charts drive home the points made much more forcefully than elaborate and laborious verbal explanations.

Integrated multimedia presentations using PowerPoint, videotapes, videodiscs, CD-ROM, and other visuals are quite common in this technological age. Digital whiteboards facilitate digital storage of intricate diagrams that can be used in conjunction with electronic projective systems to serve as electronic flipcharts, as was described in Chapter 3. When planning a presentation using Power Point or integrated multimedia, it is important to ensure before the presentation starts that the related equipment are properly hooked up and tested so that the presentation can go smoothly without interruptions.

The Presenter

An effective presentation is also a function of how "unstressed" the presenter is. The speaker should establish eye contact with the audience, speak audibly and understandably, and be sensitive to the nonverbal reactions of the audience. Strict adherence to the time frame and concentration on the points of interest to the audience are critical aspects of presentation. The display of extreme nervousness throughout the presentation, stumbling for words, fumbling with the notes or audiovisuals, speaking inaudibly and/or with distracting mannerisms, straying away from the main focus of the study, and exceeding the time limit all detract from effectiveness. One should also not minimize the importance of the impression created on the audience by dress, posture, bearing, and the confidence with which one carries oneself. Such simple things as covering the materials on the visuals until they need to be exhibited, and voice modulation, help to focus the attention of the audience on the discussion.

The Presentation

The opening remarks set the stage for riveting the attention of the audience. Certain aspects such as the problem investigated, the findings, the conclusions drawn, the recommendations made and their implementation are, as previously mentioned, important aspects of the presentation. The speaker should drive home these points at least three times—once in the beginning, again when each of these areas is covered, and finally, while summarizing and bringing the presentation to a conclusion.

Handling Questions

Concentrated and continuous research on the research topic over a considerable period of time indisputably makes the presenter more knowledgeable about the project than anyone else in the audience. Hence, it is not difficult to handle questions from the members with confidence and poise. It is important to be nondefensive when questions are posed that seemingly find fault with some aspect of the research. Openness to suggestions also helps, as the audience might at times come up with some excellent ideas or recommendations the researcher might not have thought of. Such ideas must always be acknowledged graciously. If a question or a suggestion from a member in the audience happens to be flawed, it is best addressed in a nonjudgmental fashion.

The question and answer session, when handled well, leaves the audience with a sense of involvement and satisfaction. Questioning should be encouraged and responded to with care. This interactive question and answer session offers an exciting experience both to the audience and to the presenter.

As may be readily seen, a 20-minute presentation and a short question and answer session thereafter do call for substantial planning, anticipation of audience concerns, psychological preparedness, and good impression management skills.

Reporting has to be done in an honest and straightforward manner. It is unethical to fail to report findings that are unpalatable to the sponsors or that reflect poorly on management. As suggested earlier, it is possible to be tactful in presenting such findings without withholding or distorting information to please the sponsors. Internal researchers, in particular, will have to find ways of presenting unpopular information in a tactful manner. It is also important to state the limitations of the study—and practically every study has some limitation—so that the audience is not misled.

SUMMARY

The Research Proposal and the components of various types of written research reports were discussed in this chapter. It was emphasized that the purpose of the report and the composition of the intended audience are critical factors in deciding what aspects of the study will be stressed the most. Examples of different kinds of reports were offered and additional examples can be found in the Appendix to this chapter. Ways of making effective oral presentation were also discussed, stressing both the contents of the presentation and the style of delivery.

In the next and concluding chapter of the book, we will take a final look at business research and decision making.

DISCUSSION QUESTIONS AND POINTS TO PONDER

1. What is the purpose of the Research Proposal?
2. Why is it necessary to have the letter of authorization in the report?
3. Discuss the purpose and contents of the Executive Summary.
4. What are the similarities and differences of basic and applied research reports?
5. How have technological advancements helped in writing and presenting research reports?
6. Why is it necessary to specify the limitations of the study in the research report?
7. What aspects of a class research project would be stressed by you in the written report and in the oral presentation?

EXERCISES

Exercise 13.1   Critique Report 4 in the Appendix. Discuss it in terms of good and bad research, suggesting how the study could have been improved, what aspects of it are good, and how scientific it is.

Exercise 13.2   Write a Research Proposal for conducting a study on the efficiency of the manufacturing teams in a company.

Exercise 13.3   Give a title to and write the introductory section of any study you might like to conduct.

APPENDIX

REPORT 1: SAMPLE OF A REPORT INVOLVING A DESCRIPTIVE STUDY

SEKRAS COMPANY

TO: Mr. L. Raiburn, Chairman
Strategic Planning Committee

FR: Joanne Williams
Public Relations Officer

RE: Report requested by Mr. Raiburn

Attached is the report requested by Mr. Raiburn.
If any further information or clarification is needed, please let me know.

Encl: Report

REPORT FOR THE STRATEGIC PLANNING COMMITTEE

Introduction

Vice President Raiburn, Chairman of the Strategic Planning Committee, requested two pieces of information:

1. The sales figures of the top five retailers in the country in 1997 and in 2000.
2. Customers' ideas of what improvements can be made to Sekras to enhance their satisfaction. For this purpose, he desired that a quick survey of the company's customers be done to elicit their opinions.

Method Used for Obtaining the Requisite Information

Figures of sales of the top five retailers in the country for 1997 and 2000 were obtained from *Business Week,* which periodically publishes many kinds of industry statistics.

To obtain customers' inputs on improvements that could be made by the company, a short questionnaire (specimen in Appendix A) was mailed to 300 of our credit card customers—100 who had most frequently used the card in the last 18 months, 100 who most infrequently used it during the same period, and 100 average users. Questionnaires in three different colors were sent to the three groups. Respondents were offered a complimentary magnet for responses received within a week.

The questionnaire asked for responses to three questions:

1. What are some of the things you like best about shopping at Sekras?
2. What are some of the things that you dislike and would like to see improved at Sekras? Please explain in as much detail as possible.
3. What are your specific suggestions for making improvements to enhance the quality of our service to customers like you?

Findings

I. Sales Figures of the Top Five Retailers in 1997 and 2000

Information regarding sales of the top five retailers in 1997 and 2000 is provided in Table 13.1 below. As can be seen, Walmart retained its top position, and Home Depot, which was not among the top five in 1997, occupied the second place in 2000. Sears had dropped from second to third position, and Kmart slid from third position to the fourth in 2000. Target emerged as the fifth top retailer. JC Penney and Dayton Hudson did not find a place among the top five retailers during 2000.

It may be observed that Walmart had increased its sales by about 1.75 times during the 3-year period, while Kmart had marginally increased its sales, and Sears had dropped a little during the same period.

II. Customer Suggestions for Improvements

Of the 300 surveys sent out, 225 were recieved, a 75% response rate. Of the 100 most frequent users of our credit card to whom questionnaires were sent, 80 responded; among the most infrequent users, 60 responded; and among the average users, 85 responded.

Table 13.1

Comparative Sales Figures of the Five Top Retail Companies During 1997 and 2000

Top Retailers in 1997			Top Retailers in 2000		
Company	Sales in Billions of $	Share Among Top Five	Company	Sales in Billions of $	Share Among Top Five
Wal-Mart Stores	113.4	47%	Wal-Mart Stores	191.33	54.7%
Sears, Roebuck	41.5	17%	Home Depot	45.74	13.1%
Kmart	32.1	13%	Sears, Roebuck	40.94	11.7%
JC Penney	29.2	12%	Kmart	36.50	10.3%
Dayton Hudson	26.9	11%	Target	35.51	10.2%

Source: *Business Week*

About 75% of the respondents were women. The majority of the customers was between the ages of 35 and 55 (62%).

The responses to the three open-ended questions were analyzed. The information needed by the Committee on the Suggested Improvements is tabulated (see Table 13.2). Responses to the other two questions on features liked by the customers, and their specific suggestions for improvement, are provided in the two tables in the Appendix. The following are suggestions received from one or two respondents only:

1. Have more water fountains on each floor.
2. The pushcarts could be lighter, so they will be less difficult to push.
3. More seats for resting after long hours of shopping would help.
4. Prices of luxury items are too high.

From looking at Table 13.2, it is seen that the most dissatisfaction stems from (1) out of stock small appliances, and (2) inability to locate the store assistants who could guide customers in locating what they need (44% each). The need for child care services is expressed by 38% of the customers. Twenty percent also indicate that the cafeteria should cater to the international spicy type of foods. The next two important items pertain to the temperature (18%) and billing mistakes (16%). Some customers (16%) also wish the store would be open 24 hours.

Table 13.2
Suggested Areas for Improvement

Features	Frequent Users No.	Medium Users No.	Infrequent Users No.	Total No.	Total %
1. Small appliances such as mixers, blenders are often not in stock. This is irritating.	30	48	22	100	44
2. The cafeteria serves only bland, uninteresting food. How about some spicy international food?	26	14	5	45	20
3. Often, we are unable to locate where the items we want are!	3	6	14	23	10
4. It would be nice if you could have a child care service so we can shop without distractions.	28	32	25	85	38
5. It is often difficult to locate an assistant who can help us with answers to our questions.	29	49	22	100	44
6. I wish it were a 24-hour store.	17	13	7	37	16
7. Sometimes, there is a mistake in billing. We have to make some telephone calls before charges are corrected. This is a waste of our time.	4	12	14	20	16
8. Allocate some floor space for kids to play video games.	2	—	4	6	2
9. Import more Eastern apparel like the kimono, sarees, sarongs.	—	8	4	12	5
10. Regulate the temperature better; often, it is too cold or too hot.	15	12	17	44	18

The rest of the suggestions are offered by less than 10% of the customers, and hence, can perhaps be attended to later.

A note of caution is in order at this juncture. We are not sure how representative our sample is. We thought that a mix of high, average, and infrequent users of our credit card would provide us some useful insights. If a more detailed study obtaining information from a sample of *all* the customers who come to the store is considered necessary, we will initiate it quickly. In the meantime, we are also interviewing a few of the customers who shop here daily. If we find anything of significance from these interviews, we will inform you.

Improvements Indicated by These Suggestions

Based on the current sample of customers who have responded to our survey, the following improvements and actions seem called for:

1. Small appliances need to be adequately stocked (44% complained about this). An effective reorder inventory system has to be developed for this department to minimize customer dissatisfaction and avoid loss of sales for lack of sufficient stock. The research team can help in this, if requested.

2. Customers seem to need help to locate store items and would appreciate help from Store Assistants (44% expressed this need). If providing assistance is a primary concern, it would be a good idea to have liveried store personnel with badges to indicate they are there to assist customers. During idle hours, if any (when there are no customers seeking help), these individuals can be deployed as shelf organizers.

3. Need for child care has been expressed by more than a third of our customers (38%). It would be a good idea to earmark a portion of the front of the building for parents to drop off their children while shopping. The children will have to be supervised by a trained child care professional recruited by the organization. An assistant could be recruited later if needed. From the cost–benefit analysis in Exhibit 7, it may be seen that these additional expenditures will pay off multifold in sales revenues, and at the same time, create a fund of goodwill for the company.

4. Adding to the variety of foods served in the cafeteria (a need expressed by 20%) is at once a simple and a complex matter. We need further ideas and details as to what types of food need to be added. This information can be obtained through a short survey, if Mr. Raiburn so desires.

5. Billing errors should not occur (16% indicated this). The billing department should be warned that such mistakes should be avoided and should not recur. Performance assessment should be tied to such mistakes.

6. Regulation of temperature (16% identified this) is easy. This, in fact, could be immediately attended to by the Engineering Department personnel.

I hope this report contains all the information sought by Mr. Raiburn. As stated earlier, if the non–credit card customers also have to be sampled, it can be easily arranged.

REPORT 2: SAMPLE OF A REPORT WHERE AN IDEA HAS TO BE "SOLD"

MUELLER PHARMACEUTICALS

June 15

TO: The Board of Directors

FR: Harry Wood, VP.
(Through: President Michael Osborn)

RE: Sabbatical for Managers

Enclosed is a brief report on the need for a sabbatical policy for our managers and R & D personnel, for discussion at our next board meeting. We will also plan on a more detailed presentation at that time

WHY SABBATICALS FOR MANAGERS ARE NECESSARY

Introduction

At the company's board meeting last month, the members were concerned that no new products have been developed during the past 4 years and that the profits of the company are considerably down. One of the board members suggested that a sabbatical given to the managers and key staff of our company might rejuvenate them, and help creativity flow again. At that time, the matter was treated casually and not given any further consideration. Sensing the need to consider this option seriously, I have since talked to a few companies who do offer this benefit to their managers. I have further obtained some data from them, which demonstrate the efficacy of sabbaticals.

Based on the available information, there is a strong case for introducing a sabbatical policy in our company. Details of my discussions with other companies and their data are presented below.

Gist of Telephone Conversations with Vice Presidents and Presidents of Companies

I talked to the presidents, vice presidents, and directors of IBM, Tandem, Apple Computers, Eli Lilly, and Time Warner Inc. All these companies have had sabbatical policies for at least the past 9 years. Some presidents to whom I spoke said they initiated the policy because they found that their own productivity went up after they had had some time away from their jobs doing different kinds of things. Some said that they introduced the sabbatical because they felt that their managerial staff experienced burnout after long years of nonstop work at a hectic pace and became ineffective.

Without exception, everyone said that it makes good business sense to offer managers a chance to refurbish their lives and recharge their batteries every 6 years or so, so that they come back to work with renewed vigor. Among the many advantages recounted by those to whom I spoke are:

1. More enthusiasm and zest for work.
2. Better working relationships with staff.
3. A fresh approach to problem solving with less competitiveness among the different departments.
4. More creative flow of ideas, new marketing strategies, and product development ideas.
5. A more dynamic workplace in terms of interpersonal interactions, interdepartmental collegiality, and joint problem solving.

Some Hard Data

The Appendix, which contains the information provided by two companies, shows that the number of new products developed quadrupled in one company and increased fivefold in the other during the years following the introduction of the sabbatical. As they themselves acknowledge, the increase cannot be attributed to the sabbatical alone, but they have also documented that most of the new products developed were under the leadership of the managers after their return from a 3-month sabbatical. You will note that new product development statistics for these managers, *before* and *after* their sabbatical, are indeed compelling! Reinforcing our theory is also the decline in the figures after the fourth or fifth year of their return from sabbatical and the pickup again after the next sabbatical. Noteworthy too is that the "pickup" years were no different from the others in terms of the economic environment, technology advancement, or other factors that might have a direct impact on innovation!

I have also placed in the Appendix a copy of the article on Executive Life, which appeared in a top journal on July 3, 2000, which you have probably already read. Is it not astonishing and amusing that many of the executives who try something new during the sabbatical, ultimately want to get back to their old jobs? The case cited of the law firm partner, Axinn, who missed the rigors of his old job and could just not shake off the lawyer in him when he tried to be a rabbi-in-training during his sabbatical, is particularly interesting.

Benefits of Sabbatical

The benefits of sabbatical to the managers are obvious; they refresh themselves trying their hands at new things or doing the things they have dreamed of (such as learning to play the flute or paint or write). These activities seem to offer them a new lease on their professional lives, but the benefits to the corporation seem to be even greater, as experienced by the companies that already have this scheme in place. Apple Computer's revenues are stated to have quadrupled under the leadership of Mr. John Sculley, who took 9-week sabbaticals. Again no one is attributing a cause-and-effect relationship, but there might be a strong correlation possible there! Mr. Lerman, partner of Wilmer, Cutler & Pickering, strongly affirms that when managers come back from sabbatical, they are more effective and invigorated.

Recommendation

Given the qualitative and quantitative evidence generated from a number of organizations that have implemented the sabbatical policy, I strongly recommend that we also establish a sabbatical policy in our company. The suggestion is to offer a paid, 3-month sabbatical for all our R & D scientists, and managerial and executive staff, after every 6 years of service. The costs of implementing this with respect to our senior scientists, managers, and executives are worked out and shown in Exhibit 4. The likely benefits within 10 years of our initiating such a policy in terms of new product development, increased sales, and joint problem-solving endeavors due to higher energy levels of department heads, are also shown in the same exhibit.

I will ask the HRM Director to collect information from more companies having sabbatical policies and ask him to make a presentation to the Board at our next meeting. In the meantime, if you need more information or clarification, feel free to give me a call.

In conclusion, our company is at the crossroads and our scientists and managers need to be energized to enhance their performance and productivity. Constant pressure and ceaseless toil are wearing them out. Many are frustrated by the demands imposed by the jobs. "All work and no play" has banished their zest for working and drained them of their creative ideas. It is high time we inject some vitality into our system through sabbaticals.

REPORT 3: SAMPLE OF A REPORT OFFERING ALTERNATIVE SOLUTIONS AND EXPLAINING THE PROS AND CONS OF EACH ALTERNATIVE

TO: Mr. Charles Orient, CEO
Lunard Manufacturing Company

FR: Alex Ventura, Senior Researcher
Beam Research Team

RE: Suggestions on alternative ways of cutting costs in anticipation of recession.

Enclosed is the report requested by Mr. Orient. If any additional information or clarification is needed, please let me know.

Encl: Report

REPORT ON ALTERNATIVE WAYS OF HANDLING RECESSIONARY TIMES WITHOUT MASSIVE LAYOFFS

Introduction

The Beam Research Team was asked to suggest alternative ways of tiding over the anticipated recession over the next several months, when a slowdown of the economy is expected. A recent article in *Business Week* titled "Hunkering Down in a Hurry" indicated that executives in a large number of companies are slashing costs mostly through layoffs and restructuring. Mr. Orient wanted the Beam Research Team to suggest other alternatives besides layoffs.

This report provides five alternatives citing the advantages and disadvantages of each.

Method Used for Developing the Alternatives

The Team studied the economic indicators and the published industry analyses, read the Federal Reserve Board Chairman's speeches, examined the many ways in which companies cut costs during nonrecessionary periods as well as recessions, and based on these, suggested the following five alternatives.

Alternatives Suggested

1. A moratorium on all capital expenditure.
2. Hiring freeze.
3. Recovery of bad debts through sustained efforts.
4. Trimming of operating expenditures with substantial reduction in travel and entertainment expenditures.
5. Discontinuance of the manufacture of low profit margin products.

Advantages and Disadvantages of Each of the Above

Itemized details of the cost–benefit analysis for each of the above suggestions are furnished in the Appendix which may be referred to. We give only the net benefits for each alternative here.

1. Moratorium on all capital expenditure

It makes good sense to desist from all capital expenditure since manufacture of most of the items will slow down during recession. Except for parts for existing machines, there is no need to buy capital equipment, and all proposals in this regard should be shelved.

This strategy will cut down the expenditure to the extent of 7 to 10% of revenue. See Appendix for full details. A reserve fund can be created to catch up with future orders when the economy returns to normal.

2. Hiring Freeze

The annual increase in the strength of staff during the past four years has been about 15%. With a slowdown of the economy, a hiring freeze in all branch offices will save over $10 million annually.

This might initially result in some extra workload for the staff and cause some job dissatisfaction. But once they get used to it, and the impact of the actual recession hits them, employees will be thankful for the job they have. It will be a good idea to explain in advance the reasons for the hiring freeze to the employees so that they understand the motive behind the company's policy, and appreciate having been informed.

3. Recovery of Bad Debts through Aggressive Efforts

Bad debts of the company have been on the increase over the past three years, and no intensive efforts to recover them seem to have been made hitherto.

We suggest that collection agents who have successfully recovered bad debts for other companies be hired immediately. Such agents may have to be paid more than other collection agents, but the extra cost will be well worth it. About a billion dollars can be collected within a few weeks of their being on the job, and this will help the financial cash flow of the company.

4. Trimming of Operating Expenditures

Several operating expenses can be cut down—the travel expenses of managers in particular—as shown in Exhibit 4 of the Appendix. Videoconferencing costs much less and is quicker, and should be encouraged for most of the meetings and negotiations. This alone will result in savings of more than $175,000 per month.

Another way of considerably curtailing expenditure is to restrict entertainment expenses only for such purposes and to such managers as actively promote the business of the company or is essential for public relations.

These changes will have a negative impact on morale, but managers understand the economic situation, and will adjust to the new system once the initial mental resistance wears off.

5. Eliminating the Manufacture of Low Margin Products

The team found from a detailed study of the company records of manufacturing, sales, and profits figures for the various products that all the items listed in Exhibit 5 of the Appendix have very low profit margins. It is evident from the data provided that considerable time and effort are expended in manufacturing and selling these items.

It will be useful to phase out the discontinuance of manufacture of these items and divert the resources to the high profit items suggested in Exhibit 6. From the cost–benefit analysis in Exhibit 7, it may be seen that several billions can be saved through this strategy.

It is possible to put into effect all of the five alternatives above and handle the onslaught of the recession with confidence.

REPORT 4: EXAMPLE OF AN ABRIDGED BASIC RESEARCH REPORT

FACTORS AFFECTING THE UPWARD MOBILITY OF WOMEN IN PUBLIC ACCOUNTING

Introduction

A substantial number of women have entered the public accounting profession in the past 15 years or so. However, less than 4% of the partners in the Big Eight accounting firms are women, indicating a lack of upward mobility for women in the accounting profession. Against the backdrop of the fact that the women students perform significantly better during their academic training than their male counterparts, it is unfortunate that their intellectual ability and knowledge remain underutilized during their professional careers. The recent costly litigation and discrimination suits filed make it imperative for us to study the factors that affect the upward mobility of the women and examine how the situation can be rectified.

A Brief Literature Survey

Studies of male and female accounting majors indicate that the percentage of women accounting students has increased severalfold since 1977 (Kurian, 1998). Based on the analysis of longitudinal data collected over a 15-year period, Mulcher, Turner, and Williams (2000) found that women students' grades in senior accounting courses were significantly higher than those of the male students. This higher level of academic performance has been theorized as due to the higher need and desire that women have to achieve and overcome stereotypes (Messing, 2000), having higher career aspirations (Tinsley et al., 1999), or having a higher aptitude for accounting (Jones & Alexander, 2001; Riley, 2001). Empirical studies by Fraser, Lytle, and Stolle (1998), and Johnson and Meyer (1999), however, found no significant differences in personality predispositions or behavioral traits among male and female accounting majors.

Several surveys of women accountants in the country pinpoint three major factors that hinder women's career progress in the public accounting field (see for instance, Kaufman, 1986; Larson, 1999; Walkup & Fenman, 2001). They are (1) the long hours of work demanded by the profession (a factor that conflicts with family demands), (2) failure to be entrusted with responsible assignments, and (3) discrimination. In sum, the lack of upward mobility seems to be due to factors over which the organization has some control.

Research Question

Do long work hours, failure to be handed greater responsibilities, and discrimination account for the lack of upward mobility of women in public accounting?

Theoretical Framework

The variance in the dependent variable, **upward mobility,** can be explained by the three independent variables: long hours of work, not handling greater responsibilities, and discrimination. As women are expected to, and do indeed take on responsibility for household work and childrearing, they are not able to work beyond regular work hours at the workplace. This creates the wrong impression among higher-ups in the organization that women are less committed to their work. Because of this perception, they are not entrusted with significant responsibilities. This further hinders their progress as they are not afforded exposure to the intricacies of accounting practices as much as men. Hence women are overlooked at the time of promotion.

Deliberate discriminatory practices due to sex-role stereotypes, as evidenced in the well-known case of *Hopkins vs. Price Waterhouse & Co.,* also arrest women's progress. If women are not valued for their potential and are expected to conform to sex-typed behavior (which confines them to inconspicuous roles), their chances of moving up the career ladder are significantly reduced.

Thus, the three independent variables considered here would significantly explain the variance in the upward mobility of women in public accounting. The impracticability of putting in long hours of work, lack of opportunities to handle greater responsibilities, and sex role stereotyping all negatively impact upward mobility.

Hypotheses

1. If women spend more hours on the job after regular work hours, they will be given greater responsibilities.
2. If women are entrusted with higher level of responsibilities, they will have more opportunities to move up in the organization.
3. If women are not expected to conform to stereotypical behavior, their chances for upward mobility will increase.
4. All three independent variables will significantly explain the variance in women CPAs' upward mobility.

METHOD SECTION

Study Design

In this cross-sectional correlational field study, data on the three independent variables and the dependent variable were collected from women CPAs in several public accounting organizations in the country through mail questionnaires.

Population and Sample

The population for the study comprised all women CPAs in the country. A systematic sampling procedure was first used to select 30 cities from the various regions of the country from which a sample of accounting firms would be drawn. Then, through a simple random sampling procedure, five CPA firms from each of the cities were chosen for the study. Data were collected from all the women in each of the firms so chosen. The total sample size was 300 and responses were received from 264 women CPAs, for an 88% response rate for the mail questionnaires, which is pretty good. The unit of analysis was the individuals who responded to the survey.

All respondents had, as expected, the CPA degree. Their ages ranged from 28 to 66. About 60% of the women were over 45 years of age. The average number of children in the house below the age of 13 was two. The average number of years of work in the organization was 15, and the average number of organizations worked for was two. The average number of hours spent daily at home on office-related matters was 1.4.

Variables and Measures

All demographic variables such as age, number of years in the organization, number of other organizations in which the individual had worked, number of hours spent at home on office-related matters, and number of children in the house and their ages, were tapped by direct single questions.

Upward Mobility. This dependent variable indicates the extent to which individuals are expected to progress in their career during the succeeding 3 to 10 years. Hall (1986) developed four items to measure this variable, a sample item being: *I see myself being promoted to the next level quite easily.* The measure is reported to have convergent and discriminant validity, and the Cronbach's alpha for the four items for this sample was .86.

Sex-Role Stereotyping. This independent variable was measured using Hall and Humphrey's (1972) 8-item measure. An example item is: *Men in this organization do not consider women's place to be primarily in the home.* Cronbach's alpha for the measure for this sample was .82.

Responsibilites Assigned. This was tapped by three items from Sonnenfield and McGrath (1983), which asked respondents to indicate their levels of assigned responsibility to (a) make important decisions, (b) handle large accounts, and (c) account for the annual profits of the firm. Cronbach's alpha for the three items was .71 for this sample.

Data Collection Method

Questionnaires were mailed to 300 women CPAs in the United States. After two reminders, 264 completed questionnaires were received within a period of 6 weeks. The high return rate of 88% can be attributed to the shortness of the questionnaire and perhaps the motivation of the women CPAs to respond to a topic close to their heart.

Questionnaires were not electronically administered for various reasons, including the advantage it afforded to the busy respondents to reply without switching on the computer.

Data Analysis and Results

After determining the reliabilities (Cronbach's alpha) for the measures for this sample, frequency distributions for the demographic variables were obtained. These may be seen in Exhibit 1. Then a Pearson correlation matrix was obtained for the four independent and dependent variables. This may be seen in Exhibit 2. It is to be noted that no correlation exceeded .6.

Each hypothesis was then tested. The correlation matrix provided the answer to the first three hypotheses. The first hypothesis stated that the number of hours put in beyond work hours on office-related matters will be positively correlated to the responsibilities assigned. The correlation of .56 ($p < .001$) between the number of hours spent on office work beyond regular work hours and the entrusted responsibilities substantiates this hypothesis.

The second hypothesis stated that if women are given higher responsibilities, their upward mobility would improve. The positive correlation of .59 ($p < .001$) between the two variables substantiates this hypothesis. That is, the greater the entrusted responsibilities, the higher are the perceived chances of being promoted.

The third hypothesis indicated that sex-role stereotyping would be negatively correlated to upward mobility. The correlation of −.54 ($p < .001$) substantiates this hypothesis as well. That is, the greater the expected conformity to stereotyped behavior, the less the chances of upward mobility.

To test the fourth hypothesis that the number of hours spent beyond regular work hours on job-related matters, assignment of higher responsibilities, and expectations of conformity with stereotyped behavior will significantly explain the variance in perceived upward mobility, the three independent variables were regressed against the dependent variable. The results, which are shown in Exhibit 3, indicate that this hypothesis is also substantiated. That is, the R^2 value of .43 at a significance level of $p < .001$, with df (3,238), confirms that 43% of the variance in upward mobility is significantly explained by the three independent variables.

Discussion of Results

The results of this study confirm that the variables considered in the theoretical framework are important. By focusing solely on the number of hours worked, ignoring the quality of work done, the organization is perhaps not harnessing the full potential and encouraging the development of the talents of the women CPAs adequately. It seems worthwhile to remedy this situation.

It would be useful if the top executive were to assign progressively higher levels of responsibilities to women. This will utilize their abilities fully, and in turn, enhance the effectiveness of the firm. If executives are helped to modify their mental attitudes and sex-role expectations, they would tend to expect less stereotypical behavior and encourage the upward mobility of women CPAs. Knowing women bring a different kind of perspective to organizational matters (Smith, 1999; Vernon, 2001), it is quite possible that having them as partners of the firm will enhance the organizational effectiveness as well.

Recommendations

It is recommended that a system be set up to assess the *value* of the contributions of each individual in discharging his or her duties, and use that, rather than the number of hours of work put in, as a yardstick for promotion.

Second, women CPAs should be given progressively more responsibilities after they have served 3 to 5 years in the system. Assigning a mentor to train them will facilitate smooth functioning of the firm. Third, a short seminar should be organized for executives to sensitize them to the adverse effects of sex-role stereotyping at the workplace. This will help them to beneficially utilize the talents of women CPAs. If viewed as professionals with career goals and aspirations, rather than perceive them in stereotyped ways, women CPAs will be enabled to handle more responsibilities and advance in the system. The organization would also stand to benefit by their contributions.

In conclusion, it would be worthwhile for public accounting firms to modify their mental orientations toward, and expectations of, women CPAs. It is a national waste if their potential is not fully tapped and utilized.

CHAPTER 14

MANAGERIAL DECISION MAKING AND RESEARCH

TOPICS DISCUSSED

- Role of Research and Common Sense in Managerial Decision Making
- Decision-Making Process in Applying Different Types of Research Results
- Description of a Qualitative Case Study and Another Case That Should Have Been Studied, but Was Not

CHAPTER OBJECTIVE

After reading this chapter you will be able to appreciate the fact that both qualitative and quantitative investigations have their place in business research. Sometimes, qualitative research may be the only way to attempt to solve certain types of problems, though it may not stand up to the rigors of testability and replicability.

We started the book saying that scientific research helps managers to make good decisions. This is because of the knowledge they acquire on each aspect of research and its significance, as has been brought out throughout the book.

SCIENTIFIC RESEARCH AND MANAGERIAL DECISION MAKING

Managers wrestle with a multitude of problems—big and small—in their everyday work life. The difference between a successful and not so successful organization lies in the quality of decisions made by the managers in the system. We have seen that scientific thinking equips managers with an awareness and comprehension of the multiplicity of factors operating in their work environment. It also gears managers to problem solving with objectivity, after taking calculated risks, and all in all, making good decisions after weighing the alternatives. Does this mean that once the manager applies scientific research results to decision making, that the decisions so made are *always* going to be right?

No, for various reasons. First, there is always a 5% chance of making a Type I error; that is, accepting the null hypothesis when it should be rejected. Second, though research results may offer the directions for change, sound common sense should be the guiding light for good decision making. For example, research results may indicate that operating costs have to be cut. The recommendations made to achieve this might be to cut down on staff, close a couple of departments, and so on. Does the manager then make the decision to follow these recommendations? A great amount of thought would have to center on the implications of following the recommended suggestions. Questions such as the immediate and long-term effects of following these strategies to cut costs, and the ripple effects on the rest of the system if mass layoffs and closing certain operations were resorted to, would loom large in the mind of the manager. These and other important aspects will then have to be carefully weighed by the manager before a final decision is made in choosing the right alternative to cut costs. Thus, good decision making entails a common sense approach to applying research results.

To sum up, research is the scientific path that leads the manager to decision making, and experience and commonsense are the beams of light that guide managers to solve problems sensibly. Experience is the cumulative knowledge gained from the outcomes of past problem-solving endeavors—a treasure filed away in a part of the brain, to be readily recalled whenever necessary. Such experience might be the result of a trial-and-error mode of operation in the past, leading to an understanding of what works and what does not. The question then arises, why not be guided by past experience and common sense alone? Why go through the rigorous scientific process of research?

Scientific research is important for several reasons. It is only through a scientific thinking process that we come to understand, and take into consideration, the complex set of factors that operates in any given problem situation. A viable and parsimonious model of theory building is enabled by the preliminary interviews and the literature review processes. We test the relevance of the model for solving the issue at hand, by scientifically testing the various hypotheses that logically flow from it. For this purpose, we collect data in a scientific manner, using the sampling design that is appropriate for the situation. The results of our data analysis then tell us how good our conceptualized theory is, and how the problem at hand can be solved, using a combination of alternatives generated by the results of statistical data analysis. It is at this stage that the manager uses good judgement by using both the research findings and drawing on the personal invaluable resources of past experiences. In sum, research indicates the direction to problem solving; experience and common sense, in conjunction with scientific research results, contribute to good managerial decision making. One without the other is not completely effective.

Research also exposes us to the ever increasing advances in technology. Today, the manager can find facts that are material to the business—nationally and globally—by simply using the Internet. Vast masses of company data also become available to managers, on practically any aspect of the company's multifarious operations, through a good Information System and Data Warehouse installed in the company's Information Technology system. Managers also solve simple, repetitive problems by using the menu-driven Expert System. Such technology was not perfected even a couple of decades ago.

True, managers cannot solve every problem by doing scientific research themselves. Often, internal research teams help in conducting research to find the answers to problems, or outside researchers are hired for the purpose. In either case, knowledge of research and the scientific thinking process helps the manager to understand each step taken by the researcher, and enhances the quality of the decisions made. This is primarily due to the fact that the contents of the research report, on submission, are meaningfully grasped, and intelligent and useful dialogues had transpired between the manager and the researcher throughout the duration of the study. As a matter of fact, a good research report itself may very well be, at least in part, the result of a knowledgeable manager interacting effectively with the researcher. With all the requisite information provided at the beginning and throughout the duration of the study, the researcher understands the problem situation and the constraints better and is enabled to conduct a good study.

Good decision making, as we have seen, is a function of thoroughly understanding and using the findings of the research, carefully weighing the various recommendations made, taking experience as a guide, and recognizing the organizational culture and the values of the system. Ethical behavior dictates that the manager applies research findings for the benefit of the organization, even if they clash with his or her own personal goals and ambitions. As an example, it would be difficult to deny oneself the prospect of an imminent promotion to a higher position, when research findings recommend an immediate temporary halt of all organizational changes. Governed by a sense of fairness and ethics, the manager instituting the study must, in such a case, subordinate self to organizational interests.

Purposive Research

It is necessary for us to recall at this point that purposive research can be of different types, depending on the nature of the problem investigated. Sometimes descriptive studies are called for, and at other times analytical or predictive studies may be necessary. Also, some situations lend themselves only to qualitative studies and others to quantitative analysis. Though one would like to conduct scientific studies that satisfy the hallmarks of science, this may not always be possible in applied research, mainly because sufficient prior knowledge does not exist in that realm. In such cases, one may have to rely mainly on qualitative studies, until sufficient knowledge is gained to conceptualize theoretical models that can be subsequently tested.

Decision-Making Processes in Applying Results from Different Types of Research

Results of data analysis of **descriptive studies** do provide information of interest to the manager. Based on such information, the manager might contemplate some future course of action. For example, the manager might consider creating opportunities for more challenging work, if a descriptive study were to indicate that employees are bored with their jobs. No complex decision making is called for in such cases.

Results of analysis of **hypothesis testing studies** provide alternative choices for solving problems. The manager has to make a decision on the choice of alternative or combination of alternatives, and their implementation to solve the problem. Here, experience and sound judgment come into play in the decision-making process.

Qualitative studies may either describe events or offer solutions as in the case study that follows. However, in the absence of hard empirical statistical results, there is an element of hit and miss in implementing the solutions proposed in this kind of a study. The manager has to consider and judge if the recommendations made would solve the problems, and to what extent changes would be worthwhile. There is always an undetermined element of risk that the manager takes in making the proposed changes. Experience-based personal judgment, with a touch of intuition, will play a big part in decision making in the case of qualitative research.

We have given several examples of scientific research conducted in the hypothetico-deductive mode throughout this book, while discussing the process and design aspects of research. To illustrate the value and legitimacy of qualitative studies in business research, let us now conclude with two illustrations. The first is a case study that called for research and with the judicious implementation of the findings of the study by the president of the company, which is now doing very well, and another that called for research but went by the wayside because of lack of a study of the situation.

CASE 1: CASE STUDY OF THE CRADLE OF INDIAN HANDCRAFTS

Background Information

The Cradle of Indian Handcrafts is a solely owned company, specializing in the creative design of handcrafted ethnic jewelry, scarves, handbags, artifacts, and home furnishings. These are supplied to museums and big department stores in the United States and Europe. In the United States, museums like the Metropolitan Museum of Art in New York and the Los Angeles County Art Museum, and big department stores such as Saks Fifth Avenue and Neiman-Marcus, to name a few, place special orders and stock their shelves with high-end merchandise that is in great demand and sells very well.

The company, situated near San Francisco, was founded in 1984 by a naturalized American, Anisha Sekar. Sekar had worked as a senior manager in at least two retail stores prior to starting the company. The company was then run by the president, Anisha Sekar, with a staff of two. An assistant was recruited when business picked up.

Sekar's motive in starting the company was to capitalize on the increasing interest for Indian handcrafted products worldwide, and especially in the United States. An added motivation was to help the unnoticed and neglected but skilled artisans in India, who worked from their homes earning very little money. A creative mind and a place to start business in were Anisha's main assets at that time. The other advantage she had was extensive contacts with top executives, including CEOs in department stores.

The Company in 1999

In 1999 the company had become a multimillion dollar business and operated from the third floor. Anisha Sekar still remained the sole owner of the company, which was managed by a vice president and two assistants. The vice president with the help of the assistants ran the business, attending to orders, making shipments, maintaining good customer relations, trouble shooting, and attending to all other related matters. The company staff was handsomely paid, and good performance amply rewarded. The U.S. office was and is deliberately kept small, so that the company's reputation is maintained and the personal relationship with established clients is not lost. For the past 5 years, Tom, Anisha's husband, had been managing the accounting and financial side of the business.

In addition to the U.S. office, there was a small contingent of permanent staff and agents in India, Bali, and Thailand. A local manager in India supervised the artisans and ensured quality control and adherence to specifications of orders. Local agents in India attended to details connected with the shipment of goods, dealt with local customs, and oversaw the payments related to the shipment.

Method of Operation

Anisha and Tom continue to travel extensively within the United States, and make quarterly trips to India. Business also takes them frequently to the Far East, Europe, and other places. They were (and continue to be) out of town at least 3 weeks in a month, during which time the vice president was in sole charge of the company's operations. Local business travel of the couple is for purposes of (a) sales presentations, when newly designed samples are displayed and their attributes elaborated during presentations to the company's buyers, (b) taking orders, (c) exhibiting new designs in exhibitions worldwide, and the like. The trips to India, for the major part, are to personally explain to the local semiurban artisans the type of items, their design, and the production needs in terms of numbers. Prices are also negotiated since due to rampant inflation, costs are a moving target. Deadlines for completion of the work are also specified at this time. In the initial years, getting the artisans to make jewelry to custom-tailored specifications was not an easy task to accomplish. Traditional Indian artisans do not believe in changing their age-old ways of stone settings and design styles to cater to an overseas market with totally different tastes. Adherence to time schedules is not in their blood either. Though convincing the artisans to trust her judgment was a difficult and laborious task in those initial years, she overcame their resistance soon, as they started to realize the high monetary gains involved. Their egos were also stroked during special events organized to recognize their work and contributions. The artisans have been won over, now toe the line, adapt themselves to the new designs, and for the most part, deliver the goods on time.

Both the artisans and the company have gained immensely through the years. The artisans have become richer and more sophisticated, and the company's business has expanded, with more classy organizations placing big orders for different kinds of handcrafts, including specially designed decorative art objects and furnishings for the contemporary home.

Some Issues That Faced the Company in 1999

While the president and the vice president were excited about the expansion of their business, they also faced a few problematic situations with the steady growth of the business. Some of the major ones are described below.

Sometimes, after accepting the design of a sample and placing a bulky order, clients refused to accept the shipment, or cancelled the order for no justifiable reason after the goods were shipped from India. This was often so because there is a turnover in the buyers or their management, or due to a slowdown in sales. This is a particularly difficult situation to cope with, since goods are produced 6 months prior to delivery and special goods made to order by one company are not accepted by other buyers. Despite a written contract in the form of a purchase order, prudence precludes proceedings against such companies because it would affect all future business with them and others.

Refusal to accept orders was also due to other reasons. One of them was that the goods were not received on time. Missed delivery dates could be due to any of the following reasons: (1) the artisans in India did not complete making the goods within the specified time and the local manager was unable to do much about it; (2) shipments were delayed due to dock workers' strike or when cargo was offloaded in the Far East due to typhoon and other weather conditions, beyond one's control; (3) Indian customs sometimes insisted on inspection of every box sent, resulting in late shipments; and (4) the ship was not docked on time in San Francisco. These contributed to delays in clearing shipments.

Sometimes goods were also returned after being opened by clients, because they were found to be damaged. Damaged consignments include broken as well as fungus-ridden goods. The fungus problem was a function of the moisture absorbed by the goods during the rainy season in Bali, Indonesia, and India, while they remained packed in boxes for a prolonged time, awaiting shipment.

One of the frustrations for the president was that occasionally, the buyer was not ready to place an order on the scheduled date. The practice is for the president to personally meet with the buyers on an agreed upon date, set for the sole purpose of personally accepting the bulk orders that are discussed in great detail as to design, color, and so on. The situation becomes particularly aggravating when a trip is undertaken for the sole purpose of catering to the needs of a single large-volume buyer who is unprepared to place the order when the president shows up.

A matter that has been engaging Anisha's mind was that with the growing volume of business the need for an additional manager had arisen. Anisha wondered how to allocate the duties and responsibilities between the vice president and the manager such that there was a clear delineation of roles and lines of authority, without making it a centralized system.

In June 1999, as the Christmas season was approaching, and while Anisha was planning her trip to India to place the Christmas orders, she was wondering what the season would bring—a sense of accomplishment or one of problems? There was no way of telling.

Anisha felt that a consultant could offer her some recommendations on how to tackle the various issues. Without wasting further time, she called a consulting firm to study her business and suggest improvements.

THE CONSULTING TEAM AND ITS APPROACH

The Solutions Consulting Company sent a research team of three members to meet with the president and work on the assignment. After discussing the various issues for 3 days with the president and the vice president, the research team realized that it faced a unique situation inasmuch as the consulting firm had not until then worked with a solely owned company engaged in international business. The type of problems experienced by this company in a foreign country had also not been dealt with by either this consulting firm or any others with which it has liaison. For this reason, the assignment was seen as exciting and challenging, and the team members started to work on the project immediately.

Problem Delineation

Based on their interviews with the president and her staff, the team first identified the key problem areas to be investigated, as those relating to:

1. The client system in the United States
2. The artisans in India
3. The customs in India
4. The goods themselves, and
5. Reallocation of duties and responsibilities with the addition of a new manager.

They further listed the issues to be tackled under each of the above (with their own remarks noted in parentheses), as follows.

Client System:

- Not accepting goods or canceling orders after shipment has been dispatched from India. (Find out why)
- Not prepared to place orders after inviting the president for that very purpose. (Explore reasons)

Artisans

- Not completing the work on time. (Why the delays?)

Customs

- Inspection of each consignment by Indian customs delays shipments. (How can inspection be expedited?)

Goods

- Delayed shipments due to reasons beyond control, for example, dock workers' strikes in India, frequent and disruptive power outages, and late docking of ships in the United States. (Not much can be done about these)
- Damaged goods—broken and fungus ridden pieces. (Remedies?)

Reallocation of Duties and Responsibilities after Hiring a New Manager

- Assigning roles
- Specifying responsibilities
- Establishing lines of authority and reporting
- Ensuring a nonbureaucratic, decentralized setup

The Team's Method of Approach for Collecting Information

The leader of the consulting team, David, was to travel to Singapore in connection with another consulting assignment. He wanted to utilize that opportunity to visit nearby India, while the president of the company was also there. Since Anisha had no objection to this, David prepared himself for the trip. He collected and read all the relevant materials that he could obtain on Indian customs and shipping procedures, as well as the available materials available online on Indian artisans. Fortunately, the Indian Consulate in San Francisco made available to him much of the information he wanted on India. He could also gather some valuable information on the web.

The India Experience

In India, David met the local manager, many of the artisans in several different semi-urban areas, some of the shipping agents, and two of the customs officials in New Delhi. Anisha had introduced him to all of them. Meeting with the latter two parties was possible only because of Anisha's frequent work-related interactions with them through the years. It did not take David much time to realize that Indian cultural values totally discouraged egalitarian interactions between officers and those with whom they come into contact.

The Customs Issue

Given the power dynamics and the bureaucratic system, David had to wait a number of days before he could get an appointment to meet with a couple of the customs authorities. There was not much free flow of information during that meeting. However, one officer suggested that it might be possible to work out a special arrangement, whereby surprise spot checks can be made on a small percentage of the boxes on any of the shipments chosen at random. All but the boxes so picked can be shipped and the inspected boxes shipped later. This, he said, would require the permission of the Central Government Ministry, which has the authority to authorize such an arrangement in exceptional cases. He would not give any further details and abruptly terminated the meeting.

Since Anisha knew quite a few ministers in the Central Government—especially those connected with imports and exports—she started to make inquiries to find out how to go about this matter, and who should be contacted. But she had to wait until her next trip to India, 3 months later, to get any information at all.

During the next trip, Anisha pursued the matter, contacted the right people, and made a written request, detailing what she wanted. A final decision on the matter is still awaited, despite periodic reminders by the local manager. If the application is approved, it could possibly help all international small businesses.

David's Conversations with Others

David's conversations with the Indian manager, Sheila, indicated that some Indian artisans have no concept of what timely deliveries entail, and despite monthly reminders, are tardy in completing their work. David's conversations with the artisans (which were translated by a native bilinguist) did not take him very far, because the artisans felt shy and were tongue-tied in front of a foreigner, and barely answered his questions.

David, however, explored the possibility with Sheila of her monitoring the work-in-progress of the artisans who were tardy, on a fortnightly basis. If, in conjunction with the artisans, a weekly schedule of work-in-progress could be developed right after the work orders are given to the artisans, and if the artisans have in their possession this preformulated schedule, then delays can be tracked in a timely manner through more frequent monitoring. Delivery schedules can then be adhered to.

Sheila seemed to be skeptical about the success of this approach. Some artisans worked at their own pace, and the mere possession of schedules might not encourage them to stick to time schedules, she said. Sheila, however, also suggested that monetary incentives might do the trick.

The U.S. Clients

While all this investigation was going on in India, the other two members of the team were interviewing a sample of the clients who had canceled orders after the goods were shipped from India, and especially those who had canceled the Christmas orders the previous year. They also later interviewed a sample of those clients who had failed to place orders after inviting the president of the company for the purpose.

They first tabulated the information to be collected from these two sets of clients as follows:

Issue	Total No. of Clients	No. in California	No. Outside California	No. to be Interviewed In CA	Outside
Refusal to Accept	16	7	9	4	5
Not Placing Orders	12	6	6	3	3

They decided that all client organizations in and around a radius of 100 miles of San Francisco would be personally interviewed, and the rest contacted by telephone.

Their main findings from interviewing those buyers who had placed the orders, but subsequently refused to accept the shipments, were (1) a couple of the buyers who placed the orders did not have the authorization to do so; (2)

long after placing the orders, a few of the buyers decided that the goods they had ordered were not what they should have; and (3) occasionally, some infighting among the ranks within the hierarchy resulted in cancellations. For instance, one senior buyer had some dispute with the junior buyer on another order placed by her, and instructed that all the orders placed by this buyer during that week be canceled!

Not Placing the Order after Inviting the President for the Purpose

In some cases where the president was invited but the order not placed, the problem situation arose because the buyers had not done their homework on time, and hence were not prepared to place the order on the day of the scheduled meeting. Such a state of unpreparedness usually happened at the level of the chief buyer, who happened to be very busy with other pressing work.

The Fungus Problem

One of the team members who has connections with scientists in the chemical and leather industries found that a particular type of wax prevented mold and mildew formation, and was used by packers in Europe. When applied thinly over furniture and leather goods and rubbed in thoroughly, the wax protects the items from fungus formation even when goods are exposed to moisture for long periods of time. The team member who spoke to the scientists was surprised that the efficacy of this product was not more widely publicized and known.

Conversations with the Vice President Regarding Reallocation of Responsibilities When a New Manager Is Recruited

One of the team members spent a week watching the operations of the Cradle of Indian Handcrafts. He obtained job descriptions for all the staff, and discussed with the VP the possible reallocation of duties when a new manager is hired. The agreed upon goal was to keep the system decentralized and to train the newcomer to take on the responsibilities as an additional VP as business expands.

Two possibilities seemed feasible. One was to bifurcate the work and distribute the clients equally between the VP and the newcomer. The second was to place the new manager in charge of attending to matters regarding all shipments, issues that arise that relate to loading and unloading at the docks, and bill collections. The VP would be in charge of client relations, overseeing and tracking orders, and being in overall charge of operations.

In either case, one of the two assistants would help the VP and the other, the manager, with the flexibility of both attending to either, as required by the exigencies of the circumstances.

The first approach, while it helps the newcomer to take on executive responsibilities right from the start, also makes the line of authority rather fuzzy. Also, more of the VP's time, which is already stretched to its limits, will be taken up in training the new recruit in *all* aspects of the company's operations.

The advantage of the second approach is that it establishes clear lines of authority without centralizing the system. However, the training and development of the newcomer will be delayed, as the individual will have to learn the entire realm of operations by watching and seeking answers to questions.

Given all this, the team member considered that a slow, step-by-step introduction to the company's operations will help the new entrant to get acclimatized to the environment without getting unduly overwhelmed. The better the prior work experience of the newcomer, the faster will be the learning curve. In due course of time, say over the next year, the individual can take over the full responsibility of dealing with half of the clients.

List of the Team's Recommendations

On David's return from India, the team members exchanged notes and agreed upon the following list of recommendations with respect to each of the previously identified items, to be included in their report to the president of the Cradle of Indian Handcrafts.

The Client System

Cancellation of Orders

Revise company policy to state that contracts for orders placed should be signed by both the chief buyer and the vice president in charge of purchases. This is most likely to ensure noncancellation, since the signature of the VP will carry with it the moral obligation to honor commitments.

Not Placing Orders after Inviting the President for the Purpose

To avoid unfruitful trips, telephone confirmation of the meeting should be obtained directly from the chief buyer, 3 working days before the scheduled meeting. If, at this time, the party at the other end happens not to be quite prepared, or is likely to remain unprepared until the meeting date, this gives them a chance to postpone the meeting or expedite the necessary preparations. A follow-up telephone reminder of the meeting can again be given a day prior to the departure date. This would be particularly necessary in the case of those who have been unprepared in the past.

Delays in Deliveries by Artisans

By installing an automatic tracking system, whereby each artisan's progress is monitored on a weekly basis, the production schedules should be kept on track, and on-time deliveries ensured. To ensure adherence to the schedules, an incentive of Rs. 1,000 (about $20, as per existing exchange rate) should be offered to artisans, each time they deliver their assigned products on time. This would entail an additional annual expenditure of Rs. 4,000 per artisan (Rs. 1,000 × 4 delivery periods during the year). The annual maximum recurring expenditure on this account for payment to artisans will be more than amply recovered through timely sales of goods readily accepted, and increased orders placed because of enhanced customer satisfaction.

Delays Due to Customs Inspections

Things move slowly in government offices. The president of Cradle of Indian Handcrafts should continue to pursue her application with the officials in the Central Ministry vigorously, not only through her office manager in India (in addition to her personal contacts while in India), but also through international telephone calls and faxes by her U.S. office. It is expected that sooner or later the application would be approved, and surprise checks of shipments by customs officials would result in minimal shipment delays from India.

Protection of Goods from Fungus Formation

The special wax stated to be effective, yet not widely publicized and hence not known, should be used on all articles susceptible to mold and mildew build-up before the goods are packed in boxes for shipment from India. Even if the stored boxes lie in the docks for a long time awaiting shipment, the materials will remain in good condition.

In addition, a new packaging system should be introduced where all fragile handicrafts are wrapped in bubble and shrink-wrapped to protect them in transit. More careful packing with appropriate and heavier packing materials, and using the wax as indicated, will reduce rejections on account of damages to goods.

Reallocation of Duties and Responsibilities When the New Manager Is Hired

Based on the logic noted earlier, the recommendation made is to initially assign to the new manager the following job responsibilities: shipments, attending to all dock-related matters, billing, bill collections, and such other matters as the vice president feels need to be done.

This arrangement is suggested to establish a clear line of authority, while at the same time, keeping the system as decentralized as possible. This will also facilitate executive development in easy stages.

After the first or second year, the accounts of the clients can be divided equally between the VP and the manager. At this time, a team approach to management will prevail, with both the VP and the manager reporting directly to the president.

Having summarized the points, the three members of the team began to write up the report, each working on the part investigated by him.

ASSESSMENT OF THE QUALITY OF THE RESEARCH DONE

Given the above details, let us look at the type and quality of research that was done by the research team of Solutions Consulting Company. Let us also examine to what extent the study meets the criteria of scientific research, and to what extent it facilitates decision making for the president.

Nature of the Investigation

Cradle of Indian Handcrafts is a small organization where problem identification does not involve a cumbersome process. By interviewing the president and the vice president in depth, and talking to the two assistants, the team was able to pinpoint the problem areas fairly quickly. They also clearly delineated the specific issues to be studied. Thus, the problem identification part of the investigation was done right. But, since the investigation had international dimensions, and since the Indian culture is so completely different from the culture of the investigators, it was also a difficult study to conduct.

A qualitative study such as the one conducted was a good way to go about finding solutions to the issues facing the organizations. The business is small in terms of both the number of staff members and the clients (about 130 organizations). Looking at the volume of business generated and the growing profits of Cradle of Indian Handcrafts, it is obvious that the president's strategy of resorting to obtaining bulk orders from a limited number of high-end volume customers—the museums and the specialty stores—is a wise one. Since there is not much competition in this specialized "handcrafts design" field, Sekar is able to keep the business small and still have a highly profitable organization.

It is necessary to examine the work done in India and in the United States separately, to assess the quality of the research done in each area.

Investigations in India

Information had to be obtained from the local manager in India, the Indian customs officials, and from a sample of Indian artisans. It became quite clear that gaining access to the *customs officials* even for a short conversation was difficult. Hoping to obtain written responses to questions would have been wishful thinking. Under the circumstances, the researcher did the right thing in deciding to resort to interviewing as the only data collection mechanism.

Whether through systematic probing, or serendipity, the consultant found that approaching the Central Government officials might help minimize delays in inspection, which in turn, would speed up shipping. Whether the application made based on the suggestion of the consultant will bring forth the desired results or not remains to be seen. Perhaps the researcher could not have personally done much more in this area. The bureaucratic nature of the Indian system and its impenetrability are common knowledge. However, if the culture and values prevailing in the system were better understood some different approach could have been taken, as mentioned later.

Language barriers and unfamiliarity precluded obtaining useful responses from the *artisans*. Hence, the researcher had to come up with his own idea of how the delays in the delivery of the finished products could be avoided. He had to rely on the manager's suggestion that offering an incentive for timely work might accomplish the purpose—not a very scientific way of generating a solution to resolve the problem.

The information in David's handwritten notes of the several interviews with the *local manager in India* (in the Appendix) does not indicate any serious problems experienced by the Indian manager, excepting for missed shipment dates due to delays by artisans, and the unpredictable tardy inspections by customs. Noteworthy, however, is the absence of specification of a method for the Indian manager to develop individual work schedules, and a system to monitor their work progress on a frequent basis. This aspect does not seem to have received much attention.

In sum, the researcher did the right thing in resorting to interviewing as the data collection mode. But his solutions were not generated from purposeful interviews because he operated in a foreign culture that was perplexing to him and defied his understanding. Hence, his recommendations were based more on hunches than facts. His investigation cannot be called scientific.

Investigations in the United States

Information relating to three different issues was collected in the United States. One pertained to the clients who refused to accept some shipments for no apparent reason. The second related to those clients who would not place the purchase orders on the scheduled dates after the president was invited for the purpose. The third pertained to the matter of the fungus problem that resulted in returned goods.

The last problem relating to fungus seems to have been intelligently resolved, entailing minimal effort and expenditure of resources. Knowing the right sources of information in the right organizations is definitely an asset in research endeavors!

It would seem that interviewing a sample of 9 out of the total of 16 client organizations who refused to accept orders, and a sample of 6 of a total of 12 organizations that failed to place orders, was ample. The stratified sampling design used, based on the regional location of the organizations, also seems appropriate. Those client organizations that were in San Francisco, as well as those within a 100-mile radius, were personally interviewed, and those located in different regions of the country were surveyed by telephone. Interviews were also conducted with buyers at different hierarchical levels in each of the organizations with respect to both of the issues investigated.

From the interview questions (to be appended to the report), it would seem that the questions asked were on target. Whether or not the telephone interviews were appropriate for obtaining answers to such a delicate matter is, however, a moot point.

HOW SCIENTIFIC IS THIS STUDY?

If we consider the seven hallmarks of science listed and discussed in Chapter 2, this research investigation, as is generally the case with qualitative studies, does at best meet only the criteria of purposiveness and parsimony. It does not meet the criteria of *testability* (because this is not in the nature of a hypothesis testing study), *replicability* (since there is no database to repeat the results), *accuracy and precision* (because no statistical tests were done), *objectivity* (due to the fact that some of the conclusions are drawn from intuitive solutions), and *rigor* (since no scientific research design was possible to be attempted).

Does this, then, make the study useless? No, because, as we had noted earlier in various parts of the book, this kind of a qualitative study does point out solutions to remedy some of the problems (as it did in this study), though to what extent the solutions will be effective can be judged only after implementation. Several qualitative studies attempting to find answers to similar type of problems will form the basis for future theory formulation and hypothesis testing. Thus, qualitative studies have their place in scientific investigations.

WHAT ELSE COULD HAVE BEEN DONE?

Let us see if anything else could have been done to improve the quality of the study that would have enhanced its value a little more. The following seem to be some aspects that might have been useful to this investigation. We will first deal with the domestic part and then the international part of the study.

Domestic

1. It would have been better if some unstructured and structured interviews had been first conducted with a sample of the total of 132 U.S. clients across the country, to find out what *they* thought of and wanted from the Cradle of Indian Handcrafts. The more focused, problem-centered interviews could have followed later.

2. Based on the information gained through the unstructured and structured preliminary interviews, if considered necessary, a questionnaire survey could have also been done. This would have provided hard data on matters of concern to the client system. Such knowledge would be useful to enhance the effectiveness of the business operations, as well as to enhance client satisfaction.

3. It would have been preferable to have had personal rather than telephone interviews with the clients located in different regions who had rejected big shipments. The information in the appendix indicates that all the eight clients were residents of either Dallas, Texas, or Miami, Florida.

Telephone interviews serve the purpose while asking questions and seeking answers to certain types of topics. Responses to a delicate matter such as the one investigated would be better forthcoming in a face-to-face interview, where the verbal and nonverbal messages can be processed instantaneously by the researcher and appropriate follow-up questions posed.

India

4. As for the dialogue with the artisans in India, it would have been useful if the investigator had sought the help of a native researcher (there are plenty of

universities in and around New Delhi), while talking to the artisans. This would have facilitated comfortable interactions between the local artisans and the Indian researcher. By phrasing the questions in a way that relates to the experiences of the artisans, pertinent and useful information could have been obtained regarding the reasons for the delays in production by artisans. Better suggestions for taking corrective action could have then become possible. Establishing rapport, particularly while collecting data through interviews, is critical for obtaining good information from the interviewees.

5. Insofar as the investigation regarding customs inspection is concerned, the cultural nuances and politics of the situation were not taken into consideration. It would have been advisable to have approached the customs at the very beginning through one of the high level ministries entrusted with export promotion and who Anisha was familiar with. Later on, the services of a local agent who has frequent interactions with customs officials in the course of his operations should have been sought for follow-up of the application, and the job might have been quickly attended to.

The above is not relevant to the methodology, but to the politics of culture that a researcher needs to be sensitive to, particularly in a foreign country. The lesson is that when one who is not a native does research in a foreign country, it is always a good idea to link with another native researcher who knows the ropes. Problem solving would be easier and more effective that way.

HOW HAS THE RESEARCH FACILITATED THE DECISION-MAKING PROCESS FOR THE PRESIDENT OF CRADLE OF INDIAN HANDCRAFTS?

The president has to make decisions with respect to the following suggestions that will be highlighted in the report:

1. To change or not to change the current way of drafting the purchase contract, to include the signatures of both the chief buyer and the vice president of companies.

2. Should an incentive system be instituted for artisans who stick to their production schedules without any delays?

3. What should be done to expedite the approval for spot inspection from customs authorities in India?

4. Should she accept the recommended suggestion of treating goods with wax to avoid mold and mildew formation?

5. When she recruits another manager, how should the duties and responsibilities be reallocated?

The easiest decision will be with respect to item 4 above. The president would readily *accept and implement the recommendation* of treating susceptible goods with the special wax. Even if a mistake is made and the wax treatment does not work, not much expenditure would have been incurred. This particular remedy lends itself to immediate and easy implementation as well.

With regard to item 5, which is the next easiest to decide upon, the president would probably *accept the recommendation* of first giving the incoming manager limited responsibilities, and then entrusting the individual with the responsibility of handling the accounts of half of the clients. This would ensure relatively smooth transition with minimal disruption to the clients and the office.

The first item of changing the format of the purchase contract so that it includes the signature of both the chief buyer and the vice president, though apparently simple and useful, is ridden with political implications. The buyers may wonder why the change is now being made, the chief buyer may question and resent the change, and the vice presidents of the companies involved may not want to increase their workload. Under the circumstances, it would probably be best if the president first casually mentioned to the VPs the problem of the rejections after the orders are accepted, and obtain their informal reactions. She could subsequently determine how best to take care of the problem. As such, the president is *not likely to accept this recommendation.*

As for the second item of instituting an incentive system for the artisans, there may be no need to do this. The artisans are paid adequately, especially compared to the other village artisans and to the living standards in the area. If it is considered necessary to establish an incentive system, the president might consider motivating the artisans in other ways.

Given the president's philanthropic bent of mind toward furthering the progress of the families of the artisans, she may be more inclined to institute an incentive that could be tailored to the family needs of the artisans. For example, she might offer to bear the educational expenses of a child in the family, or finance the construction of a small house for the artisan and his family, when goods are produced and delivered on time over a period of a certain number of years. Such a scheme would serve the dual purpose of continuously keeping the artisans motivated, and helping their families to experience a better quality of life.

Before considering any alternative, the president is likely to elicit suggestions from the artisans themselves as to what would facilitate their adhering to schedules. Hence, this recommendation is also *not likely to be accepted.*

The third item of what she should do to get the quick approval of the customs is baffling. Maybe the best solution under the circumstance is to find an agent who is familiar with the rules and procedures of the system because of his constant dealings with export officials, and see what can be done about the application that has been submitted.

In this qualitative study, it would seem that two of the recommendations made by the consultants should be clearly acceptable to the president, and two others not. For yet another recommendation made, suggesting that the president should vigorously pursue her application with the customs, the politics of culture were not taken into consideration, and the solution offered was naive.

AN UPDATE ON THE CRADLE OF INDIAN HANDCRAFTS AT THE END OF 2001

The company is flourishing under Anisha Sekar's guidance, operating from the fourth and fifth floors of the mansion. The VP resigned for family reasons. Now a very competent general manager practically runs the business with the help of a staff of 10 who attend to orders, make shipments, maintain good customer relations, fight fires, and attend to all other related matters.

The company now has offices also in Egypt, Italy, and Taiwan, in addition to a full-fledged export office in India with a general manager and a contingent staff of six others—a spinoff of the expanded business in the past 2 years. The India office supervises the artisans, places production orders, and ensures quality control and strict adherence to the specification of the orders. It also attends to details connected with the shipment of goods, deals with the local customs, and oversees the payments related to the shipments.

The Cradle of Indian Handcrafts is a shining example of how an organization can benefit through research.

As we see, qualitative research can offer solutions but the manager has to engage in experience-based decision making to a greater extent than in the case of quantitative research. Since the solutions do not emanate from analyses of hard empirical data, one has to try different solutions, until the right one works! However, there is no alternative to qualitative research in some situations, as in the preceding case study. Gradual theory building can progress through successive qualitative studies on a given topic. This would later foster scientific hypothesis testing studies, which in turn will help to solve business problems.

A timely qualitative research analysis would have helped the second case study detailed below as well, but never got the chance to be studied.

CASE STUDY 2: CASE OF THE RISE AND FALL OF JOSUS APPAREL

Background of the Company

Joan Garcetta and Susan Meades formed a Sub Chapter S company with a small group of stockholders having limited liability and with less reporting requirements and responsibility than a regular corporation. The new entity named Josus Apparel was opened with much fanfare.

Both Joan and Susan were experienced in the apparel business, having worked in the corporate environment of a huge apparel retail company for a number of years. Both had developed extensive contacts in the apparel business and had gained business acumen in such matters as hiring the right people, setting employee goals, identifying critical markets, designing fashionable sportswear, deploying effective advertising strategies, and the like.

As per the requirements for a Sub Chapter S company, Joan Garcetta and Susan Meades installed a Board of Directors with five members. The Board was expected to meet at least once a month, and as circumstances warranted. Board members were known to the two owners while working in other organizations and were chosen primarily for their knowledge of the apparel business.

The First Year of the Company's Business

The first year of the company's business grossed over a million dollars, with a small profit for the company. By the end of the second year, the company had a turnover of more than two million dollars. The partners were very elated and congratulated themselves for having had the courage to take on the risk of starting a new venture, leaving the security of a steady job behind.

The Changing Scene

As business grew, Susan felt she had several ideas for enhancing the visibility of the company and considerably increasing its sales. When she expressed these thoughts to Joan, she was somewhat upset that Joan did not seem to fully appreciate her creative ideas. This resentment developed into full-fledged animosity as the months sped by and there was no change in Joan's attitude, who came across to Susan as more efficiency than effectiveness conscious. Susan decided to implement her ideas on her own initiative. She recruited new staff including marketers, designers, sellers, and other personnel to operationalize her dreams without consulting Joan. Not to be outdone, Joan created her own fiefdom, and the net result was that the two women were not talking to each other, and nobody was attending to the markdowns of slow-moving merchandise or ensuring that merchandise was received in time before customer preferences changed.

Trivial matters that should have been taken care of by the two owners now engaged the attention of the Board and had to be dealt with by them. Instead of mapping the strategic future of the company, the Board met several times to resolve mundane matters. The Board members became frustrated and were ready to quit.

The End of Josus Apparel

Before the end of the third year, the company had to fold due to sustained severe losses. What promised to be a bright future during the first year turned out to be the final year for the company even before the end of the third year.

As Susan Meades sat ruminating in her chair one cold rainy evening, she tried to assess what went wrong with the business. She had left a big corporation just 3 years previously because she had little opportunity for self-expression, individual creativity, and an outlet for her talents, not to mention that she was also fed up with the lack of trust and organizational politics inherent in a large system. She had started the apparel company with great expectations and enthusiasm, only to find that in less than 3 years everything went downhill. "If only Joan had been a little more appreciative and encouraging, things might have been different," she angrily muttered to herself.

For want of a simple qualitative analysis an organization was lost!

SUMMARY

After having gone through the different steps in the research process and research design of hypothetico-deductive studies, we came full circle in understanding and acknowledging the role of both qualitative and quantitative studies in research. We saw that every hypothetico-deductive study must have had its genesis in prior qualitative investigations. Hence we end this final chapter with the note that both qualitative and quantitative studies are integral parts of scientific investigations—each having its distinct role to play. In the ultimate analysis, the induction–deduction process is what leads to problem solving—an issue we examined at the beginning.

DISCUSSION QUESTIONS AND POINTS TO PONDER

1. Briefly describe a situation where, given the results of a hypothesis testing study, the manager has to extensively apply experience and common sense in making the final decision.

2. Which involves a more difficult decision-making situation for a manager—applying the results of a qualitative study or a hypothesis testing study? Why?

3. Describe, and depict through a diagram, the cycle of the research process, from the time when the area is investigated for the first time, to finding definitive answers to the problems encountered in that area.

4. In Case Study 2, what would you define the problem to be and what do you think are the factors that brought the company down? Offer a qualitative analysis of the situation.

A FINAL NOTE
TO THE STUDENT

If you have enjoyed learning about research and built up a repertoire of research skills, you are prepared and ready for your professional life. As you must have realized from the discussions in this book, research is an integral part of organizational reality that helps businesses to continuously improve and grow progressively. Though you may not have become an *expert* researcher after one semester of coursework, and perhaps a research project, I am sure you would have gained an intelligent appreciation of, and an adequate depth of knowledge for business research—great assets in dealing effectively with consultants. The ability to discriminate between the good and the not so good research will also be invaluable to you in sifting through the materials you will undoubtedly read in the practitioner and academic journals in your professional life as managers. And, more important, as you get deluged by all the information from various sources, including the Internet, newspapers, talk shows, and the like, you will be better able to evaluate the validity of the messages and judge them for what they truly represent. You are thus armed to handle the information overload that one faces in today's Information Age.

If you have satisfactorily met the following objectives, you can be confident that you have taken a giant step toward becoming even more effective as a manager:

- Developing a sensitivity to, and being able to identify, important variables operating in a particular situation.
- Being able to sense problems that may be surfacing from time to time in your environment.
- Being able to gather information quickly by asking appropriate questions of the right sources in an unbiased manner.
- Locating and being able to extract relevant information from published sources.
- Being able to clearly conceptualize the logical relationships among variables in any given situation.
- Becoming sensitive to sources of biases in both published articles and project reports given to you by consultants and researchers, and thus becoming a more discriminating and sophisticated consumer of research.
- Knowing which aspects of a study could be advantageously applied to a problem encountered in your own work situation.

- Recognizing the limitations of a research study, even though they may not have been enumerated in the report.
- Being able to carry out a small research project in an organization.

Research is the excitement of exploring avenues for problem solving, and as a manager you will find the research knowledge and skills you have now acquired to be extremely useful. Scientific research, when applied with good common sense, yields the desired results.

I wish you success in your personal, academic, and professional careers!

Uma Sekaran

A REFRESHER ON SOME STATISTICAL TERMS AND TESTS

TOPICS DISCUSSED

DESCRIPTIVE STATISTICS

- Frequencies
- Measures of Central Tendency and Dispersion
- Mean, Median, Mode
- Range, Variance, Standard Deviation, Interquartile Range

INFERENTIAL STATISTICS

- Pearson Correlation
- Relationship between Two Nominal Variables: χ^2 test
- Significant Mean Differences between Two Groups: t-Test
- Significant Mean Differences among More Than Two Groups: ANOVA
- Multiple Regression Analysis

OTHER MULTIVARIATE TESTS AND ANALYSES

- MANOVA
- Discriminant Analysis
- Factor Analysis, Cluster Analysis, Multidimensional Scaling

ANALYSIS OF QUALITATIVE DATA

MANAGERIAL RELEVANCE

CHAPTER OBJECTIVES

To many, the very mention of the word "statistics" might give the jitters. You might wonder when, if ever, you would use statistics in real life. But when you think about it, we do use statistics every day without our realizing it. For example, you might wonder how many hours a week, on average, you spend in reading a particular subject, what are the highest and lowest marks obtained by students on a specific exam, and where you stand in the class relative to others. You might even wonder if the time you spend and the effort you expend in studying for a particularly difficult class are worth it, considering the grades you get in that class. In answering each of these questions, you do indeed apply the concepts of central tendencies and dispersions, and correlations—all related to statistics!

Knowledge of the use of appropriate statistical tests in data analysis will prove to be a boon to managers in intelligently understanding the implications of the findings of a study conducted to solve a problem. *The purpose of this chapter is to refresh your memory about the various terms and statistical tests that you might have studied earlier,* without getting into the details of derivation of formulas. After reading this chapter, you should be able to explain what types of analyses are appropriate, under what conditions, and for what objectives. This will help you to follow with relative ease the data analyses discussed in Chapter 12.

In research, we seek scientific data, which on analysis, provide answers to the research questions. *Data* refer to the available raw information gathered through interviews, questionnaires, observations, or secondary databases. By organizing the data in some fashion, analyzing them, and making sense of the results, we find the answers we seek.

In most organizational research, at the very minimum, it is of interest to know how frequently certain phenomena occur (frequencies), and the mean or average score of a set of data collected, as well as the extent of variability in the set (i.e., the central tendencies and dispersions of the dependent and independent variables). These are known as **descriptive statistics** (statistics that describe the phenomena of interest). Beyond this, we might want to know how variables relate to one another, whether there are any differences between two or more groups, and the like. These are called **inferential statistics** (i.e., statistical results that let us draw inferences from a sample to the population, as discussed in Chapter 11). Inferential statistics can be categorized as **parametric** or **nonparametric.** The use of parametric statistics is based on the assumption that the population from which the sample is drawn is normally distributed and data are collected on an interval or ratio scale. Nonparametric statistics, on the other hand, make no explicit assumption regarding the normality of distribution in the population and are used when the data are collected on a nominal or ordinal scale.

Both descriptive and inferential statistics can be obtained by using PC software programs designed to enter data, edit and analyze them, and produce results for various types of data analyses. Programs such as SPSS, SAS, MINITAB, Excel, and others, are used in social science research. Before discussing data analysis, it would be useful to quickly refresh your memory regarding some of the statistical concepts and their applications.

We will very briefly explain some of the terms and tests such as **frequencies, measures of central tendencies and dispersions, correlation, *t*-test, regression analysis**, and the like. The idea is to give an overview of these and their relevance, rather than offer a tutorial in statistical formulas and interpretations, which you might have studied earlier in a course on statistics.

DESCRIPTIVE STATISTICS

Descriptive statistics involve transformation of raw data into a form that would provide information to describe a set of factors in a situation. This is done through ordering and manipulation of the raw data collected. Descriptive statistics are provided by frequencies, measures of central tendency, and dispersion. These are now described.

Frequencies

Frequencies simply refer to the number of times various subcategories of a certain phenomenon occurs, from which the percentage and the cumulative percentage of their occurrence can be easily calculated. An example will make this clear. Let us say the president of a company wants to know how many African Americans, Hispanics, Asians, Whites, and "others" (subcategories of the phenomenon "employees") are on its payroll. A frequency count of these distinct subcategories of employees would provide the answer and might look something like the figures in Table M 1.

The president now knows that there are 8 African Americans, 2 Hispanics, 6 Asians, 182 Whites, and 2 Native Americans (others) in the company. He also has the percentages and cumulative percentages for each category. This information can also be presented in the form of a **histogram** or a **bar chart.** If the president desires to have at least 10% African Americans without increasing the total number of employees, then at a minimum, 12 more African Americans have to be recruited, and a decision has to be made as to which 12 of the other employees should have their services terminated.

Other instances where frequency distributions would be useful are when (1) a marketing manager wants to know how many units (and what proportions or percentages) of each brand of coffee are sold in a particular region during a given period, (2) a tax consultant desires to keep count of the number of times different sizes of firms (small, medium, large) are audited by the IRS, and (3) the financial analyst wants to keep track of the number of times the shares of manufacturing, industrial, and utility companies lose or gain more than 10 points on the New York Stock Exchange over a 6-month period.

In all the foregoing cases, it may be noted that we desire to obtain the frequencies on a **nominally scaled** variable. That is, these variables will be grouped into various nonoverlapping subcategories, such as the different brands of coffee, sizes of firms, and types of companies. The number of occurrences

Table M 1

Frequency Distribution of Categories of Employees

Category	Frequency	Percent	Cumulative Percent
African Americans	8	4.0	4.0
Hispanics	2	1.0	5.0
Asians	6	3.0	8.0
Whites	182	91.0	99.0
Others (Native Americans, etc.)	2	1.0	100.0
Total	200	100.0	

under each category and their respective percentages will then be determined. In management research, frequencies are generally obtained for nominal variables such as gender and educational level.

Measures of Central Tendencies and Dispersion

It is often useful to describe a series of observations in a data set parsimoniously, and in a meaningful way, which would enable individuals to get an idea of, or "a feel" for, the basic characteristics of the data. Measures of central tendencies and dispersions enable us to achieve this goal. There are three measures of central tendencies: the **mean,** the **median,** and the **mode.** Measures of dispersion include the **range,** the **standard deviation,** and the **variance** (where the measure of central tendency is the mean), and the **interquartile range** (where the measure of central tendency is the median).

Measures of Central Tendency

The Mean. The mean or the *average* is a measure of central tendency that offers a general picture of the data without unnecessarily inundating one with each of the observations in a data set. For example, the production department might keep detailed records on how many units of a product are being produced each day. However, to estimate the raw materials inventory, all that the manager might want to know is how many units per month, *on an average,* the department has been producing over the past 6 months. This measure of central tendency, that is, the *mean,* might offer the manager a good idea of the quantity of materials that need to be stocked.

Likewise, a marketing manager might want to know how many cans of soup are being sold, *on an average,* each week, or a banker might be interested in the number of new accounts that are opened each month, *on an average.* The mean or average of a set of say, 10 observations, is the sum of the 10 individual observations divided by 10 (the total number of observations).

The Median. The median is the *central item* in a group of observations when they are arrayed in either an ascending or a descending order. Let us take an example to examine how the median is determined as a measure of central tendency. Let us say the annual salaries of nine employees in a department are $65,000, $30,000, $25,000, $64,000, $35,000, $63,000, $32,000, $60,000, and $61,000. The mean salary here works out to be about $48,333, but the median is $60,000. That is, when arrayed in the ascending order, the figures will be as follows: $25,000, $30,000, $32,000, $35,000, $60,000, $61,000, $63,000, $64,000, $65,000, and the figure in the middle is $60,000. If there are an even number of employees, then the median will be the average of the middle two salaries.

The Mode. In some cases, a set of observations would not lend itself to a meaningful representation through either the mean or the median, but can be signified by the *most frequently occurring phenomenon.* For instance, in a department where there are 10 White women, 24 White men, 3 African American women, and 2 Asian women, the most frequently occurring group—the **mode**—is the white men. Neither a mean nor a median is calculable or applicable in this case. There is also no way of indicating any measure of dispersion.

As is evident from the above, nominal data lend themselves to description only by the mode as a measure of central tendency. It is possible that a data set could contain bimodal observations. For example, using the foregoing scenario, there could also be 24 Asian men who are specially recruited for a project. Then we have two modes, the White men and the Asian men.

We have illustrated how the mean, median, and the mode can be useful measures of central tendencies, based on the type of data we have. We will now examine dispersions.

Measures of Dispersion

Apart from knowing that the measure of central tendency is the mean, median, or mode (depending on the type of available data), one would also like to know about the variability that exists in a set of observations. Like the measure of central tendency, the measure of dispersion is also unique to nominal and interval data.

Two sets of data might have the same mean, but the dispersions could be different. For example, if Company A sold 30, 40, and 50 units of a product during the months of April, May, and June, respectively, and Company B sold 10, 40, and 70 units during the same period, the average units sold per month by both companies is the same—40 units—but the variability or the *dispersion* in the latter company is larger.

The three measurements of dispersion connected with the mean are the range, the variance, and the standard deviation, which are explained below.

Range. Range refers to the extreme values in a set of observations. The range is between 30 and 50 for Company A (a dispersion of 20 units), while the range is between 10 and 70 units (a dispersion of 60 units) for Company B. Another more useful measure of dispersion is the variance.

Variance. The variance is calculated by subtracting the mean from each of the observations in the data set, taking the square of this difference, and dividing the total of these by the number of observations. In the above example, the variance for each of the two companies is:

$$\text{Variance for Company A} = \frac{(30 - 40)^2 + (40 - 40)^2 + (50 - 40)^2}{3} = 66.7$$

$$\text{Variance for Company B} = \frac{(10 - 40)^2 + (40 - 40)^2 + (70 - 40)^2}{3} = 600$$

As we can see, the variance is much larger in Company B than Company A. It makes it more difficult for the manager of Company B to estimate how much goods to stock than it is for the manager of Company A. Thus, variance gives an indication of how dispersed the data in a data set are.

Standard Deviation. The standard deviation, which is another measure of dispersion for interval and ratio scaled data, offers an index of the spread of a distribution or the variability in the data. It is a very commonly used measure of dispersion, and is simply the square root of the variance. In the case of the above two companies, the standard deviation for Companies A and B would be $\sqrt{66.7}$ and $\sqrt{600}$ or 8.167 and 24.495, respectively.

The mean and standard deviation are the most common descriptive statistics. The standard deviation, in conjunction with the mean, is a very useful tool because of the following statistical rules, in a normal distribution:

1. Practically all observations fall within three standard deviations of the average or the mean.
2. More than 90% of the observations are within two standard deviations of the mean.
3. More than half of the observations are within one standard deviation of the mean.

Applying this to the case of Companies A and B, what is indicated to the manager of Company A is that when the average is 40 units, and the standard deviation is 8.167, very simplistically (i.e., without calculating the standard error and taking into consideration the z score for the confidence level) he would need anywhere between 15 and 65 units for the next month [$40 \pm (3 \times 8.167)$]. In other words, in all probability, he would need no more than 65 units. For Company B, on the other hand, the demand could be as high as 114 units. The demand could vary anywhere between 0 and 114 [$40 \pm (3 \times 24.495)$]—a much wider spread.

As can be readily seen, if an estimate has to be made of the optimum number of units to be manufactured for the next month based on the 3 months' sales data, the manager of Company B will be in a greater predicament than that of Company A, even though both companies sold 40 units per month, on an average. Rather than try to estimate how many units should be produced based on the past 3 months' average, the manager of Company B might opt to trace the trends during the same months of the previous years and make them the basis of his estimation since there is so much variability in the sales!

In the foregoing example, the calculations of the **mean** (or the **average**) and the **standard deviation** were rendered possible since the observations pertained to values measured on a ratio scale—that is, they were not nominal or ordinal in nature. Whenever observations are measured either on an interval or a ratio scale, it is possible to calculate the mean. Refer to the discussion on scales and Figure 8.3 in Chapter 8, where the mean is shown to be appropriate as a measure of central tendency, and the variance and standard deviation are indicated as appropriate indicators of the dispersion, when either the interval or ratio scale is used as the basis of measurement.

Other Measures of Dispersion. When the *median* is the measure of central tendency, percentiles, deciles, and quartiles become meaningful. Just as the median divides the total realm of observations into two equal halves, the *quar-*

tile divides it into four equal parts, the *decile* into 10, and the *percentile* to 100 equal parts. The percentile is useful when huge masses of data, such as the GRE or GMAT scores, are handled. When the area of observations is divided into 100 equal parts, there are 99 percentile points. Any given score has a probability of .01 that it will fall in any one of those points. If John's score is in the 16th percentile, it indicates that 84% of those who took the exam scored better than he did, while 15% did worse.

Oftentimes we are interested in knowing where we stand in comparison to others—are we in the middle, in the upper 10 or 25%, or in the lower 20 or 25%, or where? For instance, if in a company-administered test, Mr. Chou scores 78 out of a total of 100 points, he would be unhappy if he were in the bottom 10% among his colleagues (the test-takers), but would be reasonably pleased if he were in the top 10%, despite the fact that his score remains the same. His standing in relation to the others can be determined by the central tendency median and the percentile he falls in.

The measure of dispersion for the median, the **interquartile range,** consists of the middle 50% of the observations (i.e., observations excluding the bottom and top 25% quartiles). The interquartile range could be very useful when comparisons are to be made among several groups. For instance, telephone companies can compare long-distance charges of customers in several areas by taking samples of customer bills from each of the cities to be compared. By plotting the first and third quartiles and comparing the median and the spread, they can get a good idea of where billings tend to be highest, to what extent customers vary in the frequency of use of long-distance calls, and so on. This is done by the box-and-whisker plot for each area. The box-and-whisker plot is a graphic device that portrays central tendencies, percentiles, and variability. A box is drawn extending from the first to the third quartile and lines are drawn from either side of the box to the extreme scores, as shown in Figure M 1a. Fig. M 1b has the median represented by a dot within each box. Side-by-side comparisons of the various plots clearly indicate the highest value, the range, and the spread for each area or city. For a fuller discussion on this, refer to Salvia (1990).

In sum, we have illustrated how the mean, median, and the mode can be useful measures of central tendencies, depending on the type of available data. Likewise, we have shown how the standard deviation (and variance, which is the square of standard deviation), and the interquartile range are useful measures of dispersion. Obviously, there is no measure of dispersion associated with the mode.

INFERENTIAL STATISTICS

Thus far, we have discussed descriptive statistics. Many times, however, we would be interested in inferential statistics. That is, we might be interested to know or infer from the data through analysis (1) the relationship between two variables (e.g., between advertisement and sales), (2) differences in a variable among different subgroups (e.g., whether women or men buy more of a product), (3) how several independent variables might explain the variance in a dependent variable

Figure M 1
(a) Box and whisker plot.
(b) Comparison of telephone bills in three Cities.

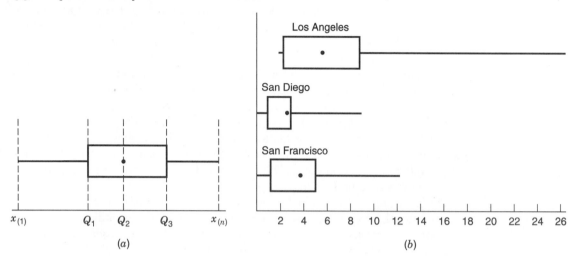

(a)   (b)

(e.g., how investments in the stock market are influenced by the level of unemployment, perceptions of the economy, disposable incomes, and dividend expectations). We will now discuss some of these inferential statistics.

Correlations

In a research project that includes several variables, beyond knowing the means and standard deviations of the dependent and independent variables, we would often like to know how one variable is related to another. That is, we would like to see the nature, direction, and significance of the *bivariate* relationships of the variables used in the study (that is, the relationship between any two variables among the variables tapped in the study). A Pearson correlation matrix will provide this information, that is, it will indicate the direction, strength, and significance of the bivariate relationships of all the variables in the study.

The correlation is derived by assessing the variations in one variable as another variable also varies. For the sake of simplicity, let us say we have collected data on two variables—price and sales—for two different products. The volume of sales at every price level can be plotted for each product, as shown in the scatter diagrams in Figure M 2a and M 2b.

Figure M 2b indicates a discernible pattern of how the two factors vary simultaneously (the trend of the scatter is that of a downward straight line), whereas Figure M 2a does not. Looking at the scatter diagram in Figure M 2b, it would seem there is a direct negative correlation between price and sales for this product. That is, as the price increases, the sale of the product drops consistently. Figure M 2a suggests no interpretable pattern for the other product. A correlation

Figure M 2
(a) Scatter diagram with no discernible pattern.
(b) Scatter diagram indicating a downward or negative slope.

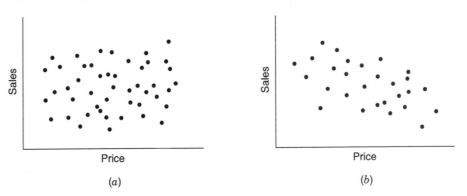

(a)   (b)

coefficient that indicates the strength and direction of the relationship can be computed by applying a formula that takes into consideration the two sets of fig-ures—in this case, different sales volume at different prices.

Theoretically, there could be a perfect positive correlation between two vari-ables, which is represented by 1.0 (plus 1), or a perfect negative correlation which would be − 1.0 (minus 1). However, neither of these will be found in real-ity when assessing correlations between any two variables expected to be dif-ferent from each other.

While the correlation could range between − 1.0 and + 1.0, we need to know if any correlation found between two variables is significant or not (i.e., if it has occurred solely by chance or if there is a high probability of its actual existence). As we know, a significance of $p = .05$ is the generally accepted conventional level in social science research. This indicates that 95 times out of 100, we can be sure that there is a true or significant correlation between the two variables, and there is only a 5% chance that the relationship does not truly exist. If there is a correlation of .56 (denoted as $r = .56$) between two variables A and B, with $p < .01$, then we know that there is a positive relationship between the two vari-ables and the probability of this not being true is 1% or less. That is, over 99% of the time we would expect this correlation to exist. The correlation of .56 also indicates that the variables would explain the variance in one another to the extent of 31.4% $(.56^2)$.

We would not know which variable *causes* which, but we would know that the two variables are associated with each other. Thus, a hypothesis that postu-lates a significant positive (or negative) relationship between two variables can be tested by examining the correlation between the two. A bivariate correlation analysis, which indicates the strength of relationship *(r)* between the two vari-ables, can be generated for variables measured on an interval or ratio scale.

Nonparametric tests are also available to assess the relationship between vari-ables not measured on an interval or ratio scale. Spearman's rank correlation and Kendall's rank correlation are used to examine relationships between two ordinal

Table M 2
Contingency Table of Skin Color and Job Type

	Job Type		
Skin Color	White Collar	Blue Collar	Total
White	30	5	35
Nonwhite	2	18	20
Total	32	23	55

variables. See Table M.3, which shows the different types of statistical analyses that data can be subjected to, when the independent and the dependent variables are measured on different scales.

Relationship Between Two Nominal Variables: χ^2 Test

We might sometimes want to know if there is a relationship between two nominal variables or whether they are independent of each other. As examples: (1) Is viewing television advertisement of a product (yes/no) related to buying that product by individuals (buy/don't buy)? (2) Is the type of job done by individuals (white-collar jobs vs. blue-collar jobs) a function of the color of their skin (white vs. nonwhite)? Such comparisons are possible by organizing data by groups or categories and seeing if there are any statistically significant relationships. For example, we might collect data from a sample of 55 individuals whose color of skin and nature of jobs, culled from a frequency count, might be illustrated as in Table M 2 in a two-by-two contingency table. Just by looking at Table M 2, a clear pattern seems to emerge that those who are White hold white-collar jobs. Only a few of the nonwhites hold white-collar jobs. Thus, there does seem to be a relationship between the color of the skin and the type of job handled; the two do not seem to be independent. This can be statistically confirmed by the chi-square (χ^2) test—a nonparametric test—which would indicate whether or not the observed pattern is due to chance. As we know, nonparametric tests are used when normality of distributions cannot be assumed as in nominal or ordinal data. The χ^2 test compares the expected frequency (based on probability) and the observed frequency, and the χ^2 statistic is obtained by the formula:

$$\chi^2 = \Sigma \frac{(O_i - E)^2}{E_i}$$

where χ^2 is the chi-square statistic; O_i is the observed frequency of the ith cell; and E_i is the expected frequency. The χ^2 statistic with its level of significance can be obtained for any set of nominal data through computer analysis.

Thus, in testing for differences in relationships among nominally scaled variables, the χ^2 (chi-square) statistic comes in handy. The null hypothesis would be set to state that there is no significant relationship between two variables (color of skin and nature of the job, in the above example), and the alternative hypothesis would be that there would be a significant relationship.

The chi-square statistic is associated with the degrees of freedom (*df*), which denotes whether or not a significant relationship exists between two nominal variables. Degrees of freedom is 1 (one) less than the number of cells in the columns and rows. If there are four cells (two in a column and two in a row), then the degree of freedom would be 1 [(2–1) × (2–1)]. The chi-square statistic for various *df* is provided in Table III at the end of the book.

χ^2 statistic can also be used for multiple levels of two nominal variables. For instance, one might be interested to know if four groups of employees—production, sales, marketing, and R & D personnel—react to a policy in four different ways (i.e., with no interest at all, with mild interest, moderate interest, and intense interest). Here the χ^2 value for the test of independence will be generated by cross-tabulating the data in 16 cells—that is, classifying the data in terms of the four groups of employees and the four categories of interest. The degrees of freedom here will be 9 [(4–1) (4–1)].

The χ^2 test of significance thus helps us to see whether or not two nominal variables are related. Besides the χ^2 test, other tests, such as the **Fisher exact probability test** and the **Cochran Q test** are used to determine the relationship between two nominally scaled variables.

Significant Mean Differences Between Two Groups: The t-Test

There are many instances when we would be interested to know whether two groups are different from each other on a particular interval-scaled or ratio-scaled variable of interest. For example, would men and women press their case for the introduction of flextime at the workplace to the same extent, or would their needs be different? Do MBAs perform better in organizational settings than business students with only a bachelor's degree? Do individuals in urban areas have a different investment pattern of their savings than those in semi-urban areas? Do CPAs perform better than non-CPAs in accounting tasks? To find answers to such questions, a *t*-test is done to see if there are any significant differences in the means for two groups in the variable of interest. That is, a **nominal** variable that is split into two subgroups (as for example, smokers and nonsmokers; employees in the marketing department and those in the accounting department; younger and older employees) is tested to see if there is a significant mean difference between the two split groups on a dependent variable, which is measured on an **interval** or **ratio** scale (as for instance, extent of well-being; pay; or comprehension level).

The *t*-test takes into consideration the means and standard deviations of the two groups on the variable and examines if the numerical difference in the means is significantly different from 0 (zero) as postulated in our null hypothesis. We examine this under **sample data and hypothesis testing** in Chapter 11.

When we compare the mean differences between two different groups on a variable, we do a *t*-test on two independent samples. We can also do a *t*-test to examine the differences in the same group before and after a treatment. For example, would a group of employees perform better *after* undergoing training than they did *before?* In this case, the formula for the *t*-test is adjusted to take into account correlation between the two scores, if any. In other words, the adjusted *t*-test for the matched sample or other type of dependent samples reflects the true mean differences.

Table II at the end of the book shows the *t* values, denoting the symmetrical bell-shaped distribution with mean = 0 and standard deviation = 1, for varying degrees of freedom [i.e., number of observations or the sample size less the number of constraints or $(n-1)$ *df*].

The Mann-Whitney U test is a nonparametric test for examining significant differences when the dependent variable is measured on an ordinal scale and the independent variable on a nominal scale.

Significant Mean Differences: Among Multiple Groups: ANOVA

Whereas the *t*-test would indicate whether or not there is a significant mean difference in a dependent variable between two groups, an **analysis of variance** (ANOVA) helps to examine the significant mean differences among more than two groups on an interval or ratio-scaled dependent variable. For example, would there be a significant difference in the amount of sales by the following four groups of salespersons: those who are sent to training schools; those who are given on-the-job training during field trips; those who have been tutored by the sales manager; and those who have had none of the above? Or would the rate of promotion be significantly different for those who have assigned mentors, choose their own mentors, and have no mentors in the organizational system?

The results of ANOVA show whether or not the means of the various groups are significantly different from one another, as indicated by the *F* statistic. The *F* statistic shows whether two sample variances differ from each other or are from the same population. The *F* distribution is a probability distribution of sample variances and the family of distributions changes with the changes in the sample size. Details of the *F* statistic may be seen in Table IV at the end of the book.

When significant mean differences among the groups are indicated by the *F* statistic, there is no way of knowing from the ANOVA results alone as to where they lie, that is, whether the significant difference is between Groups A and B, or between B and C, or A and C, and so on. It would therefore be unwise to use multiple *t*-tests, taking two groups at a time, because the greater the number of *t*-tests done, the lower the confidence we can place on results. For example, three *t*-tests done simultaneously decrease the confidence level from 95% to 86% $(.95)^3$. However, several tests, such as Scheffe's test, Duncan Multiple Range test, Tukey's test, and Student–Newman–Keul's test are available and can be used, as appropriate, to detect where exactly the mean differences lie.

The Kruskal–Wallis one-way analysis of variance is the nonparametric test used when the dependent variable is on an ordinal scale, and the independent variable is nominally scaled. Tables M 3 and M 4 provide information on the statistical techniques and tests used, as well the different nonparametric tests.

Table M 3

Statistical Techniques and Tests Classified According to Type, Number, and Measurement Scale of Variables[a]

			Criterion Variables					
			One			Two or More		
			Nominal	Ordinal	Interval	Nominal	Ordinal	Interval
Variates	One	Nominal	Chi-square test for independence Cochran Q test Fisher exact probability	Sign test Median test Mann-Whitney U test Kruskal-Wallis one-way analysis of variance	Analysis of variance			Multiple discriminant analysis
		Ordinal		Spearman's rank correlation Kendall's rank correlation	Analysis of variance with trend analysis			
	Two or More	Interval	Analysis of variance		Regression analysis	Analysis of variance		Multiple regression analysis
		Nominal		Friedman two-way analysis of variance	Analysis of variance (factorial design)			Analysis of variance
		Ordinal						
		Interval	Multiple discriminant analysis		Multiple regression analysis		Multiple discriminant analysis	Canonical correlation

[a] Adapted from R. L. Baker & R. E. Schultz (Eds.) *Instructional product research*. New York: Van Nostrand Co., 1972, p. 110.

Multiple Regression Analysis

Whereas the correlation coefficient r indicates the strength of relationship between two variables, it gives us no idea of how much of the variance in the dependent or criterion variable will be explained when several independent variables are theorized to *simultaneously* influence it. For example, when the variance in a dependent variable X (say performance) is expected to be explained by four independent variables, A, B, C, and D (say, pay, task difficulty, supervisory support, and organizational culture), it should be noted that

Table M 4
Use of Some Nonparametric Tests

Test	When Used	Function
Chi-square	With **nominal** data for one sample or two or more independent samples.	Tests for independence of variables.
Cochran Q	With more than two related samples measured on **nominal** scale.	Helps when data fall into two natural categories.
Fisher exact probability	With two independent samples measured on **nominal** scale.	More useful than χ^2 when expected frequencies are small.
Sign test	With two related samples measured on **ordinal** scale.	A good test for ranked data.
Median test	With one sample, to see if randomly drawn measurements are from a population with a specified median.	In a symmetric distribution, the mean and median will be the same.
Mann-Whitney U test	With two independent samples on **ordinal** data.	Analogue of the two independent sample t-tests.
Kruskal-Wallis one-way ANOVA	With more than two independent samples on an **ordinal** scale.	An alternative to one-way ANOVA where normality of distributions cannot be assumed.
Friedman two-way ANOVA	With more than two related samples on **ordinal** data.	A good alternative to two-way ANOVA where normality cannot be assumed.
Kolmogorov-Smirnov	With one sample or two independent samples measured on an **ordinal** scale.	Is a more powerful test than χ^2 or Mann-Whitney U.

not only are the four independent or predictor variables correlated to the dependent variable in varying degrees, but they might also be intercorrelated (i.e., among themselves). For example, task difficulty is likely to be related to supervisory support, pay might be correlated to task difficulty, and all three—task difficulty, supervisory support, and pay—might influence the organizational culture. When these variables are jointly regressed against the dependent variable in an effort to explain the variance in it, the individual correlations collapse into what is called a **multiple r** or multiple correlation. The square of multiple r, R-square or R^2 as it is commonly known, is the amount of variance explained in the dependent variable by the predictors. Such analysis, where more than one predictor is jointly regressed against the criterion variable, is known as **multiple regression** analysis. When the R-square value, the F statistic, and its significance level are known, we can interpret the results. For example, if the R^2 is .63 with an F value of say, 25.56, and a significance level of $p < .001$, then we can say that 63% of the variance has been significantly explained by the set of predictors. There is less than .001% chance of this not holding true.

In sum, multiple regression analysis is done to examine the simultaneous effects of several independent variables on a dependent variable that is interval scaled. In other words, multiple regression analysis aids in understanding how much of the variance in the dependent variable is explained by a set of predictors. If we want to know which among the set of predictors is the most important in explaining the variance, which the next, and so on, a stepwise multiple regression analysis can be done. If we want to know whether a set of job-related variables (e.g., job challenge, job variety, and job stress) would significantly *add* to the variance explained in the dependent variable (say, job satisfaction), over and above that explained by a set of organizational factors (e.g., participation in decision making, communication, supervisory relationship), a hierarchical regression analysis can be done.

Multiple regression analysis is also done to trace the sequential antecedents that *cause* the dependent variable through what is known as **path analysis.** As stated in an earlier chapter, this tracing of sequential antecedents is possible even in cross-sectional data. A detailed discussion of these types of analyses is beyond the scope of this book.

OTHER MULTIVARIATE TESTS AND ANALYSES

We will now briefly describe three multivariate techniques—**multivariate analysis of variance** (MANOVA), **discriminant analysis,** and **canonical correlations.** We will also describe, in brief, some of the other multivariate techniques, such as **factor analysis, cluster analysis,** and **multidimensional scaling.** Multivariate analyses examine several variables and their relationships simultaneously, in contrast to bivariate analyses which examine relationships between two variables, and univariate analyses where one variable at a time is examined for generalization from the sample to the population. The multivariate techniques are now presented superficially to enable you to have some idea of their use.

MANOVA is similar to ANOVA, with the difference that ANOVA tests the mean differences of more than two groups on *one* dependent variable, whereas MANOVA tests mean differences among groups across *several* dependent variables simultaneously, by using sums of squares and cross-product matrices. Just as multiple *t*-tests would bias the results (as explained earlier), multiple ANOVA tests, using one dependent variable at a time, would also bias the results, since the dependent variables are likely to be interrelated. MANOVA circumvents this bias by simultaneously testing all the dependent variables, cancelling out the effects of any intercorrelations among them.

In MANOVA tests, the independent variable is measured on a nominal scale and the dependent variables on an interval or ratio scale.

The null hypothesis tested by MANOVA is: $\mu_1 = \mu_2 = \mu_3 \ldots \mu_n$,

The alternate hypothesis is : $\mu_1 \neq \mu_2 \neq \mu_3 \neq \ldots \mu_n$.

Discriminant analysis helps to identify the independent variables that discriminate a nominally scaled dependent variable of interest—say those who are high on a variable from those who are low on it. The linear combination of independent variables indicates the discriminating function showing the large difference that exists in the two group means. In other words, the independent variables measured on an interval or ratio scale discriminate the groups of interest to the study.

Canonical correlation examines the relationship between two or more dependent variables and several independent variables; for example, the correlation between a set of job behaviors (such as engrossment in work, timely completion of work, and number of absences) and their influence on a set of performance factors (such as quality of work, the output, and rate of rejects). The focus here is on delineating the job behavior profiles associated with performance that result in high-quality production.

Other types of statistical analyses such as *factor analysis, cluster analysis,* and *multidimensional scaling* help us to understand how the variables under study form a pattern or structure, in contrast to focusing on predicting the dependent variable or tracing relationships.

Factor analysis helps to reduce a vast number of variables (for example, all the questions tapping several variables of interest in a questionnaire) to a meaningful, interpretable, and manageable set of factors. A principal-component analysis transforms all the variables into a set of composite variables that are not correlated to one another. Suppose we have measured in a questionnaire the four concepts of mental health, job satisfaction, life satisfaction, and job involvement, with 7 questions tapping each. When we factor analyze these 28 items, we should find four factors with the right variables loading on each factor, confirming that we have measured the concepts correctly.

Cluster analysis is used to classify objects or individuals into mutually exclusive and collectively exhaustive groups with high homogeneity within clusters and low homogeneity between clusters. In other words, cluster analysis helps to identify objects that are similar to one another, based on some specified criterion. For instance, if our sample consists of a mix of respondents with different brand preferences for a product, cluster analysis will cluster individuals by their preferences for each of the different brands.

Multidimensional scaling groups objects in multidimensional space. Objects that are perceived by respondents to be different are distanced, and the greater the perceptual differences, the greater the distance between the objects in the multidimensional space. In other words, multidimensional scaling provides a spatial portrayal of respondents' perception of products, services, or other items of interest, and highlights the perceived similarities and differences.

In sum, multivariate techniques such as MANOVA, discriminant analysis, and canonical correlation help us to analyze the influence of independent variables on the dependent variable in different ways. Other multivariate techniques such as factor analysis, cluster analysis, and multidimensional scaling offer meaningful insights into the data set by forming patterns of the data in one form or the other.

It is advantageous that several univariate, bivariate, and multivariate techniques are available to analyze sample data, so we can generalize the results obtained from the sample to the population at large. It is, however, important to pay attention to what each hypothesis is, and use the correct statistical technique to test it, rather than apply advanced inappropriate techniques.

ANALYSIS OF QUALITATIVE DATA

As we know, qualitative data can be obtained through many sources, prime among them being in-depth interviews, participant or nonparticipant observations, films and videotapes, projective tests, case studies, and documents and archival data. Description of the matter under study is the main essence of qualitative research and a range of interpretive techniques can be used to decode, translate, decipher patterns, and discover the meaning of phenomena that occur.

The data culled can be categorized and coded according to some meaningful classification scheme. Frequency counts can thereafter be taken, and χ^2 or other appropriate nonparametric tests done.

As an example, a manager might be concerned about the productivity at the workplace, especially since a diverse group of individuals work together. The researcher who assists the manager might want to know how people of different ethnic origins might perceive their White bosses. Would these individuals feel they are respected and treated well at the workplace, that they are not being stereotyped in different ways, and that the differences in ethnicity are valued rather than devalued? In addition, the researcher might want to know if they express any special needs based on their parenting status. For instance, women with infants and young children might like flextime or flexible workplace or part-time jobs, which might improve their productivity.

The researcher might talk to several employees about these issues, and make a note of the ethnic origin, parenthood status, and responses to a number of open-ended questions. These *interview data* may be later tabulated and coded, and then entered in the computer for nonparametric analysis. For example, if a Hispanic woman feels that communication with the boss is a problem for her, this could be coded as a communication concern. If an African American says that he is being discriminated against in the nature of the tasks assigned to him, then it could be coded under "discrimination/task," and so on. All the items coded, including the ethnic origin, parenthood status, and so on, can then be submitted for cross tabulation and a χ^2 test.

Table M 5 illustrates a tabulation of the responses obtained from 25 employees to the open-ended, unstructured interview, which posed the question: "What is your reaction to the computerized production system recently introduced?" Frequency counts can be obtained based on these tabulations and the applicable nonparametric tests used to interpret data.

When information is gathered from such sources as newspapers, journal articles, and audio and videotapes, it can be classified, tabulated, and analyzed to understand phenomena, explain them, or foretell future trends. Naisbitt's well-known

Table M 5

Tabulation of Qualitative Data Obtained from 25 Interviewees

Nature of Responses	Physical	Psychological	Substantive
Favorable	# Relieves physical exhaustion.	@ Don't have to worry about personal responsibility for meeting targets	* Production will increase.
	## Will reduce muscular pains.	@@ Mind is free to think about other things as well.	** Just-in-time systems can be easily incorporated.
	### Can sleep better at night.		+ Less supervision needed.
Unfavorable	$ Sedentary life not good for physical fitness.	x Sooner or later there will be layoffs.	& Will the heavy investment really pay off in the long run?
	= Muscles will get flabby.	xx I am not sure what I am now!	^ Maintenance costs can be very high.
		xxx Do I have to learn new things now? At my age will I be able to?	% Too much time will be spent on training—meantime, production will suffer.

Respondents	Respondents	Respondents
# 6, 8, 15, 22	@ 1, 11, 16, 17	* 4, 7, 10
## 8, 15, 19	@@ 3, 8, 9, 13, 16	** 7, 12, 18
### 6, 8, 15, 19	$ 2, 20, 24	+ 10, 12, 14, 5
	= 9	
x 1, 9, 21	& 10, 18, 25	Top Managers: 4, 7, 10
xx 2, 3, 22, 24	^ 4, 12, 18	Middle Managers: 12, 14, 18, 25
xxx 9, 23	% 7, 12, 14	Blue Collar: All the rest

forecast of the future (see *Megatrends*) could have been the result of engrossing himself in such an exercise. In analyzing qualitative information, the researcher engages in an in-depth probe and subjectively interprets the data in an effort to account for much of the variation in the phenomenon of interest.

Events, objects, persons, words, and syntax used in the various sources are frequently carefully analyzed for their content, from which several inferences are drawn and projections made for the future. Solutions for the rectification for some types of problems faced in organizations are also possible through content analysis of case studies, audio and videotape reviews, and such others.

Content analysis involves the quantification of the qualitative information obtained through a systematic analysis of the relevant information, thus providing a means for submitting it to statistical analysis. For example, a content analysis of the feedback on the effectiveness of different types of carefully manipulated media advertisements on TV, radio, newspaper, and web sites can be examined as to its efficacy on recall and subsequent purchase of a product. It is also possible to convert the qualitative data into interval-like data by developing some justifiable rational scheme, as per the following illustration.

Example M 1   Let us suppose that five open-ended questions are asked to understand how members feel about the organizational climate and we want to set up a numerical scale for the responses received for this variable. We may adopt the following categorization and coding scheme for the purpose.

1. If only one response is favorable, or if all responses are unfavorable, the variable might be categorized as the "organizational climate is experienced to be *very unsatisfactory*," and assigned code **1**;

2. If two of the five responses are favorable, the answer might be categorized as "the organizational climate is experienced as *unsatisfactory*" and assigned code **2**;

3. If three responses are favorable, the response might be categorized as "the organizational climate is experienced as neither satisfactory nor unsatisfactory," and assigned code **3**;

4. If four responses are favorable, the variable can be categorized as "the organizational climate is experienced as *satisfactory*" and coded as **4**; and

5. If all five responses are favorable, the response can be categorized as "the experienced organizational climate is *very satisfactory*" and the response coded as **5.**

These interval-like data can then be submitted for different kinds of parametric statistical analysis, as warranted, to find answers to the issues relating to the research.

In sum, while analyzing qualitative data, the notes transcribed are integrated and categorized under appropriate themes, the response categories then transformed into numbers, and subjected to appropriate data analyses. By using multiple methods such as interviewing, observing, and referring to information available with the company, the researcher establishes convergent validity and a sense of reliability for the data.

MANAGERIAL RELEVANCE

Managers make decisions every day, some of which are routine and some very critical for the organization. The ability to understand the different types of analyses as well as the probabilities associated with each projected outcome helps managers to take calculated risks (or avoid them), based on their own natural inclinations as well as the gravity of the problem situation. If, for instance, the manager decides that a significance level of .90 (or even .80) in the data analytic results is acceptable, then he or she is aware that the probability of making a wrong decision is 10% (or 20%). Such knowledge is extremely crucial for decision making on various matters of differing complexity and consequence.

Knowledge of analysis such as multiple regression reminds the manager that multiple factors influence outcomes and attention has to be paid to all the critical variables indicated by the results of the analysis. The manager also gains a new appreciation of a scientific, data-based information system that would lend itself to different types of analyses to solve problems in a sophisticated and reliable manner. More advanced multivariate analyses, when comprehended, offer managers valuable insights into developing strategies for organizational growth.

SUMMARY

We examined the use of descriptive statistics like the mean, median, and mode as measures of central tendency and the range, standard deviation, variance, and interquartile range as measures of dispersion. These descriptive statistics help managers to understand and describe the nature of the phenomena encountered in a situation, whether they relate to people, stocks, production, events, or any other feature of interest.

We also saw the need for generating frequency distributions in the case of some nominal demographic data, like educational level and number of organizations in which individuals have worked. Organizations might also like frequency distributions for certain types of occurrences such as machine breakdowns due to different specific reasons, or types of accounting errors made, or the investment portfolio during a given period.

While discussing inferential statistics, we examined (1) how correlational analysis can be done to test the relationship between two variables, (2) how χ^2 tests can detect whether two nominal variables are dependent or independent, (3) how to trace significant differences between two groups on a dependent variable, using the t-test, (4) how to trace differences among several groups, using ANOVA, and (5) how to explain and predict the variance in the dependent variable when multiple independent variables are theorized to influence it, using multiple regression analysis. We noted the roles of the χ^2, t, and F statistic as tests of significance for different types of data analyses. We also briefly described the use of multivariate analysis such as MANOVA, discriminant analysis, and canonical correlation. In addition, we saw that techniques such as factor analysis, cluster analysis, and multidimensional scaling help to detect patterns in the collected data.

We also examined how qualitative data are handled. A sophisticated categorization of the content under different heads—for example, under male and female responses as to how household finance is handled, which members of the family usually buy the necessities and luxury items, and so on—can open up a vista of ideas to financial institutions, retailers, service agencies, and others, to develop strategies. We also saw that development and adoption of a good and useful coding system using creative classification schemes can lead to valuable information that can foster further research.

Having recapitulated some statistical terms and tests, and refreshed our memory of these here, discussions on how the data are actually analyzed will become clearer and more easily understood.

DISCUSSION QUESTIONS

1. Which measures of central tendency and dispersion are appropriate in the following cases, and why?

   a. The ages of individuals who are grouped as follows:

Under 25	3
25–35	120
36–55	80
Over 55	22

b. The performance ratings (on a 100-point scale) given by the head of the department to the top six performers:

Top scorer   87%

Second   82%

Third   81%

Fourth   76%

Fifth   74%

Sixth   68%

c. The weights of eight boxes of raw materials purchased:

275, 263, 298, 197, 275, 287, 263, and 243 pounds.

2. What is the chi-square test? State a research hypothesis (not in the examples given in the book) that would call for a χ^2 test.

3. If you want to know whether three groups of employees—those who have served the organization from 4 to 6 years, 7 to 9 years, and 10 to 12 years—are to be classified as different in the number of trips they have taken outside of the city on business work, what statistical test would you use and why?

4. Explain in your own words what multiple regression analysis is. Give an organizational situation that would call for the use of multiple regression analysis.

5. The vice president of Lucas International was perplexed by the rate of turnover in the company during the past 18 months or so. She suspected that three possible factors contributed to this—the lower salaries paid to staff compared to industry average, the location of the company, and the extent of bureaucracy that pervaded the system. She was not sure if there were any differences among the four categories of employees—managers, clerical staff, machine operators, and secretarial staff—in their intentions to quit in the next 6 months. "It would be helpful to know how many of each category of staff are currently in the organization, and to have a profile of their ages, educational qualifications, and experience with the organization," she thought. Furthermore, she wanted to know which of the employees were more disgruntled—the older or the younger. She put her assistant who had taken a course on research methods to work, to gather the necessary data and give her the needed information.

Indicate the variables on which the assistant would gather data, and what kinds of analyses he will be submitting the data to, to submit a report to the VP. (It would help you to first list the information that the VP wants and then proceed with the exercise.)

GLOSSARY OF TERMS

Action Research A method of initiating change processes with an incremental focus, for narrowing the gap between desired and actual state.

Alternate Hypothesis An educated conjecture that sets the parameters that one expects to find. The alternate hypothesis is tested to see whether or not the null is to be rejected.

Ambiguous Questions Questions that are not clearly worded and likely to be interpreted by respondents in different ways.

Analytical Study A study that tries to explain why or how certain variables influence the dependent variable of interest to the researcher.

ANOVA Stands for Analysis of Variance, which tests for significant mean differences in variables among multiple groups.

Applied Research Research conducted in a particular setting with the specific objective of solving an existing problem in the situation.

Area Sampling Cluster sampling within a specified area or region; a probability sampling design.

Attitudinal Factors People's feelings, dispositions, and reactions toward the organization and factors in the work environment such as the work itself, the co-workers, or supervision.

Audit Capability Tracking functions built into software to obtain desired detailed information on actions or activities captured by the software, as for example, the number of times a web site has been visited, or a facility has been used.

Basic Research Research conducted to generate knowledge and understanding of phenomena (in the work setting) that would add to the existing body of knowledge (about organizations and management theory).

Behavioral Factors Actual behavior of employees on the job, such as being late, working hard, remaining absent, or quitting work.

Bias Any error that creeps into the data. Biases can be introduced by the researcher, the respondent, the measuring instrument, the sample, and so on.

Bibliography A listing of books, articles, and other relevant materials, alphabetized according to the last name of the authors, referencing the titles of their works, and indicating where they can be located.

Broad Problem Area A situation where one senses a possible need for research and problem solving, even though the specific problem is not clear.

Browser Software that facilitates viewing and navigating through web applications.

Case Study The documented history of noteworthy events that have taken place in a given institution.

Category Scale A scale that uses multiple items to seek a single response.

Causal Analysis Analysis done to detect cause-and-effect relationships between two or among more variables.

Causal Study A research study conducted to establish cause-and-effect relationships among variables.

Chi-Square Test A nonparametric test that establishes the independence or otherwise between two nominal variables.

Classification Data Personal information or demographic details of the respondents such as age, marital status, and educational level.

Closed Questions Questions with a clearly delineated set of alternatives that confine the respondents' choice to one of them.

Cluster Sampling A probability sampling design in which the sample comprises groups or chunks of elements with intragroup heterogeneity and intergroup homogeneity.

Comparative Scale A scale that provides a benchmark or point of reference to assess attitudes, opinions, and the like.

Comparative Study A study conducted by collecting data from several settings or organizations.

Complex Probability Sampling Several probability sampling designs (such as systematic and stratified random), which offer an alternative to the cumbersome, simple random sampling design.

Computer-Assisted Telephone Interviews (CATI) Interviews in which questions are prompted onto a PC monitor that is networked into the telephone system, to which respondents provide their answers.

Concurrent Validity Relates to criterion-related validity, which is established at the same time the test is administered.

Confidence The probability estimate of how much reliance can be placed on the findings; the usual accepted level of confidence in social science research is 95%.

Consensus Scale A scale developed through consensus or the unanimous agreement of a panel of judges as to the items that measure a concept.

Constant Sum Rating Scale A scale where the respondents distribute a fixed number of points across several items.

Construct Validity Testifies to how well the results obtained from the use of the measure fit the theories around which the test was designed.

Content Validity Establishes the representative sampling of a whole set of items that measures a concept, and reflects how well the dimensions and elements thereof are delineated.

Contextual Factors Factors relating to the organization under study such as the background and environment of the organization, including its origin and purpose, size, resources, financial standing, and the like.

Contrived Setting An artificially created or "lab" environment in which research is conducted.

Control Group The group that is not exposed to any treatment in an experiment.

Controlled Variable Any exogenous or extraneous variable that could contaminate the cause-and-effect relationship, but the effects of which can be controlled through the process either of matching or randomization.

Convenience Sampling A nonprobability sampling design in which information or data for the research are gathered from members of the population conveniently accessible to the researcher.

Convergent Validity That which is established when the scores obtained by two different instruments measuring the same concept, or by measuring the concept by two different methods, are highly correlated.

Correlational Analysis Analysis done to trace the mutual influence of variables on one another.

Correlational Study A research study conducted to identify the important factors associated with the variables of interest.

Criterion-Related Validity That which is established when the measure differentiates individuals on a criterion that it is expected to predict.

Criterion Variable The variable of primary interest to the study, also known as the dependent variable.

Cross-Cultural Research Studies done across two or more cultures to understand, describe, analyze, or predict phenomena.

Cross-Sectional Study A research study for which data are gathered just once (stretched though it may be over a period of days, weeks, or months) to answer the research question.

Data Mining Helps to trace patterns and relationships in the data stored in the data warehouse.

Data Security/Surveillance All measures taken as a safeguard against threats to unauthorized access of data on the Internet.

Data Warehouse A central repository of all information gathered by the company.

Deduction The process of arriving at conclusions based on the interpretation of the meaning of the results of data analysis.

Dependent Variable *See* Criterion Variable.

Descriptive Statistics Statistics such as frequencies, the mean, and the standard deviation, which provide descriptive information of a set of data.

Descriptive Study A research study that describes the variables in a situation of interest to the researcher.

Dichotomous Scale Scale used to elicit a Yes/No response, or an answer to two different aspects of a concept.

Directional Hypothesis An educated conjecture as to the direction of the relationship, or differences among variables, which could be positive or negative, or more or less, respectively.

Discriminant Validity That which is established when two variables are theorized to be uncorrelated, and the scores obtained by measuring them are indeed empirically found to be so.

Disproportionate Stratified Random Sampling A probability sampling design that involves a procedure in which the number of sample subjects chosen from various strata is not directly proportionate to the total number of elements in the respective strata.

Double-Barreled Question Refers to the improper framing of a question that should be posed as two or more separate questions, so that the respondent can give clear and unambiguous answers.

Double-Blind Study A study where neither the experimenter nor the subjects are aware as to who is given the real treatment and who the placebo.

Double Sampling A probability sampling design that involves the process of collecting information from a set of subjects twice—such as using a sample to collect preliminary information, and later using a subsample of the primary sample for more information.

Dynamic Panel Consists of a changing composition of members in a group who serve as the sample subjects for a research study conducted over an extended period of time.

Editing Data The process of going over the data and ensuring that they are complete and acceptable for data analysis.

Efficiency in Sampling Attained when the sampling design chosen either results in a cost reduction to the researcher or offers a greater degree of accuracy in terms of the sample size.

Electronic Mail (e-mail) The most useful of Internet services that allows one to send and receive messages from all over the world almost instantaneously.

Electronic Questionnaire Online questionnaire administered when the microcomputer is hooked up to computer networks.

Element A single member of the population.

Enterprise Resource Planning Integrated system solutions for standard business requirements for the enterprise, often supported by a single application package.

Ethics Code of conduct or expected societal norms of behavior.

Exogenous Variable A variable that exerts an influence on the cause and effect relationship between two variables in some way, and needs to be controlled.

Experimental Design A study design in which the researcher might create an artificial setting, control some variables, and manipulate the independent variable to establish cause-and-effect relationships.

Experimental Group The group exposed to a treatment in an experimental design.

Expert System An Inference Engine that uses stored knowledge and rules of if–then relationships to solve problems.

Exploratory Study A research study where very little knowledge or information is available on the subject under investigation.

Ex Post Facto Design Studying subjects who have already been exposed to a stimulus and comparing them to those not so exposed, so as to establish cause and effect relationships (in contrast to establishing cause-and-effect relationships by manipulating an independent variable in a lab or a field setting).

External Consultants Research experts outside the organization who are hired to study specific problems to find solutions.

External Validity The extent of generalizability of the results of a causal study to other field settings.

Faces Scale A particular representation of the graphic scale, depicting faces with expressions that range from smiling to sad.

Face-to-Face Interview Information gathering when both the interviewer and interviewee meet in person.

Face Validity An aspect of validity examining whether the item on the scale, on the face of it, reads as if it indeed measures that it is supposed to measure.

Factorial Validity That which indicates through the use of factor analytic techniques whether a test is a pure measure of some specific factor or dimension.

Focus Group A group consisting of 8 to 10 members randomly chosen, who discuss a product or any given topic for about 2 hours with a moderator present, so that their opinions can serve as the basis for further research.

Field Experiment An experiment done to detect cause-and-effect relationship in the natural environment in which events normally occur.

Field Study A study conducted in the natural setting with a minimal amount of researcher interference with the flow of events in the situation.

Fixed Rating Scale *See* Constant Sum Rating Scale.

Forced Choice Elicits the ranking of objects relative to one another.

Frequencies The number of times various subcategories of a phenomenon occur, from which the percentage and cumulative percentage of any occurrence can be calculated.

Fundamental Research *See* Basic Research.

Funneling Technique The questioning technique that consists of initially asking general and broad questions, and gradually narrowing the focous thereafter on more specific themes.

Generalizability The applicability of research findings in one setting to others.

Goodness of Measures Attests to the reliability and validity of measures.

Graphic Rating Scale A scale that graphically illustrates the responses that can be provided, rather than specifying any discrete response categories.

Group Videoconferencing Video transmittal technology that enables remote groups of people to participate in a conference using video cameras and monitors.

Groupware A software that enables teams on a network to work on joint projects and access data simultaneously.

History Effects A threat to the internal validity of the experimental results, when events unexpectedly occur while the experiment is in progress and contaminate the cause-and-effect relationship.

Hypothesis An educated conjecture about the logically developed relationship between two or more variables, expressed in the form of testable statements.

Hypothesis Testing A means of testing if the if–then statements generated from the theoretical framework hold true when subjected to rigorous examination.

Hypothetico-Deductive Method of Research A seven-step process of observing, preliminary data gathering, theorizing, hypothesizing, collecting further data, analyzing data, and interpreting the results to arrive at conclusions.

Independent Variable A variable that influences the dependent or criterion variable and accounts for (or explains) its variance.

Induction The process by which general propositions based on observed facts are established.

Inferential Statistics Statistics that help to establish relationships among variables and draw conclusions therefrom.

Information System The system that acquires, stores, and retrieves all relevant information for a specific group of functions (e.g., manufacturing information system).

Inkblot Tests A motivational research technique that uses colored patterns of inkblots to be interpreted by the subjects.

Instrumentation Effects The threat to internal validity in experimental designs caused by changes in the measuring instrument between the pretest and the posttest.

Interitem Consistency Reliability A test of the consistency of responses to all the items in a measure to establish that they hang together as a set.

Internal Consistency Homogeneity of the items in the measure that tap a construct.

Internal Consultants Research experts within the organization who investigate and find solutions to problems.

Internal Validity of Experiments Attests to the confidence that can be placed in the cause-and-effect relationship found in experimental designs.

Internet A vast network of computers connecting people and information worldwide.

Interrater Reliability The consistency of the judgment of several raters on how they see a phenomenon or interpret the activities in a situation.

Interval Scale A multipoint scale that taps the differences, the order, and the equality of the magnitude of the differences in the responses.

Intervening Variable A variable that surfaces as a function of the independent variable, and helps in conceptualizing and explaining the influence of the independent variable on the dependent variable.

Interviewing A data collection method in which the researcher asks for information verbally from the respondents.

Intranet A network that connects people and resources within the organization.

Itemized Rating Scale A scale that offers several categories of responses, out of which the respondent picks the one most relevant for answering the question.

Judgment Sampling A purposive, nonprobability sampling design in which the sample subject is chosen on the basis of the individual's ability to provide the type of special information needed by the researcher.

Lab Experiment An experimental design set up in an articially contrived setting where controls and manipulations are introduced to establish cause-and-effect relationships among variables of interest to the researcher.

Leading Questions Questions phrased in such a manner as to lead the respondent to give the answers that the researcher would like to obtain.

Likert Scale An interval scale that specifically uses the five anchors of *Strongly Disagree, Disagree, Neither Disagree nor Agree, Agree,* and *Strongly Agree.*

Literature Review The documentation of a comprehensive review of the published work from secondary sources of data in the areas of specific interest to the researcher.

Literature Survey *See* Literature Review.

Loaded Questions Questions that would elicit highly biased emotional responses from subjects.

Local Area Network (LAN) Computers in close proximity connected together, enabling people to share information, files, and other necessary materials.

Longitudinal Study A research study for which data are gathered at several points in time to answer a research question.

Management Information System (MIS) A generic term for information within an enterprise, facilitated by software and technology.

Manipulation How the researcher exposes the subjects to the independent variable to determine cause-and-effect relationships in experimental designs.

Matching A method of controlling known contaminating factors in experimental studies, by deliberately spreading them equally across the experimental and control groups, so as not to confound the cause-and-effect relationship.

Maturation Effects A threat to internal validity that is a function of the biological, psychological, and other processes taking place in the respondents as a result of the passage of time.

Mean The average of a set of figures.

Measure of Central Tendency Descriptive statistics of a *data set* such as the mean, median, or mode.

Measure of Dispersion The variability in a set of observations, represented by the range, variance, standard deviation, and the interquartile range.

Median The central item in a group of observations arranged in an ascending or descending order.

Mode The most frequently occurring number in a data set.

Moderating Variable A variable on which the relationship between two other variables is contingent. That is, if the moderating variable is present, the theorized relationship between the two variables will hold good, not otherwise.

Mortality The loss of research subjects during the course of the experiment, which confounds the cause-and-effect relationship.

Motivational Research A particular data gathering technique directed toward surfacing information, ideas, and thoughts that are not either easily verbalized, or remain at the unconscious level in the respondents.

Multiple Regression Analysis A statistical technique to predict the variance in the dependent variable by regressing the independent variables against it.

Multistage Cluster Sampling A probability sampling design that is a stratified sampling of clusters.

Nominal Scale A scale that categorizes individuals or objects into mutually exclusive and collectively exhaustive groups, and offers basic, categorical information on the variable of interest.

Noncontrived Setting Research conducted in the natural environment where activities take place in the normal manner (i.e., the field setting).

Nondirectional Hypothesis An educated conjecture of a relationship between two variables, the directionality of which cannot be guessed.

Nonparametric Statistics Statistics used to test hypotheses, when the population from which the sample is drawn cannot be assumed to be normally distributed.

Nonparticipant-Observer A researcher who collects observational data without becoming an integral part of the system.

Nonprobability Sampling A sampling design in which the elements in the population do not have a known or predetermined chance of being selected as sample subjects.

Nuisance Variable A variable that contaminates the cause-and-effect relationship.

Null Hypothesis The conjecture that postulates no differences or no relationship between or among variables.

Numerical Scale A scale with bipolar attributes with five points or seven points indicated on the scale.

Objectivity Interpretation of the results on the basis of the results of data analysis, as opposed to subjective or emotional interpretations.

Observational Survey Collection of data by observing people or events in the work environment and recording the information.

One-Shot-Study *See* Cross-Sectional Study.

Open-Ended Questions Questions that the respondent can answer in a free-flowing format without restricting the range of choices to a set of specific alternatives suggested by the researcher.

Operational Definition Definition of a construct in measurable terms by reducing it from its level of abstraction through the delineation of its dimensions and elements.

Operations Research A quantitative approach taken to analyze and solve problems of complexity.

Ordinal Scale A scale that not only categorizes the qualitative differences in the variable of interest, but also allows for the rank-ordering of these categories in a meaningful way.

Paired Comparisons Respondents choose between two objects at a time, with the process repeated with a small number of objects.

Panel Studies Studies conducted over a period of time to determine the effects of certain changes made in a situation, using a panel or group of subjects as the sample base.

Parallel-Form Reliability That form of reliability which is established when responses to two comparable sets of measures tapping the same construct are highly correlated.

Parametric Statistics Statistics used to test hypotheses when the population from which the sample is drawn is assumed to be normally distributed.

Parsimony Efficient explanation of the variance in the dependent variable of interest through the use of a smaller, rather than a larger number of independent variables.

Participant-Observer A researcher who collects observational data by becoming a member of the system from which data are collected.

Population The entire group of people, events, or things that the researcher desires to investigate.

Population Frame A listing of all the elements in the population from which the sample is drawn.

Posttest A test given to the subjects to measure the dependent variable after exposing them to a treatment.

Precision The degree of closeness of the estimated sample characteristics to the population parameters, determined by the extent of the variability of the sampling distribution of the sample mean.

Predictive Study A study that enables the prediction of the relationships among the variables in a particular situation.

Predictive Validity The ability of the measure to differentiate among individuals as to a criterion predicted for the future.

Predictor Variable *See* Independent Variable.

Pretest A test given to subjects to measure the dependent variable before exposing them to a treatment.

Pretesting Survey Questions Test of the understandability and appropriateness of the questions planned to be included in a regular survey, using a small number of respondents.

Primary Data Data collected firsthand for subsequent analysis to find solutions to the problem researched.

Probability Sampling The sampling design in which the elements of the population have some known chance or probability of being selected as sample subjects.

Problem Definition A precise, succinct statement of the question or issue that is to be investigated.

Problem Statement *See* Problem Definition.

Projective Methods Ways of eliciting responses difficult to obtain, otherwise than through such means as word association, sentence completion, and thematic apperception tests.

Proportionate Stratified Random Sampling A probability sampling design in which the number of sample subjects drawn from each stratum is proportionate to the total number of elements in the respective strata.

Purposiveness in Research The situation in which research is focused on solving a well-identified and defined problem, rather than aimlessly looking for answers to vague questions.

Purposive Sampling A nonprobability sampling design in which the required information is gathered from special or specific targets or groups of people on some rational basis.

Qualitative Data Data that are not immediately quantifiable unless they are coded and categorized in some way.

Qualitative Study Research involving analysis of data/information that are descriptive in nature and not readily quantifiable.

Questionnaire A preformulated written set of questions to which the respondent records the answers, usually within rather closely delineated alternatives.

Quota Sampling A form of purposive sampling in which a predetermined proportion of people from different subgroups is sampled.

Randomization The process of controlling the nuisance variables by randomly assigning members among the various experimental and control groups, so that the confounding variables are randomly distributed across all groups.

Range The spread in a set of numbers indicated by the difference in the two extreme values in the observations.

Ranking Scale Scale used to tap preferences between two or among more objects or items.

Rating Scale Scale with several responses categories that evaluate an object on a scale.

Ratio Scale A scale that has an absolute zero origin, and hence indicates not only the magnitude, but also the proportion of the differences.

Recall-Dependent Question Questions that elicit from the respondents information that involves recall of experiences from the past that may be hazy in their memory.

Reliability Attests to the consistency and stability of the measuring instrument.

Replicability The repeatability of similar results when identical research is conducted at different times or in different organizational settings.

Representativeness of the Sample The extent to which the sample that is selected possesses the same characteristics as the population from which it is drawn.

Research An organized, systematic, critical, scientific inquiry or investigation into a specific problem, undertaken with the objective of finding answers or solutions thereto.

Research Proposal A document that sets out the purpose of the study and the research design details of the investigation to be carried out by the researcher.

Researcher Interference The extent to which the person conducting the research interferes with the normal course of work at the study site.

Restricted Probability Designs *See* Complex Probability Sampling.

Rigor The theoretical and methodological precision adhered to in conducting research.

Sample A subset or subgroup of the population.

Sample Size The actual number of subjects chosen as a sample to represent the population characteristics.

Sampling The process of selecting items from the population so that the sample characteristics can be generalized to the population. Sampling involves both design choice and sample size decisions.

Scale A tool or mechanism by which individuals, events, or objects are distinguished on the variables of interest in the some meaningful way.

Scientific Investigation A step-by-step, logical, organized, and rigorous effort to solve problems.

Search Engine Software program designed to search and locate information through "keywords," typically in documents on the World Wide Web.

Secondary Data Data that have already been gathered by researchers, data published in statistical and other journals, and information available from any published or unpublished source available either within or outside the organization, all of which might be useful to the researcher.

Selection Effects The threat to internal validity that is a function of improper or unmatched selection of subjects for the experimental and control groups.

Semantic Differential Scale Usually a seven-point scale with bipolar attributes indicated at its extremes.

Simple Random Sampling A probability sampling design in which every single element in the population has a known and equal chance of being selected as a subject.

Simulation A model-building technique for assessing the possible effects of changes that might be introduced in a system.

Social Desirability The respondents' need to give socially or culturally acceptable responses to the questions posed by the researcher even if they are not true.

Software Technology that is capable of designing programs to meet the different computing needs of individuals and companies.

Solomon Four-Group Design The experimental design that sets up two experimental groups and two control groups, subjecting one experimental group and one control group to *both* the pretest and the posttest, and the other experimental group and control group to *only* the posttest.

Split-Half Reliability The correlation coefficient between one half of the items measuring a concept and the other half.

Stability of a Measure The ability of the measure to repeat the same results over time with low vulnerability to changes in the situation.

Standard Deviation A measure of dispersion for parametric data; the square root of the variance.

Stapel Scale A scale that measures both the direction and intensity of the attributes of a concept.

Static Panel A panel that consists of the same group of people serving as subjects over an extended period of time for a research study.

Statistical Regression The threat to internal validity that results when various groups in the study have been selected on the basis of their extreme (very high or very low) scores on some important variables.

Stratified Random Sampling A probability sampling design that first divides the population into meaningful, nonoverlapping subsets, and then randomly chooses the subjects from each subset.

Structural Variables Factors related to the form and design of the organization such as the roles and positions, communication channels, control systems, reward systems, and span of control.

Structured Interviews Interviews conducted by the researcher with a predetermined list of questions to be asked of the interviewee.

Structured Observational Studies Studies in which the researcher observes and notes specific activities and behavior that have been clearly delineated as important factors for observation, before the commencement of the study.

Subject A single member of the sample.

Synopsis A brief summary of the research study.

Systematic Sampling A probability sampling design that involves choosing every *n*th element in the population for the sample.

Technology Any mechanism that transforms inputs to outputs.

Telephone Interview The information-gathering method by which the interviewer asks the interviewee *over the telephone,* rather than face to face, for information needed for the research.

***t*-Test** A statistical test that establishes a significant mean difference in a variable between two groups.

Test–Retest Reliability A way of establishing the stability of the measuring instrument by correlating the scores obtained through its administration to the same set of respondents at two different points in time.

Testability The ability to subject the data collected to appropriate statistical tests, in order to substantiate or reject the hypotheses developed for the research study.

Testing Effects The distorting effects on the experimental results (the posttest scores) caused by the prior sensitization of the respondents to the instrument through the pretest.

Thematic Apperception Test (TAT) A projective test that requires the respondent to develop a story around a picture.

Theoretical Framework A logically developed, described, and explained network of associations among variables of interest to the research study.

Treatment The manipulation of the independent variable in experimental designs so as to determine its effects on a dependent variable of interest to the researcher.

Unbalanced Rating Scale An even-numbered scale that has no neutral point.

Unbiased Questions Questions posed in accordance with the principles of wording and measurement, and the right questioning technique, so as to elicit the least biased responses.

Unit of Analysis The level of aggregation of the data collected during data analysis.

Unobtrusive Measures Measurement of variables through data gathered from sources other than people, such as examination of birth and death records or count of the number of cigarette butts in the ashtray.

Unrestricted Probability Sampling *See* Simple Random Sampling.

Unstructured Interviews Interviews conducted with the primary purpose of identifying some important issues relevant to the problem situation, without prior preparation of a planned or predetermined sequence of questions.

Unstructured Observational Studies Studies in which the researcher observes and makes notes of almost all activities and behavior that occur in the situation without predetermining what particular variables will be of specific interest to the study.

Validity Evidence that the instrument, technique, or process used to measure a concept does indeed measure the intended concept.

Variable Anything that can take on differing or varying values.

Variance Indicates the dispersion of a variable in the data set, and is obtained by subtracting the mean from each of the observations, squaring the results, summing them, and dividing the total by the number of observations.

Web Site Site accessible on the Internet or Intranet, created by individuals and organizations for the purpose of sharing information.

Word Association A projective method of identifying respondents' attitudes and feelings by asking them to associate a specified word with the first thing that comes to their mind.

World Wide Web (The Web) A mass market means of communication, the web is a collection of standards and protocols used to access information available on the Internet.

REFERENCES

Abbott, C. C. (1966). *Basic research in finance: Needs and prospects*. Charlottesville, VA: University Press.

Abdel-khalik, A. R., & Ajinkya, B. B. (1979). *Empirical research in accounting: A methodological viewpoint*. Sarasota, FL: American Accounting Association.

American Psychological Association. (2001). *Publication Manual of the American Psychological Association* (4th ed.) Washington, DC.

Angell, R. C., & Freedman, R. (1966). The use of documents, records, census materials, and indices. In L. Festinger & D. Katz (Eds.), *Research methods in the behavioral sciences*. New York: Holt, Rinehart and Winston.

Baker, R. L., & Schutz, R. E. (Eds). (1972). *Instructional product research*. New York: Van Nostrand.

Balsley, H. L., & Clover, V. T. (1988). *Research for business decisions. Business research methods* (4th ed.). Columbus, OH: Publishing Horizons.

Barry, H. (1969). Cross-cultural research with matched pairs of societies. *Journal of Social Psychology, 79,* 25–33.

Bending, A. W. (1954). Transmitted information and the length of rating scales. *Journal of Experimental Psychology, 47,* 303–308.

Bentley, T. J., & Forkner, I. H. (1983). *Making information systems work for you: How to make better decisions using computer-generated information*. Englewood Cliffs, NJ: Prentice Hall.

Billings, R. S., & Wroten, S. P. (1978). Use of path analysis in industrial/organizational psychology: Criticisms and suggestions. *Journal of Applied Psychology, 63(6),* 677–688.

Blank, G. (1989, March 14). Finding the right statistic with statistical navigator. *PC Magazine,* p. 97.

Boot, J. C. G., & Cox, E. B. (1970). *Statistical analysis for managerial decisions*. New York: McGraw Hill.

Bordens, K. S., & Abbott, B. B. (1988). *Research design and methods: A process approach*. Mountain View, CA: Mayfield Publishing.

Brown, L. D., & Vasarhelyi, M. A. (1985). *Accounting research directory: The database of accounting literature*. New York: Markus Wiener Publishing.

Bruner, G. C., & Hensel, P. J. (1994). *Marketing scales handbook*. Chicago, IL.: American Marketing Association.

Campbell, A. A., & Katona, G. (1966). The sample survey: A technique for social science research. In L. Festinger & D. Katz (Eds.), *Research methods in the behavioral sciences*. New York: Holt, Rinehart and Winston.

Campbell, D. T. (1976). Psychometric theory. In M. D. Dunnette (Ed.), *Handbook of industrial and organizational psychology*. Chicago: Rand McNally.

Campbell, D. T., & Fiske, D. W. (1959). Convergent and discriminant validation by the multitrait–multimethod matrix. *Psychological Bulletin, 56,* 81–105.

Campbell, D. T., & Stanley, J. C. (1966). *Experimental and quasi-experimental designs for research.* Chicago: Rand-McNally.

Cannell, C. F., & Kahn, R. L. (1966). The collection of data by interviewing. In L. Festinger & D. Katz (Eds.), *Research methods in behavioral sciences.* New York: Holt, Rinehart and Winston.

Carlsmith, M., Ellsworth, P. C., & Aronson, E. (1976). *Methods of research in social psychology.* Reading, MA: Addison-Wesley.

Cattell, R. B. (1966). The scree test for the number of factors. *Multivariate Behavioral Research, 1,* 245–276.

Chein, L. (1959). An introduction to sampling. In C. Selltiz, M. Jahoda, M. Deutsch, & S. W. Cook (Eds.), *Research methods in social relations.* New York: Holt, Rinehart and Winston.

Chicago Manual of Style, 14th ed. (1993). Chicago: University of Chicago Press.

Churchill, G. A. (1987). *Marketing research: Methodological foundations.* Chicago: Dryden Press.

Clark, D., & Bank, D. (1998, April 8). Microsoft, Sony agree to work together to link consumer-electronic devices. *Wall Street Journal,* p. B6.

Cohen, J. (1969). *Statistical power analysis for the behavioral sciences.* New York: Academic Press.

Cohen, J. (1990). Things I have learned (so far). *American Psychologist,* 1304–1312.

Cook, T. D., & Campbell, D. T. (1979a). *Quasi-experimentation: Design and analysis issues for field settings.* Boston: Houghton-Mifflin.

Cook, T. D., & Campbell, D. T. (1979b). Four kinds of validity. In R. T. Mowday & R. M. Steers (Eds.), *Research in organizations: Issues and controversies.* Santa Monica, CA: Goodyear Publishing.

Coombs, C. H. (1966). Theory and methods of social measurement. In L. Festinger & D. Katz (Eds.), *Research methods in the behavioral sciences.* New York: Holt, Rinehart and Winston.

Cortada, J. W. (1996). *Information technology as business history: Issues in the history and Management of Computers.* Westport, CT: Greenwood Press.

Cronbach, L. J. (1946). Response sets and test validating. *Educational and Psychological Measurement, 6,* 475–494.

Cronbach, L. J. (1990). *Essentials of psychological testing* (5th ed.). New York: Harper & Row.

Cronin, M. J. (1998a, Feb. 2). Business secrets of the billion-dollar website. *Fortune,* p. 142.

Cronin, M. J. (1998b, March 30). Ford's Intranet success. *Fortune,* p. 158.

Crowne, D. P., & Marlowe, D. (1980). *The approval motive: Studies in evaluative dependence.* Westport, CT: Greenwood Press.

Davies, G. R., & Yoder, D. (1937). *Business statistics.* New York: John Wiley.

Davis, D., & Cosenza, R. M. (1988). *Business research for decision making* (2nd ed.). Boston: PWS-Kent Publishing.

Drenkow, G. (1987, April). Data acquisition software that adapts to your needs. *Research and Development,* pp. 84–87.

Edwards, A. L. (1957). *Manual for the Edwards personal preference schedule.* New York: Psychological Corporation.

Elmore, P. E., & Beggs, D. L. (1975). Salience of concepts and commitment to extreme judgements in response pattern of teachers. *Education, 95* (4), 325–334.

Emory, C. W. (1985). *Business research methods* (3rd ed.). Homewood, IL: Richard D. Irwin.

Express Computer. (1998, March 2). Data mining captures the imagination, p. 19.

Express Computer. (1998, May 11). Beyond microprocessors, p. 22.

Ferris, K. R. (1988). *Behavioral accounting research: A critical analysis.* Columbus, OH: Century VII Publishing.

Festinger, L. (1966). Laboratory experiments. In L. Festinger & D. Katz (Eds.), *Research methods in the behavioral sciences.* New York: Holt, Rinehart and Winston.

Festinger, L., & Katz, D. (1966). *Research methods in the behavioral sciences.* New York: Holt, Rinehart and Winston.

Fiedler, F. (1967). *A theory of leadership effectiveness.* New York: McGraw-Hill.

Fishbein, M. (1967). *Readings in attitude theory and measurement.* New York: John Wiley.

French, J. R. P. (1966). Experiments in field settings. In L. Festinger & D. Katz (Eds.), *Research methods in the behavioral sciences.* New York: Holt, Rinehart and Winston.

Garten, J. E. (1998, March 23). Why the global economy is here to stay. *Business Week,* p. 21.

Gaski, J. F., & Etzel, M. J. (1986, July). The index of consumer sentiment toward marketing. *Journal of Marketing, 50,* 71–81.

Glaser, B. G., & Strauss, A. L. (1967). *The discovery of grounded theory.* Chicago: Aldine.

Gorsuch, R. L. (1974). *Factor analysis.* Philadelphia: Saunders.

Gorsuch, R. L. (1983). *Factor analysis* (2nd ed.). Philadelphia: Saunders.

Green, P. E., Kedia, P. K., & Nikhil, R. S. (1985). *Electronic questionnaire design and analysis with CAPPA.* Palo Alto, CA: The Scientific Press.

Harnett, D. L., & Horrell, J. F. (1998). *Data, statistics, and decision models with Excel.* New York: John Wiley.

Hoel, P. G., & Jessen, R. J. (1971). *Basic statistics for business and economics.* New York: John Wiley.

Horst, P. (1968). *Personality: Measurement of dimensions.* San Francisco: Jossey-Bass.

Kanuk, L., & Berenson, C. (1975). Mail surveys and response rates: A literature review. *Journal of Marketing Research, 12,* 440–453.

Kaplan, A. (1979). *The conduct of inquiry: Methodology for behavioral science.* New York: Harper & Row.

Katz, D. (1966). *Research methods in the behavioral sciences.* New York: Holt, Rinehart and Winston.

Kelly, F. J., Beggs, D. L., McNeil, K. A., Eichelberger, T., & Lyon, J. (1969). *Research design in the behavioral sciences: Multiple regression approach.* Carbondale, IL: Southern Illinois University Press.

Kerlinger, R. N. (1986). *Foundations of behavioral research* (3rd ed.). New York: Holt, Rinehart and Winston.

Kidder, L. H., & Judd, C. H. (1986). *Research methods in social relations.* New York: Holt, Rinehart and Winston.

Kilmer, B., & Harnett, D. L. (1998). *KADDSTAT: Statistical analysis plug-in to Microsoft Excel.* New York: John Wiley.

Kirby, C. (2001, Oct. 23). Snail mail's loss could be e-mail's gain. *San Francisco Chronicle,* p. B1.

Kirk, R. E. (1982). *Experimental design: Procedures for the behavioral sciences.* Belmont, CA: Brooks/Cole.

Kish, L. (1965). *Survey sampling.* New York: John Wiley.

Kish, L. (1966). Selection of the sample. In L. Festinger & D. Katz (Eds.), *Research methods in the behavioral sciences.* New York: Holt, Rinehart and Winston.

Knechel, W. R. (1986). A simulation study of the relative effectiveness of alternative analytical review procedures. *Decision Sciences, 17* (3), 376–394.

Kornhauser, A., & Sheatsley, P. B. (1959). Questionnaire construction and interview procedure. In C. Sellitz, M. Jahoda, M. Deutsch, & S. W. Cook (Eds.), *Research methods in social relations.* New York: Holt, Rinehart and Winston.

Krejcie, R., & Morgan, D. (1970). Determining sample size for research activities. *Educational and Psychological Measurement, 30,* 607–610.

Kuder, G. F., & Richardson, M. W. (1937). The theory of the estimation of test reliability. *Psychometrika, 2,* 151–160.

Labaw, P. (1980). *Advanced questionnaire design.* Cambridge, MA: Abt Books.

Lazarsfeld, P. F. (1935). The art of asking why. *National Marketing Research, 1,* 26–38.

Leedy, P. D. (1985). *Practical research: Planning and design* (3rd ed.). New York: Macmillan Publishing.

Leshin, C. B. (1997). *Management on the World Wide Web.* Englewood Cliffs, NJ: Prentice Hall.

Likert, R. (1932). A technique for the measurement of attitudes. *Archives of Psychology,* No. 140.

Lombardo, M. L., McCall, M., & DeVries, D. L. (1983). *Looking glass.* Glenview, IL: Scott Foresman, Co.

Luconi, F. L., Malone, T. W., & Scott Morton, M. S. (1986). Expert systems: The next challenge for managers. *Sloan Management Review, 27* (4), 3–14.

Luftman, J. N. (1996). *Competing in the Information Age: Strategic alignment in practice.* New York: Oxford University Press.

Marascuilo, L. A., & McSweeney, M. (1977). *Nonparametric and distribution-free methods for the social sciences.* Monterey, CA: Brooks/Cole.

Martin, M. H. (1998, Feb. 2). Smart managing: Best practices, careers, and ideas. *Fortune,* p. 149.

McClave, J. T., & Benson, P. G. (1988). *Statistics for business and economics* (4th ed.). San Francisco: Dellen Publishing Co.

McNeil, K. A., Kelly, F. J., & McNeil, J. T. (1975). *Testing research hypotheses using multiple linear regression.* Carbondale, IL: Southern Illinois University Press.

Meltzer, M. E., (1981). *Information: The ultimate management resource.* New York: Amacom.

Merton, R. K., & Kendall, P. L. (1955). The focused interview. In P. F. Lazarsfeld & M. Rosenberg (Eds.), *The language of social research.* New York: The Free Press.

Mitchell, R. E. (1969). Survey materials collected in developing countries: Sampling, measurement, and interviewing obstacles to intra- and international comparisons. In J. Boddewyn (Ed.), *Comparative management and marketing,* (pp. 232–252). Glenview, IL: Scott, Foresman & Co.

Mittal, B., & Lassar, W. M. (1996). The role of personalization in service encounters. *Journal of Retailing, 72,* 95–109.

Muehling, D. D. (1987). An investigation of factors underlying attitude-toward-advertising-in-general. *Journal of Advertising, 16* (1), 32–40.

Murdick, P. G., & Cooper, D. R. (1982). *Business research: Concepts and guides.* Columbus, OH: Grid Publishing.

Namboodiri, N. K., Carter, L. F., & Blalock, H. M. (1975). *Applied multivariate analysis and experimental designs.* New York: McGraw-Hill.

Norusis, M. J. (1998). *SPSS 8.0 Guide to data analysis.* Englewood Cliffs, NJ: Prentice Hall.

Oppenheim, A. N. (1986). *Questionnaire design and attitude measurement.* Great Britain: Gower Publishing.

Osborn, R. N., & Vicars, W. M. (1976). Sex stereotypes: An artifact in leader behavior and subordinate satisfaction analysis? *Academy of Management Journal, 19,* 439–449.

Payne, S. L. (1951). *The art of asking questions.* Princeton, NJ: Princeton University Press.

Peak, H. (1966). Problems of objective observation. In L. Festinger & D. Katz (Eds.), *Research methods in the behavioral sciences.* New York: Holt, Rinehart and Winston.

Pedhazur, E. J. (1982). *Multiple regression in behavioral research: Explanation and prediction* (2nd ed.). New York: CBS College Publishing.

Pelosi, M. K., Sandifer, T. M., & Letkowski, J. J. (1998). *Doing statistics with Excel™ 97: Software instruction and exercise activity supplement.* New York: John Wiley.

Perrier, C., & Kalwarski, G. (1989, Oct. 30). Stimulating simulations: Technique shows relationship between risk, funding. *Pensions and Investment Age,* pp. 41–43.

Price, J. L. (1972). *Handbook of organizational measurement.* Lexington, MA: D. C. Heath.

Rao, C. R. (1973). *Linear statistical inference and its applications* (2nd ed). New York: John Wiley.

Resta, P. A. (1972). *The research report.* New York: American Book Co.

Riley, M. W., & Nelson, E. E. (1974). *Sociological observation: A strategy for new social knowledge.* New York: Basic Books.

Rizzo, J. R., House, R. J., & Lirtzman, S. L. (1970). Role conflict and role ambiguity in complex organizations. *Administrative Science Quarterly, 15,* 150–163.

Roscoe, J. T. (1975). *Fundamental research statistics for the behavioral sciences* (2nd ed.). New York: Holt, Rinehart and Winston.

Runkel, P. J., & McGrath, J. E. (1972). *Research on human behavior: A systematic guide to method.* New York: Holt, Rinehart and Winston.

Salvia, A. A. (1990). *Introduction to statistics.* Philadelphia: Saunders.

Schmitt, N. W., & Klimoski, R. J. (1991). *Research methods in human resources management.* Cincinnati, OH: South-Western Publishing.

Sekaran, U. (1983 Fall). Methodological and theoretical issues and advancements in cross-cultural research. *Journal of International Business,* 61–73.

Sekaran, U. (1986). *Dual-career families: Contemporary organizational and counseling issues.* San Francisco: Jossey-Bass.

Sekaran, U., & Martin, H. J. (1982, Spring/Summer). An examination of the psychometric properties of some commonly researched individual differences, job, and organizational variables in two cultures. *Journal of International Business Studies,* 51–66.

Sekaran, U., & Trafton, R. S. (1978). The dimensionality of jobs: Back to square one. *Twenty-fourth Midwest Academy of Management Proceedings,* 249–262.

Selltiz, C., Jahoda, M., Deutsch, M., & Cook, S. W. (1959). *Research methods in social relations* (rev. ed.). New York: Holt, Rinehart, and Winston.

Selitiz, C., Wrightsman, L. S., & Cook, S. W. (1981). *Research methods in social relations* (4th ed.). New York: Holt, Rinehart and Winston.

Shurter, R. L., Williamson, J. P., & Broehl, W. G., Jr. (1965). *Business research and report writing*. New York: McGraw-Hill.

Smith, C. B. (1981). *A guide to business research: Developing, conducting, and writing research projects*. Chicago, IL: Nelson-Hall.

Smith, P. C., Kendall, L., & Hulin, C. (1969). *The measurement of satisfaction in work and retirement*. Chicago: Rand McNally, 79–84.

Stern, N. B., & Stern, R. A. (1996). *Computing in the information age* (2nd ed.). New York: John Wiley & Sons.

Steufert, S., Pogash, R., & Piasecki, M. (1988). Simulation-based assessment of managerial competence: Reliability and validity. *Personnel Psychology, 41*(3), 537–557.

Stone, E. (1978). *Research methods in organizational behavior*. Santa Monica, CA: Goodyear Publishing.

Tomaski, E. A. (1970). *The computer revolution: The executive and the new information technology*. New York: Macmillan.

Turabian, K. L. (1996). *A manual for writers of term papers, theses, and dissertations,* (6th ed.). Revised by J. Grossman & A. Bennett. Chicago: University of Chicago Press.

Turban, E., McLean, E., & Wetherbe, J. (1998). *Informational technology for management: Making connections for strategic advantage*. New York: John Wiley.

Webb, E. J., Campbell, D. T., Schwartz, P. D., & Sechrest, L. (1966). *Unobtrusive measures: Non-reactive research in the social sciences*. Chicago, IL: Rand-McNally.

Wetherbe, J. C. (1983). *Computer-based information systems*. Englewood Cliffs, NJ: Prentice Hall.

White, J. K., & Ruh, P. A. (1973). Effects of personal values on the relationship between participation and job attitudes. *Administrative Science Quarterly, 18*(4), 506–514.

Wildstrom, S. H. (1998, Jan. 26). Web sites made simpler. *Business Week*.

Williams, C. T., & Wolfe, G. K. (1979). *Elements of research: A guide for writers*. Sherman Oaks, CA: Alfred Publishing.

Zetterberg, H. (1955). On axiomatic theories in sociology. In P. F. Lazarsfeld & M. Rosenberg (Eds.), *The language of social research*. New York: The Free Press.

STATISTICAL TABLES

Table I
Cumulative Normal Probabilities

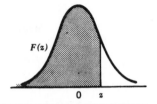

$F(z)$

z	$F(z)$	z	$F(z)$	z	$F(z)$
.00	.5000000	.30	.6179114	.60	.7257469
.01	.5039894	.31	.6217195	.61	.7290691
.02	.5079783	.32	.6255158	.62	.7323711
.03	.5119665	.33	.6293000	.63	.7356527
.04	.5159534	.34	.6330717	.64	.7389137
.05	.5199388	.35	.6368307	.65	.7421539
.06	.5239222	.36	.6405764	.66	.7453731
.07	.5279032	.37	.6443088	.67	.7485711
.08	.5318814	.38	.6480273	.68	.7517478
.09	.5358564	.39	.6517317	.69	.7549029
.10	.5398278	.40	.6554217	.70	.7580363
.11	.5437953	.41	.6590970	.71	.7611479
.12	.5477584	.42	.6627573	.72	.7642375
.13	.5517168	.43	.6664022	.73	.7673049
.14	.5556700	.44	.6700314	.74	.7703500
.15	.5596177	.45	.6736448	.75	.7733726
.16	.5635595	.46	.6772419	.76	.7763727
.17	.5674949	.47	.6808225	.77	.7793501
.18	.5714237	.48	.6843863	.78	.7823046
.19	.5753454	.49	.6879331	.79	.7852361
.20	.5792597	.50	.6914625	.80	.7881446
.21	.5831662	.51	.6949743	.81	.7910299
.22	.5870604	.52	.6984682	.82	.7938919
.23	.5909541	.53	.7019440	.83	.7967306
.24	.5948349	.54	.7054015	.84	.7995458
.25	.5987063	.55	.7088403	.85	.8023375
.26	.6025681	.56	.7122603	.86	.8051055
.27	.6064199	.57	.7156612	.87	.8078498
.28	.6102612	.58	.7190427	.88	.8105703
.29	.6140919	.59	.7224047	.89	.8132671

(*continued*)

Table I (Continued)

z	F(z)	z	F(z)	z	F(z)
.90	.8159399	1.37	.9146565	1.84	.9671159
.91	.8185887	1.38	.9162067	1.85	.9678432
.92	.8212136	1.39	.9177356	1.86	.9685572
.93	.8238145	1.40	.9192433	1.87	.9692581
.94	.8263912	1.41	.9207302	1.88	.9699460
.95	.8289439	1.42	.9221962	1.89	.9706210
.96	.8314724	1.43	.9236415	1.90	.9712834
.97	.8339768	1.44	.9250663	1.91	.9719334
.98	.8364569	1.45	.9264707	1.92	.9725711
.99	.8389129	1.46	.9278550	1.93	.9731966
1.00	.8413447	1.47	.9292191	1.94	.9738102
1.01	.8437524	1.48	.9305634	1.95	.9744119
1.02	.8461358	1.49	.9318879	1.96	.9750021
1.03	.8484950	1.50	.9331928	1.97	.9755808
1.04	.8508300	1.51	.9344783	1.98	.9761482
1.05	.8531409	1.52	.9357445	1.99	.9767045
1.06	.8554277	1.53	.9369916	2.00	.9772499
1.07	.8576903	1.54	.9382198	2.01	.9777844
1.08	.8599289	1.55	.9394292	2.02	.9783083
1.09	.8621434	1.56	.9406201	2.03	.9788217
1.10	.8643339	1.57	.9417924	2.04	.9793248
1.11	.8665005	1.58	.9429466	2.05	.9798178
1.12	.8686431	1.59	.9440826	2.06	.9803007
1.13	.8707619	1.60	.9452007	2.07	.9807738
1.14	.8728568	1.61	.9463011	2.08	.9812372
1.15	.8749281	1.62	.9473839	2.09	.9816911
1.16	.8769756	1.63	.9484493	2.10	.9821356
1.17	.8789995	1.64	.9494974	2.11	.9825708
1.18	.8809999	1.65	.9505285	2.12	.9829970
1.19	.8829768	1.66	.9515428	2.13	.9834142
1.20	.8849303	1.67	.9525403	2.14	.9838226
1.21	.8868606	1.68	.9535213	2.15	.9842224
1.22	.8887676	1.69	.9544860	2.16	.9846137
1.23	.8906514	1.70	.9554345	2.17	.9849966
1.24	.8925123	1.71	.9563671	2.18	.9853713
1.25	.8943502	1.72	.9572838	2.19	.9857379
1.26	.8961653	1.73	.9581849	2.20	.9860966
1.27	.8979577	1.74	.9590705	2.21	.9864474
1.28	.8997274	1.75	.9599408	2.22	.9867906
1.29	.9014747	1.76	.9607961	2.23	.9871263
1.30	.9031995	1.77	.9616364	2.24	.9874545
1.31	.9049021	1.78	.9624620	2.25	.9877755
1.32	.9065825	1.79	.9632730	2.26	.9880894
1.33	.9082409	1.80	.9640697	2.27	.9883962
1.34	.9098773	1.81	.9648521	2.28	.9886962
1.35	.9114920	1.82	.9656205	2.29	.9889893
1.36	.9130850	1.83	.9663750	2.30	.9892759

Table I   (*Continued*)

z	F(z)	z	F(z)	z	F(z)
2.31	.9895559	2.45	.9928572	2.59	.9952012
2.32	.9898296	2.46	.9930531	2.60	.9953388
2.33	.9900969	2.47	.9932443	2.70	.9965330
2.34	.9903581	2.48	.9934309	2.80	.9974449
2.35	.9906133	2.49	.9936128	2.90	.9981342
2.36	.9908625	2.50	.9937903	3.00	.9986501
2.37	.9911060	2.51	.9939634	3.20	.9993129
2.38	.9913437	2.52	.9941323	3.40	.9996631
2.39	.9915758	2.53	.9942969	3.60	.9998409
2.40	.9918025	2.54	.9944574	3.80	.9999277
2.41	.9920237	2.55	.9946139	4.00	.9999683
2.42	.9922397	2.56	.9947664	4.50	.9999966
2.43	.9924506	2.57	.9949151	5.00	.9999997
2.44	.9926564	2.58	.9950600	5.50	.9999999

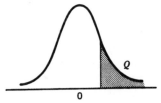

Table II
Upper Percentage Points of the *t* Distribution

v	$Q = 0.4$ $2Q = 0.8$	0.25 0.5	0.1 0.2	0.05 0.1	0.025 0.05	0.01 0.02	0.005 0.01	0.001 0.002
1	0.325	1.000	3.078	6.314	12.706	31.821	63.657	318.31
2	.289	0.816	1.886	2.920	4.303	6.965	9.925	22.326
3	.277	.765	1.638	2.353	3.182	4.541	5.841	10.213
4	.271	.741	1.533	2.132	2.776	3.747	4.604	7.173
5	0.267	0.727	1.476	2.015	2.571	3.365	4.032	5.893
6	.265	.718	1.440	1.943	2.447	3.143	3.707	5.208
7	.263	.711	1.415	1.895	2.365	2.998	3.499	4.785
8	.262	.706	1.397	1.860	2.306	2.896	3.355	4.501
9	.261	.703	1.383	1.833	2.262	2.821	3.250	4.297
10	0.260	0.700	1.372	1.812	2.228	2.764	3.169	4.144
11	.260	.697	1.363	1.796	2.201	2.718	3.106	4.025
12	.259	.695	1.356	1.782	2.179	2.681	3.055	3.930
13	.259	.694	1.350	1.771	2.160	2.650	3.012	3.852
14	.258	.692	1.345	1.761	2.145	2.624	2.977	3.787
15	0.258	0.691	1.341	1.753	2.131	2.602	2.947	3.733
16	.258	.690	1.337	1.746	2.120	2.583	2.921	3.686
17	.257	.689	1.333	1.740	2.110	2.567	2.898	3.646
18	.257	.688	1.330	1.734	2.101	2.552	2.878	3.610
19	.257	.688	1.328	1.729	2.093	2.539	2.861	3.579
20	0.257	0.687	1.325	1.725	2.086	2.528	2.845	3.552
21	.257	.686	1.323	1.721	2.080	2.518	2.831	3.527
22	.256	.686	1.321	1.717	2.074	2.508	2.819	3.505
23	.256	.685	1.319	1.714	2.069	2.500	2.807	3.485
24	.256	.685	1.318	1.711	2.064	2.492	2.797	3.467
25	0.256	0.684	1.316	1.708	2.060	2.485	2.787	3.450
26	.256	.684	1.315	1.706	2.056	2.479	2.779	3.435
27	.256	.684	1.314	1.703	2.052	2.473	2.771	3.421
28	.256	.683	1.313	1.701	2.048	2.467	2.763	3.408
29	.256	.683	1.311	1.699	2.045	2.462	2.756	3.396
30	0.256	0.683	1.310	1.697	2.042	2.457	2.750	3.385
40	.255	.681	1.303	1.684	2.021	2.423	2.704	3.307
60	.254	.679	1.296	1.671	2.000	2.390	2.660	3.232
120	.254	.677	1.289	1.658	1.980	2.358	2.617	3.160
∞	.253	.674	1.282	1.645	1.960	2.326	2.576	3.090

Table III
Upper Percentage Points of the χ^2 Distribution

ν	0.995	0.990	0.975	0.950	0.900	0.750	0.500
1	$392704 \cdot 10^{-10}$	$157088 \cdot 10^{-9}$	$982069 \cdot 10^{-9}$	$393214 \cdot 10^{-8}$	0.0157908	0.1015308	0.454937
2	0.0100251	0.0201007	0.0506356	0.102587	0.210720	0.575364	1.38629
3	0.0717212	0.114832	0.215795	0.351846	0.584375	1.212534	2.36597
4	0.206990	0.297110	0.484419	0.710721	1.063623	1.92255	3.35670
5	0.411740	0.554300	0.831211	1.145476	1.61031	2.67460	4.35146
6	0.675727	0.872085	1.237347	1.63539	2.20413	3.45460	5.34812
7	0.989265	1.239043	1.68987	2.16735	2.83311	4.25485	6.34581
8	1.344419	1.646482	2.17973	2.73264	3.48954	5.07064	7.34412
9	1.734926	2.087912	2.70039	3.32511	4.16816	5.89883	8.34283
10	2.15585	2.55821	3.24697	3.94030	4.86518	6.73720	9.34182
11	2.60321	3.05347	3.81575	4.57481	5.57779	7.58412	10.3410
12	3.07382	3.57056	4.40379	5.22603	6.30380	8.43842	11.3403
13	3.56503	4.10691	5.00874	5.89186	7.04150	9.29906	12.3398
14	4.07468	4.66043	5.62872	6.57063	7.78953	10.1653	13.3393
15	4.60094	5.22935	6.26214	7.26094	8.54675	11.0365	14.3389
16	5.14224	5.81221	6.90766	7.96164	9.31223	11.9122	15.3385
17	5.69724	6.40776	7.56418	8.67176	10.0852	12.7919	16.3381
18	6.26481	7.01491	8.23075	9.39046	10.8649	13.6753	17.3379
19	6.84398	7.63273	8.90655	10.1170	11.6509	14.5620	18.3376
20	7.43386	8.26040	9.59083	10.8508	12.4426	15.4518	19.3374
21	8.03366	8.89720	10.28293	11.5913	13.2396	16.3444	20.3372
22	8.64272	9.54249	10.9823	12.3380	14.0415	17.2396	21.3370
23	9.26042	10.19567	11.6885	13.0905	14.8479	18.1373	22.3369
24	9.88623	10.8564	12.4011	13.8484	15.6587	19.0372	23.3367
25	10.5197	11.5240	13.1197	14.6114	16.4734	19.9393	24.3366
26	11.1603	12.1981	13.8439	15.3791	17.2919	20.8434	25.3364
27	11.8076	12.8786	14.5733	16.1513	18.1138	21.7494	26.3363
28	12.4613	13.5648	15.3079	16.9279	18.9392	22.6572	27.3363
29	13.1211	14.2565	16.0471	17.7083	19.7677	23.5666	28.3362
30	13.7867	14.9535	16.7908	18.4926	20.5992	24.4776	29.3360
40	20.7065	22.1643	24.4331	26.5093	29.0505	33.6603	39.3354
50	27.9907	29.7067	32.3574	34.7642	37.6886	42.9421	49.3349
60	35.5346	37.4848	40.4817	43.1879	46.4589	52.2938	59.3347
70	43.2752	45.4418	48.7576	51.7393	55.3290	61.6983	69.3344
80	51.1720	53.5400	57.1532	60.3915	64.2778	71.1445	79.3343
90	59.1963	61.7541	65.6466	69.1260	73.2912	80.6247	89.3342
100	67.3276	70.0648	74.2219	77.9295	82.3581	90.1332	99.3341
z_Q	-2.5758	-2.3263	-1.9600	-1.6449	-1.2816	-0.6745	0.0000

(*continued*)

Table III continued

Q v	0.250	0.100	0.050	0.025	0.010	0.005	0.001
1	1.32330	2.70554	3.84146	5.02389	6.63490	7.87944	10.828
2	2.77259	4.60517	5.99147	7.37776	9.21034	10.5966	13.816
3	4.10835	6.25139	7.81473	9.34840	11.3449	12.8381	16.266
4	5.38527	7.77944	9.48773	11.1433	13.2767	14.8602	18.467
5	6.62568	9.23635	11.0705	12.8325	15.0863	16.7496	20.515
6	7.84080	10.6446	12.5916	14.4494	16.8119	18.5476	22.458
7	9.03715	12.0170	14.0671	16.0128	18.4753	20.2777	24.322
8	10.2188	13.3616	15.5073	17.5346	20.0902	21.9550	26.125
9	11.3887	14.6837	16.9190	19.0228	21.6660	23.5893	27.877
10	12.5489	15.9871	18.3070	20.4831	23.2093	25.1882	29.588
11	13.7007	17.2750	19.6751	21.9200	24.7250	26.7569	31.264
12	14.8454	18.5494	21.0261	23.3367	26.2170	28.2995	32.909
13	15.9839	19.8119	22.3621	24.7356	27.6883	29.8194	34.528
14	17.1170	21.0642	23.6848	26.1190	29.1413	31.3193	36.123
15	18.2451	22.3072	24.9958	27.4884	30.5779	32.8013	37.697
16	19.3688	23.5418	26.2962	28.8454	31.9999	34.2672	39.252
17	20.4887	24.7690	27.5871	30.1910	33.4087	35.7185	40.790
18	21.6049	25.9894	28.8693	31.5264	34.8053	37.1564	42.312
19	22.71578	27.2036	30.1435	32.8523	36.1908	38.5822	43.820
20	23.8277	28.4120	31.4104	34.1696	37.5662	39.9968	45.315
21	24.9348	29.6151	32.6705	35.4789	38.9321	41.4010	46.797
22	26.0393	30.8133	33.9244	36.7807	40.2894	42.7956	48.268
23	27.1413	32.0069	35.1725	38.0757	41.6384	44.1813	49.728
24	28.2412	33.1963	36.4151	39.3641	42.9798	45.5585	51.179
25	29.3389	34.3816	37.6525	40.6465	44.3141	46.9278	52.620
26	30.4345	35.5631	38.8852	41.9232	45.6417	48.2899	54.052
27	31.5284	36.7412	40.1133	43.1944	46.9630	49.6449	55.476
28	32.6205	37.9159	41.3372	44.4607	48.2782	50.9933	56.892
29	33.7109	39.0875	42.5569	45.7222	49.5879	52.3356	58.302
30	34.7998	40.2560	43.7729	46.9792	50.8922	53.6720	59.703
40	45.6160	51.8050	55.7585	59.3417	63.6907	66.7659	73.402
50	56.3336	63.1671	67.5048	71.4202	76.1539	79.4900	86.661
60	66.9814	74.3970	79.0819	83.2976	88.3794	91.9517	99.607
70	77.5766	85.5271	90.5312	95.0231	100.425	104.215	112.317
80	88.1303	96.5782	101.879	106.629	112.329	116.321	124.839
90	98.6499	107.565	113.145	118.136	124.116	128.299	137.208
100	109.141	118.498	124.342	129.561	135.807	140.169	149.449
z_Q	+0.6745	+1.2816	+1.6449	+1.9600	+2.3263	+2.5758	+3.0902

Table IV

Percentage Points of the F Distribution: Upper 5% Points

v_2 \ v_1	1	2	3	4	5	6	7	8	9	10	12	15	20	24	30	40	60	120	∞
1	161.4	199.5	215.7	224.6	230.2	234.0	236.8	238.9	240.5	241.9	243.9	245.9	248.0	249.1	250.1	251.1	252.2	253.3	243.3
2	18.51	19.00	19.16	19.25	19.30	19.33	19.35	19.37	19.38	19.40	19.41	19.43	19.45	19.45	19.46	19.47	19.48	19.49	19.50
3	10.13	9.55	9.28	9.12	9.01	8.94	8.89	8.85	8.81	8.79	8.74	8.70	8.66	8.64	8.62	8.59	8.57	8.55	8.53
4	7.71	6.94	6.59	6.39	6.26	6.16	6.09	6.04	6.00	5.96	5.91	5.86	5.80	5.77	5.75	5.72	5.69	5.66	5.63
5	6.61	5.79	5.41	5.19	5.05	4.95	4.88	4.82	4.77	4.74	4.68	4.62	4.56	4.53	4.50	4.46	4.43	4.40	4.36
6	5.99	5.14	4.76	4.53	4.39	4.28	4.21	4.15	4.10	4.06	4.00	3.94	3.87	3.84	3.81	3.77	3.74	3.70	3.67
7	5.59	4.74	4.35	4.12	3.97	3.87	3.79	3.73	3.68	3.64	3.57	3.51	3.44	3.41	3.38	3.34	3.30	3.27	3.23
8	5.32	4.46	4.07	3.84	3.69	3.58	3.50	3.44	3.39	3.35	3.28	3.22	3.15	3.12	3.08	3.04	3.01	2.97	2.93
9	5.12	4.26	3.86	3.63	3.48	3.37	3.29	3.23	3.18	3.14	3.07	3.01	2.94	2.90	2.86	2.83	2.79	2.75	2.71
10	4.96	4.10	3.71	3.48	3.33	3.22	3.14	3.07	3.02	2.98	2.91	2.85	2.77	2.74	2.70	2.66	2.62	2.58	2.54
11	4.84	3.98	3.59	3.36	3.20	3.09	3.01	2.95	2.90	2.85	2.79	2.72	2.65	2.61	2.57	2.53	2.49	2.45	2.40
12	4.75	3.89	3.49	3.26	3.11	3.00	2.91	2.85	2.80	2.75	2.69	2.62	2.54	2.51	2.47	2.43	2.38	2.34	2.30
13	4.67	3.81	3.41	3.18	3.03	2.92	2.83	2.77	2.71	2.67	2.60	2.53	2.46	2.42	2.38	2.34	2.30	2.25	2.21
14	4.60	3.74	3.34	3.11	2.96	2.85	2.76	2.70	2.65	2.60	2.53	2.46	2.39	2.35	2.31	2.27	2.22	2.18	2.13
15	4.54	3.68	3.29	3.06	2.90	2.79	2.71	2.64	2.59	2.54	2.48	2.40	2.33	2.29	2.25	2.20	2.16	2.11	2.07
16	4.49	3.63	3.24	3.01	2.85	2.74	2.66	2.59	2.54	2.49	2.42	2.35	2.28	2.24	2.19	2.15	2.11	2.06	2.01
17	4.45	3.59	3.20	2.96	2.81	2.70	2.61	2.55	2.49	2.45	2.38	2.31	2.23	2.19	2.15	2.10	2.06	2.01	1.96
18	4.41	3.55	3.16	2.93	2.77	2.66	2.58	2.51	2.46	2.41	2.34	2.27	2.19	2.15	2.11	2.06	2.02	1.97	1.92
19	4.38	3.52	3.13	2.90	2.74	2.63	2.54	2.48	2.42	2.38	2.31	2.23	2.16	2.11	2.07	2.03	1.98	1.93	1.88
20	4.35	3.49	3.10	2.87	2.71	2.60	2.51	2.45	2.39	2.35	2.28	2.20	2.12	2.08	2.04	1.99	1.95	1.90	1.84
21	4.32	3.47	3.07	2.84	2.68	2.57	2.49	2.42	2.37	2.32	2.25	2.18	2.10	2.05	2.01	1.96	1.92	1.87	1.81
22	4.30	3.44	3.05	2.82	2.66	2.55	2.46	2.40	2.34	2.30	2.23	2.15	2.07	2.03	1.98	1.94	1.89	1.84	1.78
23	4.28	3.42	3.03	2.80	2.64	2.53	2.44	2.37	2.32	2.27	2.20	2.13	2.05	2.01	1.96	1.91	1.86	1.81	1.76
24	4.26	3.40	3.01	2.78	2.62	2.51	2.42	2.36	2.30	2.25	2.18	2.11	2.03	1.98	1.94	1.89	1.84	1.79	1.73
25	4.24	3.39	2.99	2.76	2.60	2.49	2.40	2.34	2.28	2.24	2.16	2.09	2.01	1.96	1.92	1.87	1.82	1.77	1.71
26	4.23	3.37	2.98	2.74	2.59	2.47	2.39	2.32	2.27	2.22	2.15	2.07	1.99	1.95	1.90	1.85	1.80	1.75	1.69
27	4.21	3.35	2.96	2.73	2.57	2.46	2.37	2.31	2.25	2.20	2.13	2.06	1.97	1.93	1.88	1.84	1.79	1.73	1.67
28	4.20	3.34	2.95	2.71	2.56	2.45	2.36	2.29	2.24	2.19	2.12	2.04	1.96	1.91	1.87	1.82	1.77	1.71	1.65
29	4.18	3.33	2.93	2.70	2.55	2.43	2.35	2.28	2.22	2.18	2.10	2.03	1.94	1.90	1.85	1.81	1.75	1.70	1.64
30	4.17	3.32	2.92	2.69	2.53	2.42	2.33	2.27	2.21	2.16	2.09	2.01	1.93	1.89	1.84	1.79	1.74	1.68	1.62
40	4.08	3.23	2.84	2.61	2.45	2.34	2.25	2.18	2.12	2.08	2.00	1.92	1.84	1.79	1.74	1.69	1.64	1.58	1.51
60	4.00	3.15	2.76	2.53	2.37	2.25	2.17	2.10	2.03	1.99	1.92	1.84	1.75	1.70	1.65	1.59	1.53	1.47	1.39
120	3.92	3.07	2.68	2.45	2.29	2.17	2.09	2.02	1.96	1.91	1.83	1.75	1.66	1.61	1.55	1.50	1.43	1.35	1.25
∞	3.84	3.00	2.60	2.37	2.21	2.10	2.01	1.94	1.88	1.83	1.75	1.67	1.57	1.52	1.46	1.39	1.32	1.22	1.00

(continued)

Table IV (*continued*)

Upper 2.5% Points

v_2 \ v_1	1	2	3	4	5	6	7	8	9	10	12	15	20	24	30	40	60	120	∞
1	647.8	799.5	864.2	899.6	921.8	937.1	948.2	956.7	963.3	968.6	976.7	984.9	993.1	997.2	1001	1006	1010	1014	1018
2	38.51	39.00	39.17	39.25	39.30	39.33	39.36	39.37	39.39	39.40	39.41	39.43	39.45	39.46	39.46	39.47	39.48	39.49	39.50
3	17.44	16.04	15.44	15.10	14.88	14.73	14.62	14.54	14.47	14.42	14.34	14.25	14.17	14.12	14.08	14.04	13.99	13.95	13.90
4	12.22	10.65	9.98	9.60	9.36	9.20	9.07	8.98	8.90	8.84	8.75	8.66	8.56	8.51	8.46	8.41	8.36	8.31	8.26
5	10.01	8.43	7.76	7.39	7.15	6.98	6.85	6.76	6.68	6.62	6.52	6.43	6.33	6.28	6.23	6.18	6.12	6.07	6.02
6	8.81	7.26	6.60	6.23	5.99	5.82	5.70	5.60	5.52	5.46	5.37	5.27	5.17	5.12	5.07	5.01	4.96	4.90	4.85
7	8.07	6.54	5.89	5.52	5.29	5.12	4.99	4.90	4.82	4.76	4.67	4.57	4.47	4.42	4.36	4.31	4.25	4.20	4.14
8	7.57	6.06	5.42	5.05	4.82	4.65	4.53	4.43	4.36	4.30	4.20	4.10	4.00	3.95	3.89	3.84	3.78	3.73	3.67
9	7.21	5.71	5.08	4.72	4.48	4.32	4.20	4.10	4.03	3.96	3.87	3.77	3.67	3.61	3.56	3.51	3.45	3.39	3.33
10	6.94	5.46	4.83	4.47	4.24	4.07	3.95	3.85	3.78	3.72	3.62	3.52	3.42	3.37	3.31	3.26	3.20	3.14	3.08
11	6.72	5.26	4.63	4.28	4.04	3.88	3.76	3.66	3.59	3.53	3.43	3.33	3.23	3.17	3.12	3.06	3.00	2.94	2.88
12	6.55	5.10	4.47	4.12	3.89	3.73	3.61	3.51	3.44	3.37	3.28	3.18	3.07	3.02	2.96	2.91	2.85	2.79	2.72
13	6.41	4.97	4.35	4.00	3.77	3.60	3.48	3.39	3.31	3.25	3.15	3.05	2.95	2.89	2.84	2.78	2.72	2.66	2.60
14	6.30	4.86	4.24	3.89	3.66	3.50	3.38	3.29	3.21	3.15	3.05	2.95	2.84	2.79	2.73	2.67	2.61	2.55	2.49
15	6.20	4.77	4.15	3.80	3.58	3.41	3.29	3.20	3.12	3.06	2.96	2.86	2.76	2.70	2.64	2.59	2.52	2.46	2.40
16	6.12	4.69	4.08	3.73	3.50	3.34	3.22	3.12	3.05	2.99	2.89	2.79	2.68	2.63	2.57	2.51	2.45	2.38	2.32
17	6.04	4.62	4.01	3.66	3.44	3.28	3.16	3.06	2.98	2.92	2.82	2.72	2.62	2.56	2.50	2.44	2.38	2.32	2.25
18	5.98	4.56	3.95	3.61	3.38	3.22	3.10	3.01	2.93	2.87	2.77	2.67	2.56	2.50	2.44	2.38	2.32	2.26	2.19
19	5.92	4.51	3.90	3.56	3.33	3.17	3.05	2.96	2.88	2.82	2.72	2.62	2.51	2.45	2.39	2.33	2.27	2.20	2.13
20	5.87	4.46	3.86	3.51	3.29	3.13	3.01	2.91	2.84	2.77	2.68	2.57	2.46	2.41	2.35	2.29	2.22	2.16	2.09
21	5.83	4.42	3.82	3.48	3.25	3.09	2.97	2.87	2.80	2.73	2.64	2.53	2.42	2.37	2.31	2.25	2.18	2.11	2.04
22	5.79	4.38	3.78	3.44	3.22	3.05	2.93	2.84	2.76	2.70	2.60	2.50	2.39	2.33	2.27	2.21	2.14	2.08	2.00
23	5.75	4.35	3.75	3.41	3.18	3.02	2.90	2.81	2.73	2.67	2.57	2.47	2.36	2.30	2.24	2.18	2.11	2.04	1.97
24	5.72	4.32	3.72	3.38	3.15	2.99	2.87	2.78	2.70	2.64	2.54	2.44	2.33	2.27	2.21	2.15	2.08	2.01	1.94
25	5.69	4.29	3.69	3.35	3.13	2.97	2.85	2.75	2.68	2.61	2.51	2.41	2.30	2.24	2.18	2.12	2.05	1.98	1.91
26	5.66	4.27	3.67	3.33	3.10	2.94	2.82	2.73	2.65	2.59	2.49	2.39	2.28	2.22	2.16	2.09	2.03	1.95	1.88
27	5.63	4.24	3.65	3.31	3.08	2.92	2.80	2.71	2.63	2.57	2.47	2.36	2.25	2.19	2.13	2.07	2.00	1.93	1.85
28	5.61	4.22	3.63	3.29	3.06	2.90	2.78	2.69	2.61	2.55	2.45	2.34	2.23	2.17	2.11	2.05	1.98	1.91	1.83
29	5.59	4.20	3.61	3.27	3.04	2.88	2.76	2.67	2.59	2.53	2.43	2.32	2.21	2.15	2.09	2.03	1.96	1.89	1.81
30	5.57	4.18	3.59	3.25	3.03	2.87	2.75	2.65	2.57	2.51	2.41	2.31	2.20	2.14	2.07	2.01	1.94	1.87	1.79
40	5.42	4.05	3.46	3.13	2.90	2.74	2.62	2.53	2.45	2.39	2.29	2.18	2.07	2.01	1.94	1.88	1.80	1.72	1.64
60	5.29	3.93	3.34	3.01	2.79	2.63	2.51	2.41	2.33	2.27	2.17	2.06	1.94	1.88	1.82	1.74	1.67	1.58	1.48
120	5.15	3.80	3.23	2.89	2.67	2.52	2.39	2.30	2.22	2.16	2.05	1.94	1.82	1.76	1.69	1.61	1.53	1.43	1.31
∞	5.02	3.69	3.12	2.79	2.57	2.41	2.29	2.19	2.11	2.05	1.94	1.83	1.71	1.64	1.57	1.48	1.39	1.27	1.00

Upper 1% Points

v_2 \ v_1	1	2	3	4	5	6	7	8	9	10	12	15	20	24	30	40	60	120	∞
1	4052	4999.5	5403	5625	5764	5859	5928	5982	6022	6056	6106	6157	6209	6235	6261	6287	6313	6339	6366
2	98.50	99.00	99.17	99.25	99.30	99.33	99.36	99.37	99.39	99.40	99.42	99.43	99.45	99.46	99.47	99.47	99.48	99.49	99.50
3	34.12	30.82	29.46	28.71	28.24	27.91	27.67	27.49	27.35	27.23	27.05	26.87	26.69	26.60	26.50	26.41	26.32	26.22	26.13
4	21.20	18.00	16.69	15.98	15.52	15.21	14.98	14.80	14.66	14.55	14.37	14.20	14.02	13.93	13.84	13.75	13.65	13.56	13.46
5	16.26	13.27	12.06	11.39	10.97	10.67	10.46	10.29	10.16	10.05	9.89	9.72	9.55	9.47	9.38	9.29	9.20	9.11	9.06
6	13.75	10.92	9.78	9.15	8.75	8.47	8.26	8.10	7.98	7.87	7.72	7.56	7.40	7.31	7.23	7.14	7.06	6.97	6.88
7	12.25	9.55	8.45	7.85	7.46	7.19	6.99	6.84	6.72	6.62	6.47	6.31	6.16	6.07	5.99	5.91	5.82	5.74	5.65
8	11.26	8.65	7.59	7.01	6.63	6.37	6.18	6.03	5.91	5.81	5.67	5.52	5.36	5.28	5.20	5.12	5.03	4.95	4.86
9	10.56	8.02	6.99	6.42	6.06	5.80	5.61	5.47	5.35	5.26	5.11	4.96	4.81	4.73	4.65	4.57	4.48	4.40	4.31
10	10.04	7.56	6.55	5.99	5.64	5.39	5.20	5.06	4.94	4.85	4.71	4.56	4.41	4.33	4.25	4.17	4.08	4.00	3.91
11	9.65	7.21	6.22	5.67	5.32	5.07	4.89	4.74	4.63	4.54	4.40	4.25	4.10	4.02	3.94	3.86	3.78	3.69	3.60
12	9.33	6.93	5.95	5.41	5.06	4.82	4.64	4.50	4.39	4.30	4.16	4.01	3.86	3.78	3.70	3.62	3.54	3.45	3.36
13	9.07	6.70	5.74	5.21	4.86	4.62	4.44	4.30	4.19	4.10	3.96	3.82	3.66	3.59	3.51	3.43	3.34	3.25	3.17
14	8.86	6.51	5.56	5.04	4.69	4.46	4.28	4.14	4.03	3.94	3.80	3.66	3.51	3.43	3.35	3.27	3.18	3.09	3.00
15	8.68	6.36	5.42	4.89	4.56	4.32	4.14	4.00	3.89	3.80	3.67	3.52	3.37	3.29	3.21	3.13	3.05	2.96	2.87
16	8.53	6.23	5.29	4.77	4.44	4.20	4.03	3.89	3.78	3.69	3.55	3.41	3.26	3.18	3.10	3.02	2.93	2.84	2.75
17	8.40	6.11	5.18	4.67	4.34	4.10	3.93	3.79	3.68	3.59	3.46	3.31	3.16	3.08	3.00	2.92	2.83	2.75	2.65
18	8.29	6.01	5.09	4.58	4.25	4.01	3.84	3.71	3.60	3.51	3.37	3.23	3.08	3.00	2.92	2.84	2.75	2.66	2.57
19	8.18	5.93	5.01	4.50	4.17	3.94	3.77	3.63	3.52	3.43	3.30	3.15	3.00	2.92	2.84	2.76	2.67	2.58	2.49
20	8.10	5.85	4.94	4.43	4.10	3.87	3.70	3.56	3.46	3.37	3.23	3.09	2.94	2.86	2.78	2.69	2.61	2.52	2.42
21	8.02	5.78	4.87	4.37	4.04	3.81	3.64	3.51	3.40	3.31	3.17	3.03	2.88	2.80	2.72	2.64	2.55	2.46	2.36
22	7.95	5.72	4.82	4.31	3.99	3.76	3.59	3.45	3.35	3.26	3.12	2.98	2.83	2.75	2.67	2.58	2.50	2.40	2.31
23	7.88	5.66	4.76	4.26	3.94	3.71	3.54	3.41	3.30	3.21	3.07	2.93	2.78	2.70	2.62	2.54	2.45	2.35	2.26
24	7.82	5.61	4.72	4.22	3.90	3.67	3.50	3.36	3.26	3.17	3.03	2.89	2.74	2.66	2.58	2.49	2.40	2.31	2.21
25	7.77	5.57	4.68	4.18	3.85	3.63	3.46	3.32	3.22	3.13	2.99	2.85	2.70	2.62	2.54	2.45	2.36	2.27	2.17
26	7.72	5.53	4.64	4.14	3.82	3.59	3.42	3.29	3.18	3.09	2.96	2.81	2.66	2.58	2.50	2.42	2.33	2.23	2.13
27	7.68	5.49	4.60	4.11	3.78	3.56	3.39	3.26	3.15	3.06	2.93	2.78	2.63	2.55	2.47	2.38	2.29	2.20	2.10
28	7.64	5.45	4.57	4.07	3.75	3.53	3.36	3.23	3.12	3.03	2.90	2.75	2.60	2.52	2.44	2.35	2.26	2.17	2.06
29	7.60	5.42	4.54	4.04	3.73	3.50	3.33	3.20	3.09	3.00	2.87	2.73	2.57	2.49	2.41	2.33	2.23	2.14	2.03
30	7.56	5.39	4.51	4.02	3.70	3.47	3.30	3.17	3.07	2.98	2.84	2.70	2.55	2.47	2.39	2.30	2.21	2.11	2.01
40	7.31	5.18	4.31	3.83	3.51	3.29	3.12	2.99	2.89	2.80	2.66	2.52	2.37	2.29	2.20	2.11	2.02	1.92	1.80
60	7.08	4.98	4.13	3.65	3.34	3.12	2.95	2.82	2.72	2.63	2.50	2.35	2.20	2.12	2.03	1.94	1.84	1.73	1.60
120	6.85	4.79	3.95	3.48	3.17	2.96	2.79	2.66	2.56	2.47	2.34	2.19	2.03	1.95	1.86	1.76	1.66	1.53	1.38
∞	6.63	4.61	3.78	3.32	3.02	2.80	2.64	2.51	2.41	2.32	2.18	2.04	1.88	1.79	1.70	1.59	1.47	1.32	1.00

INDEX